SALES MANAGEMENT

SALES MANAGEMENT

Gordon R. Storholm

West Chester State College

Prentice-Hall, Inc., Englewood Cliffs, N.J. 07632

Library of Congress Cataloging in Publication Data

STORHOLM, GORDON R.
Sales management.

Includes index.
1 Sales management. I. Title.
HF5438.4.S86 658.8'1 81-15717
ISBN 0-13-787747-1 AACR2

Editorial/production supervision and
interior design by *Richard C. Laveglia*
Cover design by *Wanda Lubelska*
Manufacturing buyer: *Ed O'Dougherty*

Printed in the United States of America

10 9 8 7 6 5 4 3 2 1

ISBN 0-13-787747-1

Prentice-Hall International, Inc., *London*
Prentice-Hall of Australia Pty. Limited, *Sydney*
Prentice-Hall of Canada, Ltd., *Toronto*
Prentice-Hall of India Private Limited, *New Delhi*
Prentice-Hall of Japan, Inc., *Tokyo*
Prentice-Hall of Southeast Asia Pte. Ltd., *Singapore*
Whitehall Books Limited, *Wellington, New Zealand*

To Jeanne, Paul, Larry, Ann, and Frank

The Complete Salesperson

Self-starter: dasher/doer/self manages time/likes the job, the people, the tangible & intangible rewards/wants to grow and will

Authority: knows the "what's what" of your products and theirs (what's good, what's not-so-good, what the difference is)/gathers and absorbs market information/applies intelligence inputs to generate new selling opportunities

Strategist: maps the big picture out of lots of little ones/pin-points decision makers across the board/wins their business by being able to talk business

Problem solver: fits data and dynamics, numbers and nuances to create ideas that bridge the gap between what is and what could be

Administrator: writes his own ticket by getting the things done that customers and company need to have done, on time

Persuader: convinces with credibility/not merely a seller of goods but a filler of needs

CONTENTS

PREFACE

The purpose of this book is to provide a basic understanding of the practice of sales management, its functions and techniques. It is introductory in the sense that it assumes no previous knowledge on the part of the reader, but it also includes material that is fairly sophisticated regarding certain functional problems and opportunities that are peculiar to the field of sales management.

The book attempts to give a realistic account of what sales managers actually do, how they behave, and the problems they contend with. It also attempts to describe and explain the skills used by sales managers in achieving their objectives. As in any profession where human interaction is a major element of the job, there are few pat formulas or unfailing maxims for getting results through the efforts of others. This book, therefore, is not a "how to do it" approach to solving specific problems. I do attempt to draw on ten years of experience as a sales manager in presenting what I have always thought should be taught in a graduate or undergraduate course in sales management.

This book reflects certain judgments that I have formed as to what constitutes a good textbook in sales management. I have become convinced that a somewhat different approach to this important discipline is not only justifiable, but might even be welcome in certain quarters. Essentially, I have attempted to provide a text that is easy to read and places the art and business of sales management in a contemporary perspective.

One way in which this book is different from texts currently on the market is that it approaches sales in terms of four separate types of selling: direct, commercial, technical, and consultative. It has long been known that a successful salesperson in one type of selling may not, and indeed *probably* will not, perform well in a different selling mode. An analysis of these four distinct types of selling is conducted in some depth, and this distinction is highlighted throughout the text.

A second point of departure from existing texts is the broad coverage given to manufacturer's representatives. It has been estimated that over half of all sales managers will work with "reps" sometime during their careers. Yet very little has been written about this important channel of distribution. Since manufacturers' representatives account for a significant proportion of the selling population, an entire chapter is devoted to this group.

The interview with Frank Smith, a sales manager, that precedes each chapter is intended to provide the reader with a general understanding of the kinds of questions that are going to be addressed in that chapter.

The text begins with a review of marketing functions and of the selling process, two areas that must be understood by the reader before attempting to digest the practice of sales management. The remainder of the book deals with the functions of the sales manager, and all chapters reflect current thinking, plus insights gained in the many interviews I conducted in writing this text. Many of the sources used are personal interviews rather than current literature. The anecdotal incidents presented here were related to me by sales managers from various backgrounds and industries. The final chapter on careers in the sales field attempts to provide a current assessment from a professional standpoint.

The cases in this text are intended to be basic in nature. Having taught a sales management course more times than I care to remember, I have concluded that the shorter case allows the instructor to bring out a basic review of the major points of each chapter, and yet have enough flexibility to spend as little or as much time as he or she wants. Occasional levity is admittedly attempted in a few of the cases. Most good sales managers seem to have a sense of humor in spite of, or possibly because of, the enormous pressure that exists in the profession. The would-be sales manager would be well advised to develop a sense of humor.

In gathering material for this text I conducted numerous interviews with sales managers, many of whom belong to the Philadelphia Chapter of the Sales and Marketing Executives International. I also distributed a questionnaire requesting certain company and industry practices regarding training, planning, control, and other functional areas. The response to my requests for interviews and written data was beyond my expectations, and I am greatly indebted to the many sales executives that gave so freely of their time.

In this text, as in life, I try to maintain an up-front approach and call the shots as I see them. As a result, I take total responsibility for views expressed, facts, omissions, deletions, and the like.

It would be impossible to acknowledge all those who helped with this text. I would, however, like to thank a few. Until one undergoes the process of writing a book, he or she cannot understand why authors always mention the patience and forebearance shown by their spouses and children. My greatest acknowledgment is to my wife Jeanne, and my children Paul, Larry, Ann, and Frank for the environment they provided that allowed me to write this textbook. Without the encouragement of Connie Masley and Ross Webber, I would not have undertaken the project. My editor, John Connolly, provided constant help, and when I had a need, he always responded like the gentleman person of quality that he is.

Phyllis Knaupf did the typing and layout and made the manuscript a work of art. Additional typing and editorial support were provided by Karen Protivnak, Denise Blair, Phyllis McDonald, and Larry Storholm. Finally, I would like to thank Professors William Ashford, William Lundahl, Garvin Williams, and Robert Collins for reviewing the manuscript and offering many constructive comments. The manuscript was also reviewed by Frank Sirch of Xerox Corporation, Sally Stevens of the Chally group, Frank Blee of Smithkline Corporation, Robert Graf, Robert Gill of DuPont Corporation, David Vaughan, and David Morehouse of the SAI group. Additional ideas were provided by Steven X. Doyle, President, SXD Associates, Harold Laxman, President, Bionic Concepts Ltd., and James Elliott, vice-president, National Liberty Corporation. All these fine people volunteered their valuable insight, and I am deeply indebted to them as professionals and as friends.

Gordon Storholm
Ocean City, NJ

INTRODUCTION: INTERVIEW WITH A SALES MANAGER

Frank Smith is sales manager of the Wilmington, Delaware, branch of Micron Corporation. Frank grew up in Philadelphia and graduated from the University of Pennsylvania in 1955, majoring in marketing. His first job out of school was with Prudential Insurance in Newark, New Jersey, as a marketing analyst. After several years in an office, Frank decided that he wanted a faster pace. Contrary to what he had heard other students say, a lot of people with "pencil-pushing" positions told Frank that there was both money and excitement in sales. He was hired by Micron in Port Washington, New York, as a sales representative in 1962 and he led the office in 1965 in total unit sales. The next year, Frank was promoted to marketing team manager in the Philadelphia branch office, where he supervised seven other salespeople. In 1970, Frank was promoted to branch manager of the twenty-five salesperson office in Wilmington. This Introduction records an interview with Frank Smith and his reactions to certain important questions regarding sales management.

Interviewer: Why don't we start off with a general question that ought to lead into specifics? Frank, what do you like and what don't you like about the job of sales manager?

Frank Smith: That is certainly a general question. First of all, if you ever hear of a job where everything is good all the time, let me know. I want to apply for it. A few years ago, I read a book called *Working* by a man named Terkel.[1] It's a compendium of interviews with peoples in all walks of life—taxi driver, executive, waitress, prostitute, hockey player, everything. The point of the book, at least the message I got from it, is that there's no such thing as a job that you like all the time. A lot of kids coming out of college, for instance, have the idea that now they're going to get the *ideal* job, where you like everything about it. That notion is total fantasy. *Nobody* has the ideal job. If the good part outweighs the bad over 50 percent of the time, you are very lucky indeed. This job is the same way. I've been in sales management for about ten years and, believe me, there are some days, plenty in fact, when I wish I didn't have to go to work. All in all, though, it's a pretty interesting and rewarding career.

Interviewer: Well, I gave you a general question and you gave me a general answer. Now let's be specific; how about the pay, the working conditions, the hours.

Frank Smith: O.K., let's be specific. In my opinion, these factors are both good and bad; for example, I have to be away from home one or two nights a week, but the pay is good. My wife is like most American wives; she can adapt to my working crazy hours as long as I like it, and as long as it helps meet the bills. Most companies treat their salespeople pretty well. After all, who brings in the bread? I have a nice air-conditioned office, an expense account, and car expenses. Unfortunately, I am so overloaded with work, as are most sales managers, that I look upon these goodies as *necessities*, not frills. Sometimes the level of work gets so high, you feel like packing it in, but that's part of the job.

Interviewer: I think that's a pretty typical reaction of sales managers. Now how about the intrinsic factors of the job. The real meat of it.

Frank Smith: Ah! That's where this job is really and truly satisfying. As you put it—in the *intrinsic* factors. As far as real kicks are concerned, I wouldn't trade this kind of job for any other. You get a sense of achievement through what your people produce. The numbers are right there to tell you how well you did or if you screwed up. The opportunity to develop people has to be right up there, too. I could never figure out whether I enjoy developing people because it helps them or because it helps my own ego; probably both. There isn't a sales manager around who likes anything better than to develop a loser into a *producer*. That is the ultimate in ego satisfaction for all of us. You get a bunch of sales managers around a table having a couple of drinks and what do you think the topic of conversation is that they all relate to? Sex? Golf? Sales? Check "none

[1]Studs Terkel, *Working: People talk about what they do all day and how they feel about what they do.* (New York: Pantheon Books) 1974

of the above." The thing that they all get excited about is how they took some nurd who couldn't close a door and made a real heavyweight out of him. I guess there's a real feeling of satisfaction in just about most facets of the job. Most sales managers are like salespeople in many respects. They hate like hell to be working inside at a desk. But that's a facility you either develop and learn to get a certain satisfaction from or you don't stay a sales manager very long.

Interviewer: Would you say that being a sales manager makes more of a conformist out of you?

Frank Smith: Definitely. I find myself chewing out salespeople for breaking rules and not turning in paper work and short cutting a lot of details. Then I realize that I did the same thing myself. Actually, I don't want my salespeople to be conformists. Most psychologists will tell you that good salespeople don't fit the corporate image conformist profile very well. That is one of the ironies of sales management. From the vice-president on down, we expect conformity, when we know that most conformists make lousy salespeople. We really need creative, imaginative, and, above all, *enthusiastic* salespeople. Yet we come down on them when they don't conform to the policies and procedures we set down. I think you will find that most sales managers try to protect their salespeople from corporate policy within reason. For example, I have a saleswoman who can never fill out this particular report the right way. No matter how many times I show her, she still does it wrong. Other than this one thing, she's an excellent salesperson. So I wind up accepting the report about 75 percent accurate. Every sales manager has cases like this.

Interviewer: Do you think most salespeople have little idiosyncracies?

Frank Smith: No, I think most salespeople have big idiosyncracies.

Interviewer: Oh?

Frank Smith: I mean, sales is a mind-blowing job. You get turned down about 90 percent of the time. You have to be a little crazy to be able to take that and still have a reasonably good attitude.

Interviewer: And that's part of the reason they pay you—to help maintain those reasonably good attitudes.

Frank Smith: Yes. You could say that is probably my major function.

Interviewer: Do you perform this function through, as the textbooks say planning, organizing, controlling, staffing and directing?

Frank Smith: Definitely. Nearly any manager will tell you that he or she performs those functions to one degree or another all day long.

Interviewer: Why don't we talk about what you do during a typical day? First, however, let me ask you something. You've been using this term *salesperson* and you mentioned a *saleswoman*. Are you one of these liberals or do you just naturally think women have a place in sales?

Frank Smith: I am not a liberal, although some of my best friends are. I think women are just *great* in sales. They don't lie on their call reports and don't have the male ego. Seriously, there's no difference from a performance standpoint. What counts is how well trained and motivated a salesperson is, not sex or race. Although some customers still harbor the old prejudices.

Interviewer: Are you saying that these thoughts are universally shared in the sales management community?

Frank Smith: Oh, I don't know. There are probably still a lot of male chauvinists and white supremicists around, but for the most part a sales manager wants somebody who can *sell*, and everything else is secondary.

Interviewer: O.K., let's come back to your day. What do you do first?

Frank Smith: I presume you mean what time do I get to the office, how do I plan my day, and so on?

Interviewer: Yes. I know there's no such thing as a "typical" day, but can you give me an example of some of the things you do?

Frank Smith: Well, I can give you something pretty typical, I guess. First of all, I get to the office about 7 A. M. on a lot of days. This is not unusual for a sales manager because it's about the only time you can get your paper work done. I usually have a lot of reports on territorial analysis, sales figures, competitive activity, and so on. Each month I have a summary of all sales and call activity. It's due on the fifth of each month, so I *insist* that everybody have theirs in by the thirtieth of the preceding month. I have to analyze the data because my boss is liable to call me up and ask me about some particular salesperson's activity. This report and the analysis associated with it takes me about ten or fifteen hours every month, so if it's between the thirtieth and the fourth, I usually work on that thing from about 7 to 9 A.M. Normally, I spend from about 8 to 8:30 talking to Woody Woodward, the service manager. He has responsibility for all maintenance. You can imagine how many rush jobs he has where a salesperson promises, and he, meaning of course, Woody, has to deliver, even though the salesperson has no authority to commit the service department. We always get it worked out, but normally before 8:30 and after 6 P.M. Incidentally, in sales management, there's no "company" time and "my own" time; you work as long as you have to. That's one of those factors that you referred to earlier. I never saw a sales manager *ever*, anywhere, who worked 9 to 5 hours and succeeded.

From about 8:30 to 10 I try to get out any correspondence I have. I'm rarely successful at it, because the sales force starts coming in at about 8:30 and about half of them have some important matter (to them) to see me about. No matter how trivial it is to me, I *make* it important, because if they think I don't care about them, they aren't going to care about me. I try to remember that *I'm* here to help *them*, not the other way around.

At 9, I go out to the sales room. All the chairs are empty. They know I come out at 9 to look. They are all at Duffy's having coffee together. I know it. They know I know it. I have never gone there in my life. They leave there at 9:15 unless they have an earlier appointment. They also know if they aren't out of there by 9:15 that I'll find out and then maybe I'll go there sometime.

Usually, at least three days a week, I go out with a salesman or saleswoman from about 9 to 11. I make it a rule to tell them in advance. If they want me to help them cold call, I go. If I think they want to talk because of a problem or even just for the hell of it, we go have coffee for about a half hour, even longer, maybe. I get to know enough about them so I can figure out what makes them tick. I want to know what they want, so I can help them get it. Some want the money, some want to be promoted, some don't know what they want. They *all* want recognition. Everybody does. I try to help them understand that they can get what they want, and try to help them do what has to be done to get it.

The other days, between the fifth and about the twenty-fifth of the month I normally come in to the office at about 8 o'clock. I am constantly interviewing salespeople. I interview about five people every month because I find that I have about five or six openings every year. These openings come as a result of promotions, someone leaving the company, or because of office expansion. I explain to the applicant whether or not we have an available slot. This way I have a backlog of talent available to at least *offer* a job in case an opening comes. It takes them about two months for training and orientation, so you can't just wait for an opening to occur and then go out and start looking. It would be six months that the territory would be open. So I spend a lot of time in the morning interviewing salespeople. The other days of the month I spend filling out reports such as budgets, forecasts, and control sheets. When I make a sales forecast, there's a lot of data from the sales records that I analyze, so these reports can take four to six weeks to prepare if I work on them an hour or two every morning. Also, we have a district meeting for sales managers every month so that just about covers my mornings.

One way or the other, I'm back in the office by 11 and then I begin to answer my morning messages. I always try to get some work done at lunch, so I usually go with Woody and go over service problems or sometimes I go with a salesperson and a customer, usually one with a complaint where the salesperson doesn't have the authority to give the customer what he wants.

By the time I get back from lunch, if some new problem hasn't come up, I try to work on whatever paper work I left in the morning. Normally, by 3 o'clock my boss calls to talk about a sales meeting or about some particular problem. He never calls with solutions, only with problems.

If it's possible, I like to meet with one of the salespeople sometime in the afternoon for about two hours. This is pretty much a repeat of what happened in the morning. I usually get back by about 4 o'clock or 4:15, which is about when a lot of the salespeople come back. Obviously, many stay out much later. If it takes until 6 P.M. to clear up some business with a customer, then they stay until 6 P.M. There's kind of an unwritten rule here. If a salesperson went over the quota last month, he or she isn't expected back at the office every day. I never say anything about it and nobody abuses the privilege. By 4:45 they start coming in to see me again, for the same reasons they came in during the morning. I stay as long as they do, and I usually leave about 6, unless there's some important paper work that needs doing. I seldom take work home with me.

Interviewer: That's a pretty long day, Frank. Is that typical?

Frank Smith: Yes, except for Thursday night. Every Thursday night we have a sales meeting. It starts at 5 o'clock and lasts until 6 during the months of June, July, and August. The rest of the year the meeting starts at 5:30 and lasts until about 8:30 or 9 P.M. I buy roast beef sandwiches and beer out of the office budget, and there is never anybody expected into the office on Friday morning. They can go right to Duffy's without stopping here first. Just so they're out on the pavement by 9:15.

Interviewer: Some nonsales types might think that a meeting every Thursday night might not be necessary.

Frank Smith: I know. My own feeling is that if you hold an unnecessary meeting, it causes a lot of cynicism and resentment. I make sure that every meeting is a good one. The important thing is that I can gauge everyone's attitude at that Thursday night meeting. Another plus about the meeting is that they get a feeling of belonging to something. I pick one of the salespeople to run the meeting about a month in advance. It gives him or her plenty of time and they always look good. Of course, I also make sure that I look good when I'm in front of the group. The rest of the time I just watch. You'd be surprised how much you can learn about how *they* feel at these meetings. Also, believe it or not, we make it a pretty fun thing; I always pick a "Star of the Week," where I bring attention to some sale that was made. It's always embellished with a lot of B. S., but you'd be surprised at how everybody anticipates who the "star" is going to be. I always give him or her a prize worth about ten bucks. Not much, but they all wish they had won it when everybody's applauding.

Interviewer: You feel that the recognition is important. Don't the meetings ever get dull?

Frank Smith: No, because about twice a year we have a contest and once in a while I cancel the meeting. Also, I spend a certain amount of time in sales training in these meetings. Everybody participates, and that keeps them on their toes. We have a big Christmas party, too. Everybody brings their spouse and we all have a good time. The important thing, as I said before, is that it gives them a sense of belonging to something.

Interviewer: On a more somber note, what about the ones that aren't doing a good job?

Frank Smith: Right. That's the part *no* sales manager likes. We have a formal performance appraisal once a year, but they know how they are doing every month not only from the sales figures, but also from their own perception and from some of my own input. In a sense, the burden is on me because I'm supposed to help them make their quotas. This is probably the one area I work on right from the textbook. I have a very scientific way of setting up sales potential, and I have it double-checked by the staff people at the home office about four times a year. If a salesperson isn't cutting the mustard, we make some mutual agreement and he or she leaves. It's not really that cut and dried, of course. I work with them and work with them. They know when they aren't doing well. Naturally, it's not always *my* fault, but I think most sales managers always figure they did something wrong when they have to terminate a salesperson.

Interviewer: I guess a lot of it has to do with how well you hire, right?

Frank Smith: You better believe it! I think at least 50 percent of the whole thing is how good a hiring job the sales manager did. You wouldn't believe how hard it is to find a good salesperson. We all pride ourselves on how well we can spot a top salesperson, but we're not always that good at it. Believe me, when you hire salespeople, you need all the help you can get. We use tests, a battery of interviews, tight reference checks—everything. It's still not that easy to pick the right one. How they perform in your office during a hiring interview isn't always how they perform in the field. They're all stars on paper. Millions of dollars of products have been sold in this office during employment interviews.

Interviewer: Do you think different types of sales jobs require different types of people?

Frank Smith: Yes, definitely. There are certainly different types of selling jobs. I think the four-category breakdown of *direct sales, commercial sales, technical sales* and *consultative sales* is probably as good a way to classify salespeople as any. For example, the person who sells to a husband and wife, say an auto salesman, uses different techniques in selling his or her product than does a medical instrument salesperson who sells to hospital buying committees. Not only are the techniques different, but normally their personality characteristics and motivations are also different. There is no guarantee at all that a successful salesperson selling an "intangible" like life insurance will be equally successful selling computers to a bank. This is where psychological testing and multiple interviewing can be very important tools in helping to identify the right kind of salesperson for the right type of selling.

Interviewer: What are the prospects for the good sales manager of moving up the organizational ladder?

Frank Smith: One factor that I think is important to recognize is that you don't become the national sales manager overnight. What I mean by this is that most good sales managers tend to spend a lot of time in the lower levels of management before moving up. I think this is good because it takes several years to really understand any business, whether it's office equipment, insurance, or whatever. It's a natural thing to become impatient, because most successful sales managers typically feel that if they were running the whole operation they could bring in more sales. Unfortunately, it's really necessary to understand the whole *marketing* concept of the firm. For example, it isn't practical to bring in more sales unless *profits* are increasing, too. Believe me, most sales managers who are promoted to more responsible positions usually find that different kinds of problems exist that they weren't aware of before. You talk to any high-level sales executive about their job and they'll talk about the pressures. The only way to prepare for this kind of situation is to get a lot of experience at the lower level. Naturally, you have to set a timetable for yourself—where you want to be in five years, ten years, and so forth. I think you will find that most organizations *want* to see you meet your personal objectives and will help you accomplish them. Realistically, if there are five sales managers competing for one job at a higher level, only one person will get the job. At that point, what the other four people do becomes a subjective decision. I can assure you though, the best way to get ahead is to become very proficient in all the functions that a sales manager is supposed to perform.

Interviewer: Are politics normally a big factor in promotion decisions?

Frank Smith: This depends upon the company. I feel that my company promotes people because they earn it. I'm a firm believer that people in business usually get breaks because they make the breaks happen. That might sound naive, but I think you will find this attitude to be very prevalent in the sales management field. Most people in it are pretty optimistic by nature. Let me tell you, if you don't have a positive attitude in sales management, you are either with the wrong company or else you should do some serious soul searching about whether you are in the right field. One nice thing about this field is that, if you're good, there is always a wide market for your talents; there are plenty of competitors who would be delighted to hire you.

Interviewer: If you had to break down what you do into separate compartments, how would you do it?

Frank Smith: Well, I think we covered almost everything that a sales manager does, although this interview would last a week if we went into depth. But I've thought about this, and I think I'd break down my functions into two general areas, and several subcategories.

The two main areas I'd call *personal* and *interpersonal*. By *personal*, I mean *administrative*, *planning*, and *organizing* functions, things I do by myself. By *interpersonal*, I mean *motivating, hiring, performance evaluation*, and *training*, in other words, things I do with other people. You'll notice though, that when I went over some of the things I do, that I hit all the old textbook functions; planning, organizing, controlling, staffing, and directing, even though some of them were performed at the same time.

Interviewer: I think that's a good, simple breakdown, and a good observation on the management functions. Let me ask you one last question, Frank. You hear about *marketing* a lot. Ads in the paper for *marketing managers*, companies *marketing* products, and so on; tell me, what is the difference between *marketing* and *sales* as you see it?

Frank Smith: Well, in my opinion, *marketing* is the "big picture"; *sales* is part of it. I don't know that I'd want to be a marketing manager, but I know that as a sales manager I get involved in a lot of marketing decisions. Marketing includes, for example, not only sales, but advertising, distribution, market research, and product planning. All these functions are tied in with each other and with sales. A sales manager, for example, gets involved in advertising, product planning, and all the other marketing functions. I'd even go so far as to say that if a sales manager doesn't understand and appreciate the importance of the other marketing functions he or she will find it pretty tough to do a complete job. As a matter of fact, let's take a look at the field of marketing before we get into anything else. If we can, I'd like to at least examine its general functions; I think it will give us a good background for the rest of the book.

Interviewer: O.K., let's do it.

CHAPTER 1

MARKETING

OBJECTIVES

To provide the reader with an understanding of the field of marketing, which is vital to the field of sales management.

To provide the reader with a general understanding of the following subject areas:

* The marketing-oriented approach
* The marketing organization
* Advertising and sales promotion
* Product planning
* Distribution
* The marketing mix

To put into perspective the importance of the integration of sales management with the preceding subject areas.

For the reader to acquire a true understanding of the field of *sales management*, it is necessary for him or her to acquire at least a general understanding of the broader field of *marketing*. Only through an understanding of its integration with such fields as *advertising*, *sales promotion*, *marketing research*, and other functional areas of marketing can the field of sales management be learned. This chapter is designed to provide the background material for the reader who has not studied marketing, and to provide a review for those who have.

NATURE AND IMPORTANCE OF MARKETING

Three eminent authorities give three different definitions of marketing:

> The analyzing, organizing, planning and controlling of the firm's customer impinging resources, policies, and activities with a view of satisfying the needs and wants to chosen groups at a profit.[1]
>
> The performance of those activities which seek to accomplish organization's objectives by anticipating customer or client needs and directing a flow of need satisfying goods and services from producer to customer or client.[2]
>
> The performance of business activities that direct the flow of goods and services from producer to consumer.[3]

Further examination of these definitions should provide additional understanding as to what marketing *is*, regardless of which definition you select. Certainly, marketing encompasses much more than the sales function. It includes all those functions involved in the process of getting goods and services from producer to consumer: *distribution*, *product planning*, *marketing research*, and others.

Marketing-Oriented Approach

Marketing is such an important function that most larger firms and many smaller ones (but not enough, unfortunately) have taken what is known as a *marketing-oriented* approach to business.[4] This approach is based upon the concept that a firm's efforts should be focused upon the needs and wants of its customers. The alternative is a *production-oriented* approach, where a company's prime concern is with efficient production of goods and services, the customer's requirements being of secondary importance. The type of approach taken by a firm will determine to a great extent the interdependence of its various departments. In a marketing-oriented firm, managers of individual departments subordinate their individual goals to a company-wide effort to fulfill the customer's needs *at a profit*. A production-oriented firm is characterized by department managers going their own separate ways and placing departmental goals ahead of overall company goals.

Although corporate profits in 1978 reached a record high, there has been a continuing squeeze on the *individual* company's profit potential over the past several decades. It is safe to say that the marketing-oriented firm stands not only a

TABLE 1-1

Marketing Orientation versus Production Orientation

Marketing Orientation	Attitudes and Procedures	Production Orientation
Customer needs determine company plans	Attitudes toward customers	They should be glad we exist, trying to cut costs and bring out better products
Company makes what it can sell	Product offering	Company sells what it can make
To determine customer needs and how well company is satisfying them	Role of marketing research	To determine customer reaction, if used at all
Focus on locating new opportunities	Interest in innovation	Focus is on technology and cost cutting
A critical objective	Importance of profit	A residual, what's left after all costs are covered
Seen as a customer service	Role of customer credit	Seen as a necessary evil
Designed for customer convenience and as a selling tool	Role of packaging	Seen merely as protection for the product
Set with customer requirements and costs in mind	Inventory levels	Set with production requirements in mind
Seen as a customer service	Transportation arrangements	Seen as an extension of production and storage activities, with emphasis on cost minimization
Need-satisfying benefits of products and services	Focus of advertising	Product features and quality, maybe how products are made
Help the customer to buy if the product fits his needs, while coordinating with rest of firm, including production, inventory control, advertising, etc.	Role of sales force	Sell the customer, don't worry about coordination with other promotion efforts or rest of firm

Source: E. Jerome McCarthy, *Basic Marketing* (Homewood, Ill.: Irwin 1978)

better chance of higher profits in the future, but even a greater chance of survival in the face of increasing competition. An example of some differences in outlook between adopters of each approach is shown in Table 1-1.[5]

Marketing Manager

Because of the tremendous impact of marketing decisions on the firm's competitive position, the top marketing executive typically carries vice-presidential responsibility, although his title may simply be marketing manager. In most larger firms, the chief marketing executive manages about five or six other managers in functional areas. A typical organization breakdown (or in very large firms, a divisional breakdown) is shown in Figure 1-1.

In most organizations, the top marketing executive comes from the ranks of the functional area that is considered to be the most critical to the firm's success. For this reason, the *sales* function is the most frequently used source of marketing managers. The most critical functions to a firm, however, depends upon the nature of that firm's product or service. For example, some consumer product companies that depend heavily upon advertising to move their product appoint the top marketing executive from the advertising and sales promotion function. Most consumer product companies obtain their marketing managers from marketing functions other than sales.

The marketing manager's job consists of carrying out the classic functions of management (*planning, organizing, controlling, staffing, directing*) in coordinating the efforts of his or her functional managers and in making decisions related to all functional areas. Figure 1-2 shows two employment ads describing those firms' requirements for their new marketing manager.

Functional marketing areas carry varying amounts of responsibility in differ-

Figure 1-1

Typical Marketing Organization

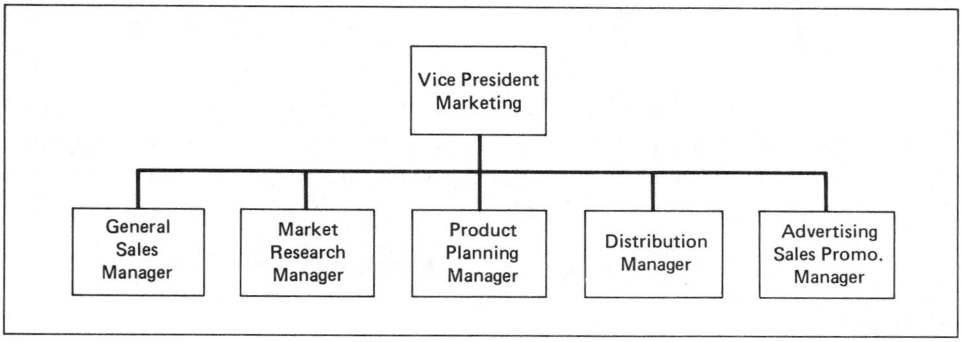

Figure 1-2

Employment Ads for Marketing Managers

DIRECTOR OF SALES & MARKETING

Fast growing Northwest Company has an immediate opening for ambitious, aggressive and experienced manager who is presently earning $100,000+ per year. Must understand marketing and sales in direct sales field and must be willing to make and follow through on commitments.

Company will do approximately 45 million in sales in 1981 with a sales force of 200. 30% growth per year over last 5 years with no end in sight! This position could lead to Vice-President within a year. An exciting and fun company to work for with tremendous unlimited potential.

If qualified please write with detailed work history to:

Box EO-72, The Wall Street Journal

MARKETING MANAGER

To $40,000

Health & beauty aid products manufacturer has an excellent opportunity for a "classic" Marketing Mgr.

This product management position will require total mgmt. of a key product group ($40MM+), to include advertising/sales promo, pricing, etc. Formulation & development of line extensions and new products is also a key area of responsibility. MBA is essential.

REPLY IN CONFIDENCE:
Box ES-257, Wall Street Journal

ent corporations. For example, the marketing research effort in company A might be considerably more elaborate than in company B, and the product planning effort in company B might likewise be more elaborate than in company A. It is also possible that certain firms might have different reporting structure from that shown in Figure 1-1. For the most part, the majority of larger firms tend to break down the marketing department into five major functional areas: *sales*, *advertising and sales promotion*, *product planning*, *marketing research*, and *distribution*. Let us now examine each of these functions in detail.

SALES

Since the subject of this text is sales management, it is important to have a good understanding of its parameters. As indicated earlier, the sales function is normally the most critical function in the marketing organization. Many managers would insist that it is the most important function in the entire organization, because it is the only function that generates revenue and profits. We have already said that implementation of the "marketing concept" requires a combined effort in which all business functions act as a team to achieve a common goal of *customer satisfaction at a profit*. Selling, therefore, plays the key role in this effort, since the customer is not satisfied nor is a profit earned until the product or service is actually sold.

Selling is loosely described as *personally assisting or persuading a prospect to buy goods or services*. The type of salesperson, sales manager, and sales strategies that a firm employs are therefore dependent upon the type of customer and the type of goods or services being sold. There is, nevertheless, a general sales process that applies in most cases. This process includes (1) setting an appointment with a prospective customer, (2) making a sales presentation to solve one or more problems for the prospect, (3) closing the sale, and, (4) providing follow-up service for the customer. This process is considerably more complex than described here, and the next chapter will be devoted to an analysis of the sales process.

The functions of sales management will likewise be examined in the remainder of this book; therefore, an in-depth discussion of the sales manager's duties and responsibilities will not be examined here. Basically, the functions of sales management include the *hiring*, *training*, *evaluating*, and *motivating* of the sales force. Of course, there are related administrative functions performed by the sales manager in the areas of *planning*, *organizing*, and *controlling*. It is also critical that the sales manager's efforts be coordinated with other marketing functions if the marketing department is to achieve its goals.

ADVERTISING

The firm's strategy of product promotion is intended to *inform*, *persuade*, and *remind*. These objectives are met through the processes of *sales*, *advertising*, and *sales promotion*.

Advertising is a type of one-way communication transmitted through various media. The type of advertisement used and the selection of the appropriate media provide a continuing challenge, since the purpose of advertising is to influence buying habits. *Sales promotion* refers to all sorts of promotion not included in personal selling or advertising. Typical sales promotion tools include distribution of *free samples*, *premiums*, *trade shows*, *point-of-purchase displays*, and *trading stamps*. Organizations seem to be of divided opinion as to whether *direct mail* falls under the heading of advertising or sales promotion.

Together with personal selling, advertising and sales promotion form what is referred to as a *promotional blend*. The precise mixture of the three factors depends upon the type of product to be sold, the target market to be sold to, and the objectives of the firm.

In most firms the *advertising* and *sales promotion* functions are coordinated by one department, although each function may require an individual executive who assumes responsibility for each function. Figure 1-3 shows the typical breakdown of responsibility in an advertising and sales promotion department.

Over the past decade, as Table 1-2 indicates, sales promotion expenditures have been consistently higher than those of advertising, although the latter function appears to hold a certain mystique for most students and business people.[6] Let's take a look in greater detail at these two functions.

Figure 1-3

Typical Advertising and Sales Promotion Department

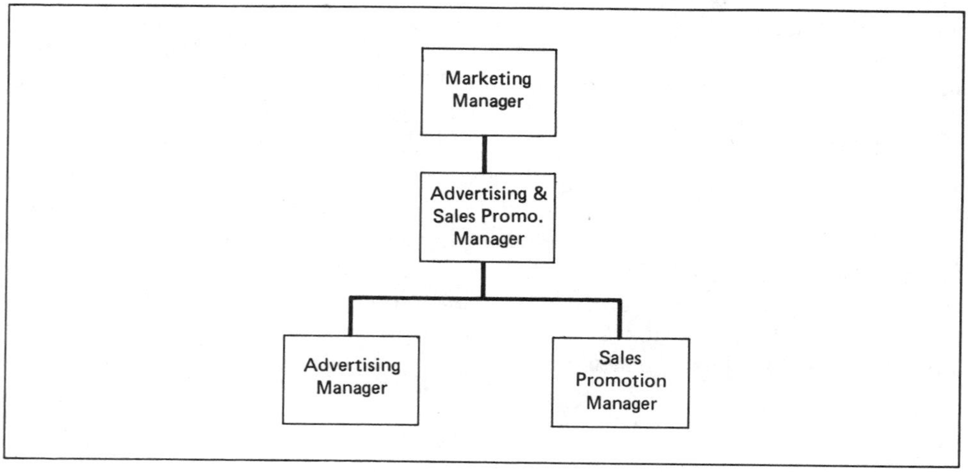

Advertising

The primary function of advertising is to influence sales revenues by directly or indirectly increasing demand for goods and services. As a result, advertising has an impact, either directly or indirectly, on a firm's sales, profits, market share, and, in turn, other firms' promotional budgets. The impact of advertising on the American scene has long been debated by leading representatives of various communities. We will not discuss the social pros and cons of advertising, but will attempt to discuss specifically the nature and functions of this marketing institution.

Types of Advertising

Most marketing professionals agree that there are five different types of advertising. The goals of the particular ad campaign will determine the type to use. Let's examine briefly the five different types.

Institutional Advertising This type of ad is typically aimed at various constituencies such as stockholders, legislators, community spokespeople, and others who have had an impact on public opinion. Usually the message of the ad is not so much to get the consumer to buy the product as it is to build up the image of the product, firm, or industry. Probably the most obvious institutional advertisements are those that promote the products of a certain industry. Examples that have been

TABLE 1-2

Ten Largest Advertisers, 1979

Rank	Firm	Millions
1	Procter & Gamble Co.	$614.9
2	General Foods Corp.	393.0
3	Sears, Roebuck & Co.	379.3
4	General Motors Corp.	323.4
5	Philip Morris Inc.	291.2
6	K Mart Corp.	287.1
7	R. J. Reynolds Industries	258.1
8	Warner-Lambert Co.	220.2
9	American Telephone and Telegraph Co.	219.8
10	Ford Motor Co.	215.0

Source: *Advertising Age*, Sept. 11, 1979, p. 3.

seen by nearly everyone are ads for milk, steel, Florida oranges, and petroleum (see Figure 1-4).

The thrust of the ad is based upon "goodness" or social benefits. Institutional ads often appear in great numbers when an industry or company has been under pressure from consumer or government groups.

Product Advertising These ads are typically very informative and are particularly effective when a new product or service has been introduced. The purpose of the ad is to inform the public of the features and benefits of the product or service. *Primary demand* (that is, demand for a type of product or service) is especially stimulated by this type of advertising (see Figure 1-5).

Competitive Advertising Compared to product advertising, where demand for the product itself was the ad objective, competitive advertising focuses upon a specific product or service. The emphasis in this type of advertising is to differentiate between a specific brand and all others. Price, emotion, and product differences are characteristic of this type of advertising (see Figure 1-6).

Comparative Advertising This type of advertising is a relatively new phenomenon. Here a particular competitive product or service is mentioned by name, and the differences between the advertiser's product and the competitive product are compared. Like most new techniques that are heavily publicized, comparative advertising has created some controversy[7] (see Figure 1-7).

Cooperative Advertising Although this type of advertising embodies the other four types, it should be mentioned here if only because of its universality.

Figure 1-4

Institutional Ad

A diamond isn't the only thing about us that sparkles.
I know love is supposed to be something personal, just between the two of us. But we can't help sharing it with the world. Sometimes we even try to hide our feelings. Especially in a crowd of people. But as soon as our eyes meet, there's a certain way we smile at each other. And anyone can look at us and tell we're head over heels in love. So we really didn't need a diamond to say what's in our future. We wanted one because it says what's in our hearts.
A diamond is forever.
To give you some idea of diamond values, the half-carat ring shown here (enlarged for detail) is worth about $670. Diamond values will vary according to color, clarity, cut and weight. Ask your jeweler for the free booklet, "A Diamond Is Forever." De Beers Consolidated Mines, Ltd.

Source: DeBeers Consolidated Mines, Inc.

Co-op advertising, as it is called, refers to expenditures by national manufacturers on local advertising in conjunction with the local outlet or distributor for the firm's products. Traditionally, the local outlet places the ad and is reimbursed for part of its expense by the manufacturer. The type of ad taken is normally of the product or competitive type. The practice of co-op advertising is so prevalent that about 90 percent of all manufacturers engage in it.[8]

Figure 1-5

A Product Ad

Advertising Media

One of the most critical questions facing the advertising manager concerns the type of media selected for the ad. Media are normally thought of to include newspapers, magazines, television, radio, billboards, catalogs, and other lesser-used vehicles. Generally, the choice of media depends upon the objectives of the ad campaign. The cost of the ad and the target audience to be reached will shape these decisions. Table 1-3 shows the advertising expenditures in various media.

There are several other considerations in selecting the media to be used,

Figure 1-6

Competitive Ad

When you're only No.2,
you try harder.
Or else.
Little fish have to keep moving all of the time. The big ones never stop picking on them.
Avis knows all about the problems of little fish.
We're only No.2 in rent a cars. We'd be swallowed up if we didn't try harder.
Avis can't afford to relax.
There's no rest for us.
We're always emptying ashtrays. Making sure gas tanks are full before we rent our cars. Seeing that the batteries are full of life. Checking our windshield wipers.
And the cars we rent out can't be anything less than spanking new Plymouths.
And since we're not the big fish, you won't feel like a sardine when you come to our counter.
We're not jammed with customers.

Source: © 1964, Avis, Inc.

including geographical selectivity, credibility, life-span of media (for example, radio and television commercials have short life-spans because once the commercial is over, it isn't heard again; magazines have longer-life ads), and pass-along rate (number of different persons seeing an ad placed in the same media).

Newspapers Of the major media, newspapers are the most popular, primarily because of their ability to reach most people within a given area and the flexibility of timing with respect to ad placement.[9] The major disadvantage of this medium is, of course, the numbers of competing ads by local firms.

Magazines One of the greatest advantages of the magazine is the ability to specify a target market. Magazines also have a longer life-span than other media. As in newspapers, however, the number of competitive ads is very high, and the lead time required for the placement of an ad renders this medium relatively inflexible.

Television This medium has the advantage of both audio and visual features, which the other media do not have. Television is particularly effective in reaching

Figure 1-7

Comparative Ad

Source: © Volkswagen of America.

TABLE 1-3

Advertising Expenditures on Various 1979 Media, 1979 (000 omitted)

Newspapers	$10,891,700
Magazines	16,174,900
Spot television	4,244,400
Spot radio	304,200
Network radio	708,600
Outdoor	1,005,600
Total measured	33,329,400
Unmeasured	8,720,100
Estimated total	42,048,500

Source: *Advertising Age,* Sept. 11, 1980, p. 3.

mass audiences, but it is not very selective. The total cost of a television ad may be prohibitive, but the flexibility in showing an ad is extremely advantageous.

Radio Radio has had the advantage, unlike television, of adding more selectivity in attempting to reach target audiences. Commercials are relatively easy to prepare and great flexibility is offered in their playing. However, listeners do not seem to devote as much attention to the ads. Of all the media, radio is the most difficult to measure in terms of effectiveness, probably because of the large proportion of listeners who are in their automobiles when the commercials are aired.

Billboards This medium has a strong relationship to traffic on roads and highways. Measurement of effectiveness is difficult, and firms normally contract for as many as 100 billboards in a local area.[10] Generally, the condition of the billboard has an effect upon the advertiser's image. Firms that appear to derive the greatest benefits from this medium are those who sell luxury goods, alcohol, tobacco, and related products and services. Disadvantages are that the message to be conveyed must necessarily be short and that billboards are restricted or prohibited in many states.

Catalogs This medium is used primarily in retailing. Costs of printing and distributing catalogs are extremely high, but the retailer may benefit from a "built-in" customer following through dissemination of catalogs. Lead time, however, is extremely long, and as a practical measure most catalogs can only be printed once or twice a year.

The Advertising Agency

The advertising agency is essentially a consulting firm specializing in the function of increasing advertising effectiveness for its clients or, in the vernacular of Madison Avenue, helping them get "the biggest bang for the buck." The agency works with its client's advertising department and provides creative services, media services, research, merchandising counsel, and advertising campaign planning.[11] Most advertising agencies have practically unlimited input in the firm's advertising decisions. Virtually all the ads seen in major media were developed by agencies. Contrary to the caricature of the Madison Avenue agency account executive engaging in three-hour martini lunches with his or her client, the competition in the advertising world dictates results-oriented customer service. Probably because of the difficulty involved in measuring advertising effectiveness, agency-client relationships are nearly always precarious. Dropping an agency's contract is not unusual in the industry; as a result, most agencies have become more effective in their client relationships over the past decade. Formerly, the account executive (or sales representative) who serviced the account was the most influential person in the client-agency dyad. Over the past decade, the *creative* personnel, or those who design the ads, in an agency have been most responsible for retaining or losing accounts.

The compensation structure of the industry has traditionally dictated a 15 percent agency fee. However, this fee has recently been increased to 17.5 percent in some agencies. This commission is paid to the agency by the media; in other words, if a firm places a television ad for $100,000, the network keeps $82,500 and returns $17,500 to the agency. This commission system (15 percent to 17.5 percent) is for the most part used by large accounts that spend several millions each year. Some large firms, such as General Electric, own their own advertising agencies. Smaller accounts are normally charged a fee. Part of the reason for the increased use of the fee structure is that many firms tend to use only the creative services of agencies, while others use the full range of services mentioned previously. Table 1-4 shows the leading advertising agencies and their gross income in 1979.

TABLE 1-4

Leading Advertising Agencies, 1979 (gross income in millions)

Rank	Agency	1979	1978
1	J. Walter Thompson Co.	$253.9	$221.5
2	McCann-Erickson	250.4	211.0
3	Young & Rubicam	247.6	203.8
4	Ogilvy & Mather International	206.2	168.4
5	Ted Bates & Co.	181.0	133.1
6	SSC&B	153.2	133.1
7	BBDO International	144.8	120.4
8	Leo Burnett Co.	141.1	128.3
9	Foote, Cone & Belding	137.6	110.0
10	D'Arcy-MacManus & Masius	128.0	104.7

Source: *Advertising Age*, Sept. 11, 1980.

SALES PROMOTION

Sales promotion is typically used in conjunction with selling and, to a great extent, with advertising. Unlike advertising, the techniques of sales promotion are normally expected to result in fairly quick sales. Its primary objectives are to attract new customers and increase brand awareness.[12] If the firm is large enough, a separate manager is usually appointed for the sales promotion function; otherwise, this responsibility is exercised by the same executive who is responsible for advertising. The most widely used sales-promotion techniques are *premiums*, *samples*, *coupons*, *business meetings*, *conventions and trade shows*, *point-of-purchase displays*, and *audiovisual productions*.

Premiums The objective of this type of sales promotion is to draw the customer into a store or to influence the potential user to buy a certain product or service. Premiums are typically described as free merchandise or an "extra" incentive designed to speed up or influence the buying process. Examples of premiums are toothbrushes attached to toothpaste, logo-bearing T-shirts, and specialized containers such as reusable glasses. In many cases, the premium is sold at cost (T-shirts, for example, are a popular item). This type of premium is referred to as *self-liquidating* and provides free publicity for the manufacturers. In general, premiums have proved to be very effective in consumer industries.

Free Samples Distribution of free samples as a major sales promotion technique has been dying out in popularity in recent years, due primarily to its high cost. Certain manufacturers, in its place, have introduced *trial-sized* containers. This reduces the cost incurred in free sampling and reduces the risk to the consumer of trying the product. Service industries, on the other hand, still continue to use the free sample visit or free trial of the service as an effective sales promotional tool.

Coupons Coupons are probably the most widely used sales promotion technique for consumer products, the overwhelming majority of which are redeemed in supermarkets. It is estimated that about 30 percent of all coupons are redeemed.[13] In 1978 over 40 billion coupons were distributed; partially because of high food and related product prices, it is expected that the use of coupons will continue to increase in the future.

Business Meetings, Conventions, and Trade Shows It has been estimated that about 5600 trade shows are held every year, which are attended by 80 million persons.[14] The primary purpose of these gatherings is to provide information that will generate sales either directly or indirectly. Most larger firms hold periodic meetings for their salespeople, which are designed to recognize and reward performance and to provide a motivational thrust. Trade shows are designed to bring together all or most firms in an industry to a central location where they can display their product or service lines to customers and prospects who buy within the industry. Normally, trade shows are elaborately designed and provide many stimulating attractions to potential buyers. Major shows are normally held in the larger metropolitan areas, although regional shows are often held in smaller cities.

Point-of-Purchase (POP) Displays These materials typically consist of signs or other eye-catching visuals placed at the advertiser's merchandise. Rack displays, special receptacles, and special shelves are an example of POP displays for use in retail outlets. Obviously, the manager of the retail outlet must agree to use the display if it is to be effective, and herein lies the greatest impediment to the use of this sales-promotion technique. Because every foot of floor space has a dollar sales value assigned to it by the store manager, there has traditionally existed a strong resistance to untested displays.

Audiovisual Presentations Most large firms have designed modular audiovisual (AV) displays. These displays are shown in public places, ranging from the World's Fair to train and bus terminals, and are normally set up in places where a wide cross section of people is likely to see them, thereby ensuring some exposure to the desired target market. In most cases, the messages delivered by AV presentations are Institutional in nature and are designed to enhance the image of the advertiser, as well as to promote products and services.

This section has examined the functions of advertising and sales promotion and their impact on a firm's marketing policies and practices. Closely related in the marketing program is the next area to be covered, product planning.

PRODUCT PLANNING

The functions of sales, advertising, and sales promotion are combined in varying amounts to make up what is known as the *promotion blend*. The next marketing function to be studied, product planning, is associated with the firm's development of goods and services that will satisfy customer wants *at a profit*. The truly marketing oriented firm visualizes a product not as a product per se, but as the solution to a customer group's problem. Because of the necessity of the firm to develop a viable, well-positioned, line of products in order to grow (or even to meet competition), product planning is a highly critical marketing function.

Technically, a new product must be functionally or significantly different from other products performing similar functions in order to be called new.[15] A *product* should include the name, packaging, warranties, and other significant features in order to give it meaning in the eyes of potential customers.

Marketing professionals agree unanimously that products have specific life cycles. In the general sense, the product life cycle consists of four major stages: introduction, growth, maturity, and decline. Clearly every product has its own life cycle, and a classic life cycle curve is shown in Figure 1-8. Because of changing customer needs, the extent of competition, and the nature of the product itself, sales of most specific products will behave in a manner similar to the curve shown

Figure 1-8

Classic Product Life Cycle

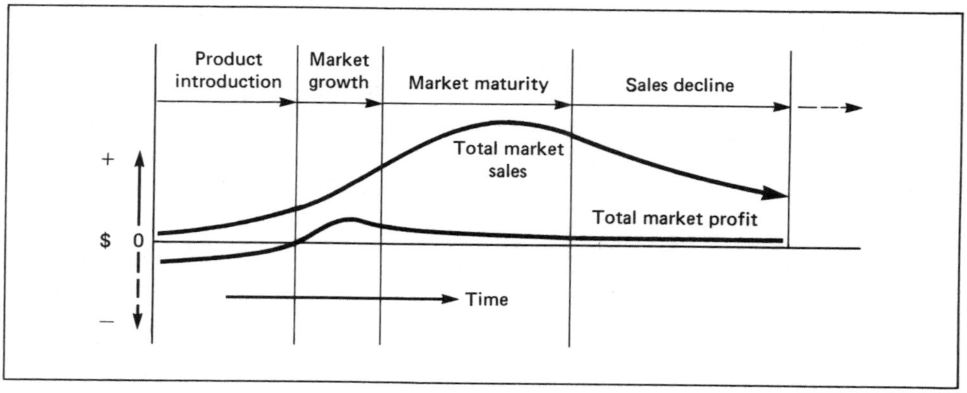

in Figure 1-8. Notable exceptions may be imagined, but generally most products will experience the four stages of *product introduction*, *growth*, *maturity*, and *decline*.

The *product introduction* stage is typically characterized by heavy expenditures in getting the product off the ground. These expenditures are exclusive of development costs, which were incurred prior to product introduction. Once the product has gained acceptance, it moves into the *market growth* stage of the life cycle. During this period, the product returns a substantial profit, which, if large enough, encourages competition to enter the field. Clearly, the time span of this stage is related directly to the success of the product. It might last several days or several years.

The third stage, *market maturity*, evolves as the overall rate of profitability begins to decrease. At this stage some competitors have come into the market, successfully reducing the original firm's sales through innovations or lower prices, and possibly causing the original firm to lower prices.

At the fourth stage, *market decline*, only a small proportion of the customer following in the growth stage remains, and because of the advanced states of most technologies, the decline may evolve quite rapidly.

Most firms do not, of course, wait until the market decline stage has set in to differentiate old products or to add new ones. The product planning department, if managed effectively, is continually working on new ideas to expand the firm's product portfolio with profitable additions, as well as to evaluate present products.

Most new ideas never make it to the back door of the factory. It is estimated that the new product failure rate is about 90 percent. In a recent study by General Foods, for example, 600 new product ideas resulted in 30 being taken to market.[16] Figure 1-9 depicts the agonizing sequence of steps involved in taking a product to market by a large chemical manufacturer.

Figure 1-9

Steps in the Development of a New Product

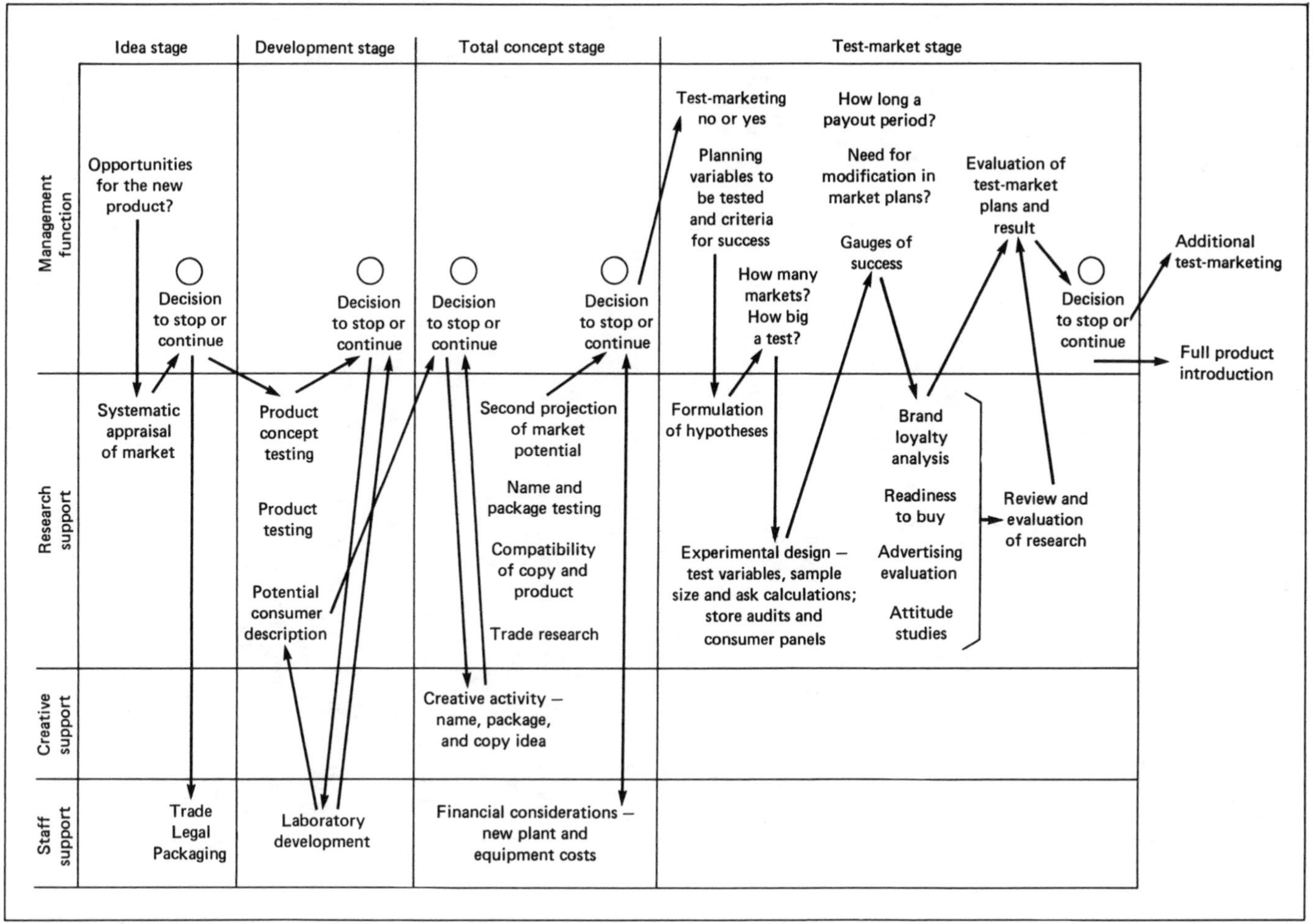

Source: *Benton & Bowles Research & Printers' Ink,* April 13, 1962, pp. 22–23.

Because of the nature of various industries, it is difficult to describe the "typical" product-planning function. Most firms, however, find that it is necessary to work with many other departments, where cooperation or lack of it has a large impact on the success of the venture. Another categorical necessity is the support and encouragement of top management.

The main reasons why products fail are not always because of physical deficiencies; they are often due to timing, inadequate marketing effort, production problems, and other conditions that could have been remedied by strong support from top management.

The role of the product planning Manager in the firm should also include the formulation of a policy with respect to new product innovation. To do so, it is necessary for him or her to develop answers for the following questions:

Does adequate market demand exist for the product?
Is it compatible with our marketing and productions capability?
Will the product result in greater profit than alternative uses of resources?
Does the product fit our image?
Is this the type of product we would be proud to advertise as ours?
Does the product help or hinder our responsibility to the communities we serve?

The sequence of elaborate preparations involved in the introduction of a new product requires a well thought out approach. Most firms use committees to evaluate the ramifications of new products from the point of view of all the important functional areas, such as finance and engineering. *Venture team* analysis is also used by some large firms. This technique consists of an interdisciplinary approach to new products by a team made up of entrepreneurally oriented members from marketing, finance, and technical areas such as engineering and design. This group evaluates and plans the firm's entry into a new business. Because of the high cost of new product development, payback periods required have grown shorter in recent years. In evaluating whether or not to field a new product, an elaborate system of screening, financial justification, and test marketing is employed by most firms.

In many firms the overall responsibility for marketing, finance, and strategy planning to ensure a new product's success in the marketplace is delegated to a product manager. This individual typically assumes his or her responsibility after the product has been introduced. The scope of the product manager's authority varies among firms.

MARKETING RESEARCH

Marketing research may be described as *a systematic and objective search for facts and data to be used in making marketing decisions.* This function, whether performed by the firm's own personnel or by outside contractors, is indispensable to marketing-oriented firms. There would appear to be an obvious competitive advantage for a firm with an effective marketing research function; indeed, in many industries the addition of such a function is necessary simply to remain competitive.

In addition to providing the data necessary to the successful conclusion of individual projects, the marketing research department typically provides management with ongoing data relating to where it stands in the industry, the size of market for specific products, sales effectiveness studies, and other data submitted on a periodic basis. Data for these reports are part of a larger process commonly known as a *marketing information system*. This concept refers to the systematic use of data collected by the company for the purpose of providing management with up-to-date information. Like most recently developed concepts, the marketing information system is no panacea to marketing management's information problems, nor is it always based on well thought out premises. The use of such systems over a period of time normally reveals the type of information managers really need and is, for the most part, quite effective.

Marketing research projects are also designed and conducted by interdependent marketing research firms. The largest of these is the A. C. Nielsen Co., probably best known for television audience analysis. Table 1-5 shows the ten largest marketing research firms. According to the American Marketing Association, about 60 percent of 3432 firms surveyed had their own marketing research departments.[17] Since the type of research conducted varied so greatly among industries and firms, there is a wide disparity in size and information functions provided by corporate marketing research departments.

Most marketing research projects, whether conducted by the firm or by an outside contractor, follow a written plan called the *experimental design*. This format shows a statement of the problem or objectives of the study, how the data will be collected, and any other pertinent details. The types of data collected are *primary data*, which consist of information from original sources, and *secondary data*, which

TABLE 1-5

The Ten Largest Marketing Research Companies, 1979

(Rank)	Firm
1	A. C. Nielsen Co.
2	IMS International
3	Selling Areas—Marketing, Inc.
4	American Research Bureau
5	Burke International Research Corp.
6	Market Facts
7	Audits & Surveys
8	Marketing Services Group, Booz, Allen & Hamilton
9	Inmarco Inc.
10	Marketing & Research Counselors

Source: *Advertising Age*

come from general published information. Most primary data are obtained either by observation or through *surveys*.

Surveys are normally conducted by interviews and by mail. Assuming that samples of a population are surveyed, various types of statistical techniques are utilized to form conclusions. Once conclusions have been drawn, these data are communicated to marketing management for use in decision making.

Over the past decade, there has been a sharp increase in the number of firms that have organized marketing research departments, and as the economic consequences of making marketing decisions continue to increase, it can be safely predicted that this tendency toward in-house marketing research departments will likewise continue to increase.

DISTRIBUTION

Distribution is concerned with the orderly flow of products and services to the ultimate consumer. Considering that distribution costs can range as high as 40 to 50 percent of some products' selling price, this function takes on enormous importance in the marketing process. Essentially, two primary functions are involved in distribution: (1) channel selection and management and (2) physical distribution management.

Channel Selection and Management

Channels of distribution are the networks or routes followed in getting the product to the consumer. These networks include the various middlemen involved in the process, such as wholesalers, distributors, brokers, and other agents. The types of middlemen needed are determined by the type of product or service being taken to market. A computer made by a major manufacturer, for example, is marketed directly from the manufacturer to the user, while the marketing of bread may involve four or five middlemen before it reaches its final destination. For every product or service there is an appropriate channel network, and each network is selected because it is deemed to be the most efficient way to bring the product or service to market. Hence, the opportunity to "eliminate the middleman" rarely exists. Wholesalers, brokers, agents, distributors, retailers, and other channel participants in the marketing system are there because they perform a necessary function. RCA, for example, would find it virtually impossible to deal directly with retailers. For this and other reasons, it sells television sets to regional *distributors*, who in turn sell to retailers. If there were no distributor, there would be no orderly market for these television sets. In the case of most agricultural products, the product is sold by the farmer to the processor, who in turn sells to the *wholesaler*, who in turn sells to the retailer. In the marketing of many products, commodities for instance, there exists a middleman, called a *broker*, who functions as an intermediary between the processor and the wholesaler. If any of these middlemen were eliminated, someone else would have to perform their function.

The particular channel network to be used is normally decided by the manufacturer. First, a decision must be made as to the type of distribution that is the most appropriate for the particular product being marketed. There are essentially four types of distribution: *direct, intensive, exclusive,* and *selective*.

Direct distribution takes place when the manufacturer uses no middlemen. An example would be a manufacturer who sells products through a sales force and delivers the products directly to the customer.

Exclusive distribution refers to a situation where the manufacturer sells to only a limited number of dealers, who sell to the final user. An example of exclusive distribution is the automobile industry; Chevrolets, for example, must be purchased from one of General Motors' authorized dealers.

Selective distribution takes place when the manufacturer sells through only a few middlemen (usually wholesalers) who have been selected because of their ability to help market the product efficiently and profitably. This type of distribution is probably the most common with respect to durable goods.

Intensive distribution is used when a manufacturer wishes to sell its product through as many outlets as possible. This type of distribution is used to sell such products as pencils, cigarettes, soft drinks, and other heavily purchased items.

There are certain exceptions to the preceding methods of distribution; for example, a firm might decide to sell its product on a direct basis as well as an exclusive basis. Many building materials firms, for example, have their own sales force, but sell through authorized dealers as well. Likewise, some firms might find that direct distribution works better, whereas competitive firms market similar products on an exclusive or selective basis, as in the office equipment industry. Most manufacturers, however, rarely make drastic changes in their distribution system, because they have determined through trial and error that there are limited options in efficiently bringing their products to the market place.

The Middleman

The most prominent type of middleman is the *wholesaler*, whose function is to buy in large quantities and to sell in smaller quantities to channel members further removed from the manufacturers. The wholesaler provides certain needed services to the manufacturer, such as providing a ready market for the products as they are made. This reduces the manufacturer's need to store and finance large inventories and reduces the number of credit risks at the lower levels in the channel network. The wholesaler in turn provides lower-level customers with the goods and services, and in many cases the credit, they require to efficiently serve their customers. Most wholesalers take title to the products they sell. There are many types of wholesalers, and their business policies and practices are based upon the type of industry they serve. Because of the functions they perform, the wholesaling function amounts to, on the average, about 10 to 15 percent of the total sales dollar.

The second most widely used middlemen are *brokers*, who facilitate the buying and selling of goods. These middlemen do not take title to the goods, but provide the indispensable service of bringing buyer and seller together. Brokers are most prevalent in the food and commodities industries. Because of their knowledge of the field in which they specialize, they are able to help maintain an orderly marketplace with respect to supply and demand factors. The majority of brokerage functions amount to about 1 to 2 percent of the sales dollar.

The last group of middlemen consists of specialized *agents*. The agent, although an independent business person, typically represents various manufacturers in the sale of their products. Agents are used by a firm in areas where sales are sporadic or where it is unprofitable to employ its own sales people. Agents' fees are a function of the established demand for the product and typically range from 2 to 15 percent of the price charged to the retailer or other user.

Physical Distribution

In addition to channel management, the *transportation* and *storage* functions are critical decision areas in the marketing process. Because of the impact of performance in these areas, more and more emphasis is being placed by firms on their importance. As a result, physical distribution is viewed by marketing-oriented firms as a total system, rather than as separate warehousing and shipping functions. Because of the interdependence of production, sales, inventory control, transportation and storage, many firms have recently developed new approaches to the concept of physical distribution.

The primary consideration in the systems approach is the determination of an optimal mixture of level of customer service and costs of distribution. This approach may dictate the location of warehouses and/or a decision to use air, rail, or truck delivery. The current trend has been to appoint a manager of distribution who reports to the marketing manager. Recent thinking seems to favor this approach because of the vast operational and integrative nature of the distribution.

This analysis has investigated the major functions of a large marketing department. The same functions are carried out in small firms, but on a less elaborate scale. We will now investigate briefly the integration of these functions into an *action* program. This is best illustrated by an examination of the *marketing mix*.

The Marketing Mix

The marketing mix is used to describe the interrelationship between the *product, place, price,* and *promotion* functions. These functions form the basis of any marketing program. It cannot be emphasized strongly enough that these four functions are carried out simultaneously. For the purposes of simplicity, however, we will analyze each function separately. *Product* refers to the total product or service that will be sold on the market and is related primarily to the product planning and market research effort. *Place* refers to the market at which the product will be directed or the specific group or groups of customers desired. Discovering this precise market is called the *segmentation process*. This market research function has a great deal to do with the *place* decision. *Price* is a decision that must be at the highest level, with appropriate input from the other levels. These decisions are often very complex and involve a great deal of testing and evaluation. *Promotion* refers to the decisions on the promotion mix of advertising, sales, and sales promotion that will be utilized to sell the product.

Each marketing mix decision area constitutes a field unto itself, and it would require an inordinate amount of space to investigate the nuances of each. Marketing management, however, must develop a suitable *mix* for its program if the firm is to achieve long-run marketing success.

SUMMARY

One of the most important business institutions is marketing. Over the years, most profitable firms have adopted the marketing concept, an approach to business that features satisfaction of customers over production priorities. The sales function is one of the basic components of the marketing process. Some of marketing's other important functions are advertising, sales promotion, product planning, marketing research, and distribution.

Marketing in business firms is normally organized by function, with the vice-president of marketing being the key executive. Managers of the other functional areas report to this individual.

Organizations promote their products and services through personal selling, advertising, and sales promotion. The product planning department has responsibility for developing new products and evaluating present ones. The distribution function is responsible for determining by which methods the firm's products are sold and how they get from producer to consumer.

Marketing research is the function that utilizes scientific methods to determine where products will be sold and who will buy them.

The marketing mix is the melding of product, price, promotion, and place to formulate marketing policy.

An understanding of marketing is critical for understanding the field of sales management.

The Sulphur City Chamber of Commerce

Sulphur City, Wisconsin, is widely known for its municipal baths. The alleged curative effects of these baths have, over the past century, attracted tourists from all over the world. Since there is no other industry in or near Sulphur City, most of the residents depend either directly or indirectly upon the baths for their livelihood. The ethnic composition of Sulphur City is overwhelmingly Scandinavian-American, and the majority of the operators of businesses and their employees wear traditional old country dress. The atmosphere has always been one of restrained gaiety, and a holidaylike feeling tends to permeate the mood of this quaint municipality. The perennial influx of visitors has been responsible for the establishment of a classic tourist business: hotels, motels, restaurants, sightseeing, and other amenities. All these places of business are, of course, dependent upon the drawing power of the municipal baths for their revenue. The Sulphur City Chamber of Commerce is an association of business people and was able to boast as recently as 1980 that 100 percent of the town's merchants were members of this body. Like most chambers of commerce, its goals and objectives are closely associated with the commercial well-being of its membership. Even its motto, *summum bonum vis medicatrix naturae*, reflects this concern. The executive director of the Sulphur City Chamber of Commerce, Mr. Peter Stockmann, recently faced the greatest crisis of his 30 year tenure. In a news release to every major wire service, the Sulphur City Municipal Baths were openly condemned as containing carcinogenic properties. To add to Peter Stockmann's consternation, this news release was made by his own brother, a physician heretofore highly respected by the local citizenry for his dedication to the medical needs of the community and his benevolent and humanitarian nature.

Once Dr. Stockmann's pronouncements became public, the outraged citizens of Sulphur City wasted no time in making known their new opinion of this once-revered neighbor. In various editorials in the local newspaper, Dr. Stockmann was roundly criticized for possessing "extreme liberal views." Even Sulphur City's Ole Olsen Post 372 of the Veterans of Foreign Wars, which had once presented Dr. Stockmann with the Man of the Year award, now denounced him as a "pinko troublemaker." As the tourist trade dwindled, the mood of the local populace became angrier and uglier until the groundswell of public opinion culminated in the siege of Dr. Stockmann's house by a rock-throwing mob. The Sulphur City police were finally able to turn away the angry crowd, but Dr. Stockmann unfortunately suffered from such emotional trauma that he was declared *non compos mentis* and was hospitalized in a rest home near Whitewater, about 200 miles away.

At the urging of the city fathers, a representative of the State Department of Health inspected the baths, and several weeks later a statement was issued to the effect that no cancer-causing substances had been discovered. Unfortunately, the tourist trade had by this time been reduced to a trickle. At an emergency session of the Executive Board of the Sulphur City Chamber of Commerce, Peter Stockmann was asked by the now desperate members what solutions he had to the problem. The words were spoken with restraint, but the meaning was clear: "get us out of this mess, or resign in disgrace."

1. If you were Peter Stockmann, what major steps would you take?
2. How do these steps relate to the basic principles of marketing covered in this chapter?

Egberts Industries

Rudy Egberts and his brother Herbie were production supervisors for one of the large auto manufacturers in Detroit. Both had attended technical high schools and the General Motors Institute. After graduation, Rudy was hired as a production trainee and Herbie followed him a year later, coming in to work as a machine engineer. During their employment period with the auto maker, they developed an enormous amount of knowledge about production techniques and general factory supervision. In 1951, Herbie developed, in his spare time, an automatic tire-breaking machine to be used in service stations. A patent was applied for, and in 1953 the Egberts brothers struck out on their own. By this time they had saved $20,000 between them. Their father, Rudy Sr., had some connections with a local bank, and they were able to come up with a loan for an additional $80,000. Egberts Industries was formed, and its first plant was the ground floor of an abandoned warehouse. Most of their capital went toward the construction of molds used to make parts for the breakers. When the molds were operational, a unique scheduling system allowed fast, efficient production. Thanks to the near-genius production talents of the Egberts brothers, the product, which had an enormous demand, became an instant success. The customers for the product, which had been secured even before the corporation was formed, were the three largest wholesaling firms in the auto aftermarket industry at a markup of about 50 percent. They in turn sold to service stations, garages, government, and institutional accounts at a markup of about 50 percent.

When the Egberts brothers produced their first machines in late 1954, there were only two other manufacturers of tire-breaking machines. By 1978 there were thirty. In January 1980, their father, Rudy Sr., chief financial officer, called the brothers to a meeting and confronted them with the following data:

TABLE 1-6

Profit and Loss, Egberts Industries 1964-1979

	1964	1967	1970	1973	1976	1979
Unit sales	30,000	25,000	20,000	20,000	15,000	15,000
Sales volume ($)	4,500,000	3,700,000	3,000,000	3,000,000	3,000,000	3,000,000
Net profits	135,000	111,000	75,000	75,000	60,000	60,000
Net profit (%)	30	30	25	25	20	20

After the brothers looked at the figures, the following conversation took place:

Rudy Sr.: This is a disgrace! You guys have had 25 years to become industry leaders and now you're just another manufacturer in a competitive industry. Another five years and you'll both be on welfare.

Rudy Jr.: Nonsense, Dad. You know we've got the best machine on the market.

The new ball traction adapter Herbie developed makes it easier to break and put together a tire on our machine than any in the industry.

Herbie: Right, Dad. You shouldn't be getting yourself excited like this. I agree that sales have been declining, but like Rudy said, the new adapter will probably make us number one in the industry.

Rudy Sr.: Gentlemen, you don't understand. There is more to making a profit than coming up with a new adapter. Let me ask you something; how many customers do you have?

Rudy Jr.: Three, Apex, United, and Car-Ease.

Rudy Sr.: How many did you have the first day you went into business?

Herbie: That's not the point, Dad. Those people are selling what they can for us. It's a tough market. I told Rudy 25 years ago that sooner or later we'd have competition.

Rudy Sr.: Gee, Herbie, that shows real forecasting genius. The Wharton econometric unit better watch out if you ever decide to go into competition with them. And what, Rudy, was your reply when our forecaster here made that apocryphal statement?

Rudy Jr.: Now I think you're being sarcastic, Dad. I said then, and I still feel today, that a customer who buys any unit except ours is foolish. We have the ball traction adapter, we have the alloy handle, we have the best machine on the market. Our competitors shouldn't be able to sell a single unit when you stack theirs up next to ours.

Rudy Sr.: Too bad somebody forgot to tell that to the competition. Look, you guys have got to get your act together. Now, as your financial advisor and as the only one in this room who doesn't think Eisenhower is still president, I'm not *asking* you, I'm *telling* you that we're going to hire a marketing manager who will turn things around.

Rudy Jr.: We can't do that. We're a machine company. Besides, we already have our customers.

Herbie: Not to mention the fact that it would cost too much money.

Rudy Sr.: O.K., fellows, I guess this is where we part company. You just lost yourself an accountant. In fact, while you're at it, find a new father; I don't like to be associated with losers.

Rudy Jr.: Wait, Dad. We'll go along with your idea. Suppose we give him six months to get results.

Rudy Sr.: What results, Rudy? Specifically.

Rudy Jr.: I don't know. I never really thought of our business in those terms.

Rudy Sr.: *Now* do you see why you need a marketing manager?

1. If you were brought in as the new marketing manager for Egberts Industries, what steps would you take?
2. What basic principles of marketing were involved in this case?

DISCUSSION QUESTIONS

1. What are the ways in which the sales function represents other (nonmarketing) segments of an organization or business?

2. What marketing support will make a sales manager more effective?

3. What are the major marketing functions and what makes them indespensable?

4. What is the role of the sales manager with regard to (a) the salesperson, (b) the customer, (c) his superiors?

5. What are the major factors of the rest of a business operation that critically affect the marketing and sales mix? How do outside factors influence these?

6. What are the advantages and disadvantages of advertising and other types of indirect selling?

7. What is the difference between *advertising* and *sales promotion?*

8. Discuss situations in which the lack of each of the following marketing functions would be disasterous to a business organization: (a) market research, (b) advertising, (c) product planning, and (d) wholesalers, dealers, distributers, and consumer outlets.

NOTES

[1]Philip Kotler, *Marketing Management* (Englewood Cliffs, N.J.: Prentice-Hall, 1967), p. 12.

[2]Jerome E. McCarthy, *Basic Marketing* (Homewood, Ill.: Irwin, 1977).

[3]Committee on Terms, Marketing Definitions. *Glossary of Marketing Terms* (Chicago: American Management Association, 1960).

[4]Robert J. Kieth, "The Marketing Revolution," *Journal of Marketing* 24 (January 1960), p. 36.

[5]T. E. Chambers and E. J. Cook, *Adoption of the Marketing Concept—Fact or Fiction?* (New York: Sales Executives Club, 1967), pp. 13–15.

[6]Roger A. Strong, "Sales Promotion, Fast Growth, Faulty Management," *Harvard Business Review,* July–August 1976.

[7]William L. Wilkie and Paul W. Furis, "Comparison Advertising Problems and Potential," *Journal of Marketing* 39 (October 1975), pp. 7–15.

[8]"Marketing Briefs," *Marketing News*, June 18, 1976, p. 2.

[9]"Newspapers See Healthy Category Gains for 1975," *Advertising Age,* June 23, 1975, pp. 3 ff.

[10]"Outdoor Made Miss America More Than Just a Pretty Face," *Advertising Age*, May 19, 1975, p. 65.

[11]David W. Nylen, *Advertising: Planning, Implementation, and Control* (Cincinnati: South-Western, 1975) pp. 80–83.

[12]Strong, "Sales Promotion," p. 122.

[13]"Premiums, P.O.P. Showing Big Gains in First Half of 1976," *Advertising Age,* July 19, 1976, p. 24.

[14]Rollie Tillman and C. A. Kirkpatrick, *Promotion: Persuasive Communication in Marketing*, rev. ed. (Homewood, Ill.: Irwin, 1972), p. 312.

[15]*Business Week,* April 22, 1967, p. 120.

[16]Ben M. Enis, R. LaGarce, and W. E. Prell, "Marketing Views," *Business Horizons 20* (School of Business, Indiana University), June 1977, pp. 46–58.

[17]Donald S. Tull and Del I. Hawkins, *Marketing Research: Meaning and Method* (New York: Macmillan, 1976), p. 3.

CHAPTER 2

SELLING

OBJECTIVES

To provide the reader with the basic concepts of selling.

To differentiate among the four basic categories of selling:

* Consultative
* Technical
* Commercial
* Direct

To discuss the basic concepts of buyer behavior.

To acquaint the reader with the processes of selling as they relate to each of four specific sales categories:

* Prospecting and lead generation
* Different types of presentations
* Handling Objections
* Closing the sale
* Follow-up

INTERVIEW WITH FRANK SMITH

Interviewer: Frank, I think before we get into the sales manager's job, it would be a good idea to take a look at selling—what the process is, different kinds of salespeople, and so on. What do you think?

Frank Smith: I agree. We should at least give a general approach to the sales process. As you know, we could write a complete book about selling, so what we can do is to just highlight the important aspects of selling.

Interviewer: That should work out pretty well. Earlier you indicated that you were in agreement that there are about four basic types of selling jobs and salespeople.

Frank Smith: Right. The designations of consultative, technical, commercial, and direct may not be used by everyone in sales, but the breakdown is pretty accurate and these four areas cover most salespeople.

Interviewer: When you were in selling, Frank, you had a very good record. Do you find that the fundamentals of selling have changed much in the last ten years or so?

Frank Smith: Oh, no. I think from time to time you hear about the need to soften the "hard sell" and the need for more concern for customer service, but the sales process has remained essentially unchanged.

Interviewer: What would you say that selling consists of?

Frank Smith: Well, it all depends on the type of product, the customer, and a lot of those things, but most people look at the selling process as consisting of *prospecting, making the presentation, handling objections, closing the sale,* and *following up* on the customer for service, referrals, and anything else that's appropriate.

Interviewer: Do you think selling is pretty much a psychological game of wits or do you think it's a case of the salesperson fulfilling needs.

Frank Smith: It's popular these days to talk about the social role that the salesperson performs by filling needs, but we also *create* needs and wants. If we didn't make the customer want goods and services, it would be kind of bad for the economy. At least that's what they taught me in macro 101. But I don't think selling is a game where one person is trying to outwit another. It's more structured than that. Partly the salesperson is there to fill a need, and sometimes, as in direct selling, you have to create a want or desire for the product in the mind of the prospect.

Interviewer: You feel, then, that selling is partly filling needs and partly creating wants.

Frank Smith: Right. And the type of selling involved determines which course the salesperson follows.

Interviewer: Let's take a look at the selling process then, and we'll try to take an overall view rather than a specific one.

Frank Smith: Fine. As I said before, you could write quite a long book on selling, and I don't think we want to do that right now. We'll just touch enough on selling to give the readers a background for the rest of the text.

THE IMPORTANCE OF SELLING

Contrary to what you may have heard, the oldest profession in the world is selling, and the phrase "nothing happens until somebody sells something" has a strong ring of credibility about it. It would be difficult to imagine what our standard of living would be like if there were no salespeople. The sales field itself employs about 7 million persons, but a larger segment of the work force continues to be employed because of the selling function.[1] In a competitive society, selling is probably the least expendable of our economic functions. Without it, the economy could not prosper or grow. Despite the magnitude of its importance, however, very little about selling other than certain myths and clichés is really known by the student. Yet as many as 50 percent of the students taking this course will probably be directly involved in selling at some time during their business career.

There seems to be a widespread image of "the salesperson" as an outgoing, aggressive, ingratiating type whose truthfulness may not always be relied upon. This image has persisted for generations, and even though it is a myth, it will continue to epitomize the salesperson to many uninformed people. Although it is true that this caricature probably does apply to a few, salespeople as a group possess the same traits of character, intelligence, and, to a lesser extent, personality as any other occupational group. The primary *difference* between sales and many other occupations is that the salesperson must possess some degree of persuasive ability. The extent to which this trait is important, however, is related to the type of selling the salesperson is engaged in. In a sense, this trait may also be attributed to a doctor, dentist, lawyer, or politician.

A common myth about selling is the widespread notion that all or most salespeople fall into a similar personality profile. Actually, there are different categories of sales requiring people with different personal characteristics and with different backgrounds. Because of this distinction, the process of selling, to be *really* understood, should be approached from the standpoints of the different categories of sales.

The type of salesperson and the techniques utilized in the selling of a product or service are determined by the customer, the nature of the product or service, the dollar expenditure on the product or service, and the length of time required to make the sale. For this reason, a salesperson selling encyclopedias to householders has more in common with an insurance salesperson than with a publisher's representative who calls on college and university professors. Likewise, a salesperson in the office equipment field calling on business executives would probably find it difficult to adapt to selling computer systems, where the decision maker is often a committee.

To facilitate an understanding of the sale process, four separate categories of selling will be discussed in this text. These categories include virtually every type of sales position. Each category requires different types of selling and different types of salespeople. We will refer to these four categories as *consultative, technical, commercial,* and *direct*.

CONSULTATIVE SALES

Consultative sales are characterized by the product or service that is sold at the higher levels of an organization. Examples of products or services that fall into the consultative category would be complex computer systems or management consulting services. The decision to make a purchase of these types of products or services may not require a high degree of technical knowledge, but must be authorized by several executives. Because of the relatively large capital outlay involved, the time span from the first sales call until the buying decision is made typically covers a relatively long period of time, often several weeks or months.

Consultative-type firms normally assign their salespeople specific accounts rather than geographical sales territories. The consultative sales process requires the salesperson to discuss the project with several people in the potential client's organization. There are many times when the progress of the sale slows down and requires a creative and sensitive effort on the part of the salesperson to get the client firm to resume interest. Sales of this type require a low-key, low-pressure type of approach by the salesperson. It requires a very strong knowledge of the product or service and the potential benefits to the user, but it also requires a strong knowledge of the workings of the potential client's organization. The successful salesperson in this field must have a personality that is compatible with achieving a few large successes periodically, as opposed to the direct salesperson, who makes sales virtually every day. Another characteristic required of the consultative salesperson is the ability to push forward for the sale without appearing to exert pressure on the prospect. As the sales manager of a well-known firm in the executive education field put it in an interview with the author,

> Our image is on the line every time one of our representatives walks into an office. That's why most of them come on more like lawyers or college professors than sales people. We can't afford to have high pressure reps who are going to antagonize the prospect. By the same token, they still have to be able to be pushy enough to make things happen. I guess the best way you could describe our people in the field is *smooth*. It's an indescribable savoir-faire that very few salesmen have and are able to capitalize on it. I guess the best way to describe it is by saying that they're selling all the way, but it seems more like a discussion of how to solve a mutual problem.

The consultative salesperson must convey not only the aforementioned "smoothness," but must also develop in the prospect a confidence in the salesperson's ability, integrity, and knowledge. To lie to a customer in consultative sales is considered to be unthinkable because of the devastating results that could occur. Most salespeople in this field, as a matter of fact, would hesitate to shade the truth or even lie by omission and are trained to be scrupulous almost to a fault.

Because of the length of time required to make a sale, most consultative salespeople are compensated by a combination of a base salary or draw plus an incentive based on sales volume or profits. More about all forms of sales compensation will be discussed in detail in Chapter 8.

Of all the sales types, the consultative is probably the most professional. Yet the nature of the selling process is such that it can also be the most frustrating. Of the four sectors of sales, consultative has the fewest salespeople in number, but has the highest average compensation. Yet for all the apparent glamour associated with this type of selling, because of its low-key atmosphere, the majority of salespeople would neither be interested nor successful in it.

TECHNICAL SALES

The most distinctive characteristic of technical sales is the product knowledge required by its salespeople. The classic industries in this field are electronic components, chemicals, and others requiring a high degree of technical sophistication to discuss intelligently the products or services being sold. Technical salespeople are often referred to as "sales engineers." Unlike the consultative area, where sophistication in organizational relationships is the salesperson's most valuable asset, the technical salesperson's product expertise normally ranks higher than persuasive ability as a predictor of success.

Most sales made in this sector require less time from introduction to purchase then in consultative sales, but the new account is rarely opened after only one or two calls. Most of the purchasing in this sector requires the approval of several people in the organization, but there are typically only one or two *real* buying influences. This buying influence is normally a purchasing administrator, engineer, scientist, or some other technical person whose opinion is valued by his or her superiors. If the technical salesperson is to convince this "buying influence" of the merits of his or her product or service, approval from higher up is usually forthcoming.

All the above is not to say that technical salespeople are strangers to the selling process. Indeed, more dollars are spent in sales training in the technical sector than in any of the others.[2] This type of selling, however, is nearly always based upon rational buying motives, unlike, for example, automobile sales, where the sale to a great extent depends upon emotion. Salespeople, therefore, are trained to sell on a rational basis. As one would expect, the personality characteristics of technical salespeople tend toward rationality and detail, thus facilitating the training process in most cases.

Compensation of technical salespeople is typically based on salary plus bonus. Normally, a company car is provided or the salesperson's expenses are reimbursed.

As in consultative selling, this field requires a special type of salesperson, and only about 18 percent of all sales jobs are in the technical sector.[3]

COMMERCIAL SALES

Commercial sales employs more salespeople than the other three types. Accounting for about 50 percent of the personnel in selling, this field generally includes nontechnical sales to business, industry, government, and nonprofit organizations. Examples of commercial sales are office equipment, wholesale food, building products, business services, and others. Most salespeople in this field are trained to make the sale on the first or second call, although many times several calls must be made by the salesperson before he or she receives an order. Unlike consultative or technical sales, it is customary for the commercial salesperson to make many sales of low or intermediate dollar value. The level of education and training for the commercial salesperson is typically lower than for the other two areas, but the instinctive motivation required to make a sale is normally higher in successful commercial salespeople. Training in this field always stresses the importance of reaching the decision maker in the organization, making a smooth presentation, and closing the sale.

This field is composed of two types: *order takers* and *order getters*. The former group is concerned with follow-up and account maintenance. Order takers typically call on designated purchasing agents and other buyers to assess vendor products or services. The order getter is more concerned with making new sales and customarily attempts to present his or her product to executives with the power to authorize an immediate purchase.

Since order taking and order getting require essentially different approaches, it should not be surprising that the two types of salespeople normally possess different personality traits, the order getter clearly being more aggressive and more highly motivated than the order taker. The type of salesperson required depends, of course, on the nature of the buying situation. As a sales manager in the office equipment field pointed out in an interview with the author,

> A lot of salespeople have the idea that it's almost *immoral* to be an order taker, that if you can't go in and close five or six deals a week you're some kind of a weakling. Actually, we have order takers who do a *much* better job in certain accounts, mainly because they have developed a relationship with the buyer and aren't pushy and aggressive like our strong closers.

Order takers, however, are assigned to accounts that do a large volume of reordering, while new accounts are sold by order getters. Since the latter kind of sales often determines the success of the company, order getters are normally more highly paid and more appreciated than are order takers.

The method of compensation in the commercial sales field varies with the

Figure 2-1

Which Sales Types Do These Jobs Fit?

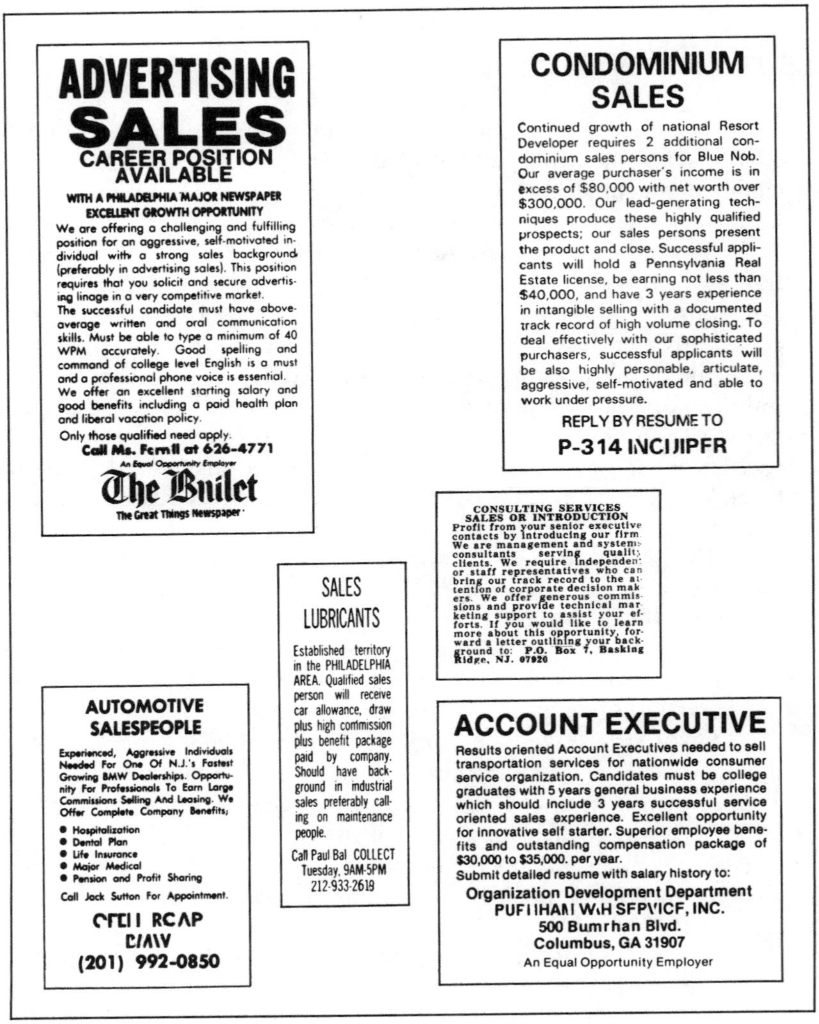
ADVERTISING
SALES
CAREER POSITION AVAILABLE
WITH A PHILADELPHIA MAJOR NEWSPAPER
EXCELLENT GROWTH OPPORTUNITY
We are offering a challenging and fulfilling position for an aggressive, self-motivated individual with a strong sales background (preferably in advertising sales). This position requires that you solicit and secure advertising linage in a very competitive market.
The successful candidate must have above-average written and oral communication skills. Must be able to type a minimum of 40 WPM accurately. Good spelling and command of college level English is a must and a professional phone voice is essential.
We offer an excellent starting salary and good benefits including a paid health plan and liberal vacation policy.
Only those qualified need apply.
Call Ms. Fcrnll at 626-4771
An Equal Opportunity Employer
The Bnilct
The Great Things Newspaper
CONDOMINIUM SALES
Continued growth of national Resort Developer requires 2 additional condominium sales persons for Blue Nob. Our average purchaser's income is in excess of $80,000 with net worth over $300,000. Our lead-generating techniques produce these highly qualified prospects; our sales persons present the product and close. Successful applicants will hold a Pennsylvania Real Estate license, be earning not less than $40,000, and have 3 years experience in intangible selling with a documented track record of high volume closing. To deal effectively with our sophisticated purchasers, successful applicants will be also highly personable, articulate, aggressive, self-motivated and able to work under pressure.
REPLY BY RESUME TO
P-314 INCIJIPFR
CONSULTING SERVICES
SALES OR INTRODUCTION
Profit from your senior executive contacts by introducing our firm. We are management and systems consultants serving quality clients. We require independent or staff representatives who can bring our track record to the attention of corporate decision makers. We offer generous commissions and provide technical marketing support to assist your efforts. If you would like to learn more about this opportunity, forward a letter outlining your background to: P.O. Box 7, Basking Ridge, NJ. 07920
SALES
LUBRICANTS
Established territory in the PHILADELPHIA AREA. Qualified sales person will receive car allowance, draw plus high commission plus benefit package paid by company. Should have background in industrial sales preferably calling on maintenance people.
Call Paul Bal COLLECT
Tuesday, 9AM-5PM
212-933-2619
AUTOMOTIVE SALESPEOPLE
Experienced, Aggressive Individuals Needed For One Of N.J.'s Fastest Growing BMW Dealerships. Opportunity For Professionals To Earn Large Commissions Selling And Leasing. We Offer Complete Company Benefits;
• Hospitalization
• Dental Plan
• Life Insurance
• Major Medical
• Pension and Profit Sharing
Call Jack Sutton For Appointment.
(201) 992-0850
ACCOUNT EXECUTIVE
Results oriented Account Executives needed to sell transportation services for nationwide consumer service organization. Candidates must be college graduates with 5 years general business experience which should include 3 years successful service oriented sales experience. Excellent opportunity for innovative self starter. Superior employee benefits and outstanding compensation package of $30,000 to $35,000. per year.
Submit detailed resume with salary history to:
Organization Development Department
500 Bumrhan Blvd.
Columbus, GA 31907
An Equal Opportunity Employer

nature of the firm's products or services. Salespeople in the office equipment industry, for example, are compensated primarily by commission, whereas most salespeople in the publishing industry are paid very little commission as a percentage of their total earnings. Although the commercial sales field is composed of many different industries having a variety of compensation plans, the *method* of selling goods and services is essentially similar.

DIRECT SALES

Direct sales are primarily concerned with the sale of products and services to the ultimate consumer. Examples of these, many of which are sold in the customer's home, are insurance, automobiles, enclyclopedias, and household services such as home improvements. There is normally some emotional appeal associated with this type of selling, and, as a result, most successful salespeople in this field possess strong persuasive ability. With few exceptions, the length of time from introduction to consummation of the sale is very short. Salespeople are trained to close the sale on the first visit, in fact.

Most sales managers feel that, if consumers are given time to consider making a purchase, they will either be "cooled off" from buying the product or service, will procrastinate on making a decision, or will buy from a competitor. A sales manager for a firm selling building lots in a vacation subdivision made these comments in an interview with the author:

> To make a sale here, you have to be a closer. Sometimes you get a real "mooch,"[4] but most of the time you have to lean on them (the prospects) a little bit. If you don't have a good story and give them a reason to buy *now*, once they're gone you'll never see them again. You get that one shot at them and, bang!, that's it! You either get them or you don't; a real heavyweight here makes himself fifteen hundred or two thousand bucks a week, but if you can't close, you're going to go home with empty pockets. There are no in-betweens.

This sales manager agreed with the overwhelming majority of his peers that this approach holds true fairly well for most types of direct sales.

Unlike the other three types of selling, there is little emphasis placed on stability of the employment situation. The turnover rate of salespeople in the direct field is probably of geometric proportion when compared to the other fields. The primary reasons for this condition are lack of financial security, inadequacy of training programs, and the difficulties encountered in developing bonafide prospects.

Most direct salespeople are paid on the basis of straight commission, although a few firms, such as insurance companies, will provide a basic income during a training period.

Some readers might be wondering where retail store sales fit into the four categories. Actually, they don't. Most retail store clerks receive a salary and are not professional salespeople but are what their title implies—clerks. "Big-ticket" furniture and appliance salespeople, however, would fit into the *direct* sales sector. Various facets of the four sales categories are outlined in Tables 2-1 through 2-3.

BUYER BEHAVIOR AND MOTIVATION

For a sale to take place, there must be a seller and a buyer. Interaction between the salesperson and the prospect is intended essentially to get the latter

Figure 2-2

Influences on Individual Buying Decisions

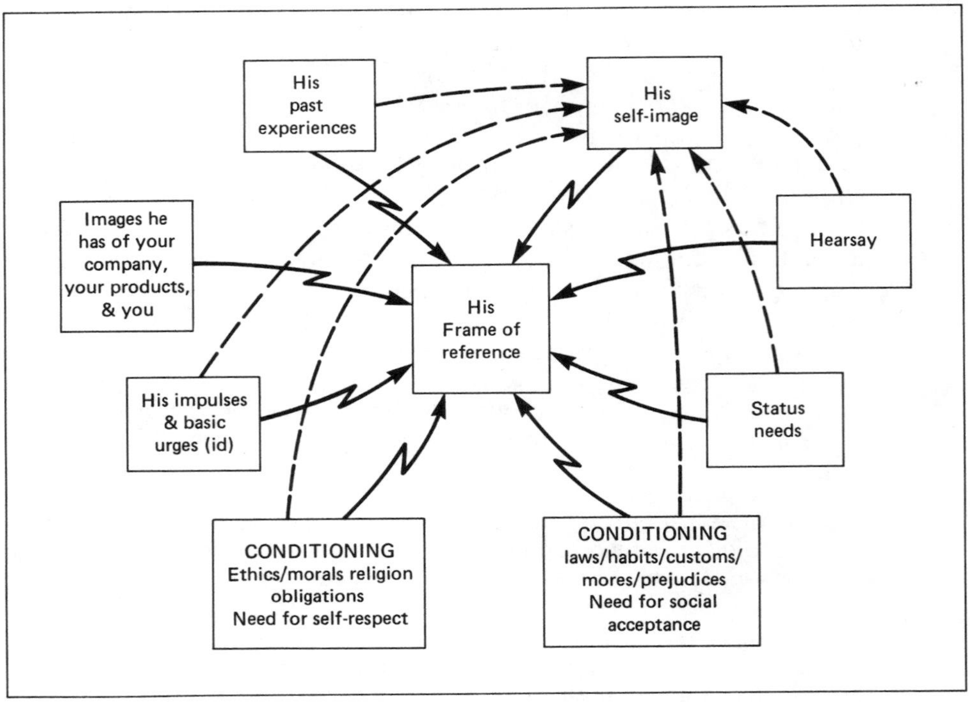

Source: Richard V. Butt, *Sales Effort and Marketing Strategy* (New York: American Management Association, 1969).

to change his or her mind about a product or service. To do this, the salesperson should have some knowledge of why the prospect will buy. A great deal has been written about buyer behavior and motivation, and not all researchers are in agreement as to what makes people buy. It should be recognized that no two persons are exactly the same; not only are people different in their views and attitudes, but the same person can be different when circumstances change. Whether a person is happy or unhappy, tired or wide awake, distracted or relaxed will have a great effect upon how he or she perceives the salesperson's presentation.

Motives to purchase a product or service range from the satisfaction of physiological needs to urges or needs for confromity, recognition, and prestige. Motives can also be classified as *primary, selective,* or *patronage*. A *primary* motive is related to those factors that motivate a person to select one general type of product or service over another. For example, a buyer may simultaneously wish to purchase a new vacuum cleaner and a new dress. Unfortunately, she does not have enough money to purchase both, so she buys the vacuum cleaner because of the

TABLE 2-1

Characteristics of the Four Sales Categories

Type of Sales	Characteristics of Sales Category	Characteristics of Successful Salespeople	Typical Mode of Compensation
Consultative	Product or service sold at higher levels of an organization. Purchasing decisions usually authorized by several executives. Salespeople assigned specific accounts rather than geographical territories. Salesperson required to discuss project with several people in client's organization.	Smooth approach. Personality compatible with achieving a few large successes periodically. Ability to gain strong confidence of the client.	Salary or base salary plus commission based on sales or profits.
Technical	Purchasing decisions require approval of several organization members but there are typically only one or two buying influences. Selling is based on rational economic buying motives.	Very strong product knowledge. Strong interest in detail. Rational approach in utilizing sales techniques.	Salary plus bonus or commission.
Commercial	Sales of a nontechnical nature to business and industry. Sales often made on first or second call. Many sales of lower dollar value than in consultative sector.	Strong self-organization. Ability to reach decision maker in organization. Ability to make smooth presentation and close sale.	Salary plus commission.
Direct	Sales of products or services to the ultimate consumer. Sale usually closed on first call or not at all. Emotional appeal to buyer. Turnover rate very high.	Strong ability to close sale on first call. Strong persuasive ability. Ability to quickly identify a prospect's buying motives.	Straight commission.

TABLE 2-2

Categories of Selling and Some Related Jobs

Consultative:	Complex computer systems
	Nuclear reactors
	Dam projects
Industrial-Technical:	Computers
	Production machinery
	Aircraft
Direct Commercial:	Food sales to chain stores
	Textiles
	Apparel
	Wholesaling
Direct Consumer:	Retail stores
	Automobile sales
	Door-to-door sales
	Restaurants

pre-eminence of household needs. *Selective* motives determine what type of vacuum she buys, and *patronage* motives determine where she will go to buy it.

Motives typically fall into two categories: rational and emotional. A knowledge of emotional motivation is clearly more important for the direct salesperson than for the other three types. Rational motives are those based on economy, durability, value, and similar benefits. To sell effectively, the salesperson should be able to determine the motives of prospects. Usually this is extremely difficult, as even the customer may not be aware of the true reasons why he or she bought a product or service. *Motivational research*, for instance, is a technique used to determine the *true* reasons why people buy a particular product or service. This technique has been popular since the 1950s. Perhaps part of the reason for its

TABLE 2-3

Preapproach Effort and Sales Type

	Consultative	Industrial Technical	Direct Commercial	Direct Consumer
Extent of preapproach effort	Long-term and very extensive effort	Long-term and extensive effort	Medium-term and moderate effort	Short-term and little or no effort
Significance of any one sale	Highly significant	---------	-----------	Little significance

popularity was the Freudian nature of the explanations given for buying behavior. One eminent authority discussed the impact of motivational research:

> Marketers were quickly fascinated by the glib, entertaining and usually surprising explanations offered for consumer behavior, especially since many of these explanations were rooted in sex . . . . Then marketers were told that cigarettes and lifesaver candies were bought because of their sexual symbolism, that men regarded convertible cars as surrogate mistresses, that women baked cakes to fulfill their reproductive yearnings. Before long, almost every advertising agency on Madison Avenue had a psychologist on its staff payroll in charge of motivational research studies.[5]

Although motivational research probably reached its peak in the early 1960s, it is still used extensively as a tool to gain insight into the question of *why* people buy. Thus, to reduce the need for the salesperson's ability to discern the buyer's motives, most sales organizations have developed presentations that attempt to cover the complete spectrum of benefits. Millions of dollars are spent annually improving sales presentations to incorporate the communication of every possible benefit of the product or service to the buyer.

There has been extensive research in recent years on what is referred to as *dyadic interaction*. It is an analysis of the roles played by buyer and seller in sales situations, type of sales interview, length of time taken, and when and where the interview takes place. Some studies have shown that the more alike the prospect and the salesperson are in such factors as age, background, and habits, the greater the probability of a sale. Other studies show that dependent persons need more assistance, and that females respond less favorably toward aggressive salespeople. If nothing else, studies of this type indicate the need for a well thought out sales presentation.

Table 2-4 classifies and characterizes basic sales motives.

TABLE 2-4

Buyer Behavior and Motivation

Classification of Motive	Characteristics of Motive
Primary	Motive that specifies *which type* of product customer will buy.
Selective	Motive that determines *which brand* of product customer will buy.
Patronage	Motive that determines *where* customer will buy product.
Rational	Motive based on utility or economy.
Emotional	Motive based upon buyer's immediate perception of product or service rather than upon long-term benefits.

THE SALES PROCESS

Different sales situations clearly require different types of salespersons, presentations, and approaches to the customer. The actual sales sequence, however, is fairly structured. Unless there exists a very unusual situation, such as a critical need for a certain product, or unless the product is being reordered, most firms find that the sales process normally requires the following elements: (1) prospecting and lead generation, (2) the presentation, and (3) persuasive techniques. These elements are necessary to achieve sales in all four sales sectors, although the *emphasis* placed on various elements might vary among sectors.

Prospecting and Lead Generation

One of the most critical elements of the sales process is the generation of potential buyers. Each type of sales force has its own time-tested method of developing prospects. Although the methods and techniques used may vary among firms, every sales organization expends considerable resources on prospecting. This section will discuss some of the methods used in the four sales sectors.

Prospecting in Consultative Sales

Although most consultative salespeople call upon a limited number of accounts, there is a constant effort to develop new accounts and to expand the depth of coverage within existing accounts. Since most selling of this type is undertaken at a very high level of an organization, the search for contacts "at the top" is often carried out in a very subtle way. An outsider's access to the top executives of a firm is typically quite limited; therefore, a creative effort must be made to establish communication with these managers. Many firms that market their products or services in the consultative sector rely on personal contact to help establish relationships at the top. The most common way of gaining an introduction to prospects is through referrals by existing clients. Management consulting firms, for example, use this method almost exclusively. Another method used successfully by many firms is through seminars and colloquiums, which are held for potential clients by invitation to establish a high level of contact. Many firms in the data-processing industry use this technique. A third technique, which yields fewer prospects than the other two mentioned here, is advertising in trade and professional journals. These ads are always low-key in nature and often indicate only the firm's specialty.

Because of the highly professional nature of consultative selling, prospecting techniques are more sophisticated than those used in the other three sectors. In summary, it can be said that probably the most effective method of getting new prospects is through word-of-mouth referral from satisfied clients. We will see how the technical, commercial, and direct fields use prospecting techniques that are less subtle in nature and more sales oriented.

Prospecting in Technical Sales

Since most technical salespeople are assigned a specific geographical territory, the prospecting function in this area is more systematic than in consultative selling. Because of the nature of the products and services sold, the technical salesperson typically has a limited number of qualified companies to call on. These accounts have, in most cases, existed in the territory for some time, and when new firms move in, it is the responsibility of the salesperson to be aware of the nature of their business and possible applications for his or her product.

Prospecting in the technical field typically requires less technique than the other three types of selling. First, users of technical goods and services have a designated buyer who is familiar with their uses and benefits. It is relatively easy for the technical salesperson to arrange an appointment with this person. Second, although all firms encourage their salespeople to sell at a high level in the organization, it is often more fruitful to establish contact with the buyer because of his or her level of expertise. In other words, even if contact *were* established with the president or vice-president of operations of a prospect firm, the salesperson would probably be referred to the buyer anyway. It is important to recognize that most designated buyers are highly sensitive about the salesperson's bypassing him or her and going to a higher level. Since it is the responsibility of the buyer to make purchasing decisions, an order from a higher-level executive is normally interpreted as an affront to the buyer's authority or skill. For this reason, it is usually fruitless for the technical salesperson to aim at a high level of contact.

Naturally, there are exceptions. If the buyer steadfastly refused to buy the product, most salespeople feel that they have nothing to lose, so they might look for another contact or, as it is known in the industry, "go in through the back door." In some cases, executives consistently override their buyer's decisions, but these cases are rare. It is also possible that the nature of the product is such that executives will specifically request its purchase. Most firms, however, have enough confidence in their buyers to delegate purchasing responsibilities.

Most technical salespeople maintain an up-to-date file on all prospect firms, their buyers, and what transpired during sales calls. If the salesperson's territory is sufficiently large, the sales manager often subscribes to services that report on the movement of established firms and the start-up of new firms on a geographical basis. *Dodge Reports*,[6] for example, provides daily communiques of new construction by territorial subdivision, and there are numerous other services that report periodically on the buying needs of firms that purchase technical products and services.

Because of the sophisticated nature of technical products and services, direct mail, advertising, and other forms of media seldom have the impact of the personal sales call for providing information and product data. Although a great deal is spent on media promotional techniques, it is considered essential by both buyer and seller that a face-to-face interview be scheduled to provide most data upon which a purchasing decision can be made. For the most part, the objective of media and direct-mail advertising in the technical field is to provide current information on the state of the art.

In summary, prospecting in the technical field is normally the responsibility of the salesperson. Because of the relative ease in making an appointment with the buyer, the personal call has been and continues to be the most common prospecting technique, although use of the technical media and, to a lesser extent, direct mail facilitates this process.

Prospecting in Commercial Sales

Most commercial salespeople are also assigned to specific geographic or account territories with availability to a finite number of prospects. As in technical sales, personal contact has been determined by most firms to be the most effective method of prospecting. Unlike technical sales, however, the commercial salesperson's access to the buyer is limited. Many salespeople canvass in commercial sales, probably because it is difficult to obtain an appointment any other way. The person charged with the responsibility of evaluating the goods and services of commercial salespeople seldom has the authority to make a purchase. Simply stated, most executives with the authority to spend money are either too busy or simply don't want to talk to a salesperson if they are not in the market for a particular product or service. It can often be assumed, then, that the individual who interviews the salesperson is *not* a decision maker with regard to making a purchase. In an interview with the author, a sales manager for a prominent manufacturer of office equipment stated

> When one of our people, or one of our competitor's people, for that matter, makes a cold call, you can be sure that they'll either be told by a receptionist that nobody wants to buy anything (even if they don't know what the product is) or at best, some guy who doesn't have the authority to go to the men's room by himself comes out. Man, this is a humiliating experience! You stand there either trying to explain to this guy the benefits of your product, and he tries to pretend he's interested when all he wants you to do is get the hell out. Maybe you ask him who has the authority to buy, and he implies that he does but he's not interested. This is the kind of stuff you have to put up with and if you don't like it, the only consolation is that *no* salesman in his right mind likes it either. But you have to do it. Sooner or later you get one who's in the market for your product and then you have a good shot at a sale. Then you finally get to see the right dude and he buys and then you're all pumped up and can go out and make cold calls for another couple of days. It's not always as bad as I make it sound and our people *do* make good money. The only thing is, it can get to be a real pain in the ass sometimes and if you can't take rejection, this is not for you.

Another unique aspect of commercial sales is relative product homogeneity and the comparison of several competitive brands that inexorably becomes part of the buying process. Nearly every salable product in the marketplace is duplicated by several competitors. As a result, salespeople representing well-known firms are often contacted by a prospect without his or her making any actual effort to locate the buyer. Many experienced salespeople understandably feel that there is a definite advantage to representing a well-known firm, even if the product's price might be higher than that of the competition.

Most commercial sales organizations require their salespeople to maintain a current file of all prospects in the territory. This file normally indicates all information considered to be pertinent to the sale, including product application, potential use, name of decision maker, and other relevant information. If updated regularly, the prospect file provides the salesperson with enough data to set up an effective system so that certain firms are not deluged with cold calls while others are neglected. The individual salesperson's prospect files provide valuable data when sales territories are realigned or salespeople move into a new territory.

In general, it may be stated that, although some telephone appointment setting is made, the bulk of prospecting in commercial sales is conducted on a face-to-face basis, and much of this prospecting utilizes "cold calling," a technique that makes selling a unique occupation.

Prospecting in Direct Sales

Probably the most well-known stereotype of direct sales is the door-to-door vacuum cleaner salesman. After sticking his foot in a closing door, he manages to get into the house, successfully demonstrates his product, and walks away with a sale. In reality, the door-to-door approach to prospecting is utilized by very few direct-sales firms today. Where it is done, cosmetics, household items, and magazine subscriptions comprise the bulk of these sales. First, many communities have local ordinances against door-to-door sales. Second, it is extremely difficult for sales organizations to hire and retain effective door-to-door salespeople. The third and probably most important reason why prospecting is not widely conducted on a door-to-door basis is because most products sold on a direct basis require a joint decision by both the husband and the wife before a sale is made. This condition imposes a strong barrier, since the chances of both parties being home during the day are slight. In some direct-sales firms, canvassers are hired to go from house to house attempting to set up appointments for salespeople. The more successful door-to-door sales firms, such as Avon and Agway, concentrate on selling products that can be sold to an individual. The price range is sufficiently low to negate the need for a joint decision. This method, however, is considered obsolete by most firms.

Most prospecting in the direct-sales field is conducted through personal referrals, direct mail, telephone canvassing, or media advertising.

Referrals This technique is unquestionably the most effective and least expensive of all direct-sales prospecting techniques. Most firms train salespeople to develop referrals through formal techniques. An insurance salesman, for example, would use a different approach to persuading a customer to refer a relative or friend as a prospect than would a home improvements salesperson. Most firms selling intangibles like mutual funds or insurance train their salespeople to elicit referrals from customers at the time of sale. This timing is considered to be propitious because the customer is presumably enthusiastic about the investment or purchase that he or she has made. The credibility of the salesperson is likewise presumed to be very high at this point; otherwise, the customer, in all likelihood, would not have agreed to make the purchase or investment. Customers are, therefore, willing to refer acquaintances because of the customer benefits that will accrue to them.

On the other hand, firms that sell a product or service requiring future performance normally train their salespeople to solicit referrals *after* the performance that has been promised has in fact been delivered. Customers are traditionally diffident to give referrals and have, in most cases, a "wait-and-see" attitude. When the firm has performed and the customer is satisfied, however, the salesperson is in a stronger position to ask for and receive referrals.

In many industries, appliances and other premiums are offered to new customers as an incentive to provide referrals. There has been very little research conducted on the effectiveness of this type of referral solicitation. The benefits of such incentives seem obvious, but a few drawbacks to this process must be considered: the cost of the premium, the possibility of a negative interpretation by the customer of such an offer, and the reluctance of many people to refer customers for a reward. Whether or not a firm uses incentives to customers, the referral method of prospecting has proved to be very effective for most direct-sales organizations.

Direct Mail There is about a 99 percent probability of your having received at one time or another a direct-mail solicitation piece from a direct-sales organization. Many firms depend almost exclusively on this technique to generate leads. This method is highly expensive and is typically used only because alternative methods are even more expensive. A direct-mail campaign, for example, is considered to be an overwhelming success if a 0.10 percent response is received. One might wonder, therefore, why some other, less expensive technique is not used. The answer is that there probably is not any. The alternative forms of lead generation are also very expensive, in some cases prohibitively so. Even in the face of high postage costs, however, it requires a very low number of replies to justify direct-mail expense.

If a firm has developed an effective direct-mail campaign, its competitors typically follow suit. After continual bombardment from several firms, prospects have little or no interest, and the reply rate normally drops precipitously. The direct-mail piece is normally designed not only to gain attention, but also to develop interest; therefore, a substantial amount of gimmickery such as free prizes and other inducements to reply are enclosed. This technique, although expensive, somewhat shopworn, and often nonremunerative, nevertheless remains a fairly effective form of direct-sales prospecting.

Telephone Solicitation One disadvantage of having one's telephone number listed in the directory is the almost inevitable probability of being solicited for an appointment by a direct-sales firm. This technique is highly expensive, yields low returns, and often the quality of leads generated is very poor. Generally, phone rooms (or in the vernacular of the direct-sales field, "boiler rooms") are used to solicit prospects for relatively expensive products and services such as food freezer services, vacation property, and home improvements. A script is prepared, which the solicitor uses in attempting to schedule an appointment. A solicitor normally works on a four- or six-hour shift and is normally considered successful if he or she schedules more than one or two appointments. As with direct mail, only a few sales are necessary to justify the expense of the phone room, but there are more problems attendant to the latter method. First, there is normally heavy pressure to schedule appointments, which results in the solicitor's scheduling very "shaky" or unqualified appointments. Then, when the salesperson calls on the prospect, he or she is often told that there is no interest in the product or service. This problem shatters the salesperson's confidence in the organization and results in high turnover. As a point of fact, many direct salespeople will not work by telephone solicitation because of the problem of poor-quality lead generation. Another problem of using a phone room is associated with the reluctance of most respondents to talk with solicitors. An increase in sophistication toward direct sales in general, a wariness of products or services sold to the home, and the high incidence of working

"You get the junk mail and I'll answer the junk telephone call."

spouses has reduced the effectiveness of this technique substantially over the past few years. In the face of these problems, however, many firms continue to use telephone solicitation with some degree of success.

Media Advertising The least common method of direct-sales lead generation is media advertising. When they are used, television and radio ads are normally presented at the local level and are intended to answer an immediate need of a prospect, for example, home improvements. Because of the high expense of these media, however, most direct-sales firms exclude this type of lead generation from their budgets. A lesser used media is magazines, where coupons and business reply cards are sometimes inserted by direct-sales firms. Most of these magazines are directed toward a particular interest group, such as auto mechanics, small business owners, or hobbyists. Television supplements to Sunday newspapers, however, have traditionally advertised direct-sales products and services successfully.

Prospecting Summary

Prospecting techniques vary according to sales type. Methods that are successful in the technical sector, for example, are hardly ever used in the direct-sales sector. Likewise, consultative-type prospecting is considerably distinct from ommercial-sales prospecting. Prospecting and lead generation are outlined in Table 2-5. It is important that the student have an awareness of the various techniques

TABLE 2-5

Prospecting and Lead Generation

Types of Sales	Four Most Widely Used Modes of Prospecting
Consultative	Referrals by existing clients
	Seminars and colloquiums
	Advertising in appropriate business and industry media
	Research of possible clients in appropriate library sources
Technical	Personal canvassing
	Direct mail
	Advertising in appropriate business and industry media
	Industrial and private lead sources
Commercial	Personal canvassing
	Prospect file follow-up
	Direct mail
	Trade shows and conventions
Direct	Direct mail
	Telephone solicitation
	Referrals by customers
	Personally developed leads

discussed in this chapter if he or she is to understand the relationship between the prospecting function and sales management.

THE SALES PRESENTATION

Most sales organizations, through research and trial and error, have developed strategic sales presentations that are intended to appeal to all or most buying motives for their goods and services. A presentation is a particular format that is used by the salesperson in selling and is often referred to as a "sales pitch." Sales presentation methods are outlined in Table 2-6 and discussed in the following.

Structurally, there are three basic types of presentations: memorized or "canned," programmed, or open-ended. The *memorized or canned* presentation is used primarily in direct sales. The salesperson is taught to memorize word for word a specific presentation of the product or service to the prospect. The main reason for having the salesperson memorize the presentation is so that he or she will not omit any important benefits or add anything that is not true. An additional reason for using this type of presentation is in situations where there is high turnover and the sales management does not have the time to provide training in greater depth. You have probably been exposed to this type of presentation with-

TABLE 2-6

Modes of Sales Presentations

Type of Sales	Extent to Which Persuasive Abilities and Techniques Normally Influence Sale	Mode of Presentation
Consultative	Low	Open ended; problem-solving approach
Technical	Low	Open ended to determine appropriate needs; programmed presentation to sell product or service.
Commercial	Moderate to high	Open ended to determine appropriate needs; programmed presentation focusing on particular feature or benefit perceived by prospect
Direct	High	Canned or programmed presentation; classic stimulus-response selling formula (AIDA) approach to sale

out being aware of it. Its use is widespread in the insurance, automobile, and encyclopedia fields.

The *programmed* presentation is similar to the canned except that the prospect participates in the discussion by answering questions or rendering opinions. For example, it may be structured so that if the salesperson asks the prospect a question, the answer must be "yes" or "no." In either case, the salesperson has a response designed to lead toward the sale. A further distinction is made in that the salesperson may normally use his or her own judgment in veering away from the script, provided that all major points are covered. Presentations of this type are used in many areas of commercial selling, such as office equipment and products to retailers.

The *open-ended* presentation is, as its name implies, an outline of steps that lead toward the sale, but with a great deal of input from the prospect. This type of presentation is used in any situation either where the benefits of the product or service are not apparent or where the salesperson is trying to help the prospect solve a problem. This type of presentation is used by all firms in the consultative and technical sectors and in many commercial selling situations.

Strategic Approaches

The canned, programmed, and open-ended type of presentations are illustrations of the *structure* or *format* used by various types of salespersons. In addition, there are three basic types of *strategic approaches* to selling that are taken in making the presentation. These are often referred to as the *stimulus-response approach*, the *selling formula approach*, and the *needs-satisfaction approach*.

The stimulus-response approach is used when the salesperson says things to prospects that are designed to elicit a favorable response. This approach is very simple and precludes any complex decision making on the part of the prospect. Examples of typical dialog used by salespeople are as follows:

You want to save money, don't you?
Wouldn't you like to have financial security?
Have you received your free gift yet?
Do you think it's worth five cents an hour to look beautiful?

It is clear that this type of approach leaves little room for any sophisticated discussion of need for the product or service. Surprisingly, this type of approach is used almost exclusively in the magazine subscription field and in the maintenance chemical and lighting fields, and some variation is used successfully in most consumer sales situations.

The *selling formula approach* is more widely used than the others because of its adaptability to any selling situation. This approach is based upon the four steps of gaining the customer's attention, developing his or her interest in the product or service, creating a desire or want for it, and, finally, closing the sale (see Table

2-7). This approach is referred to as AIDA, abbreviated for attention, interest, desire, and action. The framework of the AIDA approach divides the selling process into the four stages, and the intensity of the customer's attitude at each stage can normally be determined by the salesperson's experience and perception. Therefore, as the salesperson makes the presentation, he or she looks for "buying signals" and attempts to draw out of the prospect the benefit of the product or service that carries the most appeal. This process is known as finding the prospect's "hot button." Once this is determined, the salesperson elaborates on the ensuing benefits and attempts to close the sale. The selling formula theory is used in practically every nontechnical selling situation because of the logical pattern it follows. Conversely, this type of approach has a tendency to develop a salesman-oriented rather than a customer-oriented sales situation, a condition that can lose sales which might have been made on balance. Although the AIDA approach has received criticism in recent years, it remains a very effective and widely used approach.

The *needs-satisfaction approach* is more customer-oriented than the other two and is intended to develop demand by providing a satisfactory answer to the prospect's needs. Practically every firm that trains salespersons claims that it uses this problem-solving approach. In fact, the prospects *real* problem is not always

TABLE 2-7

Basic Sales Process, the Selling Formula Approach

Step in Selling Process	Form of Communication	Specification Initiated By Salesperson	Desired Result
Gaining attention	Statement or question	Addresses current problem	Prospect agrees that problem exists
Developing interest	Description of product or features	Brings out possibility that this product or service can help solve problem	Prospect can perceive some reason for solving problem
Creating desire	Enumeration of benefit	Recommends specific way that problem can be solved	Prospect agrees that a solution to problem is desirable
Taking action	Closing the sale	Insists that now is the time to solve the problem	Prospect agrees that this is the way to solve the problem and it should be done now

apparent to the salesperson and, in some cases, even to the prospect. An approach that is realistically based on problem solving typically requires considerably more training than most firms are willing to provide. For this reason, most firms continue to use some variation of AIDA. Consultative and technical firms, however, are more committed to problem solving and are, therefore, more willing to expend the training resources necessary to implement this approach.

Persuasive Techniques

Although the extent of human persuasion differs among the four types of sales, *handling objections* and the *close* take place in nearly every sale that is made. These two elements of the sales process do not really lend themselves as readily to segmentation by sales type as do prospecting and the presentation. Their importance, however, cannot be underestimated if a successful sale is to take place.

Handling Objections Sometime during the course of the sales presentation, most prospects are likely to raise objections or to set up barriers to the sale. Whether or not the objection seems legitimate to the salesperson is irrelevant. If the prospect has raised an objection, it must be answered before proceeding with the presentation. The fact that the objection has been raised indicates that this point is on the prospects's mind, and that his or her undivided attention cannot be expected until it has been answered. Most salespeople are trained to expect or even encourage objections, as they provide a positive step toward the sale if handled properly. The prevailing attitude of sales professions is that an objection is, in most cases, a desire by the prospect for more information, rather than his or her intentionally erecting barriers to the consummation of a sale. There are, of course, many cases where prospects are clearly not interested in the product or service and will continue to maintain resistance to the sale, in which case handling the objections raised is probably a waste of time. In most sales situations, however, certain objections are expected to arise. All sales organizations train their salespeople to expect specific objections and provide them with the answers to these objections.

Most sales organizations also train their salespeople to be cognizant of the fact that an objection raised by a prospect may not be the *true* objection. Many times this is the case when the reluctance to spend money is the true reason for the customer's sales resistance, but other objections are raised. In cases of this type, the salesperson often attempts to relate the benefits of the product versus cost or makes some attempt to minimize the cost factor.

Until about a decade ago, salespeople were trained to overcome objections in a fairly glib fashion. The emphasis on handling objections was designed to put the prospect on the defensive. An example of this technique would be to get the prospect to agree early in the presentation that he or she had the authority to make a buying decision; then, if later in the presentation the buyer indicated that he or she had to get approval from another person to buy, the salesperson referred to the earlier statement that he or she had already indicated that approval was unnecessary. Recent research has shown that tactics of this type have a tendency to weaken rather than strengthen the relationship between the salesperson and buyer. As a result, most salespeople are trained to treat objections in such a way as not to put prospects on the defensive or otherwise weaken the relationship.

The Close At some point in the sales process, the customer agrees to buy the product by issuing a purchase order, signing an agreement, or otherwise binding the sale in a tangible way. The process of consummating the sale or getting the prospect to bind the sale tangibly is known as the *close*. Although the extent of closing skill required varies among sales types, it should be recognized that unless the salesperson makes it happen the sale will either not take place or be delayed unnecessarily.

As in handling objections, many techniques are used to close the sale, and these techniques are related to the specific product or service being sold. Most sales organizations train their salespeople in one or more closing techniques, which follow as a logical culmination to the presentation. Generally, most salespeople attempt to close the sale after all apparent objections have been answered. The most direct method of closing a sale is simply asking for the order. However, several other general types of closes are typically used, each of which is related to a specific sales situation. Commercial and direct salespeople are particularly adept at closing the sale. Because of limited access to the qualified prospect, it is critical that salespeople in these fields develop strong closing skills. In the technical and consultative areas, however, closing skill is less important. The reason for this is that decisions to buy are much more rational and are often made by a buying committee.

In summary, the persuasive techniques of handling objections and closing the sale are critical elements of the sales process. Although direct and commercial salespeople are required to develop stronger closing skills, the ability to handle objections is a necessary requisite for all types of sales.

The Follow-Up Function

With the possible exception of some direct-sales companies, most firms insist that their salespeople continue to provide an ongoing customer service after the sale has been made. The main purpose of the follow-up is to ensure customer satisfaction and minimize complaints. An auxiliary function of follow-up is, of course, to generate repeat business. In many firms, technical and service personnel perform this function, leaving the salesperson free to call on accounts to generate new business. The salesperson, however, should continue to maintain contact with existing customers and follow up *immediately* on complaints or, for that matter, *any* telephone call from an existing customer. Most sales managers consider the sales process to be incomplete without adequate follow-up. This function can often make or break a sales organizations's reputation.

SUMMARY

This chapter has investigated the selling function and how it is employed in various types of sales organizations. Selling has had a great impact upon the economy and if it were not for this function, many if not most employees would not have a job. Essentially, there are four types of sales.

1. *Consultative sales:* The sale of solutions to problems; sold at very high levels of the buyer's organization.
2. *Technical sales:* The sale of products and services for which a high degree of technical knowledge is required.
3. *Commercial sales:* Sales of goods and services to businesses that do not fall into the consultative or technical category.
4. *Direct sales:* Sales of goods and services to consumers, excluding most retail store sales.

The sales process begins with prospecting for potential customers. Each type of selling utilizes different prospecting techniques. Consultative-sales prospecting is normally accomplished through referral and personal contact. Technical-sales prospecting utilizes canvassing and advertising techniques, commercial-sales prospecting consists primarily of canvassing, and direct-sales prospecting is carried out through direct mail, telephone canvassing, and personal referrals.

The selling process itself consists of the salesperson's convincing the prospect to buy through the use of various persuasive techniques. Selling in technical sales is highly rational, whereas selling in direct sales is highly emotional. The other two sales sectors rely more on economic than on emotional motives, as a rule. Some of the important persuasive sales techniques are developed to handle objections, create a desire for the product, and close the sale. These techniques are used in accordance with the type of sales presentation that is required to sell the product.

In any sales organization, follow-up is highly important to maintain credibility and customer following.

Eleanor's Employment Service

Eleanor Rigby is the owner and operator of a one-person employment agency. Her major in college was Library Science, but after several years as a research librarian for a local college, Eleanor decided she wanted a career that gave her a better chance to utilize her gregarious and assertive personality. She had taken several business courses as an undergraduate, and finally decided to open an employment service in the San Fernando Valley area near Los Angeles. At first she specialized in the placement of clerical, stenographic, and general office personnel, but she soon found that the demand for salespeople was so great that she decided to specialize exclusively in the placement of people in this profession. After about five years, Eleanor's Employment Service had become highly profitable, mainly because she handled all the applicants and dealt with all employers herself. Although many people told her she could porbably increase her business by expanding, Eleanor attributed her success to her personal attention to all clients. Another factor, she felt, was the aggravation involved in paper-work requirements for employees.

One day, to her shock, she received a telegram from her hometown in New York that her mother had been taken seriously ill. Fortunately, her husband Paul was at the apartment they rented watching television, and Eleanor was able to have Paul come to the office to fill in for her while she was gone. Paul had been unable to secure employment since his graduation from college several years before and was available for just this type of emergency. The following conversation took place prior to Eleanor's leaving for the airport:

Eleanor: Paul, I have four job requisitions that have to be filled. I want you to put an ad in the paper for applicants and send the four companies people who will fit the qualifications they want. Don't send them any applicants who don't have the background for the job. Do you understand that, Paul?

Paul: Yes, Eleanor.

Eleanor: Here are the requisitions. One is from Huron Plastics, one from Fleetwood Auto Sales, one from Ace Chemical Corporation, and one from Parker Systems Management. Do you know what these companies do, Paul?

Paul: Not really, Eleanor.

Eleanor: All right, read the annual reports I left for you. They tell all about the firm and what they do. You ought to be able to figure out the kind of people you want from these reports. If you have any problems while I'm gone, you'll have to figure them out yourself because I'm going to be tied up. Do you think you can handle it O.K., Paul?

Paul: Well, I'm not really sure, Eleanor.

Eleanor: This is a fine time to tell me. Well, it's too late now. Do the best you can, Paul, and I'll see you when I get back.

Paul: All right, Eleanor. Have a pleasant trip.

In analyzing the reports, Paul was able to summarize the functions of the four companies. His notes read as follows:

Huron Plastics: Manufactures and markets plastic office equipment. Sells to businesses, government, and institutions. Salespeople get most of their new business from canvassing and repeat business from calling on present customers.

Fleetwood Auto Sales: Dealership for Chrysler, Plymouth, and Toyota new cars. Also has an extensive array of used cars. Customers are almost exclusively consumers. Most sales are made at dealership location.

Ace Chemical: Manufactures and markets bulb chemicals such as chlorine and soda ash. Most customers are specialty chemical firms, and Ace provides its customers with a great amount of technical consulting on nature and applications of its products.

Parker Systems Management: Sells a communications system to corporations who have several offices at diverse locations. System must be adopted for an entire company. Most sales are made at the company president level.

After compiling and analyzing the preceding data, Paul is unable to determine how to advertise for salespeople. He is afraid to disturb Eleanor, but is even more afraid to have her return and find no results. In desperation , he calls you for help.

1. What qualifications would you stress in the newspaper ads for applicants?
2. Which type of salesperson fits each job?

The Graf Brothers

Bill and Tom Graf are carpenters near Pittsburgh, Pennsylvania. Most of the work they do is in private home construction. Their jobs are subcontracted from larger builders. Because of the uncertainty of the home building market, the climate, and even the financial condition of prime contractors, their annual income seldom exceeds $12,000. For some time, Bill and Tom have been looking around for a business to get into that will provide steady work, utilize their talents, and be more remunerative than their present situation. After searching the marketplace for some time, they came up with three possibilities and are now in the process of evaluating them. In each business situation, the Graf brothers are in a position to invest the necessary capital to start the business and have the supply connections to buy materials on credit. They also feel confident that they possess the technical expertise to do an outstanding job. Bill and Tom were trained by their father, a true craftsman from the old country, and their dedication to a job well done would certainly be a competitive advantage in today's world of slipshod, "take the money and run" workmanship. As the Graf brothers analyze the situation, the greatest obstacle to getting into business is their lack of knowledge of how to get customers. They feel that any customer they have will be a satisfied one, but obtaining that initial cadre of clients might be such a difficult undertaking that it could preclude them from starting their own business. Since they have always worked as employees or as subcontractors, they have never had to go out and obtain customers. Neither one feels confident about performing this function. They heard that you were taking a course related to selling and have asked your advice on what they should do. The following are the three alternatives they are considering:

Insulation: With the impact of the energy crisis and the income tax credit for insulating the taxpayer's home, the market for home insulation has been increasing steadily over the past few years. To enter this business, the Grafs would need very little additional capital, and if they were able to maintain a full pipeline of jobs, this business would be highly profitable. One of the major problems is the seasonality of the home insulation market.

Home improvements: The cost of new houses has caused many homeowners to consider additions to and the general upgrading of their present homes as an alternative to buying a new one. The Grafs have a high degree of expertise in this field and are scrupulous almost to a fault in doing this kind of work. The main stumbling block to entering this field, as the Graf brothers see it, is the long hours that are necessary because of the moderate prices they charge. Both of their wives have been adamant about their working only a 10-hour day.

Low-price tires: In the face of present-day inflation, many car owners are buying used and recapped tires at a fraction of the cost of new ones. Several companies sell franchises for $25,000 and upward to business opportunity seekers. Bill and Tom have determined that by renovating an abandoned service station and buying the necessary equipment they can estimate the "up-front" franchise fee. They also have found several suppliers willing to provide them with their inventory at favorable credit terms. The key obstacle to their entering this business is that they are both too active to sit and wait for customers to come in. They have determined that it would not be feasible to hire another person to work in the shop.

1. Based on the concepts learned so far in this course, what sales advice would you give the Graf brothers about each of the three alternatives?
2. Develop an outline for a sales presentation that the Graf brothers could give a prospect in each alternative. It must be something that they would realistically be able to handle and be comfortable with.

DISCUSSION QUESTIONS

1. What sales jobs exemplify different categories of selling?
2. What personal sales characteristics are compatible with each of these categories?
3. To what degree are these characteristics strictly necessary and attainable?
4. How can a sales manager or salesperson compensate for personal deficiencies in favorable sales characteristics?
5. What makes a service or product marketable?
6. For various consumer product situations, such as electronics, automotive, or household appliances, what are the different sales requirements from the smallest component to the finished end product?
7. For question 6, what types of prospecting are more desirable? Which are secondary?
8. Putting yourself in the role of a sales prospect, what are you looking for from the salesperson?

NOTES

[1]*Statistical Abstracts of the U. S.*, U.S. Department of Commerce (99), Washington, D.C., 1978, p. 418.

[2]Paul Lundgren, "The Cost of Sales Training," in *Management of Sales Training* ed., Jared L. Harrison, (Reading, Mass.: Addison-Wesley, 1977), p. 278.

[3]*Statistical Abstracts*, p. 418.

[4]A term used to describe a type of customer who will buy virtually anything.

[5]Leon G. Schiffman and Leslie Lazar Kanuk, *Consumer Behavior* (Englewood Cliffs, N.J.: Prentice-Hall, 1978), pp. 52–53.

[6]*Dodge Reports*, McGraw-Hill Corporation, New York.

CHAPTER 3

THE SALES MANAGER

OBJECTIVES

To provide the reader with an understanding of the organizational levels of sales management.

To describe and analyze the broad functions of the sales manager:

* Planning
* Organizing
* Controlling
* Staffing
* Directing

To describe and analyze the job requirements for the sales manager:

* Experience
* Education
* Skill
* Attitude

To put into perspective the impact of the company's policies, procedures, and politics.

INTERVIEW WITH FRANK SMITH

Interviewer: Now that we are into the area of what sales managers do, Frank, can you tell me what we're going to cover in the next chapter?

Frank Smith: Well, if you recall, we said earlier that, although sales managers work for different companies and supervise the sales of a multitude of products and services, there are still certain broad functions that are common to all sales managers. This is what we are going to talk about.

Interviewer: I remember you telling me that the functions you learned about in college are actually practiced on the job.

Frank Smith: Believe it or not, I even took a course in sales management. My instructor had been a sales manager for a long time. He was kind of cocky and got a little sarcastic once in a while, but he taught me a lot. What might really astound a lot of people is that much of the things you learn from textbooks has a practical application in the real world.

Interviewer: Do you think this is more true in sales management than in many other courses?

Frank Smith: Oh, sure. Because of its vocationallike orientation, some business departments feel that a course in sales management is even a little mundane. Personally, I think it should be taught at all schools.

Interviewer: Frank, do you think we could get into the chapter now?

Just as characteristics of salespersons and sales techniques vary among the four sales sectors discussed in the previous chapter, sales management techniques also vary among sectors. It would be difficult indeed to enumerate in one chapter a list of specific techniques that are utilized by all types of sales managers. Succeeding chapters will discuss many of these. However, many characteristics in the structure and informal environment are common to most sales organizations. Likewise, there are certain general functions that all sales managers perform. Finally, certain background characteristics are present to some degree in all sales managers. This chapter investigates the organizational, functional, and personal characteristics that are common to most sales managers. It also attempts to form a profile of the "typical" sales manager to enhance the reader's understanding of his or her strengths and limitations in dealing with the functions that will be discussed in succeeding chapters.

IMPORTANCE OF THE SALES MANAGER

In marketing their goods and services, firms that depend upon a sales force tend to place a great deal of importance on the sales management function. Since it is through selling that most revenues and profits are derived, it is not surprising that companies place such high priority on this function. Because of this emphasis, most firms are highly selective in the hiring and promotion of sales managers.

Since the individuals picked to lead the sales force make decisions that can directly affect a firm's success or failure in the marketplace, careful analysis of an individual's present and future potential is necessary before appointing him or her to the job of sales manager.

To perform effectively, a sales organization must have strong leadership. Not only should a sales manager be able to achieve a high level of sales and profits through managing the sales force, but he or she is also responsible for the growth and development of each individual salesperson. Because it is so vital that the sales manager maintain a strong rapport with *all* the sales force, he or she nearly always finds it necessary to maintain a personal relationship with each sales-force member while still remaining impartial.

Managerial decisions regarding personnel are normally very sensitive, yet the sales manager must constantly make decisions in this area. Because of the sensitive nature of most decisions a sales manager must make, a special personality is required. Most sales organizations have developed, either formally or informally, a profile of the successful sales manager, and persons who come closest to filling the profile are normally given strong consideration for the job when a sales management opening occurs. Although the functions that a sales manager must perform may vary among firms, there is an almost universal emphasis placed by firms upon the importance of his or her place in the organization.

Organizational Levels of Sales Management

Most national and multinational firms have similar organizational levels of sales managers within a given industry. This structure is normally referred to as "triangular" or "pyramidal." It consists of one key executive at the top and many first-line managers at the bottom of the structure. Most manufacturers of durable goods, for example, tend to organize the sales function by geography. This is the most common organizational form. Managers at each organizational level are responsible for a predetermined number of subordinates who report to them, and the responsibility, status, and importance of each sales manager depends upon his or her level in the organization.

In this setting, the manager responsible for the entire sales operation normally carries the title of *vice-president of sales* or *national sales manager*. The next sales level down in the hierarchy or structure normally consists of five or six *regional managers*. Each regional manager has responsibility for a large portion of the country, for example, the Southwest, the Northeast, or the Pacific Coast region. These managers normally have several *district managers* reporting to them. Each district manager has responsibility for a major marketing area, such as the New York City marketing area, or perhaps an entire state, or several small states. Reporting to the district manager are several *branch managers*. Each of these executives normally has responsibility for the sale of the company's products or services in an area corresponding to that of a medium-sized or large city. The typical branch office consists of as many salespeople as can be effectively supervised by a manager. This *span of control* averages anywhere from about six to ten salespeople. If a branch office consists of more salespeople than a manager can effectively supervise, an *assistant manager* helps the branch manager share the supervisory load. It should be pointed out here that not every firm uses the same titles; for example, the position described here as regional manager is known as *zone manager* at Xerox. Nevertheless, their responsibilities are similar.

As stated earlier, nearly every industry follows a classic breakdown of levels of sales management. Positions may be assigned on the basis of factors other than geography. In some technical firms, for example, sales managerial responsibility is assigned on the basis of customer type. Nevertheless, the classic breakdown described here applies to most industries.

National Sales Manager

The chief operating sales executive in most firms is typically referred to as the *national sales manager.* This executive has the overall responsibility for the entire sales force and normally reports to the key marketing executive of the company. If there is no marketing vice-president, the national sales manager typically reports to the president or the executive vice-president. The national sales manager, in conjunction with other key executives of the firm, helps set sales policies and is ultimately responsible for meeting sales forecasts. It is not unusual for a national sales manager to head up a sales force of several hundred men and women.[1] It would not be realistic to expect an executive at this level to have a surplus of free time. Much of this executive's time is spent traveling across the country. A job of this sort is characterized by intense pressure, and one or more assistants are often appointed to help share the enormous work load. Most national sales managers are compensated well. Larger firms often pay salaries and bonuses in excess of six figures to persons in this position of responsibility.

Regional Sales Manager

This position is similar to that of the national sales manager, with the exception of the access to the highest executives in the firm. A regional sales manager has overall responsibility for all sales operations within the sales region. Again, it would be unrealistic to assume that this executive is able to lead a "normal life." Constant travel, constant pressure, and very long days are typical. In an interview with the author, a regional manager for a sporting goods firm pointed out that

> No matter how much money you're paid, it's not enough to really compensate you. I made $65,000 last year, but it seemed like a dollar an hour. Naturally, I like the challenge my job presents, and so does everyone else in this position, otherwise you couldn't take the pace. There is a true sense of order and satisfaction one receives in this job. You have the satisfaction of being a major factor in the firm's successful attainment of its sales quotas. You also have the satisfaction of helping develop the sales managers who report to you. The negative aspect to a

job like this is that you either go at a frantic pace or you go backwards. Frankly, I don't think I could perform at this level of activity forever.

As indicated, compensation for regional managers is quite high, but one must weigh the personal and family sacrifices that are involved in performing this function.

District Manager

The district manager has reasonably close proximity to the branches that fall under his or her supervision. Most district managers are responsible for the activities of several branch offices. The function of the district manager is often one of control—doing whatever is necessary to assist branch managers in the attainment of their sales objectives. A typical span of control for a district manager is about five to ten branches, depending upon the type of product sold and the number of salespeople in the branches. Compensation for district managers is normally about 20 to 30 percent higher than that of branch managers.[2] Most district managers perceive themselves as future regional managers, either in their own firm or in some other firm. For this reason, most persons in this position are willing and eager to assume the responsibilities without an appreciable compensation differential compared to the branch level.

Branch Manager

This position is the first level of sales management and in most firms, the most critical job in the sales hierarchy. Since the branch manager must supervise the people who actually sell the firm's goods or services, he or she has a tremendous impact upon the firm's sales effort. In any firm, the majority of its sales managers operate at the branch level. This position is typically the first promotional step for salespeople; therefore, it is the most visible management position from the salesperson's point of view. In some firms a branch manager receives lower compensation than his or her more successful salespeople. Overall, however, most branch managers are well compensated, often earning in the $30,000 to $40,000 range, and in some cases, upward.[3]

The focus of this book will be from the branch manager level. This approach is most realistic because of the strong probability that any future sales manager will perform at this level sometimes during his or her career.

THE MANAGEMENT PROCESS

In the introductory interview with Frank Smith, the functions of the manager were discussed briefly. From the textbook viewpoint, management is typically viewed as a *process*. This process involves specific functions that managers perform and focuses upon basic management principles. From reading the Introduction, it should be reasonably clear that any attempt to separate a manager's functions into neat compartments is unrealistic. We have seen, for example, that a manager actually performs various functions simultaneously. As a matter of fact, if you spent a day with any sales manager and asked which *function* he or she was performing at any given time, the answer might very well be one of uncertainty.

There is, however, an advantage to studying management from a process standpoint. It allows the reader to understand what the manager's functions *are*, and at the same time it provides a framework for introducing certain concepts.[4] The managerial process is a fairly complex activity. Many managers are experts in practice but have never studied the process analytically. They can explain what they do and why they do it, but not in textbook terminology. This section will take a systematic approach and attempt to break down the process into parts so that those who have not had the opportunity to learn by trial and error can understand it.

Functions of Management

If you asked ten different managers to list their specific functions, you would undoubtedly get ten different answers. Likewise, no one function is more important than the others. But a list and description of management functions is a useful device for stressing the basic elements inherent in the job. Although different people use different names for the key functions of management, there is general agreement on most of the things a manager actually does. The functions that will be discussed here are planning, organizing, controlling, staffing, and directing.

PLANNING

Planning is the process by which a manager determines the alternative courses of action that will be available in the near future. The exact type of plans the manager makes are determined by his or her immediate objectives. Although most organizations plan years in advance, most sales managers are primarily concerned with plans and objectives for the year. The first step in any managerial planning process is a statement of specific objectives. Once the objectives have been set, the actions necessary to achieve the objectives are developed. Most managers also develop alternative plans in case unforeseen developments occur. Because of the existence of so many outside forces, such as the economy, competition, and technological change, it is especially important for managers to develop a set of alternative plans to be used if the original plans do not work out.

The Planning Function and the Sales Manager

Sales planning normally consists of the joint determination of goals, objectives, and alternative courses of action between the sales manager and the manager he or she reports to, and, in many cases, with the sales force. It can be said that planning is included in the other functions; for instance, the sales manager must plan his or her personnel needs; therefore, the manager *plans* even when fulfilling the *staffing* function. Likewise, the manager *plans* to utilize certain motivational techniques; therefore, the manager *plans* while fulfilling the *directing* function.

What we are most concerned with here are the types of formalized plans that most sales managers find are necessary to set forth in determining specific goals with respect to producing revenue, administration, and personnel.

Sales managers engage extensively in setting plans and objectives to produce revenue. Probably the most widely accepted of these is the *sales forecast*, a projection of gross sales that the sales manager expects his or her sales force to produce during a given time period, typically during the upcoming year or the upcoming quarter. Several sources of information are used by the sales manager in developing sales forecast estimates; they include analysis of existing and future sales potential, analysis of sales-force estimates, and analysis of certain uncontrollable variables such as competition, relative economic conditions, and the legislative environment. The specific nature of the sales manager's planning tools will be examined in detail in Chapter 10.

Although the "marketing concept" emphasizes *profits*, most field sales managers do not have adequate information to estimate net profit generated from their specific area of responsibility. The reason for this is that many additional home office and field expenses are not affected by the sales manager's performance. Instead, most sales managers make their revenue projections based on total sales and the expenses associated with the sales that are within their control or influence. Examples are discounts, local advertising, office expenses, and salespeople's expenses.

A second broad category of planning by sales managers is *administrative planning*. These plans include budgeting for office expenditures, travel and entertainment, and other foreseeable expenses; another important administrative planning area is the preparation of agenda and itinerary for sales meetings and sales training classes. Because of the importance of these sessions, it is critical that their format be planned well in advance. Most sales managers try to plan their daily activities well in advance, leaving a realistic number of gaps in the calender to accommodate unforeseen events. In short, the sales manager plans ahead in virtually every administrative functional area in which he or she is involved.

The third general area of sales management planning is interpersonal relations. This important planning sector is associated with the sales manager's relationships with the sales force, his or her managers, customers, and other persons with whom the sales manager comes in contact. As will be seen in the following chapters, a large portion of the sales manager's time is spent hiring, training, motivating, evaluating, problem solving, coaching, and selling with the sales force. Unless the manager has a well thought out and well-documented plan for allocation of his or her time in performing these duties, the result will be chaotic; hence the necessity to develop plans and timetables for meeting with other people according to an orderly schedule.

Realistically, most sales managers spend an inordinate amount of their time "fighting fires" or coping with unforeseen events. Therefore, simply to survive, let alone perform effectively, he or she cannot allow job requirements to pile up, even over a short period of time. It is imperative, therefore, that sales managers learn to perform effectively in planning.

ORGANIZING

Organizing is the process by which the structure or allocation of various positions of responsibility or work load is determined. The objectives of the firm become easier to achieve when the organizing process has been effectively implemented. Probably because of the increasing dependency of people on one another, problems in organization have become more complex as the modern corporation has grown over the years. In addition to allocating and structuring jobs within a firm, the organizing process is also necessary to structure and allocate work to be done. Managers spend a very large portion of their time performing this function.

The Organizing Function and the Sales Manager

It was stated earlier that organizing consists of the structuring of positions of responsibility or of the workload required to achieve objectives. Sales managers find that their job responsibilites require them to be highly organized. In an interview with the author, a sales manager in the technical products industry discusses organizing as follows:

> Organizing is the process of setting priorities and assigning a place for the work you need to do to successfully meet the goals you set. Organizing can range from deciding how many technical servicepeople we need to simply arranging for enough sales promotion brochures we give to our customers to be ordered on time. Actually, I look at planning and organizing almost as one process—when you make plans, you've got to organize your resources to meet the targets you set. There is a lot of detail associated with organization, and it's this attention to detail at the organizing level that decides whether or not you're going to make your sales quotas at the end of the year.

In addition to being a good organizer to maintain his or her effectiveness, the sales manager should also set an example for the sales force. According to a recent survey, most sales executives agreed that organizing was one of the primary factors in a salesperson's success on the job.[5] It would be difficult indeed for a poorly organized sales manager to communicate good organization skills to a sales force.

CONTROLLING

Controlling is the process by which managers measure actual performance against planned standards and make whatever adjustments are necessary to reach their goals. Naturally, certain elements are necessary if a manager is to effectively perform the control function. Before any steps are taken in the central process, plans, standards, and yardsticks must be established. Without meaningful and, if possible, operational targets, the implementation of the control function is a hit-or-miss process. The next step in a control process is the objective and impartial measurement of actual performance. Since prompt reporting of performance is essential, the control process normally includes various paper-work systems, including data-processing input.

The Control Function and the Sales Manager

One of the most critical areas of sales management performance lies in the control function. Objectives and targets in sales are based on shorter time intervals than in most functions. Therefore, the sales manager must necessarily institute tight control procedures based on quick and accurate feedback from the sales force. To execute control procedures, he or she must be continually aware of each salesperson's activities. This need for information requires that a constant flow of reporting to and from the sales manager be maintained.

Nearly every selling organization requires sales call reports to be filled out by each salesperson on a weekly basis. These reports typically indicate which customers or prospects the salesperson called on and the amount of sales made during the week. Other data, such as status of accounts, time spent traveling, expenses incurred and individuals to whom the salesperson spoke, are nearly always included. This information provides the sales manager with current data so that he or she is able to help salespeople solve problems either before they arise or soon after they occur. The information is also used by the sales manager to help spot areas of strong or weak sales performance based upon the relationship between actual performance and certain established standards. (A detailed analysis of sales control mechanisms and documents is forthcoming in Chapter 11.)

The control element of the sales manager's job is also apparent in the *performance appraisal* function, which will be examined in more detail in Chapter 12. Here, standards of performance are used to evaluate salespeople not only in sales results, but in other performance areas such as prospecting, administrative effectiveness, and organization. The sales manager also engages in control activities through the monitoring of daily or weekly sales performance as related to short-run quota expectations. An important part of the sales manager job is to do what is necessary to achieve sales quotas. To meet these objectives, each sales manager has his or her own set of control techniques. Some managers depend upon personal leadership qualities and persuasive abilities; others may lean on rewards and sanctions as their primary control tools. It is difficult to judge these techniques per se, since they are very strongly associated with the individual sales manager's personality.

In summary, it should be pointed out that relative success as a sales manager is strongly related to the control function and how effective he or she is in carrying out this function.

STAFFING

Staffing is the process by which managers fill organizational needs with people. Not only is it necessary for management to hire effective employees, but the need to promote, place, and terminate people is also of paramount importance. Staffing, then, is one of the most critical and sensitive areas of management performance. If a manager is able to perform effectively in staffing, he or she has been successful in attaining the first step toward getting things done through others.

The Staffing Function and the Sales Manager

The staffing function in sales management requires the manager to hire, place, and promote salespeople to positions where they will be most effective. Many sales managers feel that *staffing* is the most important of all the sales management functions. Their reasoning is based on the premise that effective salespeople provide solutions, and ineffective or poor salespeople provide the manager with problems. To a great extent, a sales manager is judged by the total sales performance of his or her staff; as a consequence, the presence or absence of strong performers can appreciably enhance or shorten a sales manager's career.

Selection of the right people for the job is a very complex process, and the subject is covered in depth in Chapter 5. The processes of interviewing, testing, and other steps associated with staffing a sales force provide a rigorous challenge to the manager. Likewise, the assignment of the right salespeople to the right accounts and territories has a strong impact upon the sales manager's effectiveness. As we shall see in succeeding chapters, the many complex variables associated with the staffing function provide sales managers with ongoing challenges, problems, and opportunities.

DIRECTING

Directing is the process by which the manager guides the performance of other people. There are many ways to perform this function, and nearly all people require different kinds of direction. The concept of direction includes leadership, supervision, guiding, and motivation. Different leadership and motivational styles have been identified, but all managers possess their own individual style in getting things done through others.

The Directing Function and the Sales Manager

There are very few management positions in organizations where managers become as personally involved with their subordinates as in the sales field. At the same time, there are few managers who find it as necessary to understand their subordinates' personalities. The process of getting salespeople to achieve their

"His technique may be a bit unorthodox, but he's the best sales manager I've got."

goals is known as *directing*. This process includes leadership. motivation, and any other behavioral form associated with it whereby the sales manager performs this task.

Most managers have their own leadership style; that is, managers vary the kind of behavior that is necessary to help employees perform. This style may be easy-going, paternalistic, relatively formal, or informal; or it may consist of several approaches, most which are based on the personality and temperament of the salesperson and sales manager alike. Because no two people respond identically to direction, most managers utilize different styles for different salespeople. The function of *direction* is highly complex. In Chapter 6, we examine this function from several viewpoints, including those of the manager and the salesperson.

This section has examined in a brief and general way the functions that are performed by sales managers. Obviously, only the surface has been scratched, and this text will analyze the functions in much greater detail. Let us now examine some of the necessary personal factors required for sales managers.

BASIC JOB REQUIREMENTS FOR SALES MANAGERS

Four basic requirements should be possessed by sales managers: experience, education, attitude, and skill. These factors are important in all sales management positions, and even though certain jobs require varying amounts of these requirements, all are requisites to successfully managing a sales force.

Experience

It has been estimated that sales managers average about four to five years' experience in selling before attaining management responsibility.[6] The actual length of sales experience required ranges from about two to ten years before most firms are willing to promote people to the position of sales manager. Although there are exceptions, most firms prefer to hire or promote to sales manager persons who have had selling experience either with that firm or with a firm in the same industry. This practice is based on the presumption that sales techniques in every industry tend to be unique, and that it is easier for a manager to more readily understand the nature of sales problems and opportunities if he or she has had related selling experience.

Given the choice between hiring a new sales manager with a *good* record within the industry and an *excellent* record in a different industry, most firms tend to select the candidate from within the same industry.[7] When one takes into consideration the fact that requisite personality characteristics as well as sales techniques differ among various industries, it is easy to understand why most firms tend to look for sales managers with company or industry experience. Imagine, for example, a successful sales manager for a management consulting firm being hired to manage a sales force of automobile salespeople. The length of time of the sale, the actual sales techniques used to obtain the sale, and the methods of training the sales force in the two industries are very different. Although the sales manager with the consultative sales background might perform well over the long run, the company would be taking an unnecessary chance in hiring him or her.

Another factor that normally relates to sales management experience is that most sales managers tend to stay in the lower levels of management for several years before moving up to the sales executive level.[8] There are several reasons why quick upward movement is the exception rather than the rule. The most obvious is that unless the firm is expanding at a rapid rate there are a limited number of sales executive jobs available, and if the incumbent executives are performing well, there are few reasons to replace them.

A second reason is that it normally takes several years before a sales manager is able to assimilate the vast amount of company and industry knowledge that is required before he or she can function effectively at the executive level. A great deal of experience at his or her present level is not only beneficial, but necessary to good performance at *any* level. Nearly every sales manager, in fact, is able to relate cases where he or she has seen relatively inexperienced sales manager "pushed up the ladder" too soon, only to perform poorly through lack of experience and background at a lower level.

A third and perhaps most compelling reason why firms tend to keep sales managers at the lower levels for several years is that many or most sales-oriented firms have the philosophy that the front-line sales manager is the most important person in the sales organizational structure. This belief is based on the assumption that revenues and profits must be earned in the short run and that the person who best makes this happen is the front-line sales manager. If a sales manager is performing effectively at a certain level, he or she represents the solution to certain problems. If he or she is placed in another position, two questions arise: (1) will the new sales manager perform as effectively and (2) is there any great assurance that the sales manager who has been successful at one level will perform with great effectiveness at the next level? In most cases, unless the answer to these questions appears to be "yes," most firms are reluctant to make changes. As the president of a tool company said in an interview with the author,

> In our opinion, the most important people in our firm are our branch sales managers. They hire, train, motivate the sales people and are generally responsible for our sales. If an office is doing well, it's normally because of the branch sales manager's efforts. Naturally, there are some branches that have a lot of good customers, but for the most part, you can thank or blame the branch manager for our share of the market in that area. You can replace me, you can replace the sales vice-president, and you can even replace the sales force, but if you've got a good branch manager, you *can't* replace him. You don't change sales managers around any more than you juggle the lineup on a baseball team when things are going well. We try to take care of our branch managers in other ways than promoting them when they are performing well.

Perhaps the remarks of this chief executive seems to indicate a limited opportunity for growth, but by and large, his attitude reflects that of many if not most medium- and smaller-sized firms.

Large national and multinational organizations, because of their size, normally provide more frequent opportunities for increased sales management responsibility, while at the same time providing a range of benefits for sales managers whose vertical movement tends to be slower. For the most part, however, most firms are reluctant to move sales managers into more responsible positions until there is ample reason to feel confident of his or her future success.

Practically every sales organization in American business adopts the philosophy that the best salespeople do *not* necessarily make the best sales managers; then they proceed immediately to fill most vacant management positions with their best salespeople! While a few sales managers have only limited administrative responsibility, most management positions in sales require a great deal of administrative expertise. There is little reason to expect that a superior salesperson should perform well administratively; if anything, because of the personality requirements for these respective functions, one might even expect a good salesperson to be a poor administrator. The reason why most companies persist in offering promotions to good salespeople is often the presumption that, while *anyone* can learn to fulfill paper work responsibilities, only an experienced and effective salesperson can provide leadership in selling. The extent to which this philosophy holds true depends upon the individual situation. The next chapter will analyze the administrative functions of sales managers and will deal with this question in depth.

Education

A key factor in obtaining employment in most sales-related jobs is the relative extent of one's education. Since World War II, there has been a trend toward hiring college graduates, and today there are very few large national or multinational firms that do not require a college degree for newly hired salespeople. This requirement also holds true, for the most part, for sales managers. Except in the technical sales area, advanced degrees are not as prevelant in sales management as in other fields, such as accounting, finance, or production, although given the choice between the holder of a bachelor's degree or an MBA, according to several marketing executives, most firms would prefer to hire the latter.

This is not to say that sales managers must hold strong academic credentials in order to succeed. Indeed, the quantity and quality of related experience is nearly always given more consideration when sales managers are selected. It is significant, however, to note that to become a sales *manager* the overwhelming majority of people have had experience as a sales *person*. And because most firms prefer to hire college graduates for sales positions, it logically follows that most sales managers today are college graduates. The trend in this direction likewise appears to be increasing, at least among medium- and large-sized firms.

Although college and university degrees and courses are important educational qualifications in sales management, they are by no means the only ones of importance. Most sales organizations have sales management and sales training programs. Many large firms such as IBM and General Motors have very elaborate educational centers employing highly sophisticated training programs and techniques where college curricula in marketing and courses in sales management provide the student with the theory and practical thought processes designed to provide a *general* approach to his or her career. Company training courses are designed to provide the student with the specific knowledge required to overcome problems and create opportunities within the framework of his or her present job. Most larger firms utilize advanced training techniques, often taught in a campuslike atmosphere. Most courses are taught by highly paid professionals who possess top academic credentials and many years of practical, relevant company and industry experience.

Although there appears to be a strong relationship between company size and the extent of in-house training and development programs, many medium and smaller firms provide excellent educational opportunities for their sales managers. In addition to obtaining basic academic credentials such as the bachelor's degree and the MBA, most sales managers, in fact most business professionals in general, wish to take courses and participate in programs designed to enhance their professional expertise. When asked in an interview about education and its place in sales management, one national sales manager responded,

> Although we hire college graduates almost exclusively and we like to hire marketing graduates with MBA's if possible, we still feel that the degree is only the start in a long educational process. If you will, the degree is a *qualifying* educational milestone. We feel that the real meat of sales management education is in our company training school. The professionals here are MBA's and Ph.D.'s but they've also been exposed to the challenges our students will meet on a day to day basis. A manager with our firm continues to go to one school or another as long as he or she is with the organization.

Many firms provide both in-house facilities and outside educational opportunities for sales managers. Several consulting firms specialize in the training of sales managers. These firms are utilized by many sales organizations, most of which are too small to provide their own educational staff. Seminars are also held by many firms in various cities on a "public" basis, which means that a firm might send only one or two of its sales managers at a given time. Although seminars of this type are not able to discuss specific company problems (since sales managers from several diverse companies are present), they normally concentrate on a general *scheme* or *approach* to the solution of sales management problems that are common to most organizations.

In summary, it should be pointed out that, although education is normally subordinated to experience in the selection of sales managers, its importance as a development tool ought not to be underestimated.

Skill

Skill in an occupation or profession can be broadly described as the extent to which the holder of associated education and experience is able to successfully *use* those two attributes. As in any other profession, sales management skill is developed through application of education and through experiences gained over a certain period of time. Also, as in other professions, a certain amount of skill appears to be woven into the fabric of a sales manager's personality. Although the term "skill" itself seems to convey a less than precise measurable attribute, the areas where sales management skill is required are quite discernible. The major skills required lie in the major functional areas of sales management. In other words, to be successful a sales manager needs specific skills in *planning, organizing, controlling, staffing,* and *directing,* both in dealing with other people and in dealing with administrative and paper-work problems. Specific skills must be developed in every category of each management function. A sales manager should be skilled, for example, not only in interviewing and hiring the best person for the job, but should also be skilled in the use of the hiring tools placed at his disposal, such as testing.

The acquisition of the requisite amount of skill for successful sales management comes from a combination of education, experience, and, to some extent, an innate aptitude for the job. The manager continually learns new techniques and applies them in the work environment. Through a process of trial and error, he or she can become proficient, but aptitude for the work is also important. The director of management training and development for a major firm discusses the need for skill in the following statement:

> We've found over the years that most people can help develop their sales management skills through application of the concepts they learn in college or through other formalized training programs. The extent to which they will become proficient at it also has a lot to do with their inborn ability or aptitude for the field or for the specific function. You can take a ballplayer with a lot of knowledge and experience, but you can't teach him to hit home runs like Mantle or Aaron. He has to have a certain unique aptitude to do that. But you don't have to be an Aaron or Mantile to become a good ballplayer. You need a certain amount of skill but it can be developed through coaching and simply playing on a day-to-day basis. I think there is an analogy between the skilled ballplayer and the skilled sales manager. Through learning and experience, both can become proficient, but you still need a certain amount of aptitude to become a highly skilled performer.

The extent to which skill in sales management can be developed and the extent to which it depends upon certain inborn characteristics is and is likely to remain a moot question. It is important to realize that, whether sales management skill in performing the required functions is easily learned or not, it is a critical ingredient to success.

Attitude

Because of the nature of the selling function, a positive, enthusiastic outlook or approach to sales management is necessary. There exists in selling an enormous amount of pressure to meet monthly and quarterly sales volume quotas. In many cases it is difficult for a sales manager to determine which customers, if any, will make purchases during the coming weeks or even days. Yet the quota must be met. In this type of business environment it is very important that the sales manager maintain an even disposition; to behave otherwise tends to confuse the sales force and to reduce one's image as a strong leader who can maintain his or her equanimity in the face of adversity.

Unfortunately, most sales managers find it difficult to "fake" a positive attitude or to maintain a facade of imperturbability when sales are low. But it is necessary for the sales manager to *be* positive in both difficult and favorable circumstances.

Because their performance evaluation is so inextricibly bound up in sales volume, it is not difficult for sales managers to acquire an air of cynicism. Yet, because of his or her influence upon the sales force, the sales manager often finds it necessary to support or depend upon the company's policies and procedures at unpopular times. In fact, sales managers find it almost necessary to maintain an air of naivete about the sales force's ability to sell in the face of competition, an unfavorable economy, or other adverse conditions. As a sales manager in the toy industry stated in an interview with the author,

> The prime requisite for a good sales manager is probably a strong stomach. When your Management tells you to push a product that you just *know* is about half as good as your competitors, it takes a lot of *chutzpah* to tell your sales force to get out there and move. Even though they know you're putting it on, if they believe in you, your optimism actually becomes contagious. And they produce. The positive attitude is a necessity and there's no place in Sales Management if you don't have it. Maybe that's why a lot of sales managers still have a lot of little kid in them—once you lose these sales management neuroses like "thinking positive," "I'm the best," "my people can outsell anybody," "we can always find a customer," and above all, your sense of humor—then you lost it all, bubula; you might as well pack it in.

Although attitude is the most abstract of sales management requirements, it is a necessary catalyst.

A sales manager's attitude always rubs off on the sales force, and no matter how effectively he or she is able to perform, a negative, cynical, or unenthusiastic attitude nearly always neutralizes one's positive attributes. Since sales managers constantly remind salespeople of the importance of a "good" attitude, it is incumbent upon the manager to consistently display the attitude he or she hopes the sales force to emulate.

In summary, it can be safely said that a sales manager's attitude will not only be reflected in the attitude of individual salespeople but will, in most cases, be a strong determinant of sales force performance.

POLICIES, POLITICS, AND THE SALES MANAGER

Every organization has certain policies and procedures that guide its managers' activities. There is also a certain "personality" that the organization projects to its employers. Because of the need for a cooperative and coordinated effort by its members to reach certain goals, many of its policies and procedures leave little room for flexibility. For this reason there are invariably certain reports to be periodically submitted, hiring procedures that must be followed, and company regulations regarding expenses, dress code, office procedures, and a host of other rules that are often unpopular among sales-force members. One of the less attractive functions of the sales manager is to support company policies, sometimes in spite of his or her personal opinion.

As indicated in the previous chapter, the personality characteristics required by most successful salespeople are often the exact reverse of those of successful administrators. Since many sales managers are more sales oriented than paperwork oriented, it is not surprising that a certain amount of ambivalence arises when implementing company policies and procedures. Often many administrative guidelines that must be followed appear to the sales manager as unnecessary "red tape" that interferes with the primary goal of making sales. One district manager in the building products industry made the following complaint to the author:

> My Branch Manager always tells me that a particular monthly report is too lengthy and it interferes with sales time. They say the salespeople are forced to spend too much time on it. Before I was promoted to District Manager, I was a Branch Manager and I had the same complaint. Jack, the previous District Manager, always told me it was necessary so that our production people would know what to manufacture. Jack would turn around and try to tell that to my salespeople with a straight face, but they knew I didn't believe it myself. Now that I'm District Manager, I can see why it is valuable, only now I can't convince my Branch Managers either. They all do it, but I know they think it's a waste of time.

It is also difficult for many sales managers to follow company guidelines with respect to recruiting and hiring techniques. It is natural for the sales manager to want to follow his or her instincts in hiring salespeople. Yet corporate hiring policies are often based on very wide experience and have been tested and proved over a long time period. Hiring policies developed at the corporate level are also intended to avoid discriminatory hiring practices. As with many corporate policies, however, it is often difficult for sales managers to maintain their patience with what they consider to be bureaucratic obstacles placed in the way of the achievement of their sales objectives.

Despite their personal feelings, most sales managers eventually learn how to support company policies and how to justify them to their sales force. This dilemma faces nearly every manager from the president of the United States all the way down to the lowest-level foreman, and it is not always easy to resolve. Most good managers, however, develop methods of compromise that enable them to act in a conscientious manner and still follow organizational policy.

A little discussed subject, but one of some interest, is the area of company politics. A description of politics in business should probably focus upon the personal connections and influence upon others by an individual. In nearly every function of business, politics from time to time determines who receives a promotion or who is selected from among several persons to gain some benefit. Sales management is no exception, and political factors sometime become important , particularly at the district and regional manager levels. A major advantage of the sales field, however, is its emphasis upon measurable production as a standard of performance. However, over a given period of time it is possible that sales attained may not provide the most objective measure of performance. A newly appointed sales manager, for instance, often finds that it is several months before a strong rapport is built with the sales force. And it is not unusual for a particular sales region to experience a reduction in sales because of local economic or competitive conditions. Such situations can lead to sales figures that are low relative to other offices, but the sales manager's performance may still be high. Situations of this sort tend to occur in sales management quite often, and most sales organization executives are aware of the reasons for a manager's seemingly below-average performance.

Over a relatively long period of time, however, say four or five years or possibly even less, a sales manager's ability tends to be reflected in his or her sales production. This factor is one of the most attractive features of sales management to many people who prefer to avoid company politics. To dismiss the existence of politics in sales management would, of course, be unrealistic and even naive. It is, however, less of an influence in sales management than in many other fields, primarily because of the need for the individual manager to make a measurable sales contribution on a fairly consistent basis in order to advance his or her career.

SUMMARY

This chapter has discussed the organizational, functional, and personal attributes of sales management. Most of the characteristics and relationships discussed here are common to the majority of sales managers.

Sales organizations are, for the most part, constructed according to the classic design of one overall sales executive at the top of the structure and many local or branch sales managers at the bottom. Most firms tend to rely on the lower-level sales managers as the most critical element in the successful attainment of sales and profits.

All sales managers perform the traditional management functions of planning, organizing, controlling, staffing, and directing. Many times two or even more of these functions are performed simultaneously. The extent to which the sales manager performs these functions effectively determines his or her effectiveness in the final analysis.

In performing the necessary sales management functions, certain background attributes tend to influence the overall outcome. These basic requirements are *experience, education, skill,* and *attitude*. The extent to which a manager possesses these attributes will have a strong impact upon his or her expertise and success in sales management.

Management of a sales force, like other management positions, sometimes requires the manager to implement policies and procedures with which he or she may not agree. Yet part of a manager's obligation is to represent the organization in *all* policy enforcement and implementation. Fortunately, most managers learn to overcome their ambivalence in this situation.

One of the more attractive aspects of a career in sales management is its emphasis upon attainment of sales and profit levels. Promotion is based primarily upon performance, unlike many positions for which company politics and personal characteristics are overriding factors in success.

Shelly's Uncle

The Steven Silver Paper Company is a medium-sized manufacturer of boxes. The firm either manufactures or distributes nearly every sixe of box, from large cardboard cartons to very small gift boxes. The firm has twenty branch offices located around the country. About three years ago, Stan Lewis, the branch manager in Philadelphia was promoted to the position of West Coast regional manager and now supervises five branch managers. When Stan Lewis went to California, he was replaced by Sheldon Davis, a salesman from the New York office. Shelly Davis had been with the firm for about sixteen months. His sales record in New York was very good, with three large orders from his major accounts providing about 80 percent of his sales volume. Shelly was a college graduate with a major in marketing and had taken a course in sales management for which he received an A. One of the vice-presidents of the firm was Shelly's uncle, who was instrumental in placing him with the company. Although there was some talk about nepotism, Shelly's uncle pointed to his nephew's outstanding sales record and his academic accomplishments as justification for his promotion. The average length of service in the industry for the other branch managers was about eight years.

After six months in the job, the sales figure and profits for Shelly's office were declining steadily. Furthermore, certain reports were being turned in late and were not always accurate. At the same time, all the other branches' sales were increasing. Mr. Silver, Shelly's uncle, called in Mitchell Herman, the Eastern regional manager, and told him he wanted an analysis of Shelly's problems. Mitchell drove down to Philadelphia to see Shelly, and the following conversation took place.

Mitch: Shelly, you're having problems. Why?

Shelly: Well Mitch, there are a few problems. First of all, my salespeople are just not up to par.

Mitch: You've got the same sales force that Stan had, and he was always over quota.

Shelly: That's another problem; the quota was set too high for this office.

Mitch: We use the same techniques to measure potential here that we do anywhere else, and we're right on target in every other branch.

Shelly: Maybe so, but I still say a big part of the problem is the sales force. They just can't learn what I teach them.

Mitch: *What* can't they learn, Shelly?

Shelly: Oh, everything. How to sell the little accounts, the presentation, prospecting, everything.

Mitch: How about the two new people you hired, Shelly. Why are they performing so poorly?

Shelly: Probably because they started hanging around with the wrong people. These old-time salespeople have a lot of bad habits they pick up.

Mitch: What do you think your sales will be next quarter, Shelly?

Shelly: I'm not sure, Mitch. I'll have to wait until March to figure it out.

Mitch: What are your immediate plans for how you'll spend your time next week? Maybe I can help you a little bit. I'll come down for a day a week starting either next week or the week after.

Shelly: Oh, you can come any day, Mitch. I have nothing on tap except next Thursday night when I'm going to see the Seventy-Sixers. Maybe you'd like to go. They play the Celtics.

Mitch: No thanks, Shelly. I'll probably be getting ready for the regional meeting on Friday. That reminds me, Stan used to have sales meetings on Thursday nights. Don't you hold them then, too?

Shelly: Yeah, I do, but I'm letting Gary run it this Thursday. After all, how often do you get to see Dr. J and Larry Bird all in one sitting?

Mitch: (Sighing) I guess you're right, Shelly. How often indeed?

1. If you were Mitch Herman, what would you tell Mr. Silver?
2. How would you go about restoring the Philadelphia branch to its former high level of effectiveness?

JBC Data Processing Inc.

JBC Data Processing, Inc., is a southwestern manufacturer of a special-purpose computer. The company makes three different models, but all three perform basically the same function. The primary differences in the three models are print-out speed and capacity. The JBC unit (the X-15) is programmed automatically and provides the user with an updated sales analysis report by territory. The computer is unique in that it provides a self-correcting mechanism that takes into account certain competitive influences in the marketplace and provides management with an accurate week-to-week analysis of sales. There exists a large market for a computer of this type, and the company is making plans to sell the unit on a national basis.

Prior to developing this computer, JBC has operated only in the Southwest. Unfortunately, the company has no prior experience in dealing with markets outside its own geographical area. The X-15 has generated a great deal of enthusiasm within the investment community. Three large banks have agreed to finance the company in the building of a national sales force. Market research has indicated that customers for the unit include virtually every firm that has a sales force of fifty or more persons. The bank has also agreed to provide the money for manufacturing facilities. It is expected that the new plant will be able to produce about 200 X-15s weekly.

The directors of JBC are concerned that the product should be sold quickly. They feel that it will be only a matter of 12 to 18 months before their competitors are able to develop a similar product, and they want to be able to maximize sales during this period of relative monopoly. They have no sales force at present and are convinced that the new national sales manager will have a great impact upon the future of JBC Data Processing, Inc. The directors have asked you to provide guidance in the selection of this critical executive.

1. What will be the functions of the new national sales manager?
2. What characteristics will you look for in filling this position?

DISCUSSION QUESTIONS

1. In a classical sales organization, how are the critical elements of the various levels interrelated?
2. For a given case history, outline the traditional role of the sales manager.
3. What personal resources will make the sales manager more effective?
4. Give examples of the right and wrong use of authority in performing the role of sales manager.
5. Discuss how a sales manager can help or harm a salesperson under various situations.
6. What factors influence attitude (a) among sales personnel, and (b) between a salesperson and a customer?
7. What is the purpose of company policy and standard practice?
8. What are the primary aspects of the "direction" function?
9. What is the role of the sales manager in a conflict between a customer and his or her company?

NOTES

[1]General Motors and Ford have several thousand.

[2]Phyllis K. Bonfield, "Average Manager Earns $20,000," *Management World*, vol. 8, February 1979.

[3]Twentieth Biennial Survey, *Compensation of Salesmen* (Chicago: Dartnell Corporation, 1979).

[4]See Ross A. Webber, *Management: Basic Elements of Managing Organizations (Homewood, Ill.: Irwin), 1979*.

[5]"Poor Use of Time Is Major Problem in Selling," *Marketing News*, vol. 13, October 19, 1979, p. 1.

[6]Ovid Riso, *The Sales Manager's Handbook* (Chicago: Dartnell Corporation, 1980).

[7]Ibid.

[8]Ibid.

CHAPTER 4

ADMINISTRATIVE RESPONSIBILITIES AND INTERFACE WITH OTHER MARKETING GROUPS

OBJECTIVES

To identify and evaluate the basic administrative functions of sales managers:

* Routine reporting and record keeping
* Sales budgeting and cost control
* Marketing planning

To analyze the sales manager's relationships with other departments:

* Advertising
* Product planning
* Marketing research
* Distribution

To enumerate and evaluate the public relations functions of the sales manager:

* Membership in organizations
* Business shows
* Charitable and institutional campaigns

INTERVIEW WITH FRANK SMITH

Interviewer: What do you consider the most important administrative functions, Frank?

Frank Smith: As I indicated earlier, the classic functions of management are very important. There are other functions such as the ones in this chapter that are also important.

Interviewer: I know a lot of salespeople don't like detail work. Does this hold true for sales managers as well?

Frank Smith: Again, as I said before, you don't stay a manager long if you can't handle detail work. Somebody once said that attention to detail separates artistry from mediocrity.

Interviewer: We're going to talk about the generalities of reporting and record keeping in this chapter. Do you find a contradiction between these responsibilities and selling?

Frank Smith: Not really. You'll find that, believe it or not, most good salespeople keep very good records.

Interviewer: Another area we want to touch on is cost control. What is your opinion of sales budgets in general?

Frank Smith: My own observation is that if the budget is too loose it hurts your profitability and teaches people bad habits. There's nothing wrong with being thrifty, you know. By the same token, if a budget is too tight, the whole exercise becomes a travesty.

Interviewer: An area we want to discuss there is the sales manager's relationship with other departments and with outside groups.

Frank Smith: In a lot of areas, the local sales manager is the only spokesperson the company has. This is a very important function.

Interviewer: Then let's investigate some of these more general functions in this chapter.

The previous chapter discussed the functions of planning, organizing, controlling, staffing, and directing, the classic functions of all managers. It was shown that the sales manager's functional responsibilities vary from those of other managers, and the specific nature of these responsibilities was investigated. All managers also perform certain administrative responsibilities, which are included within the framework of the major functions but are more related to "inside" or "paper-work" duties. This chapter will discuss these *administrative* functions, as well as the sales manager's relationship with other functional areas.

BASIC ADMINISTRATIVE FUNCTIONS

All administrative functions of sales managers fall under the purview of the five major management functions. These specific functions, however, are so applicable to sales management that they are identified and examined individually. These responsibilities consist essentially of three activities: (1) routine reporting and record keeping, (2) sales budgeting and cost control, and (3) marketing planning. These activities will be briefly described here and will be covered in much greater detail in ensuing chapters.

Routine Reporting and Record Keeping

All sales organizations require their managers to coordinate the activities of their salespeople through various routine reports. These reports are required to help the sales manager to detect any changes in performance and to be aware of opportunities developed by individual sales-force members. Despite an aversion to detail, most effective salespeople also keep good records and are effective in reporting. The most common examples of reports required by sales managers are discussed next.

Call Report These reports are normally required on a weekly basis and indicate which customers were seen and the results of each call. This report is usually compared to the weekly work plan as a measure of the salesperson's ability to stay with his or her plan. The weekly call report also indicates the numbers of calls made and the activity generated in various product lines.

Weekly Work Plan This report is a precall summary of which customers will be seen during the coming week and the purpose of each call. This report helps the sales manager to decide which salespeople he or she wants to travel with during the coming week. It also helps the sales force plan its priorities in an organized fashion.

Weekly Expense Report This report may be submitted on a monthly basis in some organizations. It records all expenses to be reimbursed by the company. It provides the sales manager with an opportunity to compare actual expenses to budgeted expenses and assists in determining the cost of sales.

Competitive Activity Reports These reports are usually submitted on a monthly basis and indicate which competitors are making inroads into individual sales territories. This information allows the sales manager to make changes in the product mix or in pricing to effectively compete with strong competition. In many cases, local sales managers are unable to effectively reduce competition, but can relay data on competitive activity to policy makers.

Sales Forecast This report is usually submitted on a monthly and a quarterly basis. It indicates expected sales in each territory and helps the sales manager to develop a forecast for the entire office.

Account Records These records indicate purchasing experience at individual accounts. They indicate why purchases were made, who was responsible within the customer firm, and other data. They also indicate where and why customers have not been using company products or services. These records are usually kept by salespeople and shown to the sales manager upon request. Normally, these records are exchanged as sales territories change. Effective managers usually require that these records be kept up to date.

In addition to requiring reports from his or her salespeople, managers are required to submit reports to their own supervisors on a regular basis. Most of these reports are office summaries of the preceding documents.

Sales Budgeting and Cost Control

In many industries, large sales volume is attained through effective selling and management. Yet because of high costs and uncontrolled expenses, the firm's profits turn out to be relatively low. To avoid this discouraging situation, sales managers are trained to keep expenditures within budgeted limits.

A *sales budget* is typically assigned to sales managers, and they are expected to maintain this budget. In some organizations, the budget assigned is unrealistically low and, as a result, sales managers seldom if ever stay within the required parameters. Setting such tight budgets often defeats the purpose of establishing them at all.

In other organizations, sales managers are given a bonus based on their ability to keep costs down. As long as the sales budgets imposed on managers are reasonable, this technique works well. But its effectiveness lies in its ability to *eliminate unnecessary costs*, not to strangle expenditures to the point where reasonable costs are discouraged. In situations of this type, the morale of the sales force usually suffers, because the salespeople are invariably aware of the fact that the manager receives a bonus for keeping costs to a minimum, and they tend to resent this fact, usually with justification.

The sales budgets that seem to work best are flexible budgets that vary at different sales levels. Rewarding a manager for staying within budgeted guidelines often works satisfactorily as long as necessary expenses are approved. Flexible budgets typically perform the required function more often than do inflexible budgets. Moreover, every sales-experienced manager seems to have a "feel" for the adequacy of the sales budget in his or her office. While it might not always be prudent to allow sales managers to set their own budgets, their input is often very valuable in helping organizations arrive at realistic attainable expense limits.

Cost-control techniques can likewise be realistic or can be onerous. In some instances, cost controls are so stringently placed on salespoeple that they literally interfere with effective sales management. Customer service and local advertising budgets are often reduced to an unrealistically low figure to the point where the long-term objectives of the firm are harmed. When the sales manager becomes preoccupied with cost control to the exclusion of performing his or her necessary positive functions, management effectiveness is severely limited.

Nevertheless, cost controls are an integral part of any marketing system. Without adequate limits on expenditures, a firm's profits are reduced substantially, often resulting in the inability to set long-range or even intermediate-range goals.

Marketing Planning

Chapter 10 will deal with the specifics of sales forecasting and other marketing planning techniques. It is very important for the manager to be aware of the necessity to continually plan ahead. Even though a home office marketing planning staff normally develops future plans on a corporate level, the field sales manager must be able to anticipate changes in local conditions and how to cope with them. Some external variables, for instance, might be the effects of a gasoline shortage, state and/or local legislation, or even the problems caused by an important thoroughfare being torn up by construction crews. The local branch manager must be able to develop and implement strategies designed to deal with future events. One of the most common problems facing local sales managers is the possibility of an aggressive sales campagin by a competitor in his or her sales area. Although this contingency is not only a possibility, but often a certainty, very few managers are prepared when such events occur. The administration of an effective program dealing with these kinds of variables is necessary for sales managers.

Other administrative steps toward marketing planning by the local sales manager include an in-depth analysis of future personnel needs. A knowledge of the local market for salespeople is essential, and most data must be gathered at the local level. The economy of the local marketplace must likewise be understood by the sales manager. An administrative approach to planning for the future includes data gathering of economic trends from local sources such as banks and government agencies at the federal, state, and local level. Other planning areas that should be exploited by sales managers in performing this important administrative function vary among locations.

RELATIONS WITH OTHER DEPARTMENTS

In addition to working within his or her own sales department, many if not most sales managers find it necessary from time to time to work closely with other departments. The most common outside departments with which sales managers interface are typically some of the other marketing departments such as advertising, product planning, marketing research, and distribution. There are, however, circumstances that require the sales manager to work closely with the production department as well. The extent to which a sales manager communicates with other departments depends greatly upon the manager's level of responsibility in the firm, the type of business or industry in which he or she works, and the type of selling that is involved. This section will investigate some of the situations in which sales managers work with other departments to achieve total marketing objectives.

Advertising

One of the most important outside functional areas in which the sales manager has a strong interest is advertising. Advertising forms part of a promotional mix, and with sales promotion and personal selling, combines to either "push" or "pull" the customer into making a buying decision. Because of the enormous influence of advertising in the buying process, the sales manager should quite naturally be concerned with this function. In most firms, advertisements are discussed with sales managers before they are shown to the buying community. There is a fairly consistent difference in the type of selling and the inputs to advertising expected at various levels of sales management.

It is not unusual for managers in direct-sales organizations to participate in advertising decision making *at the local level*. Most major manufacturers of products sold by direct salespeople advertise in local newspapers, catalogs, radio, and occasionally television, particularly those who use independent dealers to sell those products. In these cases, it is customary for the manufacturer and the local dealer to split the cost of the ad. Ads of this type are called *cooperative* or, more often, *co-op* ads. A typical example would be a large appliance manufacturer whose products are sold through a dealer in a particular town or metropolitan area. The local sales manager is typically invited to select the type of ad to be used from several ads that were prepared by the manufacturer. Since the purpose of co-op ads is usually to build sales, the sales manager is often in a good position to know which ads might be more effective in his or her local market.

In commercial and technical sales, most advertising decisions are made at the home office level. In companies that sell commercial and technical products, the national sales manager is often consulted to provide input. In some cases, his or her input is important and in some cases it is more perfunctory. In the consumer-products field, for example, advertising and sales-promotion decisions are typically made by professionals in these fields, although the sales manager might be consulted as a courtesy. In advertising commercial products, particularly those that are technically sophisticated, the sales manager often provides input for advertisements that is valued highly by the rest of the marketing team.

In consultative sales organizations, there is a greater tendency to utilize input from the sales manager. For one thing, most consultative firms are smaller and have less formal, less rigid organizational responsibilities in various positions of authority. It is not unusual, for example, for a firm in this type of selling to assign the responsibility for advertising, or part of the responsibility, to the sales manager or the other executives only partially associated with the marketing of the firm's products. Because of the flexibility of many consultative organizations, this seemingly disorganized decision-making process actually works quite well most of the time.

Product Planning

In some industries, the sales manager is asked, "If we make it, do you think you can sell it?" Because of the sales manager's interface with customers, he or she is often in a position to provide valuable advice with respect to the development of new products and applications of existing ones. Indeed, many firms promote lower-level sales managers and potential sales managers to various positions in product planning as a step in their career progression. One of the many auxiliary functions of the sales manager is to encourage input from the sales force regarding product planning. Since the salesperson is closer to the customer than any other member of the marketing team, most organizations have reasoned that this individual is probably the most qualified to observe customer and product needs. Some organizations formally encourage feedback from the sales force with respect to new ideas. A form of incentive for activity of this kind is the *suggestion bonus*. Some firms, notably IBM, make cash awards for usable ideas to improve present products or to develop new ones. On the other hand, other organizations seemingly discourage this type of feedback by not providing a communication channel for new ideas or, in some cases, by openly discouraging such activity.

Most professional salespeople have wide exposure to the marketplace and are in a position to provide valuable, positive feedback to their organization. Because of their experience in the field, they are able to make observations regarding applications and new products that many people cannot. A sales manager in the toy industry stated to the author,

> We have this toy store we call on where this kid works behind the counter for his uncle who owns the store. The kid is kind of off the wall and is always reading gruesome stories—I guess for lack of a better word, you might call him a little *weird*. Everybody always dismisses what he says. If you listen, most people have something to say. Our sales rep took this kid Allen out to lunch a few times and got some really good ideas on how we could save a lot of money the way we package a certain game we sell. The salesman communicated the idea to me, I told our people in New York, and they adopted the idea. The salesman got a nice bonus, I got recognition. Of course, Allen got nothing but the satisfaction of knowing that his idea was a good one, but who ever said life was fair?

The previous anecdote, although somewhat cynical, is indicative of the unusual ways in which product information is communicated. The sales manager telling the story also added that he strongly encouraged his salespeople to investigate new concepts or ideas in the marketplace.

Marketing Research

In addition to providing information on products, the sales manager is also a source of knowledge for the marketing research function. Many firms are deeply interested in his or her grass-roots contact with customers. The behavior of certain classes of buyers and the ability to predict this behavior is one of the primary functions of a marketing research department. In many cases, the only real contact with customers is made by the sales force, and it is important that there be high-quality feedback to the marketing research department from this source. The primary link between these two parties is the sales manager. He or she typically acts as a liaison and has responsibility for a variety of nonroutine reports that provide data on customer behavior. A marketing research manager in the office products field made the following comments to the author:

> The demand for the kind of equipment and supplies we sell is more elastic than most people realize. A change in price does not necessarily evoke a strong customer reaction. There are many reasons why a customer stays with us or goes to a competitor. It may be design, it may be service, it may be delivery or a variety of other reasons. We have found that the sales force is best able to determine what these reasons are. Unfortunately, we don't have time to talk with too many salespeople. The way we are able to achieve our goal, which is finding out what the customer buys and why, is by sitting down with sales managers and getting their input, which is of course a compendium of feedback from the many sales force members. The manager usually knows whose opinions should be more heavily weighted. I would say that in our business, the sales manager is a critical member of the Marketing Research team, even though he or she isn't a formal member.

As in product planning, local and district sales managers tend to be included in marketing research decision making in the commercial and technical fields more often than in the consumer-products field. Because of the wide disparity of goods and services sold in the direct-sales field, it is difficult to make a general statement with regard to sales management's participation in marketing research decisions in this sector. In the insurance field for example, much input is sought from local managers, whereas in the automobile field, most marketing research is conducted by specific departments within a company or by organizations outside the company.

Distribution

The distribution process includes more than simply the physical delivery of goods and services, although that is a very important factor. Most sales organizations include an office manager who is responsible for physical delivery. The role of the sales manager in the distribution process is vital in certain industries and in other industries it is less pronounced. The extent of the sales manager's involvement in distribution is normally a function of the importance of distribution in the sales process. In the air-freight business, for example, the "product" sold is a distribution service. Customers are obtained by a firm's ability to solve their distribution problems. Most air-freight firms have the additional handicap of having to absorb very high labor costs. In such an environment, effective sales management is often the most critical variable in the firm's ability to make a profit or even to survive.

Besides the air-freight industry, there are others whose chief "product" is distribution. Freight forwarding, parcel delivery, railway transportation, airline passenger service, and over-the-road trucking are some examples. Since there are complex government regulations that dampen somewhat the competitiveness of some of these industries, the importance of sales management varies somewhat among them. As a sales manager for one of the major airlines indicated to the author,

> Airline passenger service is a very complex field. Even though most private firms resent government regulation as interference, you have to realize that they [the government] do make a pretty good case for the presumption that it is in the public interest to maintain an organized fare structure. The central issue is safety, and anything that directly or tangentially affects safety is probably a legitimate area for government to become interested in.
>
> As you've noticed, we advertise competitively but don't disparage our competitors. For example, we don't put ads in papers, like "don't fly on X airline. They just had a crash that killed a lot of people." We tend to be a little more subtle in our approach to obtaining customers. I suppose you just can't sell as aggressively as you would like to in the airlines business, is what it comes down to.

Most of the distribution industries are regulated by government in terms of schedules and rates. This tends to reduce aggressive sales management. On the other hand, the role of the sales manager is critical in policy making in these industries, because sales and distribution are so tightly interrelated.

In service industries the term "delivery" has a different meaning than in industries where a physical product is manufactured and distributed to the ultimate user through a network of channels of distribution. In most service industries, distribution is directly influenced if not controlled outright by the sales department. The competitive nature of services and the need for the marketing concept has literally forced service organizations to depend upon sales management for distribution.

THE PUBLIC-RELATIONS FUNCTION OF THE SALES MANAGER

Every organization prefers to present a favorable image to the public. The term used to describe the process of presenting this image is called *public relations*. For many reasons, some organizations are more conscious of their public image than others. For example, manufacturing organizations are open to criticism because of possible pollution problems, consumer-products firms are sensitive about truth in packaging, and gas and electric companies are more than a little concerned over adverse reaction to nuclear-energy installations. Not every sales manager is faced with the prospect of defending his or her firm against armies of crusading consumers, but there is an implicit, if not an explicit, responsibility for sales managers to help enhance the organization's image on a continuing basis. Rather than defending the company against its detractors, most sales managers utilize more positive public-relations techniques. Three of the most common public-relations devices will be discussed here: membership in organizations, business shows, and association with public nonprofit institutions.

Membership in Organizations

During the decades of the 1940s, 1950s, and even 1960s, the typical convention-goer was stereotyped as an overweight, loud, rude, and often tipsy individual with a silly hat. This image was unfortunately imputed to many people who held membership in various business organizations. For the most part, however, organizations composed of various business people tend to perform a positive function. There is an organization for members of individual firms in nearly every occupation; for example, credit managers in each industry have an association, as do purchasing managers, accounting managers, and nearly every other kind of manager. Part of the reason for the existence of such organizations is to address problems common to all members, and part of the reason is to enhance the image or visibility of the occupational field.

Such organizations for sales managers exist in many diverse industries. Industry-wide organizations for sales managers often develop an industry-wide set of standards and an ethical code for transacting business. In addition, certain problems common to sales managers, such as effective recruiting, time management, and compensation management, are addressed through seminars, colloquiums, and committees. Often a higher-quality approach to the marketplace results from membership in such groups. When the sales manager must meet his or her competitor at lunch every third Tuesday, the temptation to pirate salespeople or to disparage the competitor's product is lessened considerably. To be sure, such groups may also develop strategies to fix prices and engage in other questionable activities if they perceive the customer as their common enemy. The majority of sales managers' organizations, however, engage in highly constructive activity.

One of the largest membership organizations for sales managers is the Sales and Marketing Executives International (SMEI). This organization is an independent world-wide club whose membership consists of sales managers from virtually every industry. Local chapters exist in most metropolitan areas and many smaller cities as well. The SMEI has a total membership of over 15,000 members in over 300 separate chapters. SMEI publishes a bimonthly magazine, *Marketing Times*, and sponsors many self-improvement seminars and colloquiums open to members and nonmembers alike. It also sponsors the SMEI graduate school of sales management, a full-time program designed to improve the effectiveness of sales managers. Some of the most widely known and highly respected academicians, consultants, and practitioners comprise the faculty of this school. In addition to these objectives, SMEI chapter membership lists usually include sales managers from most companies in any given marketing area. Somewhat surprisingly, this organization does not act as a pressure group, and although its membership would realistically appear to consist of politically conservative individuals, there is no political stance taken and a strong effort is made to discourage such potentially polarizing influences. SMEI is the largest independent sales managers' organization, but most cities have one or more local groups with similar objectives. In areas less urbanized, there are often county-wide organizations. Chester County, Pennsylvania, and Suffolk County, New York, have sales managers' clubs sponsored by the respective Chambers of Commerce. Although membership is voluntary, most sales managers belong to some organization of the type mentioned here.

Business Shows

Business shows are expositions, usually sponsored by an industry or trade organization, where all or most firms in the industry display their products or services. Customers and prospects are invited to attend, and buyers are given the opportunity to investigate several competitive product lines at the same time.

From the sales manager's point of view, he or she is given the opportunity to enhance the firm's image to its customers and to the customers of competitors. Most shows consist of booths staffed by company personnel. The salespeople who staff the booth are usually selected from the local sales office and are trained by the sales manager in techniques and protocol. Since many key executives of the firm are in attendance, the local sales manager usually receives a great deal of visibility. If the booth is well run and the objectives of the company in the show as perceived by the top executives are achieved, the sales manager is usually remembered by those executives for his or her contribution. As one sales manager in the toy industry recalls, however, recognition can sometimes be a two-edged sword:

> We had this show in the Coliseum in New York when I just came with the firm. At that time, a lot of companies used to hire these scantily-clad models to show the products. Like any other gimmick, its value was pretty limited. Anyway, our sales manager thought it would be a good idea to dress up these two chicks in very brief costumes to promote these two new toys we just came out with. It just happened that the Board Chairman and his wife showed up for the show. To make matters worse, one of the girls keeps calling him "cutie" or some such name. The Chairman and his wife were both outraged. The first thing he does is tell the two girls to get the hell out and the second thing he does is ask me who's responsible for the idea. I told him I didn't know, but predictably, some jerk trying to make points tells him who it was: Needless to say, *that* show didn't help our sales manager very much. I think if he had been at the booth, the Chairman of the Board would have fired him!

For the most part, business shows give sales managers the opportunity to act as a spokesperson for the organization and its objectives to competitors and with representatives of firms in allied industries. Most sales managers welcome the opportunity to represent their firm through this vehicle.

Charitable and Institutional Campaigns

A third way in which sales managers act in a public relations capacity is through participation in charitable and institutional campaigns. Such fund-raising extravaganzas as the United Way provide the opportunity for the sales manager to represent his or her organization to the public at large through identification with a well-known and highly constructive drive for charitable contributions. Such an association, as well as providing help to the needy, also provides help to the individual sales manager who enhances the company's image. It is interesting that most sales managers, who as a group tend to discourage public assistance as a way of life, tend to pursue the goals of charitable campaigns with a vengeance. Whether this is because of the innate achievement motivation that seems to exist in most sales managers or whether it is a concern for one's fellowman that makes them effective fund raisers is a moot point. However, one might question their motives; the recipients of charitable programs are seldom concerned with *how* their needs were met. As one sales manager in a small town where funds were being raised for a boy who was severely burned told the author,

> I'm sure you could say that a lot of the managers are running this drive to get their names or their company's names in the paper. And it would probably have been true of many of us. When some of us met the mother and father of the boy and saw their concern, we were all aware that it could have happened to any of us. I can assure you that whatever anyone gained in publicity, they gained more by knowing that poor kid was going to pull through because of our efforts.

Another common public-relations vehicle in which the sales manager enhances his or her organization's image is through association with fund-raising for nonprofit institutions such as hospitals or colleges. Such institutional drives receive a great deal of publicity, and successful participation in one or more of them usually ensures the sales manager's firm of favorable public reaction. The effect of the association of a company's name with a socially benevolent activity should not be discounted. Contrary to popular belief, organizations and people responsible for these benefits are well remembered, if not by the recipients themselves, by those who often influence buying habits or local legislation.

The sales manager's role as a public-relations representative for his or her company is manifested in various ways other than those mentioned here. It could be stated from a broad point of view that all salespeople are public-relations representatives of their organizations, also. In many instances, however, sales managers are expected to play a very specific public-relations role for their firms.

SUMMARY

In addition to the regular management functions of planning, organizing, controlling, staffing, and directing, certain administrative functions are common to most sales managers. These functions include *routine reporting and record keeping, sales budgeting and cost control,* and *marketing planning.*

Certain reports from salespersons are used by sales managers in most organizations. These reports might vary among firms with respect to terminology or frequency. The most commonly used reports of the type described here are *weekly call reports, weekly work plan reports, weekly expense reports, competitive activity reports, sales forecasts,* and *account records.*

The *sales budgeting and cost control* functions are performed by all sales managers. Budgets imposed by the firm are often too stringent and work in a manner counterproductive to the objectives of the firm. In the final analysis, however, tight cost control is necessary to ensure high profitability.

The *marketing planning* function depends to a great degree upon local conditions. The branch manager is in a better position than home office personnel to plan for unexpected or uncontrollable factors in the local marketplace.

The sales manager also maintains an interface or a relationship with other marketing groups. *Advertising and sales promotion, marketing research, product planning,* and *distribution* practices are all affected to some extent by the sales manager.

Micro Industries

Bob Simons is the National Sales Manager for Micro Industries, a manufacturer of children's electronic toys and games. Unlike most competitors who sell through manufacturer's representatives, Micro employs its own direct salespeople and has branch offices in thirty-eight cities. Sales of the various products made by the corporation had been increasing at the rate of about 50 percent each year until last year, when one of its new toys, the Star Ship Ray Gun, was taken off the market by several state consumer protection agencies. These agencies claimed that the rays emitted by the gun contained some properties found to be detrimental to children's health.

In a meeting of the key executives of the corporation, an independent consultant retained by the firm made a presentation regarding an investigation of the toy game's emission properties. According to this expert in the field, "if the rays were fired at a child every second for a year, he or she might develop a slight headache." In short, the amount of harmful properties in the gun were effectively zero.

Micro nevertheless took the gun off the market, but a certain amount of damage to the firm's image had already occurred. The president of the firm showed the executives a series of institutional advertisements intended to emphasize the safety of Micro's products. In addition to this public-relations campaign at the corporate level, the president asked each executive to be prepared to present in the near future a plan to supplement the corporate media plan stressing the safety and security of the Micro line.

1. If you were Mr. Simons, what are some of the steps that you would take to enhance Micro's image as a safety-oriented manufacturer?
2. Which other marketing departments would you communicate with to provide support for your program? How could these other departments help?

Mayfair Products

Marilyn Kennedy is the general sales manager for Mayfair Products. The firm markets various toys on a wholesale basis. The toys are imported from overseas and sold to department stores, toy stores, large drugstores, discount houses, and general merchandise stores. The method of selling each type of account varies; for example, the lead time in obtaining an order from a national department store account is considerably longer than from a drugstore account. Most of the salespeople agree that selling different kinds of accounts requires a different sales approach.

During recent years the company has grown considerably, and the sales force has increased from six in 1976 to forty-two in early 1981. Marilyn has been concerned recently that sales productivity has been falling steadily. A further concern is that most salespeople seem to be experiencing difficulty selling to large department stores. Marilyn is also perplexed over rising sales costs.

In a meeting with her sales supervisors, Marilyn discovered that the following additional problems were perceived by the group to be significant:

An adequate reporting system does not exist.
Communications between supervisor and salespeople are inconsistent.
Adequate accounting for sales expenses does not exist.
Salespeople appear to be wasting time.

1. If you were Marilyn, what steps would you initiate to help alleviate these problems?
2. What would you do to help solve the problem of sales productivity?

DISCUSSION QUESTIONS

1. What are the primary functions of salespeople's call reports?
2. What types of sales budgets are the most functional? Why?
3. What are the major outside departments with which sales managers interface?
4. What is the role of the sales manager in public relations?
5. What is the function of co-op advertising?
6. What are the basic administrative functions of sales managers?
7. What is the role of the sales manager in marketing research?
8. Why are sales managers encouraged to join outside organizations?

CHAPTER 5

RECRUITING AND HIRING SALESPEOPLE

OBJECTIVES

To familiarize the reader with the goals and techniques used in the recruiting process.

To explain the philosophy and attitude of the Equal Employment Opportunity Commission and its impact on the hiring process.

To introduce the basic techniques of interviewing applicants for sales positions.

To acquaint the reader with all aspects of the sales hiring process.

To enumerate and explain specific selection requirements for salespeople in each of the four sales categories.

To discuss different types of sales employment tests and the impact of the Equal Employment Opportunity Commission on testing.

To explain the postselection functions of reference checking and placement of the new salesperson in his or her job.

To discuss briefly the budgeting of selection procedures.

INTERVIEW WITH FRANK SMITH

Interviewer: Shall we take a look at what is involved in hiring salespeople, Frank?

Frank Smith: Yes, I think we ought to examine the recruiting, selection, and placement functions now. This is one of the most important managerial functions. If you pick the right people, they will make your life a lot easier. Pick the wrong ones, and they'll keep you very, very busy.

Interviewer: What's involved in the selection of the right people, Frank? I notice that you seem to do a good job in this area. Is it an instinct, or have you been trained to spot winners?

Frank Smith: I think our company does a good job in hiring because we spend the time required in screening salespeople. Personally, I feel that there is still some subjective evaluation that you can't filter out of the process, but for the most part, our system works well.

Interviewer: What techniques do you think are the most important?

Frank Smith: As you know, this is a very tricky area. Hiring individuals always has its pitfalls. I personally think that the system that can eliminate as many subjective factors as possible is usually pretty good.

Interviewer: Are you saying *all* the subjective factors should be taken out of the hiring process?

Frank Smith: Definitely not. The sales manager's intuitive judgment has a definite place in the process. I happen to think that it's overstressed in many cases.

Interviewer: What is your opinion on testing? A lot of managers have very little confidence in its value.

Frank Smith: That's because a lot of companies use the wrong tests. If you can find one that really does what it's supposed to do—identify and isolate potential winners—then testing is valuable.

Interviewer: Do you think that there are legislative problems in hiring salespeople?

Frank Smith: Well, the EEOC laws can cause you problems, but there are fewer problems involved than many people think. You have to remember, equal opportunity laws were passed for a reason. Compliance is mandatory, so if you set up a system of compliance, which we always have, then you have very few problems.

Interviewer: How would you like to start out our investigation of the hiring process?

Frank Smith: Let's take a look at recruiting applicants first, and then we'll go right through the whole process all the way to reference checking and setting up selection budgets.

Because of their impact on not only present, but future sales and profits as well *recruiting* and *hiring* decisions are considered to be among the most critical that are made by sales managers. Effective decision making in these two areas can result in the significant saving of time, cost, and energy. On the other hand, ineffective recruiting and hiring performance by a sales manager usually results in turnover and loss of countless dollars in sales and profits. These costs are not only reflected in severance pay and the hiring, training, relocation costs, agency costs, and countless others for the salesperson's replacement, but also in the sales volume that was missed by the ineffective salesperson. These costs, in most cases, are irretrievable and reduce profits substantially. This chapter will investigate the recruiting and hiring functions as they relate to the sales manager.

THE RECRUITING PROCESS

Sales recruiting is the process of finding applicants for sales positions. The objectives of recruiting include finding the right person for the job at the lowest possible cost with the least amount of effort. It rarely happens. Good salespeople are normally employed already, and it is not an easy task for the sales manager to locate candidates who he or she feels will perform effectively. This section will discuss some regulations that apply to recruiting as set forth by the federal government, sources of applicants, and some of the techniques used in recruiting salespeople.

The Equal Employment Opportunity Movement

Before discussing the technical features of recruiting salespeople, a review of some ground rules set out by the federal government is in order. Many false notions and much confusion exist as to what the laws specifically state, what is permissible, and what is considered *not* permissible in recruiting.

The key factor in recruiting and selection techniques is *validation,* a term used to describe the extent to which an instrument or technique measures what it is supposed to measure in terms of predicting job success. If, for example, a test or interview technique selects the most qualified applicants for the job and eliminates the least qualified, then it is said to be *valid.* Individual firms are therefore in a position to validate their tests. Many sales organizations, however, are afraid of violating the law and have simply dropped testing completely.

The Civil Rights Act of 1964 established the Equal Employment Opportunity Commission.[1] This piece of legislation makes it illegal to discriminate against certain minorities and females. Essentially, where a disproportionate number of minorities and females are being eliminated, the law requires an organization to demonstrate that its selection procedures are valid. The fact that the budget of the EEOC has grown from $2.5 million to $60 million should indicate the commitment of the federal government to equal employment opportunity.[2]

Under the EEOC, the commission accepts two possible explanations for an uneven distribution of females and minorities in an organization's work force:

1. The labor market does not contain enough minorities or females qualified to perform the work.

2. The firm's selection procedures, intentionally or otherwise, tend to discriminate against these groups.

The burden of proof is on the employer to support the first explanation. In the *Griggs et al.* v. *Duke Power* case in 1970, the U.S. Supreme court ruled against an employer when the firm could not show sufficient evidence to demonstrate the validity of the tests and the requirement of a high-school education.[3] *Griggs* set the tone for the EEOC activity, and since then employers have been attempting to validate their selection procedures to measure *job-related* factors. If nothing else, sales managers are now fairly knowledgeable as to how far they can legally go to find the best applicant.

One thing is certain; equal employment opportunity legislation has forced companies to improve their recruiting and selection techniques. As a result, sales managers have benefited from EEOC legislation in that it has opened up applicant sources that were formerly closed by "gentlemen's agreement." Prior to the late 1960s, the sales manager who attempted to hire minorities and females usually had an uphill battle. Now that employers have become more sophisticated in hiring techniques, they are discovering that there is very little difference among effective salespeople, whatever their sex or color.

Despite the obvious benefits of the EEOC legislation, the need for validation of all selection techniques still exists. Accordingly, this chapter on recruiting and hiring will consider EEOC throughout the following analysis.

Sources of Applicants

There are a number of potential sources of salespeople. The specific source is normally associated with the type of selling job. For example, very few consultative salespeople are hired from newspaper ads. Conversely, this source is used almost exclusively by direct-sales organizations. This section will examine and analyze some of the more commonly used sources of sales employees: (1) internal referrals, (2) newspaper ads, (3) trade magazines ads, (4) competitive firms, (5) employment agencies, (6) placement or search consultants, (7) colleges and universities, and (8) walk-ins.

Internal Referrals This source is considered to be the least expensive. Its value lies in the fact that a salesperson is likely to refer only candidates whom he or she feels will perform effectively. The primary disadvantage to internal referrals is the problem caused by the salesperson's reaction if the referral is not hired, or if the referral is hired, but performs poorly. If the sales manager is able to assure his or her salespersons that only positive benefits will accrue from referrals, this source can be highly effective. It is used most effectively in consultative and commercial sales.

Newspaper Advertisements Placing ads in the Help Wanted section of a newspaper can be quite expensive. The advantage of the ad is that it receives exposure to a large number of people in a local market and segments the market to whatever extent the placer of the ad determines. The biggest disadvantage (besides expense) of a newspaper ad is that in many cases effective salespeople are actively working for another firm and do not read the want ads. However, direct-sales firms use want ads almost exclusively, and many commercial salespeople are hired through this source.

Trade Magazine Ads This source is most popular in technical sales, although it is more of a medium for recruiting managers. Since trade magazine ads are directed to a very specific group, a high degree of market segmentation is achieved. The main disadvantage to this recruiting source is that the ad must be prepared at least one month in advance and therefore often appears when it is no longer needed. Trade magazine ads are also expensive, and the fact that they are seen by very few people can be a disadvantage as well as an advantage.

Competitive Firms The process of proselyting employees from other firms is known as "pirating." This technique is considered unethical if an employee is approached directly by the firm. Therefore, a third party, in many cases a consultant, is used to approach the employee to advise him or her of the opening. This technique is used frequently when higher-level positions are being filled. Although the practice is considered to be unethical, it would be naive to dismiss its existence. In hiring sales personnel, the technique is used to a lesser extent, but it has proved to be a very effective means of acquiring commercial and consultative salespeople and managers.

Employment Agencies Depending upon the functions that they perform, employment agencies can be a help or a hindrance to a sales-recruiting effort. If the agency personnel (normally one person at the agency handles the firm's account) have a real understanding of the nature of the job and the type of sales applicants required, use of an agency can be very beneficial. If the applicants referred by an agency are not qualified, the sales manager can waste a substantial amount of time interviewing. As a result, most sales managers who use agencies have developed a good rapport with agency personnel so that only applicants who appear to meet the requirements are referred. Agency fees normally range from 10 to 15 percent of the starting salary, which is considered to be a reasonable fee. Provided the firm has not spent a great deal of money on other sources, employment agencies are, in the long run, one of the least expensive methods of recruiting, *provided* (1) the agency sends the right people, and (2) if the sales manager's time is valuable. Agencies are used most widely in the technical and commercial fields.

Personnel and Search Consultants The "headhunter," as the search consultant is known in the trade, is retained to explore the marketplace for qualified applicants. Most professionals in this field have many contacts and specialized in recruiting for certain occupations. When a sales manager retains a headhunter, he or she usually does not want to know *how* the initial contact was made with the applicant, but only wants results. Since an actual search for the right person is conducted, the expenses to the firm are extremely high. It is not unusual for the firm to spend an amount equal to the first year's salary by the time fees and expenses have been paid. Because of its great expense, this technique is used sparingly in the recruiting of salespeople. Its greatest application is in the highly specialized technical areas.

Colleges and Universities Most large firms in the technical and commercial fields conduct college recruiting. Most insurance firms also engage in this type of recruiting. Recent college graduates are a good source of sales talent because they are assumed to be intelligent, have shown that they are able to achieve a specific goal, and are inexperienced enough that they are susceptible to the individual company's methods, techniques, and general way of doing things. The college campus is an excellent recruiting ground for inexperienced sales trainees, but does not yield many experienced salespeople. College graduates have been traditionally reluctant to enter the sales field, but in the tight labor markets of the 1970s and 1980s, more graduates are competing for selling positions.[4]

Walk-ins This general classification refers to persons who stop in personally or contact the sales manager through the mail to indicate their availability. Walk-ins are an excellent source of talent because the process is cheap and the sales manager may be selective about who is interviewed. The primary beneficiaries of walk-ins are commercial and technical sales organizations.

Since sales managers are constantly on the lookout for talent, some lesser used sources are probably effective. The sources discussed here, however, are the most widely used and unearth the major portion of sales applicants.

After the sales applicants have been identified, it is the responsibility of the sales manager to screen them. The employment process now becomes a constant series of eliminations of unsuitable candidates. The next steps in the process are the *application blank* and *preliminary interview*.

THE APPLICATION FORM

Nearly everyone is familiar with the *application form* (see Figure 5-1). Its purpose is to elicit *useful* and *meaningful* information from the applicant to aid in the screening process. The extent to which the application blank performs this function determines the effectiveness of the instrument. Many firms use application blanks that request unnecessary information. In addition, many states limit the type of information that may be asked for. Examples are age, sex, marital status, and arrest record.

Essentially, there are three parts to an application form. The first relates to information regarding name, address, telephone number, and other "location" data. This section has the practical function of enabling the sales manager to contact the applicant.

Figure 5-1

Application Form

Please Type or Print

Date	Phone Number: Home: Office:	Social Security Number
Last Name	First	Middle

Present Address (if P.O. Box, give Street location) Zip	From To
Previous Address (if less than 2 years at present address) 1.	From To
2.	From To

What position interests you?	How did you learn of National Liberty? Which newspaper?
Any relatives employed here?	In case of emergency please notify Name Telephone Number
Have you applied before? ☐ Yes ☐ No When?	Have you worked at NLC before? ☐ Yes ☐ No When? Why did you leave?

EDUCATIONAL RECORD

High Schools Attended	Name Address	Start End Year Graduated	Major Course Average	Offices Held	Activities
	Name Address	Start End Year Graduated	Major Course Average	Offices Held	Activities
Colleges, Universities,	Name Address	Start End Year of Degree?	Major Minor Class Rank	Offices Held	Activities
Technical or Vocational	Name Address	Start End Year of Degree?	Major Minor Class Rank		
Schools Attended	Name Address	Start End Year of Degree?	Major Minor Class Rank		

U.S. MILITARY RECORD

Veteran? ☐ Yes ☐ No Reserve Status ______ Branch ______ Serial No. ______

Date entered ______ Entering Rank ______ Discharge Date ______

Rank at Discharge ______

SKILLS

Business Machine or other specialized training - please check

☐ Manual Typewriter	☐ Dictaphone	☐ Keypunch
☐ Electric Typewriter	☐ Printing Equipment	☐ Postage Machine
☐ Mag Card	☐ Adding Machine	☐ Mail Inserter
☐ MTST	☐ Calculator	☐ Switchboard

Please list Professional Accreditations and Business, Social or Professional Memberships which may relate to position applied for.

PERSONAL INTERESTS

Hobbies which may relate to position applied for :	Briefly describe your career goals :

National Liberty Corporation and its affiliates are an EQUAL OPPORTUNITY EMPLOYER

A 249 (Rev.) 7/78

EMPLOYMENT HISTORY
A MISREPRESENTATION ON THIS APPLICATION MAY BE, AT THE COMPANY'S OPTION, GROUNDS FOR DISMISSAL.

Please include complete, detailed information on all jobs held within the past 5 years. Begin with your present or most recent employment.

Firm Name ______ From ______ To ______
Address ______ Phone Number ______
Position Held ______ Starting Salary ______ Last Salary ______ Immediate Supervisor ______
Basic Functions ______ No. persons Supervised ______
What did you like best? ______
What did you like least? ______
Reasons for Leaving ______ Eligible for rehire? ☐ Yes ☐ No
May we contact? ☐ Yes ☐ No

Firm Name ______ From ______ To ______
Address ______ Phone Number ______
Position Held ______ Starting Salary ______ Last Salary ______ Immediate Supervisor ______
Basic Functions ______ No. persons Supervised ______
What did you like best? ______
What did you like least? ______
Reasons for Leaving ______ Eligible for rehire? ☐ Yes ☐ No
May we contact? ☐ Yes ☐ No

Firm Name ______ From ______ To ______
Address ______ Phone Number ______
Position Held ______ Starting Salary ______ Last Salary ______ Immediate Supervisor ______
Basic Functions ______ No. persons Supervised ______
What did you like best? ______
What did you like least? ______
Reasons for Leaving ______ Eligible for rehire? ☐ Yes ☐ No
May we contact? ☐ Yes ☐ No

Firm Name ______ From ______ To ______
Address ______ Phone Number ______
Position Held ______ Starting Salary ______ Last Salary ______ Immediate Supervisor ______
Basic Functions ______ No. persons Supervised ______
What did you like best? ______
What did you like least? ______
Reasons for Leaving ______ Eligible for rehire? ☐ Yes ☐ No
May we contact? ☐ Yes ☐ No

EMPLOYMENT OFFERS ARE CONTINGENT UPON AN ACCEPTABLE REFERENCE FROM PREVIOUS EMPLOYERS

A 249 (Rev.) 7/78

Please carefully read and sign the reverse side of this application

JOB SEEKERS RIGHTS

As an applicant for employment with National Liberty, you are guaranteed certain rights by law and by our company policy.

First, you are guaranteed consideration for employment based solely on your personal qualifications without regard for race, religious creed, color, national origin, age or sex.

Second, you are assured courteous and fair treatment by members of our personnel staff and by members of management who may interview you.

All members of our staff and of our management group are aware of your rights and are committed to your fair and courteous treatment as an applicant for employment. We are certain that these committments will be fully met. If, however, any problems in these or other areas develop while you are seeking employment with us, I want to talk with you personally. Please feel free to call me and discuss your concern.

James D. Elliott
Vice President, Employee Relations
215-648-5614

AUTHORIZATION

YOU ARE ADVISED THAT ANY INQUIRY INCLUDING EMPLOYMENT REFERENCES, PUBLIC RECORDS CHECKS AND THE LIKE MAY NOW BE MADE, WHICH WILL PROVIDE INFORMATION RELATING TO YOUR EMPLOYMENT. ANY EMPLOYMENT OFFER IS CONTINGENT UPON A REPORT ON THIS GENERAL INFORMATION. IF YOU DESIRE, UPON WRITTEN REQUEST, WE WILL PROVIDE INFORMATION AS TO THE SCOPE OF THE INQUIRY.

To Whom It May Concern

I am seeking a position with the National Liberty Group of Companies and have given them and their representatives permission to obtain all information they require on my personal background, previous employment or educational history. I request you to assist them in obtaining such information by making a full disclosure of all information requested.

A photostat of this authorization shall have full force and effect of the original.

__________________ Dated

__________________ Signed

The second part of the application, the "experience" section, indicates where the applicant has worked before and what the nature of his or her jobs were. These data help the sales manager match the skills of the applicant to the job requirements. This section of the application blank is sometimes referred to as the "qualifier" section.

The third part of the application blank is known as the "personality" section. These data include hobbies, interests, goals, achievements, and other aspects of the candidates personal makeup that can help the sales manager develop some kind of perception as to the applicants life-style.

The most important part of any application blank is the "experience" section. The form should provide space for the applicant to provide a detailed description of past jobs, nature of duties performed, success on the job, name of supervisor, and reason for leaving. Dates of employment should be scrupulously checked. Any periods of unemployment should be noted and discussed during the preliminary interview.

"Personal References" have been a part of application blanks for such a long period of time that the practice has become so institutionalized that it almost seems un-American to omit this section. Actually, this section causes a very time consuming process for both the reference and the sales manager, and it seldom performs any useful function. The assumption that applicants will submit the names of persons who will provide them with a good reference appears to be warranted.[5] Questions detrimental to the applicant, such as previous arrests (even if it is legal to ask), simply force the applicant to tell lies that can seldom be checked. Reference and background investigation will be covered in depth later in the chapter.

In summary, the application blank is essentially a *guide* to the interviewer to aid in the preliminary interview if the applicant has not been screened out already. It should not contain unnecessary data nor should it be designed to require very much additional action by the sales manager, such as checking out unnecessary character references. Most larger firms have streamlined their application blanks, but too many small- and medium-sized firms continue to live in the past with respect to this important recruiting tool.

THE PRELIMINARY INTERVIEW

In this text, we will consider the preliminary interview to be the last step in the recruiting process. The importance of this selection device cannot be minimized. The preliminary interview is the first face-to-face relationship between the sales manager and the applicant. Its purpose is to help the sales manager screen acceptable candidates for in-depth interviews and, if appropriate, employment testing.

The preliminary interview should last between 30 and 45 minutes and should be structured in such a way that all applicants are asked similar questions, and the same basic material regarding their qualifications is discussed.[6] Either a patterned interview guide should be developed or the application blank should be used as a guide. A separate guide is preferable, and it should ask basic questions that will give the sales manager an idea of the applicant's motivations, potential, experience, and personal history. Since personal appearance, verbal ability, and other traits as predetermined by the firm may also be evaluated, the preliminary interview provides an excellent basis for screening out applicants. The most important points to remember about the preliminary interview, however, are (1) all applicants should be evaluated through similar questions, and (2) this interview is intended to find obvious elimination factors and is no substitute for the in-depth hiring interviews that follow.

THE HIRING FUNCTION: STAGE 1

The hiring function is one of the most critical areas associated with sales-force effectiveness. The benefits of hiring the right person and the consequences of hiring the wrong person for the job are of sufficient magnitude to warrant a very carefully thought out employment program. Most firms employ a variety of techniques to find people who will perform well. Yet, in spite of a multitude of tools and reams of data, hiring continues to be one of the most difficult functions of sales management. This section investigates the processes and techniques used in the selection of salespeople in the modern organization and attempts to point out some of the problems and opportunities that face the sales manager.

Every sales manager attempts to hire the right person for the job. Implicit in this notion is that the hiring decision will result in a long-term, mutually productive relationship between the salesperson and the firm. Since even the efforts of inexperienced salespeople have a direct impact on the firm's revenues and profits, hiring decisions made in sales are probably more important than those made in most other departments. The sales manager must therefore be cognizant of the fact that a wrong decision can result in the loss of both present and future sales. There is also the consideration of how much more of the product or service might have been sold had a different person been hired. Stated another way, the *opportunity costs* of hiring the wrong person are probably higher in sales than in any other function.

To minimize the incidence of wrong hiring decisions, there are certain qualification stages that applicants for sales jobs must pass through. The recruiting process dictates that candidates for sales jobs be interviewed by the sales manager as one of the basic steps. There are certain job requirements or traits upon which the salesperson is judged by the sales manager during or after the initial interview. These traits are referred to as *eliminators*, because the absence of one or more of these basic requirements for the particular sales position will automatically eliminate the candidate from further consideration. This initial stage of the hiring process is based on the sales manager's observation and refers only to very basic job requirements, such as the ability to understand the job, a positive attitude, and other readily discernible traits.

The second stage of the hiring process is concerned with somewhat deeper

Figure 5-2

A Statement Attested to by All Sales Managers

Hiring a sales person who sold you a bill of goods can be embarrassing.

It all starts with the interview. Time's tight. You have other things on your mind. The person across your desk seems responsible, experienced. You need someone now. You hire. It doesn't work out.

Work with us and it will work out.

We find people with proven sales backgrounds. We interview perceptively. We screen and objectively choose only prime candidates. And from those select few, the right one. A person you can rely on. That's why thousands of firms rely on us to find sales and sales management talent.

SALES CONSULTANTS®

Finding and placing sales and sales management talent is our only business.®

attributes of concern to the sales manager. Lack of traits like *verbal communication ability, aggressiveness,* or any other factor considered vital to the sales job would also warrant elimination from the candidacy. These secondary traits, which will be examined in more detail later in this section, normally become apparent to the sales manager during the advanced stages of an in-depth interview. It is possible that the manager's evaluation of both the primary and secondary traits can be made in one interview, although most sales managers prefer to conduct two.

The third stage of the hiring process is normally concerned with an evaluation of the *extent* or *intensity* of characteristics. This stage typically requires the aid of measuring instruments such as testing and/or a battery of several interviews.

In summary, the typical selection process for most selling jobs follows the steps shown in Table 5-1. This process is normally expanded or contracted in proportion to the amount of money the firm expects to invest in the salesperson.

In seeking potentially competent and effective salespeople, the sales manager attempts to find traits in candidates that will help him or her predict whether or not the person will (1) perform effectively and (2) remain on the job for a reasonable amount of time. As a starting point, most sales managers look for certain general personal traits. Absence of one or more of these traits should normally eliminate a candidate from further consideration, but the presence of these traits simply indicates that the candidate has passed the initial step in a fairly rigorous hiring process. Although these basic traits may vary in weight, the ones most commonly looked for by sales managers are the following:

1. An *understanding* of what the job is, its functions, its requirements, and what must be done to perform successfully.
2. An indication that the candidate would be *interested* in the type of selling job that is available; whether the job would be too routine or too complex; whether or not the candidate could attain fulfillment, could grow in the job, or whether he or she would loose interest in it.
3. A basic or even superficial indication that the candidate has the *aptitude* and basic ability to perform the functions of the job.
4. A productive *attitude*. The candidate should be a positive thinker, avoid excuses and rationalizations, and have a mental and emotional orientation that will fit into the present sales program. (This trait is subjective, but can be described as the manager's perception.)
5. The candidate should have *experience* either on similar jobs or may possess sufficient sophistication required for the job through past interpersonal contact.
6. *Enthusiasm* connotes an open-minded, inquisitive, sincerely exuberant orientation that indicates a willingness to stand up in the face of adversity; it is normally an asset in any sales job.
7. The applicant should have sufficient *verbal communications ability* to express himself or herself in accordance with job requirements.

Although all the preceding traits may not be required for every sales job, most sales managers are adamant about the candidates' possessing the majority of them. Sales managers reason that, if the potential salesperson does not display these basic characteristics during an employment interview, he or she will probably not convey them to potential customers.

THE HIRING FUNCTION: STAGE 2

In addition to the foregoing traits, which apply to every type of selling, sales managers must also look for traits or characteristics that lend themselves to the particular types of sales. Although it might be clear to the student that different requirements exist for the different types of sales, let's examine some of the basic

TABLE 5-1

Recruiting and Hiring Process

1	Recruiting and preliminary interview with sales manager
2	In-depth interview with sales manager
3	Administration of test battery
4	Additional interviews with two to four different local sales managers or administrators
5	Interview with local sales manager's boss
6	Final interview with local sales manager
7	Reference check and subsequent hire

requirements in each type of selling that sales managers look for in addition to those already mentioned. A very brief summary of these trends or characteristics is shown in Table 5-2.

Consultative Although the ability to communicate verbally is an important requirement for all salespeople, applicants for consultative selling jobs should be especially articulate and "polished." The reason sales managers must make this seemingly elitist appraisal is because of the high level of customer contact in consultative selling. It is reasoned by sales managers that their salespeople should be as well groomed and as socially adaptable as the people they call on. As a matter of fact, this is probably the one type of selling where one's educational background is likely to become a point in the conversation with clients, hence the importance of this factor to most consultative sales managers.

Technical The most important characteristic in this field is the salesperson's ability to grasp the technical aspects of the products he or she sells. Because of the necessity to give complete technical presentations to customers, low technical comprehension will invariably eliminate the candidate from further consideration. Although he or she might be required to take formal technical tests in the employment process, technical sales managers are able to discern one's general technical orientation or aptitude in the employment interview. Technical sales managers also consider the candidates verbal ability to be of above average importance since he or she would be talking to, for the most part, prospects and customers with a high level of sophistication in both business and technical areas. Naturally, the technical salesperson should be detail conscious. This characteristic is also likely to be appraised by sales managers.

Commercial Although the ability to communicate is important, an aggressive attitude is the primary attribute sought after in industrial salespeople. Aggressiveness means tenacity or a continual striving to reach a goal, which in this case is

TABLE 5-2

Important Secondary Traits

Consultative	Technical
Verbal and written expression	Technical aptitude
Dress	Verbal communications
Attention to detail	Attention to detail
Educational background	
Industrial-Commercial	Direct
Aggressiveness	Aggressiveness
Dress	Physical condition
Verbal communication	
Physical condition	

a sale. Sales managers are aware of (1) the high rejection rate, (2) the great number of sales calls that must be made, and (3) the importance of a continual emphasis on closing the sale. Aggressiveness, therefore, is the sine qua non of the industrial salesperson. In fact, the chance of success for an unaggressive salesperson in this field is extremely low. Although a few sales managers tend to mistake a dominant forward attitude for aggressiveness, most are able to perceive this quality in salespeople almost immediately. Since industrial sales requires a great amount of cold-calling, dress and personal appearance are of critical importance, primarily because of the weight that peoples' first impressions carry. A factor that is considered of somewhat less importance (but nevertheless is a meaningful factor in the sales manager's eyes) is the candidates' physical condition. Industrial sales requires a very high energy level; as a result, sales managers prefer to hire reasonably strong and healthy salespeople.

Direct Since the primary goal in direct sales is *closing*, there is no question of the importance of aggressiveness as a characteristic of successful salespeople. Stated in reverse, there is really no place for unaggressive salespeople in direct sales. This factor is so important that a salesperson can virtually lack most other qualifying characteristics and still be successful in direct sales. Because of this factor and because sales managers normally do not spend much time or money training new salespeople, candidates with an aggressive attitude stand a very good chance of being hired. As in industrial sales, physical condition is an important characteristic because of the high energy level at which most salespeople work. Quite candidly, however, most direct sales managers are considerably less discerning in the quality of their applicants. As one direct sales manager indicated in an interview,

> We don't really care what they did before or who they are as long as they can close or learn to close. We hire them one week and fire them the next. Most of the time, actually, we don't *have* to fire them, they just stop coming in. This is a real numbers game [the firm this sales manager represents is in the home improvements business]. We get plenty of leads and send them [the salespeople] out. If they sell, its fine, if they don't sell, that's OK too. It's *their* gas, *their* time, and *their* aggravation.

Some readers might think that the narrator is a tough character, but, actually he's a graduate of Princeton. The cynical approach is typical of a large proportion of direct-sales managers.

THE HIRING FUNCTION: STAGE 3

In case your're wondering, the word "operational" in business jargon means "measurable". The reason this latter term is not used here is because placement professionals normally use the former term in this context.

Thus far we have discussed what might be called quasi-subjective characteristics. All the preceding traits are discernible to the experienced sales manager in an interview, and they were discussed in terms of *eliminators* rather than traits that would cause the sales manager to make an on-the-spot hiring decision (except perhaps in direct sales). We will now investigate some of the processes used to isolate *positive* characteristics and help sales managers to make decisions as to who *should* be hired rather than who *should not* be hired. The processes we will discuss here are (1) multiple interviewing, (2) testing, and (3) the trial run. The third technique is used considerably less than the first two, but many companies in certain industries have found it helpful enough to warrant its being included in this analysis.

MULTIPLE INTERVIEWING

Personal observation by a manager is in hiring (and as we will see later in performance evaluations also) a highly unreliable and dangerous basis for making decisions. Just as football coaches are notoriously poor at picking winners in football pools, many people feel that sales managers are equally poor in selecting good salespeople through subjective selection methods. A sales manager's instincts, skill, experience, and judgment are vitally necessary to the successful day-to-day operation of the sales program, and the sales manager is clearly the major part of the solution or the major part of the problem. But because of the long-term effects and the tremendous actual as well as opportunity costs involved in making a decision to hire a particular individual, the maximum possible input should be used to enhance the quality of that decision. For this reason, most sales managers prefer to have candidates undergo more than one or, in some cases, four or five separate interviews prior to the final selection decision.

The reasons for multiple interviews are numerous. Because of their importance, the major reasons will be discussed here. An ironic aspect of sales management is that many sales managers, who should know better, are consistently "sold" by unqualified candidates, the result commonly being another sales mortality statistic. Most of the reasons that appear to support a multiple interviewing procedure are the same reasons for discouragement of an interviewing procedure conducted by only one sales manager.

Halo Effect: This problem refers to a condition where an interviewer allows a single trait or characteristic to influence the evaluation of other traits or characteristics. Appearance and verbal ability, for example, often color the judgment of sales managers, the result being that other factors are overlooked. In a situation where more than one interview is conducted, a strong likelihood exists that a more objective evaluation will be conducted. (The ad in Figure 5-3 depicts an example of the halo effect.)

Premature Judgment It is not uncommon for sales managers to make a decision to hire before the interviewing process has terminated, and spend the re-

Figure 5-3

Reprinted by permission of Development Dimensions International.

mainder of the time rationalizing the decision. This situation usually occurs when the "chemistry" or rapport between the sales manager and the candidate is extremely close. When the applicant is interviewed by other sales managers, this rapport is not likely to be carried over and the weight of this factor will be reduced substantially.

Ineffective Interviewing Surprisingly, many organizations do not have formal training programs that teach sales managers how to conduct employment interviews. At a minimum, several days of intensive training are required before a sales manager can assimilate the requisite skills for effective interviewing. It is not surprising, therefore, that many poor hiring decisions result when the sales manager is inexperienced or simply has never been trained to interview correctly. The use of additional interviewers should reduce some of the problems generated through poor managerial interviewing skills, but the possibility always exists that *none* of the interviewers is qualified.

Type II Risk In statistics, the risk of rejecting a true hypothesis is less weighty than that of accepting a false one. In the legal system it is, theoretically at least, more permissible to allow a hundred guilty persons go free than to convict an innocent person. In sales interviewing, similar conditions exist for the manager; if he or she passes over a good candidate, there is little or no personal risk; but if the wrong candidate is hired, the sales manager must accept the responsibility. Therefore, where a sales manager might tend to look for negatives in a candidate, other interviewers in a multiple hiring process often tend to be less fearful of making an error and a higher-quality hiring decision will result.

Interviewer Bias Human nature being what it is, many interviewers have conscious or unconscious biases, which result from their own background and experience. Certain physical characteristics, mode of dress, or even nationality of a candidate may have an effect upon an interviewer, which may result in a subjective hiring decision, perhaps the wrong one. When the applicant is interviewed by additional sales managers, the bias or stereotype image is unlikely to be carried by all interviewers.

Loss of Control Because of the strong personality of many sales professionals, some sales managers fall into the trap of allowing the candidate to control the interview. When this happens, the information that the interviewer receives is limited and usually favorable to the candidate. The reason for this is that the candidate, wittingly or not, tells the interviewer only positive facts about himself or herself. Very often much information that is essential to making the correct hiring decision is left out. In the multiple interview process, *all* the needed information normally will be elicited at some point in the process.

Pressure Decisions In some situations, sales managers are required by their superiors to fill an opening quickly. Realistically, the manager has no alternative except to hire the best person available. Compromises of this type often result in hiring the wrong person simply because there were no available candidates who were truly qualified. The solution to the problem is, of course, to resist the pressure and not hire any candidate unless he or she fits all requirements necessary. A multiple interviewing process will not turn an unqualified applicant into a qualified applicant, but it will help mitigate the pressure from above.

The preceding factors provide some insight into the need for a multiple interviewing process. Sales executives agree almost unanimously that a single interview process can be potentially expensive and even devastating to a firm's sales effort. Unfortunately, however, many sales managers continue the practice, in spite of the fact that poor sales hiring is one of the most prevalent causes of poor sales management performance.

TESTING

Most students and, for that matter, nearly anyone who has applied for a job has probably heard some discussion of the pros and cons of testing. Like youngsters hearing "facts" about sex education from peers, rumors, anecdotes, and false notions about testing abound, while very few people seem to know the real facts concerning the subject. Most of the gossip concerning testing is of a derogatory nature. Horror stories depicting monumental hiring blunders due to "testing" seem to have found their way into American business folklore. The truth of the matter is that, *when used correctly*, testing can be a valuable aid in the selection and hiring of salespeople.

This section will discuss the general categories of tests and examine some of the specific tests used in each general category.

The EEOC and Testing

The EEOC has established standards on three key issues regarding employment testing.[7]

1. *What is meant by a test?* A test refers to any instrument used to measure eligibility for hire, including application blank, interview, or any other formal technique.
2. *What constitutes discrimination?* Any instrument that adversely affects the hiring of protected classes is considered discriminatory unless it can predict work behavior or is relevant to the job.
3. *How is validity demonstrated?* Essentially, the burden of proof is on the company to demonstrate that the instrument is valid. Validity refers to the extent to which the test measures what it is supposed to measure. Its *reliability* is the extent of consistency of results if a person took the same test more than once.

The essence of the *guidelines* is that firms must validate not only tests, but other forms of hiring techniques as well. Most companies can comply with the guidelines for application blanks, interviews, and recruiting techniques, but *testing* validation has caused such a problem that many companies, including RCA, have dropped employment testing entirely! Yet employment testing is a good sales-selection device. The major problem is finding a test that will predict success on the job. Unfortunately, companies find it necessary to experiment until the "right" test or combination of tests is found. As a general rule, companies using selection tests probably used several different tests at various times.

Testing for Sales Applicants

Because different sales jobs require different kinds of ability, aptitude, and personality, finding people who are likely to be successful in this field is a complicated problem. In addition to EEOC implications, the development of valid predictive tests has eluded psychologists for several decades. As most students are aware, several different types of psychological tests presume to measure intelligence, personality traits, special aptitudes, proficiency in specific areas, and a host of other human factors. Most tests given to salespeople have been of three specific types: personality, interest, and aptitude.

Personality Tests Since personality factors are clearly of great importance in selling, many tests involving personality characteristics have been developed in an attempt to predict success. Certain traits, such as dominance, self-confidence, and sociability, can be made to show up. Questions such as, "If someone gets in front of you in line, what would you do?" are intended to elicit answers that will reveal whether or not the applicant possesses certain traits that appear to be associated with successful salespeople. Unfortunately, most personality tests are easy to fake, and little imagination is required to guess the answer that the sales organization wants to hear. Another problem is that there is very little evidence that *possession* of traits similar to those of successful salespeople will assure success on the job. Some of the more widely used personality tests are the *California Psychological Inventory*[8] and the *Edwards Personal Preference Schedule.*[9]

Interest Inventories These tests simply ask the applicant to make systematic choices indicating his or her likes and dislikes. The implication is that if he or she likes to do the things that successful salespeople like to do, then his or her chances of being successful in sales are more likely. The problems with interest inventories are that (1) most applicants will show sales interests even if these interests are not a part of his or her makeup, and (2) that *interest* in a profession is no guarantee that the applicant will be successful at it. For example, a high school football player might have the same interests as a star athlete, but the similarity of interest means very little without the requisite *ability* to perform as well on the field. The two most commonly used interest inventories are probably the *Strong Vocational Interest Blank*[10] and the *Kuder Preference Record.*[11]

Aptitude Tests Aptitude tests are designed to determine whether or not the subject has the *abilities* to succeed in a certain field. Clerical tests, for example, measure speed and accuracy in dealing with numbers and words. An individual's performance on these tests has helped indicate whether or not he or she has the ability to perform certain clerical functions. Unfortunately, no test has been developed that can accurately measure the extent of a person's *ability* to sell. The problem becomes magnified in view of the many different types of sales jobs. According to Buros's *Tests in Print*,[12] the bible of psychological testing, the aptitude tests for salespersons listed in Table 5-3 have been developed. The fact that even more tests in this field have gone out of print attests to the difficulty of predicting success in sales through testing.

As indicated previously, there is no universal consensus as to the validity or, for that matter, the value of employment testing for salespeople. A few independent consulting firms claim to have developed tests that will predict success in sales.

TABLE 5-3

Sales Aptitude Tests

Test	Publisher
Aptitudes Associates Test of Sale Aptitude	Martin M. Bruce
Combination Inventory	Life Insurance Agency Management Association (LIAMA)
Evaluation Record	LIAMA
Hall Salespower Inventory	Hall and Liles
Homes Sales Selection Inventory	Psychometric Affiliates
Information Index	LIAMA
LIAMA Inventory of Job Attitudes	LIAMA
Personnel Institute-ESS-EY Inventory	Personnel Institute, Inc.
Sales Attitudes Check List	Science Research Associates
Sales Aptitude Test	Psychological Services Bureau
Sales Comprehension Test	Martin M. Bruce
Sales Method Index	LIAMA
Sales Motivation Inventory, Revised	Martin M. Bruce
Sales Sentence Completion Blank	Martin M. Bruce
Steward Life Insurance Knowledge Test	Steward-Mortenson Associates
Steward Occupational Objectives Inventory	Steward-Mortenson Associates
Test for Ability to Sell: George Washington University Series, since 1974	Center for Psychological Service
Sales Motivation Analysis	Hall Associates
Sales Transactional Audit	Telemetrics, Inc.

Source: Oscar Buros, *Tests in Print* (Highland Park, N.J.: Gryphon Press, 1974). This source is published once every six years; and Oscar Buros, *Mental Measurements Yearbook* (Highland Park, N.J.: Gryphon Press, 1978). This source is published once every two years and updates *Tests in Print*.

For the most part, their founders hold impressive professional credentials and professional standing in their respective fields. These firms have many enthusiastic supporters who subscribe to their services and report highly satisfactory results. The tests are proprietary and form a large portion of the revenue base for the firms that developed them. Many large psychological testing firms seem to feel that there is no known method of predicting sales success. Yet it is difficult to dismiss the claims of these specialized sales-testing consultants. Mayer and Greenberg,[13] for example, claim that under the proper conditions sales applicants tested for a combination of *ego strength* and *empathy* have performed in accordance with test results. A convincing argument for this claim was published in the *Harvard Business Review*.[14] The strength of this test appears to lie in its ability to predict success in *direct* sales.

Stevens and others[15] have developed a seventeen-trait inventory called the *Motivational Profile Analysis* that isolates the presence or absence of several motivational requirements common to successful salespeople (see Figure 5-4). This inventory measures for many of McClelland's characteristics of high achievers, which will be discussed in Chapter 6.

Unlike many tests on the market, the MPA recognizes that personality differences exist among distinct types of salespeople (for example, the four categories used in this text), and it makes allowances for these differences. The resultant score presumably predicts success or failure in the particular type of sales for which the applicant is being tested.

Perhaps the most comprehensive selection capability by outside firms is claimed by private *assessment centers*. These organizations provide both testing and interviewing services for clients who are hiring new people or promoting present employees. Many assessment centers have developed their own sales-selection tests, and virtually all of them use prescribed selection techniques that have worked for them in the past.

In summary, the only thing about sales testing that is 100 percent certain is that it has been and will continue to be a controversial subject. The use of testing can be an extremely helpful supplement to other selection procedures and, *if the right test is found for his or her purposes*, can be a powerful selection tool for the sales manager.

REFERENCE AND BACKGROUND INVESTIGATION

The process of checking references is considered by many sales managers to be of utmost importance; others treat it as a formality. As a point of fact, the background check is a highly useful and productive supplement to the selection process. The primary advantage of the background check is that it verifies data given by the candidate and provides additional information that should help the sales manager reach a higher-quality selection decision.

Sales managers nearly always like to discuss the candidate with previous employers and, if possible, with customers. Very few firms today are interested in

Figure 5-4
Motivational Profile Analysis

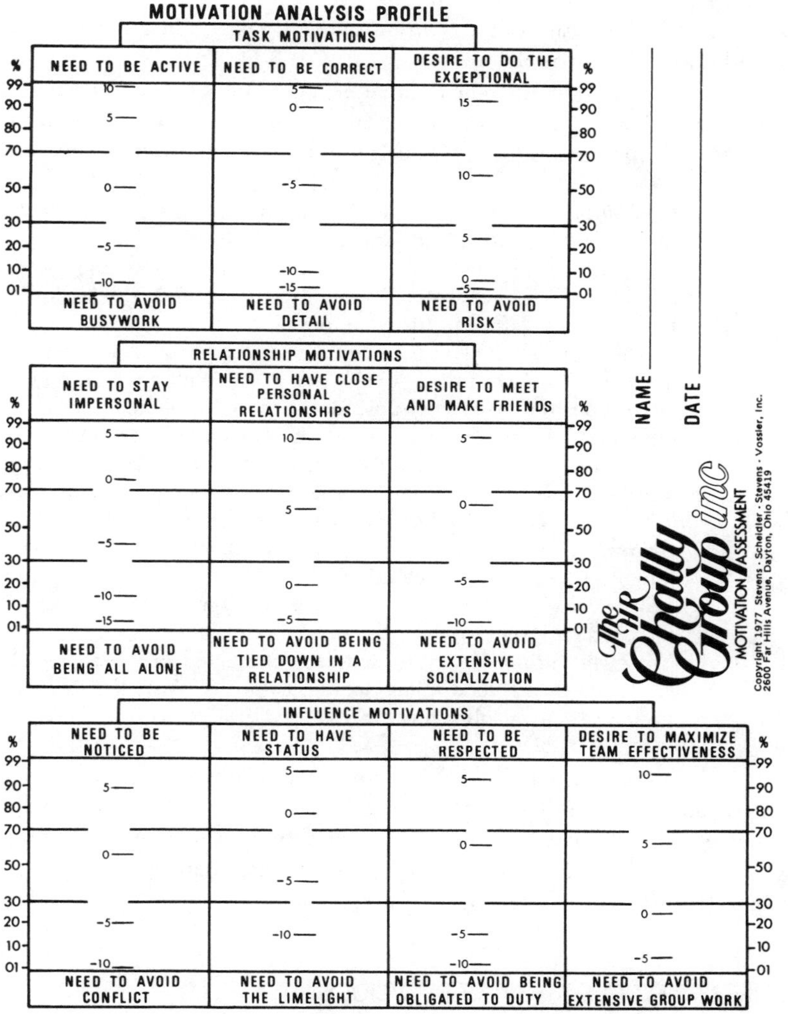

Reprinted by permission of The Chally Group. © 1979.

"personal references" suggested by the candidate, as these persons will probably provide only a positive response. Instead, the current format typically consists of a standard questionnaire that is designed to elicit as much information as possible about a candidate.

Because of various federal and state laws protecting individual privacy, it is not as simple to obtain performance data as it was in the past. Many employers are willing to provide only a former employees' dates of employment, and many customers are reticent about providing even verbal data about the candidate. A further problem lies in the need to obtain the candidates permission to seek much of the required background data. Many organizations retain outside firms to investigate a candidate's background.[16]

Assuming that the sales manager has obtained *carte blanche* to delve into the candidate's background, the following areas are most commonly covered in interviews with former employers, customers, and third parties recommended by them.

1. *Reliability:* How reliable was the salesperson in terms of meeting standards, personal requirements, or administrative requirements?
2. *Compensation history:* Did his or her earnings increase over time? Were there reductions in remuneration? If so, did they reflect greater long-run opportunities? Did the candidate state true compensation?
3. *Personal problems:* Did the candidate have personal problems that interfered with his or her job? Do the problems still exist? Who else can be contacted who would be in a position to discuss objectively these problems?
4. *Financial and credit check:* Does the candidate have a healthy need or want for money or is he or she deeply in debt? Are there any credit problems that could interfere with his or her job? Is the candidate independently wealthy with no need for income? How will this job solve his or her financial problems?
5. *Critical incidents:* Is the individual remembered for certain incidents or traits? Are they positive, negative, or neutral?
6. *Numerical scale rating:* Out of a scale of 100 with 70 as "passing," what score would the candidate receive from the interviewee?
7. *Customer rating:* Was the candidate interested in the customer's welfare? Did he or she convey a good image for the company? Was the candidate able to develop a loyal customer following?

Using a standard telephone format that provides information related to all or most of the preceding areas, a sales manager can obtain much valuable information that could influence a decision to hire or not to hire. Since a great deal of subjectivity is likely to influence many responses, as many persons as possible should be interviewed within the limits of practicality.

BUDGETING FOR SELECTION TECHNIQUES

Two primary factors relate to the sales manager's actual or perceived budgetary constraints for selection. These factors are the typical rate of turnover and the importance of hiring the right person for the position.

Most sales organizations base their selection budgets on the cost of turnover. In direct sales, where turnover is very high, selection budgets are very low. In technical sales, where turnover is low, the budget allowed for selection is quite high. In each case, the cost of making a mistake in hiring is reflected in the budget.

If a firm has been successful in selecting productive salespeople, there should be less concern than if the candidates selected have performed poorly. In the latter case, each selection technique should be evaluated, not only in terms of cost, but also in terms of effectiveness. The cheapest method is the interview, but it is also the least valid. Testing, on the other hand, is very expensive, but if a valid test *for the sales organization's purposes* can be found, the effectiveness of the selection process can probably be increased. Background investigation, particularly if it is conducted by an outside firm, is also quite expensive. If the firm has been unsuccessful in hiring effective salespeople, it is probably because the budget for selection is too low. In general, the cheaper selection techniques are less accurate.

As the cost of increasing selection success from 85 to 90 percent is probably at least as expensive as the cost of raising it from 50 to 75 percent,[17] sales management should decide upon the priority it wants to assign selection. Since effective salespeople are difficult to find, it is seldom realistic for the sales manager to assume the existence of a large pool of available talent. On this basis, research should be conducted to determine the most effective selection techniques. Once these techniques have been determined, a budget can be developed. The increased sales that result from the improved selection program should outweigh (1) the costs of the new program and (2) the opportunity costs of the former program, which resulted from hiring the wrong salespeople.

SUMMARY

Because of the high costs involved in turnover and lost sales, it is necessary for the sales manager to make high-quality selection decisions. Yet the chances of making the right decision are often impeded by the use of poor selection techniques. There appears to be no easy process developed to date that will assure or even provide low-risk hiring. Some of the major problems in recruiting, selecting, and hiring are associated with interviewing subjectivity, an irrational or poorly planned selection process designed primarily to comply with EEOC requirements, and lack of proven psychological measurement techniques. On the other hand, the use of objective and proven tools such as consistent rating of applicants, use of multiple interviews and continual upgrading and revalidation of existing viable tests is virtually certain to raise the quality of selection decisions.

After the employee is selected, it is essential that a well thought out background investigation be conducted. Federal and state privacy laws inhibit this process to some extent; therefore, it is necessary to utilize effective and efficient selection procedures.

Many sales organizations are limited in their selection process because of inadequate funds. It is of primary importance that the firm provide a large enough budget for effective selection of salespeople.

The Marketplace

Desmond Jones is the owner of an employment agency known as The Marketplace. His wife, Molly, helps with the administrative functions in running the agency and has been handling most of the recruiting advertising for sales applicants. Molly recently was offered a job singing with a band, which is her primary career interest. Because of the late hours of her new job, Molly has been unable to continue in her capacity as office manager at the agency and their children, ages 18 and 17, have been unable to lend a hand because of school.

During the first two weeks of operating the Marketplace on his own, Desmond was able to place most of the ads by himself. Last Monday, he was contacted by Mr. McCartney, president of Trans United Industries, a large conglomerate. Mr. McCartney had an immediate need for several salespeople, and he told Desmond that if several interviews could be held with applicants during the next few weeks, there would be a very lucrative fee involved. Even though he was not well versed in recruiting techniques, Desmond assured Mr. McCartney that the applicants would be found.

Mr. McCartney provided Desmond with the following sales position requirements:

Household cutlery salesperson: *Will work in the products division. The job requires selling of knives to homemakers on a door-to-door basis. The compensation is straight commission, and salespeople earn between $100 and $300 per week.*

Office equipment salesperson: *Will work in the office product division selling copy machines to businesses, government, and institutions. The salesperson receives a salary of $100 per week plus commission on copiers sold. Most salespeople earn about $350 per week. A college degree is required for this job.*

Executive salesperson: *Will work for the management and organizational consulting division. Job consists of calling on company presidents and other top-level executives selling a system of cost-reduction seminars. Salespeople earn about $35,000 per year. A college degree and five years of experience are required.*

Switchgear salesperson: *Will work for switchgear division calling on purchasing agents for manufacturing companies. Most salespeople earn about $20,000 per year with company car and annual bonus. A technical degree is required.*

Unfortunately, Molly is out of town with the band and Desmond has little experience in recruiting applicants. He only has about $300 in the bank and is anxious to bring in several applicants for Mr. McCartney.

1. How would you advise Desmond in undertaking a program to recruit applicants for these jobs?
2. What problems is Desmond liable to encounter in his search for applicants?

DISCUSSION QUESTIONS

1. Describe the profile of a successful direct salesperson.
2. What motivates most salespeople?
3. What are the legal and social aspects of the Equal Employment Opportunity programs?
4. What systematic techniques influence successful interviewing and hiring?
5. Discuss the significance and evaluation of references in the hiring process.
6. What are the major functions of the application form?
7. What are the major steps in the recruiting and hiring process?
8. Why is it considered more desirable for more than one manager to interview an applicant?

NOTES

[1]Equal Employment Opportunity Commission, *Guidelines on Employee Selection Procedures*, 9 (Federal Register) 1970 35(149:12333-12336).

[2]Lawrence O'Leary, *Interviewing for the Decision Maker* (Chicago: Nelson Hall, 1976).

[3]*Griggs et al.*, v. *Duke Power Co*. No. 124, October Term, 1970 (March 8, 1971) 401 US 424 (1971).

[4]"College Students View Selling: an Update," *Sales and Marketing Management*, March 1979, p. 104.

[5]O'Leary, *Interviewing*, p. 114.

[6] Felix Lopez, *Personnel Theory and Practice* (New York: McGraw-Hill, 1975).

[7]Equal Employment Opportunity Commission, *Guidelines*.

[8]Consulting Psychologist Press, Palo Alto, Calif.

[9]Psychological Corporation, New York.

[10]Ibid.

[11]Science Research Associates, New York.

[12]Oskar Buros, *Tests in Print* (Highland Park, N.J.: Gryphon Press, 1974), pp. 1121-1127.

[13]David Mayer and Herbert Greenberg, "What Makes a Good Salesman?" *Harvard Business Review*, vol. 42, no. 4 (July-August 1964), pp. 119-125.

[14]Ibid.

[15]H. R. Chally Group, Dayton, Ohio.

[16]"How to Select and Place Sales People," (Dayton, Ohio: H. R. Chally Group, 1979).

[17]Ibid.

CHAPTER 6

LEADERSHIP AND MOTIVATION OF THE SALES FORCE

OBJECTIVES

To provide the reader with an understanding of the following concepts of leadership:

* Leadership style
* Followership
* Situational leadership

To provide the reader with an understanding of the various theories of motivation:

* Hierarchy of needs
* Expectancy theory
* Dual factor theory
* Theory of achievement motivation

To investigate the relationship between money and motivation.

To investigation certain motivational assumptions and the four sales types.

To develop an understanding of the salesperson.

To investigate the concept of coaching.

INTERVIEW WITH FRANK SMITH

Interviewer: Well, Frank, now we're going to talk about leadership and motivation. If a sales manager understands these two concepts, I guess it's pretty hard not to succeed.

Frank Smith: You know, that might be a little bit of an overstatement, but I certainly agree that he or she has to be a good leader and motivator to succeed.

Interviewer: I often wondered how the manager learns to be a good leader without experience. Is it an inborn quality?

Frank Smith: Oh, no. Like anything else, leadership and motivation can be learned—at least the basic principles can. Then with practice, the expertise comes along with it.

Interviewer: You said earlier that a sales manager has to spend a certain amount of time as a salesperson. How effective must he or she be to become a manager?

Frank Smith: Whether you know it or not, you're touching on a very controversial subject. First of all, a lot of companies make the mistake of thinking that a good salesperson automatically makes a good manager. That is not true. By the same token, if you have two candidates equal in managerial potential, and one is a good salesperson, most companies will pick the good salesperson.

Interviewer: Do you think that most organizations adequately train their managers to be effective leaders and motivators?

Frank Smith: Probably not. We do, but I know a lot of firms just expect that the new manager will automatically be proficient in these areas.

Interviewer: You feel, then, that there is a lot to learn about being a leader?

Frank Smith: Yes. If you think it's a simple process, I have a feeling that this chapter will disabuse you of this notion.

Over the past several decades, more than 1000 studies have been conducted on the subject of leadership.[1] For the most part, these studies have attempted to develop relationships associated with effective leadership. Yet all these studies have unearthed only a few major points upon which most researchers agree:

1. There is a strong association between leadership and motivation.
2. Leadership depends upon the persons who are being led and upon the situation as much as upon the qualities of the leader.
3. There are no identifiable traits that are common to successful leaders.
4. All leaders have a particular "style." There is no single style that appears to work better than the others.
5. The ability to motivate an individual depends as much upon the characteristics of the person being motivated as the motivation technique being used.
6. There is ample evidence that the use of money has limited use as a motivation tool.

This chapter will investigate the concepts of leadership and motivation, some of the current thinking in each area, and its application to sales management.

LEADERSHIP

Broadly, *leadership is the ability to influence others to follow toward the attainment of common goals*. It is possible to be a manager or a supervisor without being a leader. Conversely, a good leader may not possess the qualities necessary to make him or her a good manager. A title of designation of authority does not guarantee that an individual will be a leader. The ingredient of his or her subordinates' *wanting* to following is critical. When we think of leaders, we tend to think of a particular *type* or personality. Yet the kind of personality required for effective leadership depends to a great extent upon the situation and upon the people being led. There exist several different types of leaders, and each type is successful in different situations.

Leadership Style

The term "style" is generally used to describe the leader's relative use of power and authority in the performance of his or her functions. This style is perceived as ranging from *autocratic* to *participative*. For our purposes, *autocratic* describes a situation where the leader makes all decisions and accepts little or no feedback from followers. A *participative* leader accepts feedback from his or her followers and even allows them to influence or to take part in decision making.

Obviously, there are additional dimensions to leadership style than *autocratic-participative*.[2] *Concern for production* and *concern for people* constitute another dimension of leadership style. *Concern for production* refers to the leader's orientation toward the work to be performed as being the primary focus of reference. The inference here is that the subordinates or followers are viewed more or less as tools to accomplish the job. Leaders who have *concern for people* tend to stress the relationship aspect of the task. They take a personal interest in followers as individuals. Although the *autocratic-participative* dimension of leadership characteristics does not mean exactly the same thing as the *concern for people-concern for production* dimension, the description of these extremes should provide an idea of the types of individual leaders were are discussing.

The *autocratic, concern-for-production* type of leader is probably best epitomized by the late Vince Lombardi, former coach of the Green Bay Packers football team.[3] Lombardi inherited a last place team, and with virtually the identical personnel, led the team to three consecutive championships. He insisted upon total authority and was a strict disciplinarian almost to the point of ruthlessness. Yet he had the total respect of his followers. We will refer to this kind of autocratic leader as *type 1* (on a scale of 1 to 10; see Figure 6-1).

Figure 6-1

Type 1	Most Leadership Styles Range	Type 10
	Somewhere Between 1 and 10	
Autocratic: Low concern for followers as individuals		Participative: High concern for followers as individuals

The other end of the spectrum is the *participative, concern-for-people* type of leader. Some recent examples of this type of leader were the late Thomas Dooley and Martin Luther King. Each had limited resources and authority, but each had a dedicated followership. These leaders epitomize a *type 10* leader.

It should be clearly understood that most leaders vary their styles from time to time. It is also possible to fluctuate in *both* dimensions; for example, a relatively autocratic leader is still capable of having high concern for his or her followers. The primary point that is being made here is that *both* types of leadership style can be eminently successful or unsuccessful.

Followership

Just as there are styles for leaders, there are also styles for followers. Some people are influenced by a particular leader, while others might be "turned off" by the same leader. How a follower reacts to a leader depends upon not only the leader's orientation toward certain values but also the psychological and emotional makeup of the person being led. There is ample evidence that highly respected and well-liked leaders find it easier to direct their subordinates.[4] On the other hand, leaders who are disliked and/or do not hold the respect of subordinates usually find it necessary to implement a style closer to type 1, primarily because they have few resources to draw upon other than their authority.

Leadership Traits

In one of the most comprehensive reviews of human behavior characteristics, Stogdill[5] found no relationship between traits such as height, intelligence or knowledge, and success as a leader. It appears that most people have some perception of what the successful leader is like. Often, the leaders typified by popular cinema favorites tend to provide a stereotype image to the public. In reality, there are *no* present traits or characteristics that are common to successful leaders. In short, there is little evidence to show that possession of any single trait or group of traits in an individual can predict effectiveness as a leader.

Situational Leadership

To further complicate matters, many if not most researchers agree that leadership is strongly affected by the situation from which the leader emerges and in which he or she operates. The follower perceives certain benefits accruing to him or her from following a particular leader. All the great leaders throughout history were able to achieve goals in certain critical situations. In business, group members are more apt to follow a leader who can likewise help them to more readily achieve their perceived objectives. Essentially, the concept of "situational leadership" is summed up by Fred E. Fiedler, one of the best-known authorities on leadership.

> Leadership performance depends then as much on the organization as it depends on the leader's own attributes. Except perhaps for the unusual case, it is simply not meaningful to speak of an effective leader or an ineffective leader; we can only speak of a leader who tends to be effective in one situation and ineffective in another. If we wish to increase organizational and group effectiveness we must learn not only how to train leaders more effectively but also how to build an organizational environment in which the leader can perform well.[6]

Leadership, then, is much more than a charisma that attracts all kinds of people and molds them into a cohesive group in pursuit of common goals. It is true that certain physical and personality traits are valuable assets at certain times. In most cases, however, there are a variety of forces (both concrete and abstract), many of which are outside the leader's control, that determine a leader's effectiveness.

MOTIVATION

To lead people effectively, a working knowledge of what leadership is and how it works is an important asset. Likewise, a knowledge of what motivation is and what is required to motivate people is equally valuable. How well a manager functions as a leader and motivator of people to a great extent determines his or her managerial effectiveness.

Theories of Motivation

Motivation is a highly complex area of study. Psychologists and psychiatrists have been formally investigating motivation for well over a century and still continue to differ on several of its basic concepts. Thus it would be both pretentious and inaccurate to attempt to explain motivation in one section of this text. There are, however, certain organizational situations in which motivation has been found to operate within classic patterns. Most of the accepted theories of organizational motivation were developed between 1940 and 1970. These theories were developed by highly credible professionals and provide a good basis for a practical, rather than a clinical, understanding of the motivation of individuals or groups within organizations. We will attempt to identify and explain some of the currently accepted thinking in the field and then examine some of these relationships within the context of the four types of selling.

The Hierarchy of Needs Maslow[7] suggests that the needs that induce all behavior are arranged in a hierarchy or are organized by level of need.

Physiological needs: *basic needs, food, shelter, and the like*
Safety needs: *needs for protection*
Social needs: *needs for friends, associates, sense of belonging*
Ego needs: *needs for autonomy, status, recognition, appreciation*
Self-actualization: *need to realize one's potential to achieve ultimate satisfaction*

According to Maslow, once a need is satisfied, the next highest need emerges to motivate the individual's behavior. There are relative degrees of satisfaction at each level. Although this theory would appear to make sense, it has been difficult to prove or disprove on an empirical basis. The primary value of the hierarchy of needs is its relevance to the motivations of employees as certain levels of these needs become relatively satisfied. For example, a straight-commission salesperson who has not been selling much would be difficult to motivate through promises of promotion and increased status. On the other hand, a highly paid salesperson could probably be motivated by an appeal to higher-level needs. In practice, this theory provides a somewhat useful *guide* in judging human motivation.

Expectancy Theory The essence of this theory is that a person will behave according to the perceived likelihood that an action will lend to a certain outcome or goal. According to Vroom, who first related the expectancy theory of motivation to business activity,

> It is reasonable to assume that most of the behavior exhibited by individuals on their jobs as well as their behavior in the "job market" is voluntary and consequently motivated.[8]

Vroom accordingly described motivation as a process that determined choices made by individuals among various forms of voluntary activity. The predictive ability of this theory has yet to be established. The value of expectancy theory is in providing insight for managers in dealing with individuals and groups. A reward system, for exmaple (money, promotion, benefits), must be wanted by the salesperson and must have a positive priority if he or she is to be motivated by it. Variations in performance level must then be perceived as leading to reward. The sales manager, therefore, must be able to vary the magnitude of the reward structure sufficiently enough to change (upward) the performance level of the salesperson. Like the hierarchy of needs theory, it is difficult to test this theory empirically, but it provides a *guide* to a better understanding of the motivation of salespeople.

Herzberg's Dual Factor Theory One of the better known and most widely studied motivational theories is the dual factor theory, developed by Herzberg.[9] There are essentially two sets of factors that evoke human behavior. The first group is termed "dissatisfiers" or "hygenic" factors. This group includes such things as salary, supervision, working conditions, job security, and company policy. Herzberg claims that these factors do not really motivate people to perform. They can only make one dissatisfied if they are not perceived as being at least acceptable to the employee. Enough dissatisfaction in any of these areas can even lead to the employee's quitting his or her job. The second group of factors consists of such things as challenge of job, opportunity for personal growth, responsibility, advancement, recognition, and, at the focal point, the job itself. These factors are known as "motivators" because they help employees to receive job satisfaction and are generally determinants of long-term changes in attitude.

Of particular interest is the place of money as a motivator in Herzberg's scheme. Essentially, this factor will evoke a short-term change in behavior or attitude, but does not constitute a long-term motivating force. The value of the dual factor theory lies in its applicability to professional careers such as sales. Although this theory is not supported by superior research practices in data gathering and analysis, it is nevertheless very widely accepted by business organizations and has formed the basis for a considerable number of job upgrading programs.

McClelland's Theory of Achievement Motivation This theory of motivation is based on more rigorous research than any of the others discussed here. McClelland's theory is based upon the chronic, persistent needs for achievement, affiliation, and power.[10] Through the administration of the Thematic Apperception Test (see Figure 6-2), an individual's need to achieve is isolated. The individual is asked to answer questions about a picture. Typically, a person who has a high need for achievement will write a story with a heavily achievement oriented theme. Persons with a high need for achievement are characterized by goal setting, the need for concrete feedback as to how well they are doing, and the willingness to take moderate risks. These characteristics are common to successful entrepreneurs and to successful salespeople in certain occupations.

Most high achievers are not aware of *why* they are constantly driven to attainment of goals. Consider the following remarks made by Dick Vermeil, a highly respected and very successful football coach:

> For me, every day is a matter of life and death in coaching football. I've never been satisfied. If I'm doing something I want to do it better than anyone else. I've been fortunate that at every level I've coached at—high school, junior college, college and professional—I've been successful to where I've been Coach of the Year. I'm excited about that. Now, I'm in a league with 27 other guys who are among the best and I want to be the best. I've always been like that and I just don't know why.[11]

Figure 6-2

Thematic Apperception Test

Look at this picture for ten or fifteen seconds. Now write a brief but imaginative story suggested by the picture and by the following questions:

1. What is happening? Who is the man?
2. What has led up to this situation? That is, what has happened in the past?
3. What is the man thinking? What is wanted? By whom?
4. What will happen? What will be done?

Reprinted by permission of the *Harvard Business Review*. Exhibit from "Business Drive and National Achievement" by David C. McClelland (July-August 1962). © 1962 by the President and Fellows of Harvard College; all rights reserved.

These remarks are typical of the orientation of high achievers.

McClelland finds that artists, teachers, scientists, and other "relationship-oriented" professionals tend to score low in need for achievement and high in need for affiliation. Persons with a high need for affiliation are, among other things, more sensitive to other peoples' feelings than people with a high need for achievement. Business managers and politicians tend to score high in need for power or the need to influence other peoples' actions. According to McClelland, these needs are shaped early in life by cultural and parental factors. The classic high achiever learns to set goals early in life and is normally raised in a culture that is receptive to individual initiative and advancement. A thorough examination of McClelland's theory would require considerably more time than we are able to devote. The points mentioned here are the most relevant to an understanding of the need for achievement and motivation of salespersons.

This enumeration of prevailing theories of motivation is by no means complete, but we have discussed briefly four theories having the most practical application to sales. Brief descriptions of each are given in Table 6-1. Most other theories dealing with organizational motivation tend to deal more with production situations than with sales.

TABLE 6-1

Some Well-known Theories of Motivation

Motivation Theory	Basic Concept
Maslow's Needs Hierarchy	People have needs ranging from the most basic (food, shelter, etc.) to psychological needs (e.g., the need for self-actualization, knowing oneself). These needs motivate individuals to fulfill the need. After the need is fulfilled, it no longer provides motivation.
Expectancy Theories	People behave in accordance with achieving their goals or objectives. They can be motivated to perform various functions to the extent that they perceive that the performance of those functions will help them achieve their objectives.
Herzberg's Dual Factor Theory	Certain factors (e.g., money, supervision, working conditions) can result in dissatisfaction, but cannot motivate employees. The real motivators are the work itself, recognition, decision-making latitude, and other *intrinsic* factors.
McClelland's Theory of Achievement Motivation	Each individual has needs for achievement, affiliation, and power. High need for achievement is characterized by certain behavior (setting goals, willingness to take moderate risks, need for concrete performance feedback) that is compatible with entrepreneurial activity. Most sales people have higher than average need for achievement.

MONEY AND MOTIVATION

The relationship between money and motivation is highly complex. There is some evidence that most sales managers tend to place money near the top as a motivator. Yet most behavioral scientists tend to assign it a low priority on the scale of motivating factors. In actuality, they are both right. The place of money as a motivator depends entirely upon the individual. It is possible for a sales manager to be in charge of several salespersons, each with a different perception of the place of money as a motivator.

One perception of money is as a "hygenic" factor in Herzberg's motivational scheme. Many managers misinterpret a salesperson's dissatisfaction with a pay plan as a signal to persuade the salesperson to sell more in order to overcome the dissatisfaction. It is incorrectly inferred by the manager that an increase in sales will result in greater satisfaction. What may really be needed by the salesperson often cannot be met by increased income. Instead of more money, perhaps the salesperson needs more challenge on the job or even a more "interesting" sales territory. In a situation of this type, money does not act as a long-term motivator.

Another perception of money is as a "scorecard" of how well an individual is performing. In this case, if the salesperson perceives himself or herself as being in competition with peers with an established dollar earnings quota, or even with himself or herself, money might very well provide a strong motivating force. In this case, the money's importance is not what it can buy, but its indication of professional standing. This factor can be a much more powerful motivator than the actual value of the money.

In many cases, it is difficult for a sales manager to determine how important money is to individual salespeople as a motivating force. Because of the traditional emphasis on monetary income as a measure of success in sales, the salesperson's customary role virtually *requires* him or her to place emphasis on the importance of money. In any sales organization, the acquisitive or "hungry" salesperson is perceived by management to represent the norm. Any utterances that tend to downgrade the importance of money are viewed with suspicion, if not with outright alarm. As a result, the sales manager must often make the assumption that the salesperson places great importance upon money as a driving force when there may in fact be other factors that would have a greater motivating effect.

In most cases, salespeople gravitate toward a particular job because they are comfortable in that type of selling *and* because of the compensation structure. If, for example, a successful salesperson in the commercial field leaves his or her job for a consultative-type selling job because of the opportunity to earn more money, it is wrong to assume that he or she is simply motivated by money. If the new job is not psychically rewarding or interesting, it will be difficult to perform well over a long period of time. Hence, money in this case is actually a *dissatisfier* (in the commercial sales situation) and not a motivator.

Despite the previous comments emphasizing nonmonetary factors, the importance of money should not be underestimated, particularly during inflationary periods. Also, circumstances arise that catapult money into the forefront for most salespeople at frequent intervals in their careers. The most common of these circumstances is when the salesperson has little or no money. At this point, money assumes a prominent place in the salesperson's order of priority, and sales managers are justified in concluding that monetary reward will probably act as a motivator, at least until the salesperson's immediate monetary needs have been met. Likewise, when a crisis situation requiring quick and substantial liquidity arises, a salesperson's primary motivation is likely to shift from a long-term motivator to monetary reward.

To conclude, there is no question that people will do many things for immediate monetary reward. The importance of money as a motivator, however, depends upon the salesperson's perception of his or her immediate need for it rather than management's decision to use it as an inducement to sell more. It is unwarranted for sales managers to assume that money itself will act as a consistent motivator of salespeople. Yet nearly every sales organization finds that, if it reduces the

"He's a good man, but it takes wild horses to get him started."

opportunity for monetary reward, salespeople complain vociferously. If that opportunity continues to be reduced, turnover follows. As David McClelland points out,

> Money is one tool among many for managing motivation. It is a treacherous tool because it is deceptively concrete, tempting many managers to neglect variables in the work situation and climate that really affect productivity. In the near future, there will be less and less excuse for neglecting these variables, as the behavioral sciences begin to define them and explain to management how they can be manipulated just as one might change a financial compensation plan.[12]

MOTIVATIONAL ASSUMPTIONS AND THE FOUR SALES TYPES

Up to now we have discussed some of the more widely accepted theories of motivation and their fundamental principles. It should be clear that some principles overlap from one theory to another, but basically there are few if any contradictions among the theories. We will examine each type of selling and apply a motivational framework to each type. It should be understood that the following analysis serves only as a *guide* to understanding the motivational structure of the four types of sales. Because of the complexity of the human mind and because of special circumstances that might prevail, there is no *guarantee* that the classic motivational assumptions for any sales type will fit the situation for all or even for most salespeople at a given time. Most sales managers would probably agree, however, that there exist certain assumptions which, if followed, enable the use of specific techniques that tend to motivate sales people *much of the time*.

Consultative Sales

The hallmark of the consultative salesperson is his or her ability to act either independently or with a modicum of technical support. Most managers of consultative salespeople are sensitive to this fact and are careful to avoid "overmanaging." At certain times, however, *all* salespeople need guidance. The ability to provide assistance without being "pushy" is a very important qualification for the consultative sales manager.

To label any salesperson as "self-motivated" would be inaccurate. Every salesperson needs recognition and approval from peers and managers. Of all the four sales types, however, consultative salespeople are the most inner directed and possibly *achievement conscious*. Because of the nature of the selling and the high level of contact that must be made, there is a strong tendency for consultative salespeople to find strong motivation in the nature of the job itself and many of the interesting opportunities to expand its scope. In terms of needs, most people in this type of selling situation have a professional orientation and are highly sensitive to the *self-esteem* needs, particularly autonomy, or the opportunity to work alone and design the job as he or she sees fit. These needs also tend to coincide with some of Herzberg's long-term motivators.

Sales managers in the consultative sector tend for the most part to understand the implications of the abundance of internal forces that operate within the occupational parameters of their salespeople, and the motivation techniques they utilize are primarily directed toward providing greater opportunities for the salesperson to grow in the job. An example of this kind of motivating is to provide the salesperson with a different kind of account. If a salesperson has been calling upon petroleum companies, the additional assignment of a steel firm provides a new challenge. The forthcoming response not only enhances the sales of the consultative firm but also provides the salesperson with fulfillment of needs.

For the most part, other motivational techniques utilized by consultative sales managers are equally undramatic. Salespeople in this category tend to set their own goals and often resent perceived interference from sales managers in attaining them. For these reasons, most sales managers make themselves available for help when called upon, but most of the support they provide is in the way of technical and organizational input. Outside of their relationships with newly hired salespersons, where the emphasis is upon orientation to company policies and practices, sales managers are extremely subtle in their use of motivational techniques.

Technical Sales

Technical salespeople, like consultative salespeople, tend to seek growth within the job. In many cases, the challenge of the job provides a long-term motivation to perform. The technical nature of the job seems to provide an inner stimulation to solve customer problems in such a way as to inspire confidence. The role of the manager in the motivation of the technical sales force is, however, often underestimated. Technical salespeople, if not directed in their efforts, sometimes tend to become involved in customer problems and technical matters to the detriment of productivity. Technical salespeople are traditionally known for their low-pressure approach, a condition that, if carried too far, can also result in lost sales. Finally, many technical salespeople have an achievement orientation similar to commercial salespeople and need to see their sales figures increase frequently to satisfy some of their most important needs. In directing a sales force with varied motivational requirements, the approach taken by the sales manager in the techniques he or she uses is critical.

Many technical sales managers work very closely with salespeople in an attempt to develop a *method* to increasing sales, rather than participating in the solution of individual problems. The ability to sell at a higher level of the customer's organization, for instance, is a common need for most technical salespeople. A second area where many technical salespeople perceive the need for improvement is in optimum utilization of selling time. Another widespread need for technical salespeople is the dissemination of immediate trends in the product marketplace, such as new techniques, concepts, and competitive accomplishments. Sales managers in this field attempt to provide their salespeople with techniques that will help them become self-sufficient in these problem areas. As more proficiency is developed, increased sales effectiveness will result, usually in a cumulative fashion, where the newly gained proficiency adds to a permanent knowledge base.

Specific techniques for short-term motivation also exist in technical sales. These techniques depend to a great extent upon the type of product and industry. In the bulk chemical industry, for example, credit extended to customers is an important profit consideration. Many times it is not in the company's interest to sell to certain firms because of the high degree of risk that the customer will not be able to pay for the products delivered. In such cases, bonus plans are often implemented to reward salespeople for selling to good customers. (Obviously, too conservative a credit policy could in certain cases tend to demotivate conscientious salespeople). Some sales managers use incentives such as the presentation of technical papers at sales meetings or seminar participation. Incentives of this type often work well in the short run and tend to appeal to needs. On a long-term basis, however, managers who can help technical salespeople develop effective selling methods are normally the most effective at motivating them.

Commercial Sales

Motivation in the commercial sales field has traditionally been based on either monetary reward or promotion possibilities. The typical office usually consists of about ten to twenty salespeople. Out of these twenty, about five or six will be compensated very well, about five or six will move into some position of greater responsibility within the company at some future time, and the remainder will eventually leave the firm. Assuming that these proportions or a similar configuration exists in most commercial sales offices, the sales manager's problem is motivating his or her people to beat these odds. For several reasons, some turnover is desirable in most sales organizations. Heavy turnover, however, impairs the effectiveness of the sales manager and is also very expensive. Since the manager must spend a disproportionate amount of time with new salespeople, it takes away from time that could be spread out among a greater number of salespeople. At the same time, interviewing and other hiring responsibilities take up even more time. If sales managers were better able to motivate existing salespeople, there is little reason to doubt that turnover could be reduced substantially.

Because of strong pressure to meet monthly sales quotas, many commercial sales managers find themselves in turn applying pressure to these salespeople through subtle comment or outright threats or implications that certain sanctions will result if sales quotas are not attained. These sanctions typically range anywhere from increases in sales quotas to loss of job. The use of fear or intimidation as a motivator often works once or twice with an individual, but does not work well over the long run; indeed, it normally results in demotivation, which is counterproductive to the overall sales effort. The reason that many commercial sales managers use negative methods is because, in most instances, they were not taught how to use positive factors or do not understand the complexity of the motivation process. One way in which organizations can enhance their motivational methods is through formal manager training programs emphasizing positive motivational techniques.

Most commercial salespeople have strong needs for achievement and recognition and, in many cases, are as concerned about money as a "scorecard" or measure of success as they are concerned about its actual value. Recognition of these needs and providing a positive route to attaining them often provide the basis for positive motivation. In many cases, it is necessary for a manager to spend a great deal of time in the field with salespeople, providing the necessary training and information. Most salespeople, if they feel that the manager's efforts are sincere and unselfish, normally expend great effort to increase sales. The sales manager must determine what it takes to *keep* salespeople expending their full efforts towards sales goals. Whatever is necessary to keep the salesperson's goals congruent with those of the company must be utilized by sales managers.

Because of the nature of the job, commercial salespeople experience a great number of rejections for each sale that is made. For this reason, it is important to hire persons who are emotionally equipped to accept this situation as part of the job. Clearly, if an individual is not able to deal with this condition, it will be extremely difficult, if not impossible, to motivate him or her over a sustained period. If, on the other hand, the individual makeup does lend itself to commercial sales, every effort should be made to help instill a positive attitude in that salesperson. A positive attitude normally results after a certain degree of success has been attained; therefore, it is necessary to help the salesperson perform effectively if a realistic motivational effort is to be made. Since effective selling is the result of a high quantity of high-quality sales calls, the commercial salesperson must be trained to achieve a high degree of proficiency in all the major sales skills.

In short, commercial salespeople must be exposed to a great deal of training and must have a high degree of product and sales knowledge before they can be motivated to perform well over a long period of time. A simple rule of thumb to be applied to commercial sales motivation is as follows:

1. Provide adequate training in necessary skills.
2. Help the salesperson achieve successful sales.
3. Determine the salesperson's needs.
4. Prove that these needs can be achieved.
5. Help him or her develop a positive attitude.
6. Continually discuss his or her needs and goals.
7. Show a high degree of effort will achieve his or her long-term goals.

This sequence is, of course, fairly general and clearly simplistic. It does, however, provide a workable framework for a commercial sales motivational framework. A primary factor to be recognized is that motivation in commercial sales is a continuing requirement for the sales manager.

Direct Sales

The turnover rate in direct sales is extremely high. Straight-commission compensation, short training periods, lack of good selection techniques, and general disinterest of management in the salesperson's future all tend to militate against stable, long-term relationships on which to build a strong motivational base. Unlike the other three types of selling, most people gravitate toward direct sales solely because of potential or perceived financial rewards. In this kind of environment, it is very difficult for sales managers to develop effective motivation techniques. As a sales manager in the franchising industry pointed out to the author,

> I've been in encyclopedias, Florida property, home improvements, you name it, and I've sold it. Every company has one thing in common—an exceptionally high markup. The company simply adds a large sales commission to the price. This entices the salesman and it doesn't cost the company a thing. When you operate this way, it's no wonder you can't keep a sales force. Most of them don't last a month. Let's face it, the biggest motivator for any of them is quick money. Any way you can help them get it is probably good motivation. I've heard so many lies in this business that the exception is a sales manager who tells the truth to his salesmen. Maybe that's a good motivator—telling your salesmen the truth.

While this statement may sound a bit harsh, it is probably quite accurate. With the exception of insurance companies, very few direct-sales organizations are concerned with long-run motivation of the sales force. Most sales offices consist of a few strong closers and a large number of relatively inexperienced salespeople. Managers attempt to develop the latter into effective salespeople, but the time and resources at their disposal are normally quite limited. The result is that managers spend much of their time interviewing new salespeople and little or no time training or otherwise developing current salespeople.

Of the relatively few salespeople who do make a career of direct selling, the majority have needs fairly similar to those in the commercial field. Because credibility is a major factor in the relationship between the manager and salesperson, it is very important that managers develop a sense of mutual trust and understanding before trying to utilize motivation techniques. A sequence similar to the one discussed in commercial sales is a good approach to motivating direct salespeople, but such a process is even more difficult to implement in direct sales. Motivation problems in the direct-sales field are widespread and will probably not be overcome until sales organizations are willing to spend the time and money that is required to develop salespeople.

UNDERSTANDING THE SALESPERSON

The preceding section pointed out certain motivational characteristics associated with the four sales types. Essentially, it was a discussion of what motivates the average or typical salesperson in each category. Unfortunately, there are few if any salespeople who conform precisely to the "average" norm. The motivational characteristics we reviewed are most prevalent in each category, but each individual has a unique need structure that is subject to change from time to time.

As this need structure shifts, so do the forces that motivate the individual salesperson. It is critical, therefore, that the manager continue to keep in close contact with all the sales force members so that he or she might have an appreciation and understanding of the salesperson's unique situation. Maintaining this contact is, unfortunately, not a simple thing to accomplish. Heavy administrative requirements often prevent sales managers from spending as much time with their salespeople as would be desirable. Most sales managers lament the fact that they are unable to spend the necessary 50 to 75 percent of their time in the field.[13] Even though other priorities emerge, however, any sales manager would be well advised to make scheduling arrangements so that adequate time always be spent with the sales force. Otherwise, there is no way in which the manager is able to gain firsthand awareness of the needs of individual sales-force members.

To truly understand the salesperson and his or her immediate and long-term needs, it is necessary to have an open and honest rapport, a condition that, because of divergent personalities, is not always possible. To achieve this rapport, it is essential that the manager maintain both trust and credibility with the sales force. This condition is achieved only after the manager has proved to the sales force that he or she is cognizant of their needs and will help them fulfill those needs. A sales manager for a large chemical firm made the following remarks to the author:

> Motivating a sales force is one of the most complex things a sales manager does. First of all, you have to spend at least two or three days a month with each salesman. Even if you're too busy, you just *have* to do it, otherwise you lose contact. Unless you are really close to them you don't know what they need or what makes them tick. I have one salesman, for instance, who needs to be built up all the time. If he thinks I'm paying attention to his efforts, he's a world beater. If he didn't get recognition, he wouldn't be able to sell anything. Everytime I see him I have to tell him how great he is. I have another salesman who wants to be left alone. I still go out with him but the only calls we go on are customer complaints or in some situation where he doesn't have to sell in front of me. He can't stand to be watched. Yet he's a top producer. I know I motivate him by being available to do whatever he wants me to do. It's like he has his own business and I'm an outside consultant. The manager here before me used to go on sales calls and critique his presentation. He [the salesman] told him flat out not to come with him anymore. Tom [the former sales manager] told me that if the salesman didn't have such a good record, he would have fired him on the spot. Instead, he respected the guy's wishes and after that, they got along fine. In another case, I have a girl who's been with us about eighteen months. I make calls with her once every two weeks because she needs the help. Yet, I don't give her any critique. I just ask her to analyze some of the calls and she always discovers her own mistakes. I just smile. A long time ago I made a rule never to directly confront a woman with criticism. Most females become resentful and defensive. Not that men don't, too. If there is any one rule in motivating salespeople, it is that no two are alike. If you don't get to know them really well, there is no way you can ever know their quirks and what it takes to make them produce.

Part of the key to understanding members of the sales force is in keeping lines of communication completely open. Accessibility to one's manager is vital to a salesperson's confidence in the organization. Because of the nature of the selling job, there are numerous unforeseen circumstances that arise and require the salesperson to be in contact with the manager. Many situations perceived by a salesperson as being of top priority are in reality not of the "crisis" proportions imagined. Nevertheless, the sales manager should always be available to communicate with salespeople who feel that it is important that he or she do so. It is also important for the sales manager to encourage an interchange of ideas with the sales force on an informal as well as on a formal level. One of the most widely used techniques to perform this function is through *coaching*.

Coaching

Coaching is a process of two-way communication that is typically carried out in the field. Sales managers should normally spend about 50 to 75 percent of their time working in the field with salespeople. Constructive feedback is given to the salesperson by the manager concerning several different aspects of the job, such as product knowledge, sales techniques, persuasive techniques, and customer relations. Like any other technique requiring person-to-person interface, many approaches can be taken by the sales manager in coaching salespeople. Since the process is intended to help the salesperson grow in the job, even "constructive" criticism often does more harm than it does good. Exposure of shortcomings or flaws in a salesperson's technique nearly always brings forth a defensive reaction, and often the "constructive" nature of the dialogue is either obscured or disappears entirely. People react differently to criticism, and it is important that a sales manager understand how each salesperson will react to coaching. Newer salespeople, for example, are more likely to accept a critique than are more experienced salespeople. Since the possibility exists that a breach of the rapport between the manager and salesperson can occur if coaching is not effectively undertaken, it is a good idea for organizations to provide formalized, in-depth training of this and other motivational opportunity and problem areas for their sales managers.

When conducted effectively, coaching is a powerful motivational tool. In many cases, simply the opportunity for two-way communication that is provided through a scheduled coaching session provides a strong basis for mutual understanding, a condition that tends to enhance motivation. Coaching is most effective when the manager and the salesperson are able to accomplish specific objectives, such as working on closing techniques, appointment setting, or some other area where the salesperson needs or requests guidance. The more coaching is viewed as a learning process rather than as a critique session, the more likely it is that the results will be beneficial.

Although coaching has been viewed by many managers as a training technique, its value as a motivational catalyst cannot be overestimated. The knowledge that one's manager is interested in the salesperson's success and is willing to help him or her achieve it ranks as an important motivating factor. The extent to which the manager communicates this interest through coaching has a strong impact upon the salesperson's motivation.[14] If the manager is highly critical and conveys an authoritarian attitude or lack of leadership skills, the salesperson normally perceives that the manager will be of little help and will respond to the manager's motivation efforts in only a superficial or even in a negative fashion. On the other hand, if the manager is able to gain the respect of the salesperson, his or her coaching efforts will normally be well received, primarily because the salesperson will perceive the manager's willingness to be of help.

In actual practice, very few sales managers spend sufficient time with their salespeople. The primary reason for this is that many organizations tend to almost literally bury their sales managers in an avalanche of reports and other paper work. In other cases, sales managers are under continual pressure to meet quotas, and they are compelled to participate in many sales calls directed at achieving sizable orders, rather than spend the time in developing the entire sales force. It is very apparent that the attitude of the top management of a sales organization determines whether or not the sales manager will spend the requisite time in the field. Unfortunately, an organization's current priorities do not always take motivation of sales people into consideration. There are very few definitive answers to such problems. Solutions such as appointing more sales managers or requiring managers to be in the field on certain days are often overly simplistic. It is a well-proved fact, however, that if sales managers cannot learn to know their salespeople, motivation is difficult to achieve.

Coaching Techniques

For a sales manager to effectively coach his or her salespeople, it is first necessary to attain credibility in the eyes of the salesperson. This credibility usually exists when the salesperson is convinced of the manager's ability and professionalism. Assuming this credibility does exist, certain coaching techniques have proved to be successful.

It is normally advisable for the manager to let the salesperson know that they will be spending a morning, afternoon, or day together. This allows the scheduling of calls in accordance with the salesperson's priorities, and the objective of the call can be communicated to the manager so that calls can be mutually planned.

In most cases, it is considered a good idea for the manager to begin by making "cold calls." This provides the salesperson with an opportunity to observe one or more approaches that have proved to be successful. After the manager has made a sufficient number of calls, the salesperson should be given an opportunity to makes sales presentations. During the course of these presentations, the salesperson's problem areas will normally be discerned by the sales manager.

It is in the comments following observations of sales calls that many managers lose their rapport with salespeople. In this type of situation, salespeople, for the most part, feel that they are left "naked" in front of the manager with respect to the latter's being able to observe their faults or errors. The feeling is one of high vulnerability. If the sales manager conveys a negative impression of the call, the salesperson will normally react defensively, and the original purpose of their going out together will become subverted. Nevertheless, the sales manager has an obligation to discuss points that he or she feels will affect the salesperson's performance.

There are several recognized methods of communication that are directed toward the original intent of the exercise—improvement of the salesperson's effectiveness. One method is to go over several positive aspects of the salesperson's performance before bringing out criticism. Unfortunately, this technique has been used so much that many salespeople ignore the positive comments and wait for the negative ones. A second technique is to ask the salesperson to evaluate the calls. In many cases, the salesperson will be able to identify areas for improvement. A third technique is in the use of the "we" approach. By using this term the manager attempts to shift the burden of the call solely from the salesperson. When suggestions are being made for improvement, the salesperson must recognize that it exists and must also be convinced that overcoming specific deficiencies will benefit him or her. Many sales managers use some form of checklist to note need for improvement in specific areas, such as preparation for call, control of sales presentation, handling objections, and benefit selling. Other managers take notes while observing. In giving any kind of feedback, specific points must be alluded to. This topic will be covered in greater detail in Chapter 13, but it is important to note here a few of the specific coaching techniques to show their impact upon the motivation of salespeople.

SUMMARY

This chapter has analyzed the basic concepts of leadership and motivation. Over several decades, studies have shown that no traits appear to be common to all successful leaders. The willingness of a person to follow and the person's perception of benefits that will accrue to him or her have a great influence on the leader's success. A further determinant of leadership is the situation or environmental factors that exist.

Motivational theories appear to have a place in explaining the sales manager's ability to motivate. The most applicable theories are the hierarchy of needs, the dual factor theory, and the theory of achievement motivation.

Although money has an important place in sales, it is not as strong a motivator as many people believe. Lack of it can cause a person to quit his or her job, but its use as a motivator is limited. Each salesperson responds to different motivational techniques, but there are a few classic approaches used generally in each sales sector. Before a manager is able to motivate a salesperson, an understanding of that individual is necessary. One of the most commonly used arenas for motivating salespeople is in the manager-salesperson relationship resulting from coaching. This process normally permits a better mutual understanding by both parties. The next chapter investigates the importance of sales training as a management function and as a performance tool.

Michelle Products

Joe Vigliano was promoted three months ago to branch manager of the Chicago office of Michelle Products. The company sells a variety of products, primarily to beauty shops, and the tempo of selling is very competitive. The manager before Joe had been fired for low production. Joe was convinced that the main problem was lack of motivation of the sales force. His predecessor was very close to the salespeople he managed and was sometimes accused of being too soft.

Joe's first actions were to raise all quotas by 10 percent and to require a minimum call rate of twelve per day. To show that his policies were not to be taken lightly, he fired the three lowest producers in the office during his first week as branch manager. Three weeks later, Marty Glickman, the highest producer in the office made some sarcastic remarks about the new call minimum. Joe took exception and in front of the entire office fired Marty on the spot. Although he knew he acted rather hastily, Joe felt he had to set an example and let the sales force know that he could not be intimidated.

After Marty's departure, most of the salespeople were very quiet, very seldom asking Joe for advice or help of any kind and speaking to him only when he addressed them first. Sales continued to drop.

In time, Joe's boss announced a six-week divisional sales contest that included Joe's office and four others. In a morning meeting the day the contest began, Joe announced that anyone not making his or her sales quota during the six-week contest period would be fired.

When the contest ended, Joe's office finished in last place. Joe received a call from the division manager's secretary that day telling him that the division manager would be visiting his office during the new few days.

1. If you were Joe, what would you do?
2. What problems in motivation exist in this case?

Apex Records Corporation

Jack Barrett is the Chicago branch manager for Apex Records Corporation. Apex manufactures and markets cabinets and other furniture used for storage of records and electronic data-processing output gear. During periods of high business activity, the salespeople in the Chicago office have high productivity. In periods of relative recession, however, business is very bad.

The salespeople receive high commissions and a good fringe-benefit program. During a good month, a salesperson can earn as much as $4000 to $5000. Of the eight salespeople who report to Jack Barrett, two have been with the firm for more than two years. Each of these persons worked for a competitor before joining Apex. The remaining six salespeople had selling experience in the following industries:

Wholesale food, 1
Ethical pharmaceuticals, 2
Textbooks, 1
Management consulting services, 1
Used automobiles, 1

By July, the top two salespeople were doing well, but the others were performing very marginally. Jack Barrett made the following comments regarding the Chicago Branch sales force:

> If it weren't for Lou and Eileen, I'd think there was something wrong with the way we're doing things around here. These other six people are like the rest—they

can't close a door! When you have a staff of weaklings like this, it's no wonder we're not doing well here. I can't go out with them much because I don't have the time. Lou and Eileen do a good job in this area anyway. Every time I tell them something, they forget it, particularly in closing the deal. They are all college graduates and all have experience, so they can't be *stupid*. I'm beinning to think college people just aren't hungry or else they can't follow directions.

1. Do you think there might be any motivation problems at Apex?
2. What would you suggest to Jack that might help improve sales?

DISCUSSION QUESTIONS

1. Discuss advantages and disadvantages of autocratic leadership. Describe specific situations that exemplify each.
2. Relate Maslow's hierarchy of needs to corresponding aspects of the sales manager's job.
3. Give examples of successful organizations in which each of the following leadership styles predominates: (a) authoritative; (b) planning; (c) individuality; (d) creativity; (e) teamwork.
4. What are some examples of the importance of the various styles of question 3 in the role of the sales manager?
5. How do salespeople obtain job satisfaction?
6. What are the special opportunities of training and motivation in the process of the sales manager making "cold" sales calls with a new salesperson?
7. When should a salesperson invite the sales manager to accompany him or her?
8. What are the needs and goals of effective sales communications? Give examples of achieving this in a constructive and positive manner.

NOTES

[1]Ralph M. Stogdill, *Handbook of Leadership* (New York: Free Press, 1974).

[2]Robert Tannenbaum and W. H. Schmidt, "How to Choose a Leadership Pattern," *Harvard Business Review*, vol. 36, no. 2 (March-April, 1958), pp. 95-101.

[3]Jerry Kramer, *Instant Replay*, (New York: Doubleday, 1972).

[4]Fred E. Fiedler, *A Theory of Leadership Effectiveness* (New York: McGraw-Hill, 1967), p. 151.

[5]Ralph M. Stogdill, "Personal Factors Associated with Leadership: A Survey of the Literature," *Journal of Psychology* 25 (1948), pp. 35-71.

[6]Ibid., p. 261.

[7]Abraham H. Maslow, "A Theory of Human Motivation," *Psychological Review*, July 1943, pp. 370-396.

[8]Victor H. Vroom, *Work and Motivation* (New York: Wiley, 1964), p. 9.

[9]Frederick Herzberg, B. Mausner, and B. Snyderman, *The Motivation to Work* (New York: Wiley, 1959).

[10]David C. McClelland, *The Achieving Society* (Princeton, N.J.: J. D. Van Most and Company, 1961).

[11]"Today," *The Philadelphia Inquirer*, November 11, 1979.

[12]David C. McClelland, "Money as a Motivator: Some Research Insights," *McKinsey Quarterly*, Fall 1967.

[13]Robert Whyte, "Sales Training and Motivation—A Special Report," *Sales and Marketing Management*, July 1977, p. 4.

[14]Orville C. Walker, Jr., Gilbert A. Churchill, Jr., and Neil M. Ford, "Selected Cultural and Empirical Issues Concerning the Motivation and Performance of the Industrial Salesforce," Proceedings of the Tenth Annual Meeting, American Institute of Decision Sciences, October 10, 1978.

CHAPTER 7

SALES TRAINING

OBJECTIVES

To provide the reader with an understanding of the basic functions of sales management.

To investigate the major areas of sales training:

* Sales skills
* Product knowledge
* Prospecting and lead generation
* Time and territory management
* Work habits
* Company policies and procedures
* Competitive products and services
* Administrative

To identify the major sources of sales training:

* Centralized sales training department
* Local or field sales training
* Outside firms and consultants

To analyze the major sales training techniques:

* Participative
* Nonparticipative

To examine some sales training performance criteria.

INTERVIEW WITH FRANK SMITH

Interviewer: One of the things you mentioned in the Introduction, Frank, was the need for sales training. Shall we pursue this subject in a little greater detail?

Frank Smith: Yes, this would be a good time to get into the area of sales training. As in other functional areas, a company can spend as much or as little as it wants to on sales training.

Interviewer: Do you think a company should make room for a large training budget?

Frank Smith: I don't think there is any question about it; if a firm skimps in its training budget, it will show up in the quality of its sales force. Actually, it's not so much the amount of money that is spent that's important; it's how *wisely* the money was spent.

Interviewer: Do you prefer any particular type of training Frank? By that I mean as far as home office, field training, in-house training, and other forms?

Frank Smith: No, it depends upon the kind of training that is involved and the stage of the salesperson's career. I do think that new salespeople should be exposed to a lot of training, and most of the time this is done at the home office. I don't want to get into this too deeply now though, because we'll get into it in detail in the chapter.

Interviewer: Right. Do you think the sales training people in an organization are usually aware of the firm's sales training needs, or do they live in an ivory tower like some college professors we know?

Frank Smith: Well, that could be a problem, I admit. Most companies, however, send their sales trainers out into the field on a regular basis. The reason is so that they will keep in touch with the sales force and will be able to tell firsthand what sales training needs exist.

Interviewer: I see. Before we get into the chapter, let me ask you one thing. Do you think that the average company does a good job in sales training?

Frank Smith: That really is not for me to say because I'm not what you would call an "expert witness." From what I've seen, though, I would make one or two generalizations. Large firms seem generally to do a good job in sales training because they have the bucks to do it. Even so, some companies could spend their budgets a little more wisely. As far as medium- and smaller-sized firms are concerned, I think the majority of companies still have a long way to go.

Interviewer: What can be done to alleviate this situation?

Frank Smith: I sincerely believe that sales managers have to be in communication with professionals in the field, and then *both* of them need to convince management that the investment in a substantial sales training budget will be justified. I hope a lot of future sales managers will read this chapter and remember what is said here when they get some responsibility in their companies.

Interviewer: Right on, man.

One of the most important and critical functions of sales management is training the sales force. Organizations spend a large portion of their sales budget in the implementation and administration of sales training programs.[1] Virtually every aspect of selling is included in the typical sales training format. Sales training is a continuous function, and the sales manager is responsible for training whether he or she performs the training or it is done by someone else. This chapter investigates the various aspects of this vital function.

MAJOR AREAS OF SALES TRAINING

There is an almost endless list of subjects taught in sales training courses, but the following eight major areas are usually included in most sales training programs:

1. Sales skills
2. Product knowledge
3. Prospecting and lead generation
4. Time and territory management
5. Work habits
6. Company policies and procedures
7. Competitive products and services
8. Administrative

These areas are outlined in Table 7-1 and discussed in the following paragraphs.

Sales Skills Training

Programs of this type normally address the technical aspects of the selling process. A good deal of time is spent practicing and reviewing the persuasive elements of the sales process. This training must be undertaken within the parameters of the individual salesperson's personality, a condition that requires a good deal of specialized training, often on a one-to-one basis. Some salespeople, for example, find it very easy to develop ready answers to the objections of prospects, whereas others require intensive instruction before becoming proficient at this skill. Because of the extensive amount of individualized attention required in this and other areas of persuasive ability, a combination of classroom and on-the-job training is often required. Some of the specific areas of sales skill training include getting attention, developing interest in the product or service, and closing the sale. Like handling objections, these steps in the sales process also require in-depth training before the salesperson attains proficiency. Closing skills, for example, normally require a great deal of training and practice under the supervision of a competent instructor. A variety of training situations are often utilized in sales skill training,

TABLE 7-1

Major Areas of Sales Training

Sales skill training	Teaches basic sales skills like handling objections and persuasive techniques.
Product knowledge training	Teaches features and benefits selling points of old and new products and services.
Prospecting and lead generation training	Teaches basic techniques of locating sales prospects and setting appointments.
Time and territory management training	Teaches the basic concepts of setting time priorities and optimum time utilization.
Work habits training	Teaches proper approach to development of effective work habits.
Company policy training	Teaches need for company policies and specific procedures necessary to running an orderly sales organization.
Competitive product training	Teaches features and benefits of competitive products and services necessary to develop effective professional skills.
Administrative training	Teaches the proper methods of completing basic documents and office procedures necessary to efficient operation of sales apparatus.

and it is not unusual for organizations to conduct both formal and informal training in this area on a continuing basis.

Product Knowledge Training

To be successful, it is virtually mandatory that the salesperson possess an expert knowledge of the goods and services that he or she sells. Not only is this knowledge required to answer questions raised by customers and prospects, but it has long been an accepted principle in sales management that complete product knowledge increases and reinforces a salesperson's self-confidence. Depending upon the relative degree of sophistication of the products or services being sold, the amount of training that must be provided can range from reasonably short training sessions to very lengthy and highly complex educational programs (see Table 7-2). Clearly, the more technically oriented the product or service, the more elaborate will be the product training program. Some organizations require their salespeople to attend full-time classroom training programs for several months; other organizations limit their product training to short sessions lasting no more

TABLE 7-2

Product Knowledge Requirements of each Sales Type

	Consultative	Technical	Commercial	Direct
Degree of Product knowledge	Too vast for any one individual	Extensive	Considerable	Moderate
Complexity of the purchase decision	Very complex	— — — — —	— — — — —	Least complex

than a few hours at a time. An example of the former type of training can be found in most large data-processing manufacturers. NCR Corporation, for example, has a product training school for salespeople that lasts six months. Limited product training can be found in many if not most direct-sales organizations. As a general rule, most consultative, technical, and commercial sales organizations attempt to provide ongoing product training. The training location often varies according to the nature of the products and the learning process required for the salesperson to assimilate the knowledge.

Training in Prospecting and Lead Generation

Because of the importance of maintaining a large quantity of prospects at all times, training in prospecting and lead generation is considered extremely important by sales organizations. Most firms, in fact, assign a very high priority to this function. Training salespeople to locate prospective customers often requires rigorous training methods in creative thinking ability, since trainees must be taught to expand their mental processes in developing new areas in which to seek customers. It is not unusual for organizations to conduct training in approaches to developing prospects and in the location of specific information through the use of directories, registers, lists, or other appropriate documents. In prospecting training, use of the telephone to set up appointments is typically on the agenda. Role playing and other techniques are used in this type of training, which often requires specific facilities. There are also certain telephone appointment-setting approaches that have proved successful for many firms. These techniques often require the salesperson to memorize a complete format designed to evoke a favorable response.

Training in Time and Territory Management

One of the most valuable assets to a salesperson is his or her time. During any given day, only a small portion of that day is actually spent in front of prospects or customers, and only part of this time is actually spent selling. One of the biggest problems perceived by sales executives is the inefficient use of time by salespeople.[2] (Chapter 14 will deal with this subject in greater depth.)

Many if not most sales organizations attempt to deal with time and territory management problems through formalized sales training sessions for salespeople. These sessions are usually designed to increase the student's awareness of the types of time-management problems and opportunities that arise, since most sales trainers take the approach that salespeople either take for granted or are oblivious to the time discipline required in sales. After the students have been made aware of its critical nature, specific time and territory management programs are taught. Programs of this type often follow a case-study format and generate a great deal of interaction among instructors and students. This interaction will hopefully lead to alternative approaches to time and territory management that can be taken by salespeople when they are in the field. Training programs in this subject area often increase dramatically the number of sales calls made as well as productivity in other face-to-face customer contact areas.

Work Habits Training

Because most salespeople receive relatively little supervision and are seldom observed, they tend to develop work habits and patterns that are monitored only by themselves. In circumstances of this kind, salespeople often fail to develop the most effective approach to their job or in some cases fall into a "rut" where it becomes difficult to overcome the inertia to perform at more productive levels. Work habits lend themselves to some habit-forming pattern. Training sessions in the improvement of work habits usually address such activities as prospecting, sales call planning, proposal writing, and sales follow-up. These and other performance areas normally involve a certain degree of discipline and should receive a relatively high priority in the salesperson's work scheme. Sloppy work habits in the aforementioned areas can easily develop if salespeople do not consciously monitor their own performance. Training programs specifically aimed at increasing effective work habits are normally quite successful provided they are periodically reinforced. If these programs are not continually updated, many salespeople have a tendency to allow their effective work habits to slide.

Training in Company Policy and Procedures

In recent years a great deal of attention has been given to formalized training for salespeople in company policies and procedures. Firms have traditionally outlined a plethora of rules, regulations, and edicts for their salespeople to follow when conducting company business, a practice not always consistent with effective selling. In large companies, cumbersome restrictions often have the effect of literally stifling creativity and inhibiting the sales process. While a certain amount of company policy is necessary and desirable, an excessive amount is likely to have a debilitating effect upon many effective salespeople. The nature of the sales job itself tends to attract a certain type of person. The typical salesperson requires a certain freedom from restriction in order to perform his or her functions, and company implemented policies and procedures are, for the most part, viewed as a restriction of that freedom. Salespeople are more readily willing to accept organizational policies and procedures when they understand the reasons for their existence and why they are necessary. As a result, many firms have recently made serious attempts to rationalize company rules and regulations to salespeople in a formal classroom environment. The purpose of these sessions is to reduce frustration and negativism in the sales force caused by implementation of company rules and regulations. This type of training also provides the sales force with the opportunity to provide input regarding its perceptions of company-instituted policies and procedures. Most firms that provide this type of training use the seminar method, often utilizing the presence of policy-making executives as well as sales trainers to communicate the firm's position.

Competitive Product Training

Effective salespeople, in most cases, are as knowledgeable about their competitors' products and services as they are about their own. Without a thorough knowledge of the competition, an enormous gap exists in the effectiveness of the salesperson. It would be difficult to sell, for example, an automobile or a copy machine unless the salesperson could compare the features and benefits of his or her product to those of competitive products. Knowledge of a competitor's products or services alone is not sufficient to effectively sell. The salesperson must also know how to sell against the competition without engaging in unethical or unprofessional practices. It is an accepted rule in nearly every industry that salespeople have every right to point out advantages over competitors' products but not in such a way as to denigrate or downgrade the competition. Stretching the truth, making unfair comparisons, and exaggerating claims about one's own product or a competitor's are a few of the ways in which salespeople engage in unethical and technically illegal business conduct. An outside observer might suspect that sales organizations either ignore or pay lip service to their salespeople's "knocking" competition. Such is not the case. Most sales managers are well acquainted with their competitors and nearly every industry is characterized by a written or, more frequently, verbal understanding among sales managers to refrain from unethical sales tactics. Violations often typically result in a phone call that is embarrassing to both sales managers. A further deterrent to unethical competitive selling is the obvious loss of credibility with most customers that results from making exaggerated or untruthful claims. In view of these requirements, sales training departments face an enormous challenge in training salespeople to be knowledgeable about competition and to be able to sell against competition without overstepping ethical bounds. Competitive sales training is normally an ongoing function, taking place whenever new developments in the competitive product marketplace occur.

One of the less popular functions of the salesperson is complying with administrative requirements. Most salespeople refer to this function simply as "paper work." Nearly every commercial, technical, and consultative selling organization has a core group of administrative forms to be filled out at periodic intervals, primarily on a weekly basis. The documents that are most commonly required are the following:

Call reports: *a weekly summary of all sales calls made. Information required typically includes which products were discussed, name of company called on, name of person spoken to, and other specific data. (See Figure 7-1.)*

Weekly sales plan: *a weekly report indicating who will be called on during the next week. Additional information might include products to be discussed and other specific data. (See Figure 7-2.)*

Monthly forecast: *a monthly report indicating the salesperson's forecast of who will buy during the coming month. This report normally includes sales volume expected and some indication of the probability that the customer will buy.*

Order form: *this document normally includes shipping information, terms of sale, and other data pertaining to the customer's order.*

Figure 7-1

Salesperson's Call Report Form

INPUT

SALESMAN'S CALL DATA

A LOT TO SAY . . . OR A LITTLE
If the salesman can make a full report in a few choice words, or crisp coded notations, why burden him with large, time-consuming forms? On the other hand, if his report must of necessity be detailed and comprehensive, he should have ample room to put it down.

A pocket-size folder provides a complete, detailed record of the daily activity and performance of American Photocopy Equipment Co. salesmen. A quick check of a neatly organized front page gives the sales manager all the data he needs to evaluate a man's progress in equipment and supply sales and in prospecting. Inside pages offer plenty of space for listing names and addresses of companies called on, business classification, persons contacted.

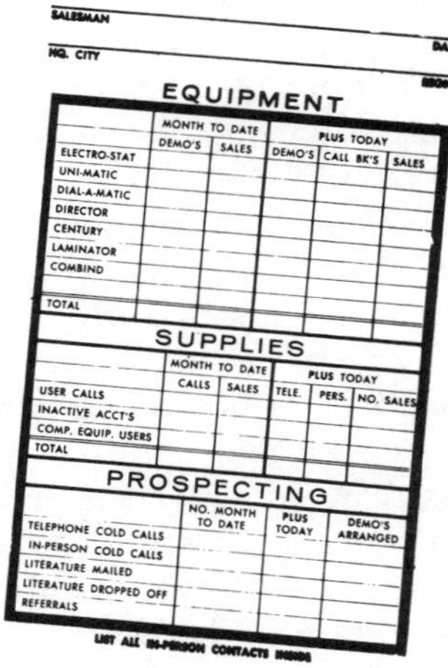

Expense form: *these are written accounts of all expenses incurred by salespeople. Account codes and other highly detailed information must be adhered to in order to comply with extensive Internal Revenue regulations. Mistakes on these forms normally result in the form's being returned to the salesperson.*

These subject areas account for the bulk of sales training. Training needs are normally determined by a consensus among sales managers at all levels. Some programs, such as analysis of competitive products or new product training, are clearly required, and the need for training in these areas is normally fairly obvious. Other areas, such as remedial training in closing a sale or in handling objections, are not as readily discernible. In some cases, coaching and practice are needed more than additional training. Most experienced sales trainers and sales managers define a training problem as one where a real deficiency of knowledge or lack of skill exists. An effort is normally made to determine how widespread a training problem is, and then programs are implemented to correct the problem.

Training programs are normally conducted at a central company-wide site by professional trainers, in the field by branch managers and sales personnel, and at outside locations such as motels or other rented facilities. In addition to company personnel, private consulting organizations or professional trainers also perform

Figure 7-2

Salesperson's Call Planning Form

FIELD REPRESENTATIVE WEEKLY ACTIVITY REPORT

DATE	TIME	APPOINTMENTS	CITY	Area Code	PHONE	H.O. Interviews	P.D.	NO SHOW	RESET	ABORTED	FULL	PART	P.D.	PROGRAM	TUITION	Reservation Fee	REMARKS
1.					-												
					-												
					-												
					-												
5.					-												
					-												
					-												
					-												
					-												
10.					-												
					-												
					-												
					-												
					-												
15.					-												
					-												
					-												
					-												
					-												
20.					-												
															$	$	

TOTAL ENR. ☐

INQUIRY INVENTORY CONTROL

B.O.H. (Last Week) .... ____
RECV'D (Home Office) .. ____
P.D. (Home Office)........ ____
RECV'D (Mgr.)............ ____
Total A ____
ENROLLED .... ____
WORKED .... ____
Total B ☐
Total A – Total B = B.O.H ☐

P.D. ACTIVITY SOURCES

STUDENT REFERRAL ..... ☐
REPLY CARD (D.M.)...... ☐
REPLY CARD (Dispenser). ☐
TELEPHONE .... ☐
DIRECT APPROACH ..... ☐

(Report amounts in SHADED AREAS to Div. Manager by PHONE)

NAME	REP. #	REG.	DIV.	WEEK ENDING

M174-510

sales training. These trainers are most often retained by medium-sized and smaller firms, although large companies have been using their specialized programs on a more frequent basis over the past few years. In general, the training site, the relative elaborateness of facilities, and the professionalism of the trainer are determined by the particular training need involved and the size of the firm's sales training budget. The following sections will cover the three most widely used modes of sales training: home office sales training, local or field sales training, and use of outside sales training firms.

HOME OFFICE SALES TRAINING

Most large firms have a centralized sales training department that acts as the nerve center for all sales training activities undertaken by the company. Training policies and procedures for the entire sales organization emanate from this department. Among its many functions, the central sales training department coordinates field programs and acts as a liaison between home office and field. The sales training department reports to either the national sales manager or the vice-president of sales (see Figure 7-3).[3]

In some very large organizations, individual divisions have their own sales training departments. IBM, for example, has separate sales training functions for separate product divisions. These divisions, however, are as large as most individual corporations. This analysis is, therefore, essentially the same whether the sales training function is a corporate or a divisional facility.

The central sales training department is normally organized as a staff, and its budget is determined to a large extent by the top sales executives. In most firms, the personnel consist of a manager and several sales trainers. Figure 7-4 is a job description of the duties and responsibilities of a typical manager of sales training.[4]

Figure 7-3

Organizational Relationship of Sales Training Department (Corporate)

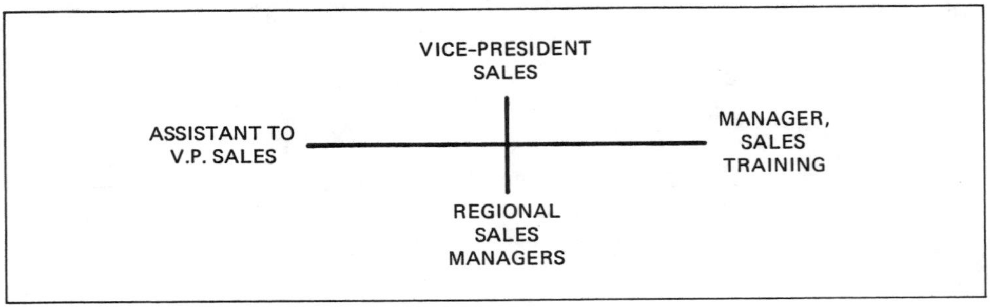

Figure 7-4

Job Description, Sales Training Manager

Date ____________________

Position Description
Manager, Training

I. *Broad Function:*

Responsible for the development, administration, and coordination of the company's sales and sales-management training and development programs.

II. *Reporting Relationship:*

Reports to Vice President of Sales. Responsible for communicating corporate sales and sales-management activities and results accomplished.

III. *Duties and Responsibilities:*

- To assist sales management in identifying training needs.
- To identify management problems to determine which are created in whole or in part in the sales sector and which of these can be remedied by sales-training efforts.
- To develop (or obtain) programs to meet the needs above.
- To organize, coordinate, and schedule the training.
- To determine who shall conduct the training, and to provide such personnel with what guidance is necessary.
- To evaluate the training and report results to operating management.
- To determine need for follow-up to insure continuing results; and to plan, organize, conduct, and administer such training.
- To coordinate with other personnel-development activities.
- To develop such long-range sales-management training programs as may be necessary to aid operating managers in developing and maintaining an effective work force.
- To coordinate and utilize the training facilities within the organization and to procure services of outside consulting services where available, necessary, and appropriate.
- To maintain an adequate system of records and progress reports.
- To submit an annual budget for approval. The budget is to contain an explanation of the need for each training program and the operating problem(s) it seeks to avoid or eliminate.

IV. *Relationships:*

Because of the staff functions of this position, there are ongoing relationships with all staff departments and the field organization.

V. *Education, Experience, and Knowledge Required:*

(Fill this section in to meet your requirements and protect your job.)

Figure 7-4 *(continued)*

VI. *Acceptabilities:*

The primary measures of the Manager, Sales Trainee are:

1. The adequacy with which the total sales and sales-management training development is administered.
2. The degree to which the sales and sales-management expenses are controlled, kept under budget, and utilized.
3. The quality and timeliness of decisions and actions regarding all responsibilities of the position, including the quality and timeliness of his or her recommendations.
4. The quality of his or her leadership in developing and executing sales-training and sales-management programs.
5. The extent to which he or she achieves and exceeds results are measured against objectives.

As indicated by the job description, close follow-up with field sales management is required. In actual practice, most sales training managers are on very close and friendly terms with the majority of field sales managers. The nature of both jobs requires a strong informal relationship, as well as a formal one. In nearly every form, sales trainers have a strong commitment to providing needed help to the sales force, and mutual respect exists between sales managers and sales trainers.

Most sales training department managers are career training professionals who have had a strong background in sales and sales management.[5] The manager is responsible for interface between the department and the key sales executive and is the one who must justify specific budgets and training programs. The other members of the department are, in most cases, former salespeople or sales managers who will perform sales training functions for a few years before returning to the field in some managerial capacity. It is not unusual for one or more of the sales trainers to spend most of his or her time traveling to field locations, either conducting training or gathering information that will help shape future sales training programs.

The home office sales training department usually has its own facilities and equipment used in training programs. Most firms have a policy of training new salespeople at these facilities using home office training personnel.[6] In some cases, these sessions are held in regional locations to reduce the expense of transporting salespeople from all over the country to one location. In either case, nearly every type of sales organization follows this approach, with the exception of most direct-sales firms. Figures 7-5 and 7-6 outline two typical home office training programs for new salespeople.

Training programs for new salespeople are extremely critical in that one of the trainees' first impressions of the firm is formed in the initial home office training. Prior to attending this session, many trainees are given a home study course.

Figure 7-5

Basic Sales Training Program for Commercial Salesperson

First day:	8:30	A.M.	Introduction
	9:30		Introduction to the company
	10:30		Buyer behavior
	12:00	noon	Lunch
	1:00	P.M.	The sales process (a comparison of three types of sales processes, i.e., stimulus-response, formula selling, and need satisfaction)
	1:45		Asking questions
	4:00		Features, advantages, benefits (lecture, exercises)
	5:30		Close
			Evening assignment: Preparation for sales call-handling objections
Second day:	8:30	A.M.	Handling objections (use of videotape feedback role play situations)
	10:30		Sales planning (movie, exercises)
	12:00	noon	Lunch
	1:00	P.M.	Psychology of selling (buyer motivation and psychology of the sale)
	3:15		The close: introduction
	5:00		Close
Third day:	8:30	A.M.	Closing (role play with customer objections)
	11:00		Selling skills practice (videotape feedback on one-to-one sales situations)
	5:00	P.M.	Adjourn
	6:30		Banquet
Fourth day:	8:30	A.M.	Selling skills practice
	10:30		Interpersonal relationships
	12:00	noon	Lunch
	1:00	P.M.	Interpersonal relationships
	3:00		Inspirational film
	3:30		Role play
	4:00		Critique
	4:30		Close
Fifth day:	8:30	A.M.	Prospecting
	10:00		Videotape replay
	12:00	noon	Lunch
	1:00	P.M.	Inspirational lecture by top executive
	2:30		Close

This course normally covers the history of the firm, its products or services, their applications, and other appropriate information. In addition to providing obviously important information, it allows the trainee to develop a list of questions in areas that are unclear or need further elaboration.[7]

It is important that the firm go all out in this first training session. Living accommodations, meals, transportation, and all facilities should be top caliber. Cutting corners to reduce expenses often conveys an impression of excessive frugality to the trainees, a condition that can negatively affect their attitude. Most organi-

Figure 7-6

Basic Sales Training Program for Technical Salesperson

First day:	8:30	A.M.	Introduction
	9:00		Introduction to the company
	9:30		Review of responsibilities and accountabilities of the Salesperson (position description)
	10:00		Discussion of the sales process
	11:00		Videotape presentations
	12:00	noon	Lunch
	1:00	P.M.	Effective listening
	2:00		Features, advantages, benefits of products
	3:00		Role-play sales situations
	5:00		Close
Second day:	8:30	A.M.	Psychology of selling
	10:00		Asking questions
	12:00	noon	Lunch
	1:00	P.M.	Handling objections
	2:00		Closing the sale
	3:00		Selling skills practice (videotape feedback)
	6:00		Close
Third day:	8:30	A.M.	Product discussion: Market segmentation
	12:00	noon	Lunch
	1:00	P.M.	Product application techniques
	6:00		Close
Fourth day:	8:30	A.M.	Territorial planning
	10:00		Product discussion: Market segmentation
	12:00	noon	Lunch
	1:00	P.M.	Product programs and how to sell programs
	4:00		Open discussion
	5:30		Close
	6:30		Banquet
Fifth day:	8:30	A.M.	Prospecting
	10:00		Product information presentation
	12:00	noon	Lunch
	1:00	P.M.	Selling skills, videotape
	3:00		Seminar evaluation, close

zations recognize this factor and attempt to provide their trainees with the best possible training and facilities.

Training programs at the home office department level are normally restricted to new salespersons and to special-purpose sessions, but the members of the department are normally quite busy throughout the year. The preparation for both home office and field training programs is an enormous task and in itself can occupy the time of one or more full-time department members. Most firms maintain a sales training Manual that includes new developments in sales techniques, product development, competition, and other areas that lend themselves to training. Continual updating of these manuals and communication with field sales personnel can also occupy the time of a full-time staff person. A multitude of other administrative functions are continually performed in the areas of planning, staffing, and directing within the department itself, which justifies the budgets of central sales training departments.

FIELD OR LOCAL SALES TRAINING

The second level of sales training is at the field or local office level. Training at this level supplements home office training and probably constitutes about 75 percent of all sales training.[8] The topics covered at local sales training sessions are the same as those that were discussed at the beginning of the chapter.

Most training at this level is conducted to upgrade sales skills and product knowledge. Much of the material covered at formal sessions is developed by the home office training staff, and the format is sent to branch locations. Training in the field tends to become less formalized as it moves from the regional level to the branch level. A typical regional training meeting includes rented facilities and training personnel from the home office, in short, a fairly big production, whereas branch training is normally conducted at regular sales meetings or on a one-to-one basis.

The typical branch sales training meeting is normally conducted by the sales manager and, in many cases, by senior salespeople. Meetings of this type are designed, for the most part, to share techniques and information through interactions of the sales force. Even more beneficial is the individual sales training that is conducted on a one-to-one basis. Most local training is *participative* in nature and requires salespeople to take part in the process. Field sales training has come a long way over the past few decades. An example of a typical field sales training program that existed in the direct-sales field during the 1930s is described in the following anecdote related by Maynard Stoddard about his first sales job.

> I won't deny that being a college freshman right off the farm, one whose knowledge of lingerie came out of a Sears catalogue, might have been a contributing factor. Certainly the "training" I received didn't add a whole lot to my one forte—the ability to distinguish between a girdle and a horse harness.
>
> The fellow in charge of this crucial phase of my indoctrination as a salesman spent the entire 10 minutes showing me how to measure a woman for "personal fit" hosiery by wrapping a tape measure about his secretary's ankle, calf, and so help me, thigh. For the correct length, he had her stick her foot through a loop fashioned at one end of the tape and, so help me again, ran the other end up her leg.
>
> "We go from 26 to 37 inches—or until she hollers 'Whoops!' " he said with an insinuating chuckle. It was pretty obvious that his secretary had never hollered "Whoops!" in her life. His implication that measuring would be one big satyrical ball did little to relieve my apprehension. . . .[9]

Budgets for sales training are normally part of the branch administrative budget. Facilities are rented sparingly, and most sessions are held at the branch office. Equipment such as videotape machines and screens is normally rented as needed. Although most branch sales training budgets are modest, programs can be highly effective if the sales manager expresses a strong commitment to training. Most home office training departments enthusiastically support traditional and innovative local sales training programs and are usually more than willing to provide whatever help is required to make the local program a success. On the other hand, if local sales management expresses a perfunctory or indifferent approach, the benefits of sales training at the local level will probably be minimal.

SALES TRAINING BY OUTSIDE ORGANIZATIONS

Many sales organizations use outside firms to help provide sales training, but it should be emphasized here that, no matter how extensively these resources are used, ultimate responsibility for sales training always rests with the first-line sales supervisor. There are several reasons why outside help is used, the most common being the limited resources of the firm. These resources normally take the form of limited training personnel or limited funds. Small companies, for example, often find it difficult to justify the use of a full-time sales trainer.

Because of the few formalized sales training programs scheduled and because of the relatively few new salespeople who are hired, most small firms find it financially unrealistic to organize and staff a training facility. Some larger firms find that certain consultants provide expertise in narrow subject areas. In other cases, urgent training needs might not be able to be met because of time demands on the firm's sales training department. Situations such as these dictate the use of outside sales training organizations as a viable alternative.

Private Consulting Firms

Many private consulting firms provide sales training seminars, which are aggressively sold to business and industry. These seminars are conducted by professional trainers who have, in most cases, extensive experience in the course subject areas they teach. These firms obtain their clients in the classic consultative-sales tradition. Original contacts are often made through direct mail, but the bulk of their business is obtained through word-of-mouth from satisfied clients; hence it is very important that the seminars fulfill their stated objectives.[10] Most private consultants who provide sales training services develop custom-made programs tailored to the client's products, personnel, and sales policies. These programs are given periodically, and the charge to the firm is normally negotiated on a per student basis. Some firms in this field who are recognized for expertise in sales training are Xerox Learning Systems, Inc., Greenwich, Connecticut, University Programs, Cherry Hill, New Jersey, and Bill Publications' Sales Builders Division, New York, New York.

Colleges and Universities

Many schools of business at institutions of higher learning provide sales training programs for businesses on both a customized and an "off-the-shelf" basis. The latter type of program is designed primarily to emphasize fundamentals that can apply to nearly any salesperson. The sales seminars are attended by one or more representatives from several firms. The teachers at college- and university-sponsored training programs are typically selected from business school faculty. In fact, there is a strong probability that the instructor of your course in sales management has participated in programs of this type. In recent years, many colleges and universities have been motivated to provide training of this kind not only as a service to the business community, but as a partial answer to financial exigency. Of the programs provided by this source, the overwhelming majority are of the off-the-shelf type, and the price of most programs is similar to that charged by private firms.

Nonprofit Organizations

In addition to private consulting firms and higher learning institutions, nonprofit organizations provide many sales training programs. These programs are primarily of the off-the-shelf type and are provided by business organizations as a service to their members. Although the sponsoring organizations are nonprofit, the tuition costs for these programs are similar to those of the other two groups. Some of the more widely recognized sales training programs are provided by Sales and Marketing Executives International (SMEI), an association of sales and marketing executives, the American Management Association, and The Conference Board. The latter two groups are associations for business executives and provide similar programs in other management areas. Figure 7-7 is an outline of a format for basic sales training.

SALES TRAINING TECHNIQUES

Sales training techniques are the means used to teach trainees. Most sales trainers are familiar with a large variety of sales techniques. The appropriate techniques to be used depend upon the purpose of the training, the number of salespeople to be trained, and the relative amount of experience of the salespeople in the subject area. Training techniques are divided into two general types, participative and nonparticipative.

Nonparticipative techniques are normally used to teach theory, very much like college classroom situations. Participative techniques are utilized for the appli-

FACULTY

John E. Flaherty, professor, Graduate School of Business Administration, Pace University, has served as a consultant for such firms as General Foods, Hunt Food and Nabisco. Author of many articles on corporate environment, Mr. Flaherty received his B.A. from Union College and his M.A. and Ph.D. from New York University.

Gil D. Harrell, professor of business administration, Michigan State University, co-authored a text on applications of behavioral principles to marketing. His articles have appeared in several business journals including, *The Journal of Marketing and The Journal of Marketing Research*. He received his B.B.A. and M.B.A. from Michigan State University and his Ph.D. from Pennsylvania State University.

James F. Robeson, associate dean of the College of Administrative Science, Ohio State University, has consulted many firms including Celanese Plastics, Frigidaire, Mead Paper and National Steel. Co-author of two books and author of several articles for professional and trade journals. Mr. Robeson received his B.B.A. and M.B.A. from the University of Cincinnati, and his Ph.D. from Pennsylvania State University.

John L. Schlacter, associate professor of marketing, Arizona State University, management consultant for industrial and commercial firms, has published many articles in publications such as *Academy of Management Journal* and *Public Relations Quarterly*. He received his B.B.A. from Western Reserve University and his M.B.A. and Ph.D. from Ohio State University.

William Wachs, consultant in sales, marketing and management and author of four books on sales and marketing published by Prentice Hall, received his B.S. and M.S. degrees from the City University of New York, his L.L.B. from New York Law School and his Ph.D. from New York University. He is a member of the New York State Bar.

Robert M. Fulmer, professor of management and director of executive education, School of Business Administration, Emory University. His current responsibilities include the Executive M.B.A. Program as well as all other executive education activities at Emory. He holds an M.B.A. from the University of Florida and a Ph.D. from the University of California, Los Angeles.

Stephen G. Franklin, is assistant professor of business administration at Emory University in Atlanta, Georgia. He attended the University of Florida, received his B.S. degree from Abilene Christian University (Texas), M.B.A. from Georgia State University, his M.A. and Ph.D.degrees in Management from the University of Oklahoma with minor areas in marketing and public administration.

Jack Schiff, executive vice president and professor of marketing at Pace University. Author of *Salesmanship Fundamentals* and co-author of *Strategic Management of the Sales Territory*. Also teaches at SMEI Graduate School of Sales Management and Marketing.

HOW TO ENROLL

REGISTRATION: Complete the registration from on the reverse side, and mail it today to: *Sales & Marketing Executives International, 380 Lexington Avenue, New York, NY 10017:* or call toll free (800) 223-7752 (Continental U.S.A. and Puerto Rico); New York State residents and all others call (212) 986-9300.

FEES: Complete fee of $450 for SME members, $495 for non-members, includes tuition, the course workbook and other instructional materials, lunches, refreshments and a Certificate of Completion. Make checks payable to *Sales & Marketing Executives International.*

TEAM DISCOUNT: If three of more register from the same company ***at the same time:*** member rate is $400; non-member rate is $450.

HOTEL RESERVATIONS: SMEI will arrange for accomodations at the minimum rate available at the time your reservation is made. Check whether you want a single or double room; a single will be reserved unless otherwise requested.

CANCELLATIONS: Full refund will be made if cancellation is received at least one week prior to the start of the program.

TRANSFERS AND SUBSTITUTIONS: Transfers and substitutions may be made at any time. If for any reason you cannot attend, the entire tuition fee will be credited to any other program over the following twelve-month period.

TAX DEDUCTION: Because the Sales Management Institute is an educational expense, registration fees, cost of travel, meals and lodging are tax dedictible under Treasury Regulation 1.162-5.

CONTINUING EDUCATION UNITS: All participants who complete the Sales Management Institute program will receive three CEUs and a Certificate of Completion.

SMEI is a not-for-profit organization since 1936

SALES MANAGEMENT INSTITUTE SCHEDULE

Each Year SMEI conducts programs in major cities from coast to coast, making it economical for executives to attend the program closest to their respective areas:

SMEI . . . in cooperation with

PACE UNIVERSITY
New York City, N.Y.
November 10-12, 1980

EMORY UNIVERSITY
Atlanta, Georgia
November 17-19, 1980

MICHIGAN STATE UNIVERSITY
Lansing, Michigan
December 1-3, 1980

cation of training theory and can be thought of as simulating a college chemistry or biology laboratory session. No matter how effective the nonparticipative techniques a trainer uses, learning the sales process can only take place through direct experience. In sales training, therefore, nonparticipative techniques are used to supplement participative ones. The most commonly used participative techniques are role playing, programmed learning, coaching and counseling, and various team or group activities. The most widely utilized nonparticipative training techniques are the lecture, the audiovisual presentation, and reading or study assignments.

Participative Techniques

Role Playing This technique is frequently used by sales trainers to help trainees simulate various sales situations. Characters are usually cast to represent the prospect or customer and the salesperson. By acting out scenarios, the salesperson will become more aware of his or her skill level, product knowledge, strong points, and weak points. A criticism of role playing is that the participants are put into an unreal or "phony" setting. Sales trainers attempt to dampen this effect by grading the participants or in some other subtle or overt way letting the participants know that the role-playing situation is to be taken seriously. Good trainers can instill an exceptional amount of enthusiasm for role-playing situations in nearly any salesperson under the right circumstances. There are several variations of role playing. In recent years, many firms have made extensive use of the videotape machine in role-playing situations. Analysis of videotape replays allows salespeople to study and evaluate their calls on simulated prospects and customers. In most cases, provided, of course, that the participants take the role-playing seriously, the analysis, discussion, and critique of the videotaped situations provide valuable insight to the sales force.

Coaching and Counseling This technique is the most widely used participative technique. It is also the most important because it consists of interaction between the sales manager and the salesperson before and after actual sales situations. The basic concepts involved in this process revolve around the discussion that takes place between the manager and trainee regarding how the sales call will be approached, the sales call, and the post-call analysis and discussion. It is critical that sales managers have a strong expertise in coaching and counseling salespeople, since these discussions have an enormous impact upon both morale and motivation. Many sales organizations spend a great deal of time in training their managers in the counseling process, often on a periodic basis so that these skills do not get stale. Coaching is an area of sales training that sales managers cannot delegate, and their effectiveness in performing this function can greatly influence the future performance of trainees.

Programmed Learning Techniques The primary purpose of programmed learning is to provide the trainee with information in printed form (see Figure 7-8). The main difference between this method of instruction and normal reading material is that in the programmed mode the reader controls the amount of material that is covered. Most programmed learning texts consist of a short amount of material, for example, the equivalent of three or four written pages known as a "frame" with a series of questions to be answered at the end of each frame. If errors are made, the student goes back to the beginning of the frame. One advantage of this type of learning is that the reader is not forced to read material he or she already knows. This type of learning technique is particularly effective for salespeople. As a group, they are relatively impatient, and an instructional mode

Figure 7-8

Sales Training Evaluation Form

APPRAISAL
(We welcome your constructive comments)

Name of course ______________________ Location ______________

Length of course (Circle one) *Too Long* *Too Short* *Satisfactory*

Comments: ____

____

Subjects that should be deleted and why: ______________________

____

Subjects that should be added and why: ______________________

____

Present subjects that should be expanded or shortened and why: ______________

____

Quality of instruction (Circle one) *Poor* *Fair* *Good* *Excellent*

Comments: ____

Motel accommodations (Circle one) *Poor* *Fair* *Good* *Excellent*

If Fair or Poor—Why? ______________________________________

____

Additional overall comments: ______________________________

____

____

____

____

—DO NOT SIGN—

of this type allows them to speed up the learning process, thus assimilating a greater amount of information than would normally be the case.

Group Techniques The essence of group training is that small groups of approximately seven people or less work together on certain problems and develop high-quality solutions. The advantages of these techniques are that (1) exchange among fellow trainees provides each individual with a valuable learning experience and (2) when each individual is required to participate, the results are normally well thought out. The most common group technique is *brainstorming*. In this technique, members of the group are encouraged to volunteer information on a random basis with a group leader documenting all contributions. When a time limit has been reached, the group analyzes each contribution until a consensus has been reached. As a rule, the longer a group practices this technique, the higher becomes the quality of emergent solutions, thus reinforcing in the participants' minds the value of peer learning experiences.

Nonparticipative Techniques

Lecture Method This sales training technique is used to provide trainees with information. Most theory is taught via this method. As in the college classroom situation, its effectiveness is limited by the attention span of the trainee. Even the most stimulating sales trainers find that the amount of learning that the trainee can absorb is often a function of conditions beyond the control of the lecturer. Any college student will readily attest to the fact that outside factors like personal problems, lack of money, hunger or daydreams including members of the opposite sex tend to cause one's attention to drift. The same phenomena hold true in sales lecture training, and for this reason participative techniques are typically used in conjunction with the lecture to maintain attention.

Audiovisuals No sales training session is complete without one or more inspirational films featuring some sports celebrity, usually drawing an analogy between sales and football, exhorting the audience to "fight for that last yard." Surprisingly, films of this type are still popular and still draw favorable comments from viewers. Salespeople as a group, although having higher intelligence than most occupational groups,[11] also tend toward a less sophisticated approach to professional success. The salesperson tends to view the extent of his or her professional attainment by sales volume achieved rather than by more abstract yardsticks. In such a black-or-white milieu, it is not surprising that films and other audiovisuals are attention-gaining training techniques. As in other nonparticipative techniques, the audiovisual is more effective if used in conjunction with participative techniques. Its main advantage is that it tends to hold the audience's attention and that it exposes the audience to the same message every time. Its effectiveness is a function of its ability to entertain the audience, how well it reinforces the material learned, and how much it increases its retention. Motion pictures and videotapes are the most widely used audiovisuals. Over the past few years 16mm cameras have been made easier to use, but require a darkened room. On the other hand, video cassettes can be hooked up to any television set. These aids are fairly expensive, but if programs are well prepared, they achieve favorable results.

Reading and Study Assignments Most sales training programs require a certain amount of homework to be completed by the trainee. New salespeople in particular are normally assigned a great deal of study material to be learned either before or during their initial sales training. The value of home study material is limited by the student's ability to absorb what he or she has read. For this reason, many firms develop programmed learning materials to be used in place of traditional study material. Many trainers feel that the use of this participative technique increases the effectiveness of the home study programs.

EVALUATING SALES TRAINING

In business and government alike, there are many jobs where the performance of the jobholder is difficult to measure. In these cases, a judgment of the person's performance is made by his or her supervisor or possibly by a consensus of various individuals with whom he or she comes into contact on a regular basis. If the jobholder has a good working relationship and good personal rapport with those who judge his or her performance, they will probably give a good performance evaluation, and vice versa. In either case, very few people feel comfortable in entrusting their future to political factors. In such situations, the jobholder normally seeks criteria that can be used to point out specific accomplishments to those who evaluate his or her performance.

To a great extent, professional sales trainers fall into these circumstances. The trainer can do an excellent job in conducting programs, but unless there are criteria that can be used to show his or her accomplishments, evaluation of the trainer's performance must be based upon a consensus of sales managers and the trainer's supervisors. Surprisingly, many sales trainers and sales training managers depend to a great extent upon such a consensus when it comes time for their performance to be evaluated. On the other hand, many professionals in the sales training field prefer to set up standards of performance by which to be judged, thus reducing the impact of politics on their career development.

Most firms that evaluate sales training personnel use some or all of the following criteria:

Sales trainee tests: *These tests are given to trainees before and after sales training to measure how much of the training material was retained. This factor has been judged to be a partial measure of the effectiveness of the trainer.*

Questionnaires: *Trainees fill out prepared forms dealing with the organization, preparation and general effectiveness of the training program. The participants in effect rate their trainers in a manner similar to professors evaluations given at many colleges and universities.*

Trainer evaluation forms: *These forms are completed by the participants and have reference to teaching attributes of trainers such as personality, enthusiasm, voice characteristics, and other evaluation criteria.*

Program appraisal: *Participants complete forms that refer to the training course. Aspects of the program such as subjects taught, length of course, training techniques and other programmatical elements are rated for effectiveness.*

Observation by supervisor: *In some organizations, the Training Director observes training sessions and rates the trainer's performance based on predetermined criteria. The primary disadvantage of this method is that several visits are required for each trainer and the process becomes very time consuming for the Training Director.*

Examples of forms used to evaluate sales training are shown in Figures 7-9 through 7-11. These and other criteria are used to evaluate professional trainers. In local field situations, formal evaluations of training effectiveness are seldom required by the branch manager's immediate supervisor. Instead, the branch manager must develop his or her own criteria that will point out the relative effectiveness of branch sales training. Most managers find that the performance of individual salespeople is the most valid measure of training success.

In the final analysis, the sales manager's success will be greatly influenced by how well the sales training function has been performed; therefore, it is incumbent upon him or her to maintain ongoing sales training with tight follow-up procedures.

SUMMARY

Training of the sales force is one of the essential functions of sales managers. The major areas of sales training are sales skills training, product knowledge training, training in prospecting and lead generation, time and territory management work habits, company policies and procedures, competitive products or services, and administrative or "paper-work" training. Although other subject areas are covered in sales training programs, the above are the most widely covered areas.

The majority of sales training programs are given at the home office, in the field at local branches, and at outside rented locations. Certain sales training programs are also conducted by outside organizations, such as consulting firms, colleges and universities, and various nonprofit associations.

The most widely used sales training techniques are either participative or nonparticipative. The former are characterized by role playing, coaching and counseling, programmed learning, and group techniques. Nonparticipative techniques are lectures, audiovisual presentations, and reading and study assignments. Of the two types, participative techniques are most critical because of the benefits of learning while doing.

As in most occupations, sales training personnel attempt to develop meaningful criteria by which their performance can be evaluated. Some of these criteria are training rating forms, course evaluation forms, questionnaires, sales trainer tests,

Figure 7-9

Sales Training Evaluation Form

APPRAISAL SHEET

To help us refine and improve our future seminars, would you please give us your impressions and reactions.

Be specific and frank, and give honest opinions—*no signatures*.

My objective in coming to the Advanced Product Seminar was:

____

____

____

Was this objective achieved:

Well Achieved ( ) Moderately Achieved ( ) Not Achieved ( )

I feel the following additions or changes should be made in future seminars (Product area, Organization, Procedure, etc.)

1. ____
2. ____
3. ____

In general, how do you rate the seminar?

Excellent ( ) Good ( ) Fair ( ) Poor ( )

Comments: ____________________________________

____

____

____

____

Figure 7-10

Sales Training Evaluation Form

TRAINER EVALUATION SHEET

Trainer's Name ______________________

VOICE			
Volume	Low	Good	High
Rate	Slow	Good	Fast
Pauses	Few	Good	Many
Bridges	(Use of ands, ah's, etc.)	______________________ Repeat words used	
PERSONALITY			
Enthusiasm	No	Ave.	Yes
Sincerity	No	Ave.	Yes
Confidence	No	Ave.	Yes
DELIVERY			
Poise	No	Ave.	Yes
Eye contact	Fair	Ave.	Good
Gestures	Fair	Ave.	Good
Use of props	Fair	Ave.	Good
DISTRACTIONS	(Jingles coins, etc.)	______________________ List here	
FEATURE BENEFIT			
	FAIR	AVE.	GOOD

COMMENTS: ____

____

____

____

Figure 7-11

Sales Training Evaluation Form

Page: ______________

Day No. __________ Date __________

Location

General subject:	Specific topic: Code:
Scheduled time	Scheduled speaker(s)
Start: ______________	Primary: ______________
Finish: ______________	Back-up: ______________

Department responsible for this session:

Prereading
Required or recommended:

Brief outline of
this session:

Reaction by participant—basic

Date: __________ Topic: __________ Code: __________

Speaker(s)

Time started: ______________ Time ended: ______________

Figure 7-11 (*continued*)

	Rating		
	Excellent	Good	Fair
Was this session well prepared?			
Was the presentation well organized?			
Were you involved?			
Were your questions adequately answered?			
Were the tests or feedback effective?			
Was the session relevant to the selling task?			

Specific comments on how this session might be improved:

and observation by the training director. Criteria for evaluation of branch sales managers are more subjective and, in the final analysis, are determined by the effectiveness of the sales force. Sales training is a continuing job for the branch sales manager and has a great impact upon his or her career.

Goodbody Engine Corporation

Larry Zeidel is the newly hired manager of sales training for Goodbody Engine Corporation, a firm that manufactures and markets all kinds of small- and medium-sized engines. Goodbody engines are used in lawn mowers, power saws, and many other kinds of equipment. Fifty percent of their engines are sold to the OEM (original equipment manufacturers) market, about 30 percent to engine wholesalers, and about 20 percent directly to end users, such as machine shops, small manufacturers, and a variety of other applications. Although the units of sale are typically smaller in this category than in the other two applications, profits are very lucrative, and there has been an increased emphasis on selling to these more diverse markets.

The sales force consists of about 180 people spread out over the United States and Canada. The majority of the sales representatives are hired directly from college and then put into the field. Sales training had been performed entirely at the branch offices. Trainers usually consisted of the sales manager and several different sales people at each branch. Training programs were informal, and there was no standard training pattern. Since salespeople have a variety of college backgrounds, from technical degrees to the social sciences, it has been felt that different people would require different lengths of time in training.

Larry is located at the home office in Chicago. He had worked with a competitive firm as a sales trainer. His duties in his new job have not as yet been defined. He was hired to set up a sales training program at Goodbody and to recommend a complete outline containing objectives, functions, and staff of the new sales training department to top management. In determining what approach will be taken, Larry has compiled the following information:

1. The average length of time spent with the company by a sales representative is three years.
2. About 30 percent of the sales force attain their assigned annual quota.
3. Engineering and quality control of the products the company offers are as good as any other firm in the industry.
4. Service and follow-up on customers has been poor.
5. Most salespeople have little or no company loyalty, even though the compensation and benefit package is excellent.
6. Sales managers complain that people at the home office are not aware of what takes place in the field and cannot adjust to customer needs quickly enough.
7. Product knowledge by one half of the sales force is good, but the other one half of the sales force has poor product knowledge.

Larry is about to make a report to top management, indicating the need for a centralized sales training department in Chicago.

1. Based on the information given, what advice would you give Larry in determining sales training objectives for the coming year?
2. How would you organize and staff the new department?

The Drane Corporation

Bill Rae is general manager for the Drane Corporation. The company markets, installs, and services air conditioning and heating in residences. The firm is located in Westchester County, New York, a beautiful area characterized by woods, vistas, and lovely homes. The county has been long known as an extremely affluent area; indeed, its residents include people known the world over.

There are many large homes in the county, and in recent years there has been quite a large demand for centrally air conditioning a large number of these homes. The process of installing a system in an old, large, mansion-type house is fairly complex, and as a result, Bill, whose background includes a degree in mechanical engineering from Penn State, had been estimating most of the homes by himself. As requests for more and more estimates came in, it became apparent that Bill was simply spreading himself too thin and was unable to provide the estimates himself.

The sales organization consisted of Chuck Stuart, Ray Hannigan, his brother Gordy, Pete Backer, Frank Kuzma, Phil Samis, and Mary Sims. All members of the sales force were recently recruited and none of them had prior experience in the air conditioning industry. Ray and Gordy were insurance salesmen, Pete had been a retail salesman in a men's clothing store, Frank had sold encyclopedias, Phil's former affiliation was with a used-car dealer, and Mary sold cosmetics door-to-door.

The busiest months in the industry are traditionally from April through July, during which time about 50 percent of annual sales are made. This year, Bill wants to provide his sales force with product knowledge, as well as sales expertise. Based upon certain information in the files, Bill expected that about 20 percent of the sales calls would be made upon prospects in the high-income category ($100,000 or more per year), and the remaining 80 percent of the prospects would be in an income category of roughly $30,000 and up.

Last year only about 10 percent of qualified prospects called on became customers. It is hoped that this year the rate will be raised to about 30 percent. Part of the reason given by many of the prospects for not buying was that the price was too high. The Drane organization is totally convinced that their higher prices are justified because of the quality of materials used and the services provided to customers.

Bill has decided to set up a sales training program this year and has called you in to help him.

1. What are Drane's greatest sales training needs?
2. Outline the program you would recommend to Bill.

DISCUSSION QUESTIONS

1. Describe the purpose of the various areas of sales training and how these might vary with skill and experience.
2. What are the sources of sales training? Discuss the possibilities of role playing in sales training.
3. Discuss the relative merits of on-the-job training versus classroom training.

4. Write a two-day program for a sales training seminar.
5. Prepare a questionnaire for evaluating the sales trainees (a) before the seminar, and (b) after the seminar.
6. Prepare an appraisal form to evaluate the seminar (a) instructors and (b) content.
7. What are some of the uses of videotaped replays in sales training?
8. Who has the ultimate responsibility for sales training? Why?

NOTES

[1]Estimate based on cost of training sales personnel, maintaining training staff, and sales training materials.

[2]"Poor Use of Time Is Major Problem in Sales," Marketing News, October 19, 1979, pp. 1–2.

[3]*Training the Sales Force: A Progress Report*. Report No. 737. (New York: The Conference Board, 1978)

[4]Job description courtesy of Dartnell Corporation, Chicago, Ill.

[5]Programs based on format for a McGraw-Hill Information Systems division sales training meeting.

[6]Conference Board, *Training*.

[7]Joseph F. Bova, "Pretraining Home Study Programs," in Jared F. Harrison, ed, *The Management of Sales Training* (Reading, Mass.: Addison-Wesley, 1977), p. 175.

[8]Curt Davis, "The Limitations of Sales Training," *Mark II*, vol. 17, September 1976, p. 18.

[9]Maynard F. Stoddard, "Confessions of a Door-to-Door Salesman," *Sales and Marketing Management*, April 11, 1977.

[10]"Back to School: More Executives Take Courses," *Wall Street Journal*, March 3, 1980, p. 1.

[11]B. A. Jerome, "Salesmen Are Trained, Not Born," *Missouri Press News*, vol. 14, June 1976, p. 10.

CHAPTER 8

SALES COMPENSATION

OBJECTIVES

To discuss the various types of sales compensation:
* Straight salary
* Combination plans
* Straight commission

To investigate some of the traditional problems of sales compensation.
* To enumerate some nonmonetary rewards.
* To discuss some company benefits.

INTERVIEW WITH FRANK SMITH

Interviewer: What do you think of money, Frank?

Frank Smith: It's not everything, but it's way ahead of whatever is in second place.

Interviewer: That statement sounds a little uncharacteristic for you, Frank. I never knew you to be avaricious.

Frank Smith: Have you seen the papers recently? Inflation up, interest rate up, everything up but my paycheck.

Interviewer: Come on, Frank, I hear you need a wheelbarrow to take it to the bank.

Frank Smith: I make a living. Seriously though, people are more money conscious today than ever. Husbands and wives both work, and it's still hard to make ends meet.

Interviewer: How does this affect your ability to keep salespeople motivated?

Frank Smith: Well, we certainly have to maintain a competitive compensation framework. You have to realize, though, money is only one of several things that motivate salespeople. When we get to the chapter on motivation later in the book we can go into those factors. Clearly, however, you can't separate money and motivation entirely.

Interviewer: You hear about all of this research on money as not being that great a motivation. Then why do they pay commission?

Frank Smith: We can get into the nitty gritty in the chapter, but to answer your question, firms don't always pay commission. There are a few other options open to management and if incentives are considered to be important, there are a lot of options open with respect to incentives.

Interviewer: Do organizations change pay plans very often?

Frank Smith: I think organizations *have* to change pay plans occasionally to shift with conditions. In fact, this is explained pretty thoroughly in the chapter.

Interviewer: What do you think of sales contests?

Frank Smith: It depends entirely on the situation. We have them periodically and they usually work out pretty well, but we don't have any illusions, either. Not everyone responds to contests, and if we ever found out that they weren't effective, we'd stop having them. I think this is an important point and the chapter gets into this in some depth.

Interviewer: I understand you are also going to talk about fringe benefits. I doubt if most people realize how much they cost an organization.

Frank Smith: Interesting point. I'd like to talk a little bit about how they started with union contracts, then were extended to white-collar employees, and so on. Unfortunately, we won't have time to get involved in the history or the philosophy of so-called "fringe" benefits. What we're going to do instead is show some general relationships and some specific benefits that salespeople receive.

Interviewer: Where did we steal the data for this chapter, Frank?

Frank Smith: You really know how to hurt a guy. You're right, though. In this one chapter we did use a lot of data from one source. In my opinion though, it's the best source, so our information is right up to date.

Interviewer: Does the chapter tell how much salespeople earn?
Frank Smith: Let's read it and then you can stop asking all these questions.
Interviewer: O.K.

The perfect sales compensation plan has existed only as a mirage to sales managers for decades and possibly even for centuries. Unfortunately, sales management has yet to develop *the* compensation plan that will have a long-term appeal for the salesperson and the company alike. For various reasons, few if any firms have a reward plan that has been considered equitable to all parties concerned over a long period of time. Individual motivations, values, and needs change over time, often resulting in a shift in one's perception of the current pay plan. Whatever the reasons, about one-quarter of all sales compensation plans have changed approximately every two years.[1] This chapter will investigate the fundamental types of compensation schemes and will study in some depth the impact of these plans on the attainment of sales objectives.

TYPES OF SALES COMPENSATION

Essentially three different types of compensation plans are used by sales organizations: straight salary plans, straight commission plans, and combination plans.

Each type has its usefulness, and each fits into certain applications. Among the major factors that determine the type of pay plan to be used are the following:

1. Influence of the salesperson on the outcome of the buying decision.
2. Dollar volume of typical sales order.
3. Extent to which salesperson is required to be engaged in nonselling activities.
4. "Logic" of plan dictated by situation.
5. Industry practices.

Influence of the Salesperson on the Outcome of the Buying Decision Many organizations decide to purchase goods and services irrespective of the influence of a vendor's salesperson. Buying committees or individual buyers often simply prefer a particular product on its own merits and place orders for it, sometimes even without the salesperson's making a call upon the customer. In other situations, certain products are not well known and are purchased only because of aggressive follow-up by the salesperson. In the first case, the salesperson has little influence on the buying decision, and in the second the salesperson has a great deal of influence. The particular plan used by the organization to compensate its salespeople should reflect these influences.

Dollar Volume of the Sales Order In certain industries, particularly in industrial or OEM (original equipment manufacturer) markets, sales of enormous dollar value are made. An example of this would be a multimillion dollar order placed for a certain quantity of steel or concrete. Even if the salesperson does have an influence on the outcome through aggressive follow-up, his or her company is unlikely to pay a high rate of commission on the entire order, since the firm's profits are dependent upon certain costs. Orders of this type are normally acquired only after preparation of complex proposals, often involving several people other than the salesperson. In other industries, particularly in durable equipment, the firm selling the product normally adds on a per unit commission rate to its price. In cases of this type, a multimillion dollar order can and does often result in a constant per unit commission rate for the salesperson. A salesman with a large manufacturer of automatic typewriters once earned a commission in excess of half a million dollars from an order placed by a firm with a government contract. The supplier afterward set a limit upon earnings for its salespeople during a calendar year. In most cases, however, large dollar volume sales do not pay a consistent rate of commission.

Extent to Which Salesperson Is Required to Be Engaged in Nonselling Activities We have already investigated some of the nonselling activities that salespeople must pursue. Meetings, training sessions, service calls, and filling out paper work are only some of the time-consuming "nonproductive" functions of most salespeople. As a rule, most pay plans reflect the need for salespeople to be taken out of the field, and a base salary is provided as compensation for performance of nonselling tasks.

"Logic" of Plan Dictated by Situation Certain special situations require special decisions as to sales compensation. These decisions are dictated by logic or by common sense more than by any inflexible policy written at headquarters. As an example, salespeople the world over have claimed, probably for thousands of years, that the area where *they* sell is the most difficult. Salespeople in New York claim that there is nowhere exactly like New York in which to sell. Likewise, salespeople from Baltimore, Philadelphia, or for that matter anywhere complain that their locale is somehow different. Most sales managers agree that although these observations are mythical for the most part, there are certain areas that literally are different. One example is Detroit. When the auto industry is prospering, it is very easy for salespeople to "sell," and when the auto industry is in recession, salespeople find it all but impossible to "sell." As a result, many firms adjust their sales compensation plans accordingly, since both extremes are out of the salesperson's control. In many cases, certain external or exogenous factors have such an impact upon sales that simple common sense dictates a change in the compensation plan. New product breakthroughs or restrictive government regulation often result in conditions that warrant a reevaluation of the compensation structure.

Industry Practices Many industries, particularly those characterized by an oligopolistic market structure, use a "follow the leader" approach to sales compensation. Although this practice is not always the best for an individual firm, it has the effect of standardizing sales costs to some extent throughout the industry. Obviously, productivity is the most important consideration to be taken into account, and, predictably, some firms with less productive sales forces often have much higher sales costs than the industry leaders. This can also be a dangerous practice since it can result in the loss of good salespeople. Nevertheless, there is some merit to the establishment of benchmark compensation jobs through industry surveys. Realistically, whether there is merit to this practice or not, it is carried on extensively and is the basis for many compensation plans.

In addition to the preceding factors that influence a firm's choice of compensation plans, many other factors, such as ability to pay, salesperson's length of time with firm, and others, are unique to individual companies. Taking all these factors into account, we will investigate the various types of compensation plans and the current dollar amounts paid to salespeople as estimated by various sources.

Straight Salary

It has been estimated that about one quarter of all salespeople are compensated on the basis of straight salary.[2] In the strictest sense, very few sales jobs can be classified as "straight salary" because most sales organizations provide occasional bonuses, prizes, or other short-term and low-value incentives. For the purposes of this analysis, the salaried salesperson receives about 90 percent or more of his or her income from a basic salary.

There are certain sales jobs to which the salary method of compensation applies; in most cases, the salesperson either has little control over the buying decision, the salesperson does not really "sell," or economic and business conditions militate against some other mode of compensation. In other cases, a clear relationship between sale and responsibility for the sale does not exist, as in the air freight industry, where it is difficult to identify who is responsible for which sale.[3]

Salary plans work particularly well in situations where the salesperson functions as an "order taker" rather than an "order getter," and there is no requirement for aggressive pursuit of sales. Salary plans also work out well in cases of national account sales, where the salesperson coordinates a large customer's requirements for his or her company's products. Normally, in such situations the salesperson has little influence over individual orders, but is in a position to perform service functions, solve problems, and to eliminate problems before they manifest themselves.

Certain technical sales situations lend themselves to team selling, a situation where technical personnel, company systems and methods analysts, and even corporate executives join forces to make a sale. In sales of this type, where it is very difficult to determine the precise contribution of the salesperson, a salary plan appears warranted.

An interesting point about salary plans is that there is no *one* type of salesperson who is compensated by this method. As a matter of fact, the reverse is true. The "type" of salesperson compensated by straight salary ranges from the barely literate order filler to the well-trained and highly articulate account representative. There is an implicit notion in the sales field that if a salesperson is compensated by salary he or she cannot be a very good salesperson. This notion, although obviously accurate in certain instances, tends to be overly simplistic in the general case. As will be seen in Chapter 9, a strong body of evidence seems to support the contention that monetary incentive is only one of several factors involved in the sales-motivation process. Many commercial and technical firms, for example, are successful in the use of a straight salary plan to compensate salespeople. On the other hand, many firms using high commission and bonus incentives are unsuccessful in motivating salespeople. To conclude, the salary plan can be successful in several types of sales jobs rather than in only the traditional order-*taking* situation.

There are several advantages to compensating salespeople on a salary basis. First, the guarantee of a regular income allows salespeople to confidently approach their duties without the worry of whether or not he or she will be paid this week. This type of plan typically results in a relatively high degree of loyalty compared to the salesperson who gets paid only when he or she produces, although this sense of loyalty is often more prevalent in salespeople who have been exposed to the other types of compensation plans. In the case of the *coordinator* salesperson, who performs many nonselling functions, the salary plan is a viable compensation vehicle, since the salesperson can focus attention on the most important details of the moment without the constant feeling that it is costing money to perform one's job priorities according to importance.

The salary approach, assuming that motivational forces are *not* being impeded, is also advantageous to management in many respects. For one thing, sales managers have flexibility with respect to shifting salespeople in and out of territories and accounts. Traditionally, changes of this type are met with resistance, since salespeople typically perceive that a loss of income will result from such changes. Assuming productivity to be a constant (which might not always be a warranted assumption), sales costs remain fixed over relatively long periods of time, a condition that allows for accurate forecasting and accounting.

On the other hand, unless the basis of the compensation plan has been well thought out and proved to be workable, the straight salary plan can have several disadvantages. First, it is almost mandatory that the motivation of each salesperson be determined to be strong even in the absence of a financial incentive system. But it is highly unlikely that an entire sales force will be composed of such types. More likely, a significant percentage of the sales force will develop the notion that inferior salespeople are being rewarded on the same basis as effective salespeople. They are also likely to conclude that little or no importance is perceived by management to be attached to incremental sales efforts. In any event, these salespeople typically develop the attitude that there exists little or no reason to put forth an extra effort to sell. Unfortunately, the salespeople who react in this manner to a salary plan are typically the more aggressive, more "numbers-oriented" personnel, the kind of salespeople that are otherwise highly desirable members of the sales force.

According to the Dartnell Sales Compensation Survey, there are two basic types of salary plans: (1) straight salary, and (2) salary plus discretionary bonus. The latter form of compensation is very common in many industries, such as building materials, bulk chemicals, and utilities, although not all sales jobs in these industries are compensated by this mode. Although averages are sometimes misleading, all salaried salespeople in 1979 earned a mean income of $21,549, while salespeople who received a discretionary bonus earned almost $2000 more (see Figure 8-1).

Between the years 1964 and 1979, the typical experienced salaried salesperson's earnings increased from $9700 to $22,265. Figure 8-2 shows the annual increases over the last 15 years.

In summary, the goals of the company, the functions of the sales force, and the motivation of sales-force members will to a great extent determine whether or not a salary plan is appropriate.

Straight Commission

In this type of compensation plan, sales-force members are paid only for what they sell. Straight commission is almost the exclusive form of payment in direct sales and is also prevalent in certain other fields such as apparel. To some extent, in every industry there are a few firms that compensate their salespeople on the basis of straight commission. Approximately 20 percent of sales organizations pay on the basis of straight commission, although this figure is an estimate, and since the actual number of direct-sales organizations and sales personnel at any given time is not known, this figure could vary as much as 40 to 50 percent.

For the few salespeople who succeed in straight commission jobs, the rewards are undoubtedly higher than for those who succeed in straight salary jobs. According to the Dartnell survey, mean commission-based income was about $32,000 in 1979, an average figure substantially higher than salary or, for that matter, any other compensation plan.[4] Figure 8-3 shows the historical pattern of commission earnings over the past 15 years.

Figure 8-1

Salary Plan Analysis

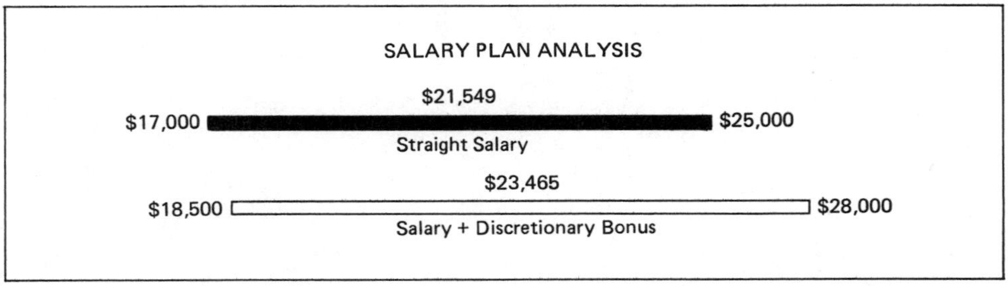

Source: *Compensation of Salesmen: Dartnell's 20th Bienniel Survey* (Chicago: Dartnell Corporation, 1980), p. 29.

Figure 8-2

Average Earnings of Experienced Salaried Salespeople

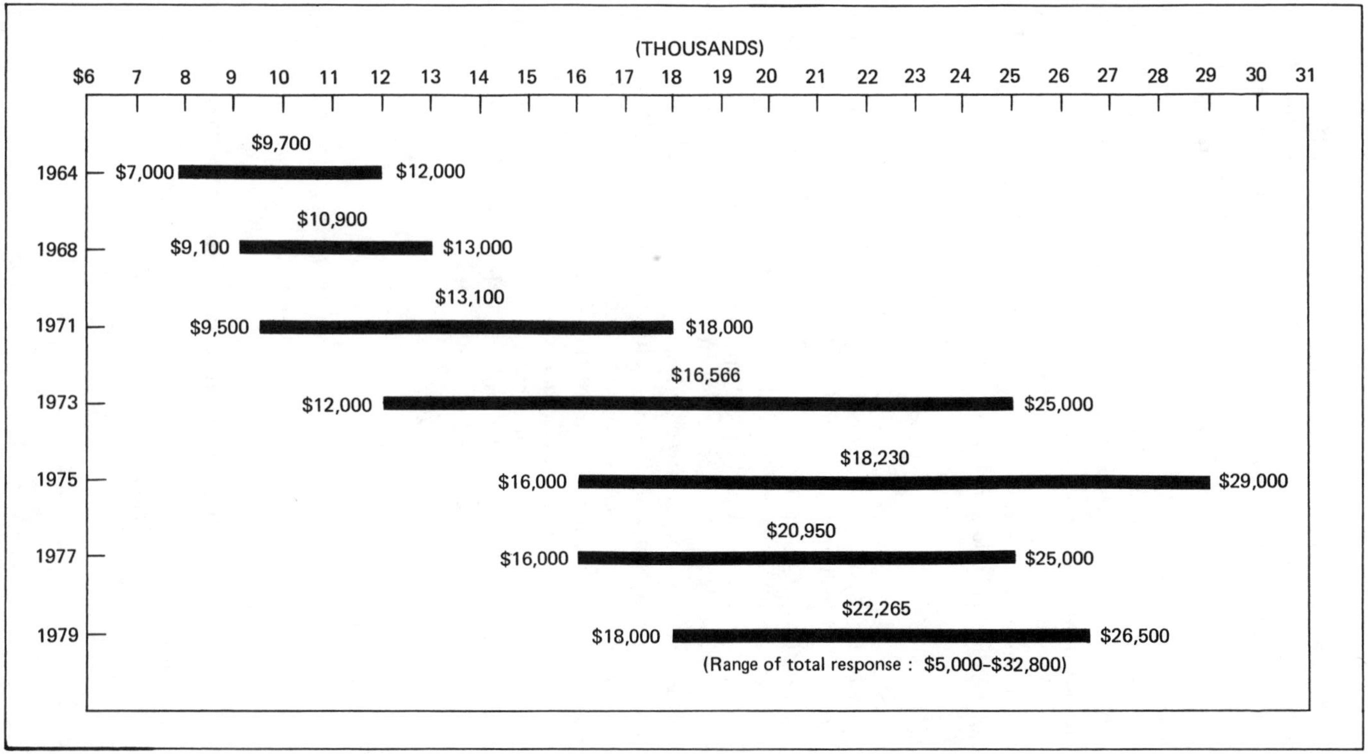

Source: *Compensation of Salesmen: Dartnell's 20th Bienniel Survey* (Chicago: Dartnell Corporation, 1980), p. 40.

Figure 8-3

Average Earnings of Experienced Commission Salespeople, Range of the Middle Half, Full Range for 1979

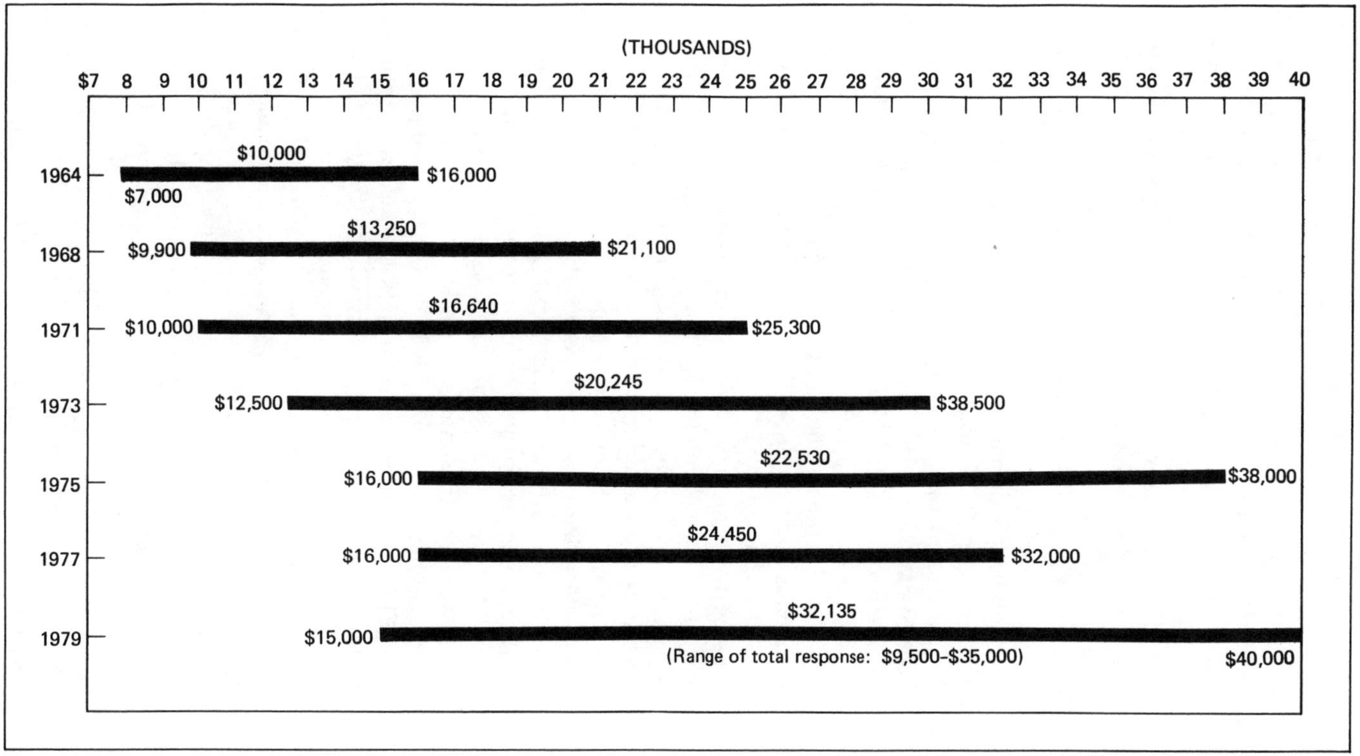

Unfortunately, averages tend to obscure the true picture. Although *experienced* salespeople in commission jobs appear to fare better than other salespeople, these figures do not take into account the large numbers of new people who go in and out of direct-sales jobs every few months. If these figures were taken into account, the "average" straight commission would undoubtedly be lower.

There exist several reasons why commission selling is advantageous to management and very few reasons why this form of compensation is favorable to salespeople. Very often there is an implied attitude on the part of management to the effect that good salespeople do not need a salary. The argument, when carried farther, states that straight commission provides the ultimate incentive—a somewhat nihilistic viewpoint. While there is no question that *some* straight commission salespeople earn unusually large incomes, there is little or no evidence to support the contention that, as a group, commission salespeople are better paid. In fact, most commission salespeople receive few or no "free" fringes from their firm, and given current hospital and dental care costs, the absence of these income supplements has a downward effect on commission sales earnings.

On the other hand, straight commission payment is advantageous to certain companies but provides little or no advantage to others. Traditionally, many direct-sales firms have been quick to adopt this type of compensation plan, primarily because their financial base is very weak. Other direct-sales firms that are in a healthier financial condition often pay straight commission because any other type of payment would result in a "loss" for the majority of their salespeople. The reason for this is the exceedingly high turnover that exists in direct sales, which results from either insufficient training or because the products and services marketed by direct-sales firms are often very difficult to sell. As was indicated in Chapter 2, many, if not most, direct-sales firms utilize a somewhat cynical approach, spending as little money as possible on training or other sales costs and seldom displaying in a tangible way any regard for the salesperson as an employee or as a person. When a firm attempts to minimize its sales costs in such a way, turnover is bound to be extremely high, sometimes as high as 300 to 400 percent in one year.

Firms in the direct-sales field that are well financed and have a more solid reputation and cash flow typically pay on the basis of straight commission because it is the most practical way. Insurance companies, for example, pay straight commission because their salespeople are almost literally set up in their own businesses. Most insurance firms provide adequate income for their new salespeople during the first one or two years until the new agent is on solid financial footing. Although the turnover in insurance sales is very high compared to other selling jobs, it should be taken into consideration that new businesses also have an extremely high mortality rate. Insurance sales, in this respect, should be equated to business starts rather than to other selling jobs for a realistic assessment, a point that very few people consider. An insurance firm typically provides the training, office, telephone, secretarial, and other facilities for the salesperson to use in selling. He or she is also given a great deal of help in obtaining licenses and other certification necessary to the conduct of business. At some point, however, the salesperson must take responsibility for the performance of the selling process, and it is at this point that the only practical compensation scheme is straight commission.

Outside the insurance industry, there are few established industries where unmodified straight commission is the accepted form of payment to salespeople. Firms that do pay straight commission typically have some modification that helps the salesperson through slack periods. The most common form of modification is the *drawing account*, more commonly referred to simply as *draw*. In this situation, money is advanced to the salesperson against future commissions and is deducted from commissions that are paid at a later date. Suppose, for instance, that a salesperson has no sales during June. The company advances the salesperson \$1000. An account is set up and the salesperson is debited \$1000. Suppose during July the salesperson has another bad month and the company provides another advance of \$1000. The debit is now \$2000. Sales pick up in August and the salesperson earns \$5000 in commissions. The company would then deduct the \$2000 advance and pay the salesperson \$3000. This example is somewhat simplistic since most firms typically set up a formula for deduction of draw advances from commissions on a staggered basis so that the impact on the salesperson's earnings during a given month is spread out. The principal, however is a simple one and is used by most firms that pay straight commission and have a need or desire to retain their salespeople as permanent or regular employees. Obviously, the disadvantage of the drawing account is the possibility that the salesperson can leave the company with a debit account. In these cases, the firm writes off the debit as a sales cost. Companies as a rule do not attempt to recover the money from the salespeople.

For most companies that wish to retain their salespeople *and* do not experience chronic cash flow problems, the straight commission approach probably has more disadvantages than advantages. First, it is unrealistic for the company to expect salespeople to perform any nonselling functions. Any duties that are not directly related to the salesperson's maximizing earnings will either be ignored or, at the very best, be performed under great protest. Another disadvantage of the commission approach is that salespeople tend to perceive the job as temporary until something better comes along. Loyalty to an organization may not necessarily be for sale, but some trade-off appears to be a *sine qua non*, and, unfortunately for the organization, most salespeople require the trade-off to be of a tangible nature.

An even more serious problem generated by the straight commission approach is that the sales manager finds it very difficult to exercise control over the sales force. Shifting accounts or changing territories is difficult at best, and in many cases salespeople have less respect for the sales manager, since they often perceive him or her to be incapable of selling effectively.

To summarize, straight commission payment is invariably associated with high turnover. Any firm that uses this mode of payment always has a compelling reason to do so, and in most cases the reason is either underfinancing or poor cash flow.

Compensation Plans

It has been estimated that over one half of all sales payment plans are of the *combination* type.[5] A combination plan pays a base salary plus one or more supplements, usually of an *incentive* nature. An *incentive* relates to a monetary payment based on performance. The effectiveness and even the use of the term "incentive" could be open to some question. This topic will be explored later in this chapter, but for the purposes of this presentation, an incentive payment typically includes a commission or bonus paid in addition to a base salary.

From an intellectual standpoint, the logic of the combination plan is irrefutable. Since the duties and responsibilities of the salesperson are of both a selling and a nonselling nature, it is right and just that he or she be compensated for both. From the sales manager's point of view, the salesperson is provided an incentive to sell aggressively while still remaining a subordinate subject to the evaluation and direct supervision of the manager. From the salesperson's point of view, he or she is appropriately rewarded at every level of performance, while at the same time not feeling "cheated" for performing nonselling duties.

A typical combination plan would be a typewriter firm that pays its salespeople a base salary of $1000 per month plus a commission on each unit sold. Office equipment firms often pay higher per unit commissions as more units are sold. According to this format, the commission structure might be as follows:

Commission Schedule

First six units per month	$50 per unit
Seventh through twelfth unit	$75 per unit
Over twelve units	$100 per unit

Assume that a salesperson is paid a salary of $1000 per month and he or she sells nine units during the month. His or her income would be

Salary + 6 units at $50 + 3 units at $75

$1000 + 300 + 225 = $1525 monthly income

On the other hand, such pay plans are usually based on annual performance, and the first six units must be sold each month to qualify for the next higher level commission. If it is April, for instance, the salesperson must have sold at least six units during January, February, and March each, or a total of at least 18 units if he or she is to qualify for the extra $25 commission during April for sales over the first six units. Assume that the salesperson has sold 12 units during January, five units during February, and only four units during March. Now during April he or she sells 12 units. April earnings would be as follows:

Commission Schedule	
First six units during April	$50 per unit
Seventh through twelfth units	$75 per unit

$300 + $450 = $750 April commission

However, the salesperson "owed" the company three units because he or she did not reach six units in either February or March, and the company must be "paid back" before the salesperson is eligible for the higher commission rate. Now the commission for April will be:

First six units during April	$50 per unit
Three units owed to company	$50 per unit
Seventh through twelfth units less units "owed" to company	$75 per unit

$300 + (3 × $50) + (3 × $75) = $675 April commission

While the determination of the salesperson's compensation may or may not have been easy for the reader to understand, there are many combination plans that are very complex and are nearly impossible to determine by sales manager and salesperson alike. Also, it may or may not have been apparent to the reader that an important reason existed for the salesperson to reach the 24 units cumulatively before becoming eligible for the $75 per unit commission. Without the cumulative requirement, a salesperson could delay processing all orders received in January, February, and March, and then submit them during April, thereby "beating" the company out of $25 on three units. As one sales manager in commercial sales related to the author,

> There is no way that a company can figure out a simple pay plan. They always have to make them complex. Whether it's because they want to confuse me or if it's as they say, that changing conditions and complex sales strategies require a complex pay plan, I don't know. One thing I do know; the first thing three-fourths of the salespeople in this country do when a new pay plan comes out is try to figure out some way to beat it and rip off the company. It's like a game, it's not even the money. Just the satisfaction of knowing that *you* beat *them*. I used to feel the same way when I was a saleswoman. It never works, though. They have it figured out and there's no way that you can ever beat the system.[6]

From the standpoint of good management, it is no joking matter that many of the combination plans of even major corporations are literally too complex to understand. A precept of incentive reward systems that has existed for nearly a century is that, for an incentive to be effective, it should be understandable and should be paid quickly. In today's business world, most salespeople are intelligent and highly educated. It is not expected that a compensation plan necessarily need assume that the salesperson coping with it have less than average intelligence. The *bases* of many compensation plans, however, are often too complex for even highly intelligent people to comprehend. To the extent that this complexity tends to waste an inordinate amount of a salesperson's, sales manager's or administrator's time in arriving at an interpretation, the plan is less than effective.

One of the most difficult aspects of designing a combination plan is determining the relative salary portion versus the incentive portion of earnings. Clearly, the objectives of the sales organization should dictate this dichotomy.

The particular weight given each factor is typically a function of how aggressively management wants its salespeople to pursue new sales. The office equipment example given earlier appeared to lend itself to a split of approximately 60 percent base salary/40 percent commission. In a situation where a good deal of servicing is required, for example, in many technical sales situations, a higher percentage of income should be the salesperson's salary.

The decision to pay an incentive of *commission* or *bonus* normally is a function of management's perception of what constitutes an appropriate *time period* over which to measure sales performance. If one month is the commonly used period during which sales results are summarized, commission is nearly always used. If sales take a long time to be consummated, for example, in consultative sales, then a *bonus* is the most frequent form of incentive payment. Bonus incentive plans are normally more difficult to design and administer than commission plans. Some bonus plans pay the salesperson quarterly; others pay semiannually or annually. If the original principle of paying incentives quickly after performance is adhered to, bonuses cannot be relied upon to act as a motivating factor. Bonuses are typically set at a lower-than-objective figure. For example, if a salesperson's annual quota is 1000 units, then bonuses would normally be paid upon attainment of 800 or 900 units. It is felt by most sales managers that if bonuses are not received until the 100 percent goal is achieved, salespeople could become discouraged.

A common combination plan includes salary, commission, *and* bonus. Plans of this type are typically most effective in situations where aggressive selling is required, *and* where the length of time of sale from appointment to sale is relatively short, such as in the office equipment industry, where this type of compensation plan abounds. Normally, a quarterly bonus is available to salespeople who have met certain sales criteria during the previous three months. This bonus allows the salesperson to compensate for poor performance during any given month by better performance during the other two months.

As one would expect, the 1979 average combination plan income was estimated to be lower than the straight commission plan and higher than the straight salary plan. Income broken down by salary plus bonus was $27,146, by salary and commission was $29,506, and by salary, commission, and bonus was $26,887 (see Figure 8-4).

Historically, combination plan earnings have increased at about the same rate

Figure 8-4

Compensation of Salespeople

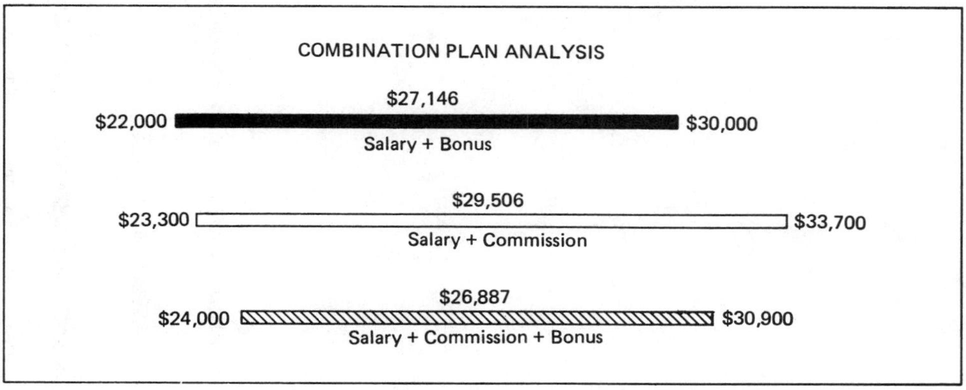

COMBINATION PLAN SPLIT

	Salary + Bonus	Salary + Commission	Salary + Bonus + Commission
Base	$21,800	$18,900	$16,300
Incentive	5,616	10,606	10,587
	$27,416	$29,506	$26,887

as the other two plans over the past 15 years. Figure 8-5 shows the pattern of combination plan earnings since 1964.

In summary, the combination plan is the most widely used sales compensation scheme. It offers the advantages of both the salary and commission plans and, if well conceived, can provide a motivational stimulus while at the same time providing security.

TRADITIONAL PROBLEMS OF SALES COMPENSATION

The preceding analysis provided the reader with the basic mechanics of the major types of sales compensation, their advantages and disadvantages, and some current income figures in each category. While every company must determine its pay plan in light of current objectives, establishment of the plan does not guarantee that the plan will work. The observation that "you can't please everyone" has no better application than in sales compensation. It is a fact worth repeating that very

Figure 8-5

Average Earnings of Experienced Combination Plan Salespeople, Range of the Middle Half, Full Range for 1979

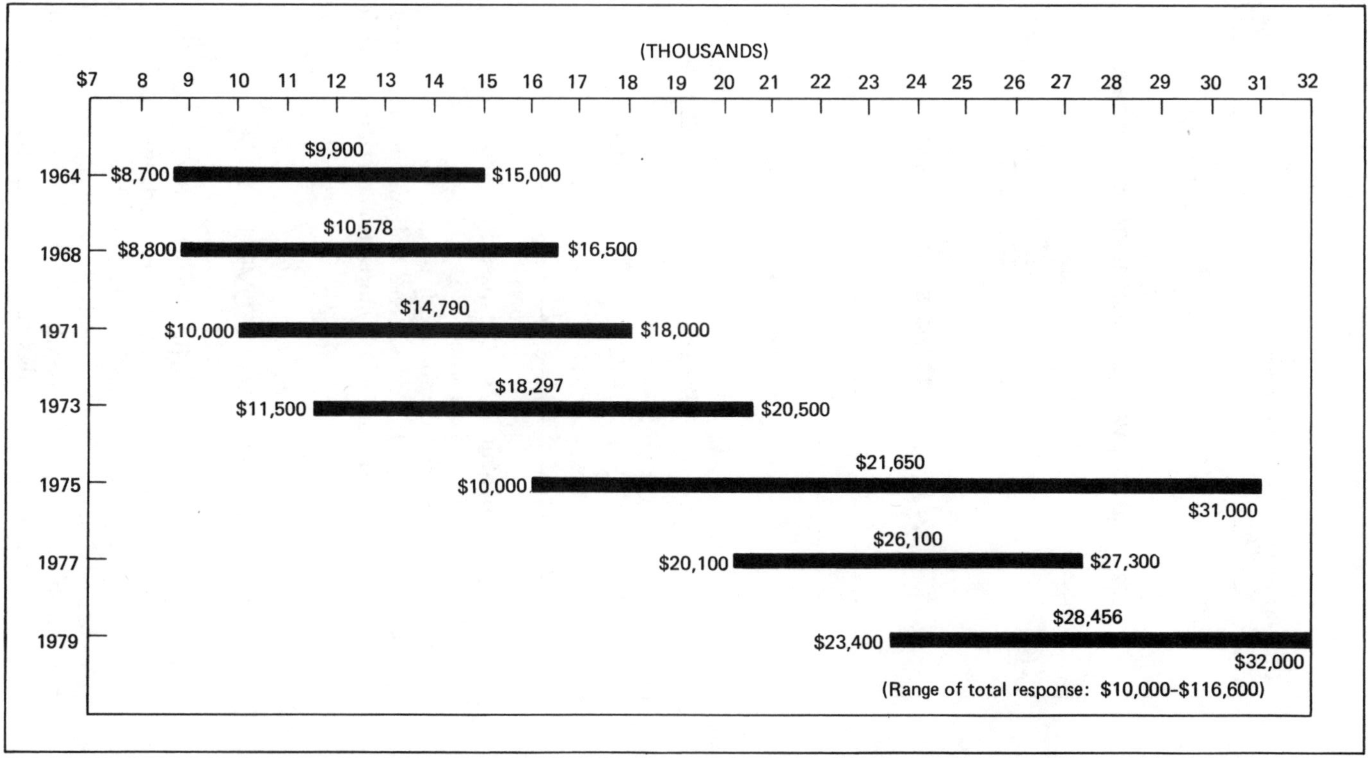

few salespeople or very few managers will express satisfaction with their compensation plan at any given time. Unfortunately, a committee composed of even the greatest authorities in the field would probably find it difficult to design a viable sales compensation for any given sales force, and there is every reason to believe that once the scheme was formulated, it would require an overhaul in the near future.

Disclosure of this fact is not by any means intended to be a monument to the lack of creativity on the part of American marketing management. On the contrary, sales organizations have shown their effectiveness by adapting to changing times by recognizing the obsolescence of compensation plans and by making the appropriate revisions when indicated. The major shortcoming of most pay plans is that, as conditions change, certain fundamental problems evolve that tend to call for a reassessment of the plan's effectiveness. This section will examine some of the problems without necessarily providing a solution in each case.

There are probably as many individual compensation dilemmas as there are individual compensation plans. However, several pervasive problems appear to exist more frequently than others. The following analysis will document some major problem areas and the typical causes of each. Where possible, both the management and the salesperson's points of view will be shown. An arbitrary listing of these problems suggests the following three to be the most common.

1. Payment plans that favor too few people.
2. Inaccurate assessment of relationships between incentive pay and motivation.
3. Reducing salespeople's income to reduce sales costs.

Payment Plans That Favor Too Few People Most if not all sales organizations employ one or more salespeople who have a great deal of seniority and who have also been effective salespeople over the years. It is not unusual that sales managers tend to "reward" these persons with sales territories or accounts that have inordinately high sales potential. Unless economic conditions are particularly bad or some other unforeseen contingency arises, these salespeople typically earn considerably more than the average sales-force member. Although this practice might seem somewhat unfair, most managers look upon the assignment as both a reward for loyal and effective service by the older salesperson and also as an incentive to the rest of the sales force. To add to the manager's justification, it should be noted that the territory is usually worked, if not harder, at least "smarter," so that close to optimal sales are generated. Unfortunately, managers often tend to single out a few senior people for the best accounts or territories to the point where the remaining sales-force members are given territories with too little potential. This situation subverts the manager's original intent and often creates division and personal enmity among the salespeople. This practice, although subtle, seems to exist in every type of sales and in every industry.

A discriminatory practice that is equally virulent is providing the most effective salespeople with the best compensation opportunities. The reasoning behind this practice is that the better salesperson is more likely to close sales, so by providing the leads or by giving the best accounts to the "heavyweights," a higher percentage of sales will be made for the office as a whole. This practice is analogous to the strategy of the New York Yankees baseball teams during the 1950s, where the best pitchers were always selected to pitch against the worst opposing teams. In either case, the total record is predictable, but younger professionals are put into a situation where they are easily discouraged.

In any situation where the compensation scheme discriminates in favor of a few people, albeit effective ones, the negative impact upon the remainder of the sales force will nearly always outweigh whatever positive effects the system produced.

Inaccurate Assessment of Relationship between Compensation and Motivation In recent years there has been a restructuring of ideas with regard to the true motivational value of "incentive compensation."[6] The earliest research of note, conducted by Harrington Emerson in the United Kingdom and Frederick Taylor in the United States drew a strong relationship between financial reward and productivity. The inference was that a person as a rational animal desires the basic necessities of life (and more) and will be motivated to work harder and produce more if a financial reward is offered.

The next significant voice to be heard on the subject was from Elton Mayo in the 1930s.[7] Mayo contended that people are social animals and that social needs may prevent them from chasing the carrot because of their need to belong. Serious investigation of this question during the 1960s centered primarily upon reasons why the individual does not work harder with incentives, even when financial reward is offered.[8] Current theory, however, focuses upon the *salesperson* rather than the incentive.[9] There appears to be a substantial amount of evidence to support the contention that the motivation of many if not most salespeople, particularly in the commercial, technical, and consultative fields, comes from *within*, and that incentive compensation is only a *part* of a larger group of motivating factors.[10] Based on substantial investigation of the role of financial incentives in the motivation process, which was covered in Chapter 6, it appears that sales organizations have relied too heavily upon bonuses, commissions, and other forms of monetary rewards to provide a stimulus when that stimulus in fact emanates from within the salesperson. If this point is valid, and there is strong evidence that it is, many sales compensation plans need to be reexamined.

Reducing Salespeople's Incomes to Reduce Sales Costs Many organizations view sales-force compensation strictly as an expense, the assumption being made that this expense should be reduced as much as possible, culminating in a positive result on the profit and loss schedule. As a result, many firms set salaries at an unrealistically low level, hoping that the incentive portion of the pay plan will induce salespeople to sell more. This is a common practice, often even used by leading firms. The result of this manipulation of the pay plan income is that salespeople's incomes often depend on the luck of the incentive plan, not their own abilities. John K. Moynahan, one of the leading experts on sales compensation, describes this situation as follows:

> That is a common rationalization of a value system that applies to far too many salesmen in American industry. The system characteristically is combined with a conventional salary administration approach that, in effect, says the amount of increase granted any salaried employee is not geared to change in the marketplace for the person's skills. Instead, changes are likely to reflect (1) The company's ability to pay (as expressed in an overall merit-increase budget); (2) The length of time since the employee's last increase; and (3) The percent of current salary that the proposed increase represents.
>
> There is even more restraint on salesmen's salary increases than on other employees' because, after all, "a salesman can always earn incentives to make up the difference." Companies tend to view incentives for salesmen as a no-lose situation: if sales are not there, costs are reduced; conversely, costs are increased only when sales volume rises and thus they are affordable. Unfortunately, that type of reasoning is false.[11]

The consequences of such policies are that the high performers leave the company and the low performers stay behind, some of whom will even be promoted to management positions. The obvious solution to this situation is the installation of a performance evaluation system where performance is rewarded and mediocrity ceases to be rewarded. Since incentives remain constant, sales compensation costs do not rise appreciably.

An equally self-destructive practice is the institution of a ceiling on sales earning in a commission-oriented environment. This problem exists in many commercial sales organizations where the commission structure is billed explicitly or implicitly by the company as a great opportunity for salespeople to "be in their own business without making a capital investment," a phrase used continually by managers in incentive-oriented sales organizations. As indicated previously, it is not unusual for customers to make a purchase decision without being sold by the salesperson. Also, changes in a customers' needs might result in an order of inordinately high dollar value. The organization's viewpoint is that, as long as the salesperson did not influence the sale to any great extent, he or she should share in the reward only to the extent of the company's largesse, the result being a dollar limitation or "pegging" of the salesperson's earnings for the calendar year. The logic of this approach notwithstanding, the salesperson's incentive is effectively sapped, since he or she gains no benefit from further sales. It is not unusual for salespeople in this situation to feel victimized by a policy engineered by greedy administrators. And, as will be seen in Chapter 11, once a salesperson sincerely feels that he or she has been treated unfairly by the company, a resignation cannot be far behind, particularly if the salesperson has been a consistently effective performer. As a rule, earnings ceilings are set by nonsales executives, their rationale being that it is bad for the morale of other employees to see salespeople benefit disproportionately to their efforts. The real reason is that either the company wants to save the incremental income or that certain executives feel that lower-level employees should not earn more than higher-level executives. However, in many highly effective firms, company presidents like to comment at gatherings that some of their salespeople's earnings exceed their own.

To enumerate all problems of compensation plans would require a great deal of time. The general cases indicated here, however, are among the most prevalent in American industry and are generally representative of the kinds of compensation problems that confront sales managers.

NONMONETARY REWARDS

One of the most widely discussed aspects of sales management is the administration of nonmonetary payment. Two major areas will be discussed here: sales contests and company benefits.

Sales Contests

There is a great deal of controversy over the efficacy of sales contests. The focal points of discussion seem to center on (1) whether or not the contest pays for itself through increased revenue, (2) whether or not the contest actually provided motivation to the sales force, and (3) whether or not the positive effects of the contest greatly outweigh the negative ones. The sales contest is a traditional tool used by sales managers to stimulate incrased sales through competition among sales-force members to achieve certain rewards. The psychic rewards have always been considered to be as important as the tangible rewards. Recognition by others and a feeling of personal achievement are perceived by most managers to be important priorities to salespeople, especially in light of their aggressive, ego-oriented, and competitive natures. Within this framework, sales contests are expected to result in not only an enthusiastic sales force but in additional sales *that the company would normally not have had otherwise*. The logic of the sales contest is based on its bringing in additional revenue with only a slight increase in variable costs.

Skeptics, on the other hand, claim that sales contests create an artificial or "phoney" air of enthusiasm, resulting in sales the majority of which would have been made anyway, and can also result in reduced morale through too heavy an emphasis on competition or through a thinly disguised, cynical process of manipulation.

In practice, sales contests have been characterized by both of the preceding situations, as well as by a complete range of results between the two. The success of the contest depends upon its objectives, the manner of competition used, and the type of people taking part in the contest. As can be readily imagined, organizations have used every kind of reward possible to make contests successful, but the results have been mixed.

Essentially, a sales contest succeeds when the sales-force members perceive the possible benefits as realistically attainable and worth the effort involved to achieve the desired reward. For this reason, it is not unusual that sales organizations often provide a carnivallike atmosphere and go to great lengths to promote contests. Yet in many cases they could have saved their time, energy, and money if sales-force members were not convinced that they would personally benefit. There is an enormous literature on sales contests, and a few general principles have evolved over the years.

Sales contests are more effective in direct-sales and commercial-sales organizations.

Contests are more effective when everyone *can win.*

A poorly administered contest is worse than no contest at all.

Money is probably the worst reward to give in a sales contest.

Possibly because of the ego needs peculiar to a certain sales type, contests seem to have more appeal to direct and commercial salespeople than to those in the consultative or technical fields. This group is further divided between order-taking and order-getting types of commercial salespeople. Predictibly, it is the latter group that responds more readily to contests. The most widely accepted explanation of this phenomenon is that the *recognition* factor, one of the critical elements of the sales contest, has more appeal to people who depend upon their persuasive ability for a livelihood than to those who sell on a more rational, well-ordered basis.

Because of differences in territory potential, no two salespeople have the same opportunity to win in an all-out competition for a reward. In addition, certain salespeople have a knack for performing well in contests, either because of a competitive attitude, because of knowledge of their customers, or for other reasons not readily discernible. Given these circumstances, it is clear that some antipathy can be expected if a contest is conducted without regard to handicaps. To avoid these problems, most contests are set up so that each salesperson is in competition with himself or herself rather than with the rest of the sales force. Certain targets are set, and when the salesperson reaches those objectives, the reward is provided. In any sales contest, however, the value of recognition cannot be underestimated. In many cases, it is more important to the recipient than the tangible reward.

Given the ups and downs of the selling profession, salespeople tend to become highly sensitive to other people's actions and reactions. Associated with this intensified sensitivity is a wariness of any attempt on the part of management to make changes in the normal routine. Probably because most salespeople at one time or another have been "burned" when management changed a compensation plan, redesigned territories, or initiated various changes, a veiled skepticism typically exists among most experienced salespeople whenever a sales contest is announced. The unfortunate aspect of this condition is that it tends to be a self-fulfilling prophecy when problems arise in sales contests. Unsuccessful or poorly thought out contests almost invariably provoke cynicism and negativism that would normally not exist. There are many aspects of contests that, if the sales force perceives them as being unfair, have the effect of undermining the contest. The rewards, for instance, should be worthwhile. Many organizations would prefer to spend too much money on prizes rather than to risk being called cheap by the sales force. If the targets are not realistic and attainable, management's credibility is also lessened. Many firms make the mistake of offering very valuable rewards, but at some level of sales that could only have been attained through some fortuitous windfall sale. In summary, when a sales force has become "turned off" by a sales contest, it normally takes at least several months before their confidence in management is restored.

Current thinking with regard to rewards in sales contests is that people will often respond to recognition with greater effort than other types of incentives. Of the more tangible incentives, it has been found that travel and, to a lesser extent, luxury items are most favored as premiums. The number of organizations whose function is to organize and maintain sales contests and provide the prizes is quite large. Most organizations in this business have determined that salespeople are not particularly motivated by cash rewards. Part of the reason for this is that in periods of inflation the money will simply be used to pay another bill, and part of the reason is that the salesperson's spouse will spend the money. In either case, the salesperson views the contest with a twist of irony. In essence, the extra effort he or she puts in is tantamount to working overtime because the rewards are identical. With vacations and luxury premiums, however, the salesperson views the process as providing the opportunity to win something that he or she would not otherwise have.

In summary, it can be said that contests can be very beneficial to both management and salesperson alike. Unfortunately, not every sales organization will gain the same degree of benefit from them.

Company Benefits

As various elements of our social system become less reticent to look for government to provide for many of their needs, so do employees look to firms in the private sector. Benefits have passed the stage of being a "fringe" of the compensation package; indeed, in many firms, the employee benefit costs run anywhere from 25 to 50 percent of monetary income. Hospitalization insurance no longer only provides for minimum care while confined, but covers dental care, eyeglass care, and many other health needs not envisioned even a decade ago. Table 8-1 shows various company benefits paid by sales organizations from a sample of 330 companies.

A summary of the benefits offered by firms participating in this survey revealed the following information:

97% paid all or part of the salesperson's hospitalization.
89% provide some sort of life insurance.
81% pay all or part of the salesperson's accident insurance.
34% allow salespeople some sort of profit sharing.
54% allow personal use of company car.
41% pay for memberships in clubs and associations.
63% pay all or part of educational expenses.
63% provide a salary continuation program.
43% provide dental insurance.
70% pay all or part of moving expenses.

One of the more important aspects of a compensation plan is that nonmonetary compensation should be taken into consideration when comparing compensation of two different jobs. In direct sales, for example, where very few benefits are paid, a salesperson would be required to earn nearly twice as much as a salesperson working with a large firm in order to duplicate the total package received by the latter. Part of this is because of lower group costs, but the major part is due to the relatively high income tax rate, which does not deduct a significant amount of

TABLE 8-1

Percentage of Companies Paying All or Part of Company Benefits

	Salary Plan		Commission Plan		Combination Plan	
	1979	1977	1979	1977	1979	1977
Hospital insurance	100%	99%	80%	94%	100%	99%
Accident insurance	89	85	65	74	89	88
Life insurance	99	94	69	85	96	93
Dental insurance	60	35	39	15	53	27
Educational assistance	74	65	40	38	76	68
Profit sharing	49	38	29	38	47	40
Pension plan	69	59	34	30	72	66
Stock purchase	22	21	26	13	28	22
Personal use of company car	53	58	28	26	62	57
Club/association membership	55	48	19	28	40	36
Salary continuation program	68	72	31	36	63	68
Moving expense	67	64	42	40	74	74

Source: *Compensation of Salesmen: Dartnell's 20th Bienniel Survey* (Chicago: Dartnell Corporation, 1980) p. 74.

fringe benefit premiums. Even though the 1040 form does indicate that certain deductions for health insurance may be taken, closer inspection of the IRS formula reveals that the de facto deduction is quite small.

Each benefit carries a different value for every salesperson, but the array of benefits adds a significant amount to the total pay package and must be taken into consideration in any type of compensation analysis.

SUMMARY

There are essentially three types of payment plans for salespeople: straight salary, straight commission, and combination plans. Straight salary is paid in situations where the firm finds it difficult to trace a direct link between a salesperson's efforts and his or her quantitative productivity. The prevailing notion that salaried salespeople have less motivation than other sales types has never been proved or disproved; however, very successful firms pay their salespeople on the basis of straight salary. Straight commission is typically paid either by companies in poor financial condition or by companies that essentially set up their salespeople in an independent business. Insurance companies are the best example of this. Combination plans consist of a salary and an incentive payment based on productivity. About half of all companies use a combination plan when compensating salespeople. This method of payment combines the positive features of both the other plans.

Certain major problems are common to many compensation plans. Some plans favor only a few salespeople, in other firms there exists too great a reliance on incentives as a motivating factor, and a third major problem is the company's reduction of sales salaries to reduce costs, a practice that inexorably leads to turnover.

There are essentially two important kinds of nonmonetary incentives: (1) prizes and premiums awarded for performance in sales contests and (2) company benefits. Current research indicates that sales contests are not only sometimes ineffective, but can actually have negative consequences if not administered properly. It is the opinion of many professionals that money is not an effective reward in sales contests. While company benefits are relatively intangible and even abstract, they are nevertheless an important part of any compensation package, sometimes costing as much as 50 percent of the salesperson's monetary payment.

Bob and Mike

Bob Pitts is sales manager for a branch of a well-known uniform supply firm. The salespeople reporting to him are provided with a company vehicle and are located in geographical territories. Each salesperson has several large accounts and is expected to add new accounts every week. Since competition is very brisk, it is not unusual for even good salespeople to lose accounts from time to time. Most firms in the industry have similar prices and similar services. The majority of the sales-force members have been with the firm for several years and are good at what they do. There is no question in Bob's mind, or anyone else's, for that matter, that the sales representatives have established an informal set of rules among themselves with respect to what constitutes a good day's work. It is not unusual to drive by one or two bars at certain times, particularly when a big horse race or ball game is being televised, and see several of the firm's trucks parked within a discreet distance. What disgusts Bob is that there are also several of his competitors' trucks parked in the same general area.

In discussing the situation with Mike Parker, the vice-president of marketing, it was pointed out to Bob that even, if some of the salespeople were fired to set an example, others would come in and take their place. "Besides," Mike advised, "most of our people are very knowledgeable. You'd just be cutting off your nose to spite your face."

The compensation plan as it exists presently consists of a base salary, which constitutes about 90 percent of their income; the remainder is a bonus paid on sales volume.

Bob has given the problem consideration and has decided that a sales contest might solve the problem, at least temporarily.

1. What do you think of Bob Pitts' idea of the sales contest as a possible solution to the problem?
2. What would you advise Bob to do?

The Last Compensation Plan

J. D. Purran is the national sales manager for Band Stereo Corporation, a distributor of audio components, located in San Francisco, California. The corporation recently acquired distribution rights to an imported line of mobile communications equipment that is manufactured in Japan. Mr. Purran and his regional managers, Joe Farrell, Earl McIntyre, Howard Shaw, and Garth Hudson, have been considering dissolving the sales organization, since the existing line has not been particularly profitable. Unfortunately, a different type of expertise is required, so it will be necessary to hire about thirty new salespeople. Mr. Purran and his colleagues are interested in developing a compensation plan that will provide an incentive to salespeople. They are convinced that part of the problem with Band Stereo was that the sales effort was less than it should have been.

The former compensation provided salespersons with a salary, all expenses, a company car, and a bonus equal to about 10 percent of annual salary. Most salespeople made the majority of their sales to large accounts. Because of quantity discounts, the profit margin on these sales was considerably lower than that realized in selling to smaller users. An analysis of records showed that very few small users had been contacted on a regular basis. During the meeting, one of the managers remarked that most of his salespeople were good enough golfers to qualify for the PGA tour. It was generally conceded that the compensation plan did little to stimulate a concentrated effort. The managers want to develop a plan now that will be equitable to the salespeople, will stimulate deeper penetration, and will be profitable to the company. They want this compensation plan to be a permanent one.

1. Based on the preceding information, what kind of compensation plan would you suggest?
2. What other types of sales compensation plan might you consider as alternatives?

DISCUSSION QUESTIONS

1. What are the major factors that determine the type of pay plan used for salespeople?
2. What are the three major types of compensation plan?
3. What are the two major types of salary plan?
4. What are the advantages and disadvantages of the straight commission type of sales compensation plan?
5. What are the advantages and disadvantages of the combination type of sales compensation plan?
6. What are the major problems associated with sales compensation plans?
7. What are the advantages and disadvantages of sales contests?
8. What major trends exist with respect to benefit programs?

NOTES

[1]John K. Moynahan, "How to Direct Your Sales Compensation Program toward Specific Goals," *Sales and Marketing Management*, Sept. 20, 1979, p. 94.

[2]"A Better Way," *Sales and Marketing Management,* April 9, 1979, p. 14.

[3]Steven X. Doyle and Benson P. Shapiro, "What Counts Most in Motivating Your Sales Force," *Harvard Business Review,* May–June 1980, p. 133–140.

[4]Compensation of Salesmen: Dartnell's 20th Bienniel Survey (Chicago: Dartnell Corporation, 1980), p. 40.

[5]Dartnell, ibid

[6]Ross A. Webber, Management: basic elements of managing organizations (Homewood, Ill. Irwin, 1979) p. 64.

[7]F. J. Roethlisberger and W. J. Dickson, *Management and the Worker* (Cambridge, Mass.: Harvard University Press, 1939).

[8]William F. Whyte, *Money and Motivation,* (New York: Harper, 1955).

[9]David C. McClelland, "Money as a Motivator: Some Research Insights," *The McKinsey Quarterly*, Vol. 3 (Fall, 1967) pp. 10-21.

[10]G. W. Hofstede "The Colors of Collars" *Columbia Journal of World Business*, Vol. 7, No. 5 (1972) pp. 72-79.

CHAPTER 9

ORGANIZING THE SALES FORCE

OBJECTIVES

To examine the classic organization structures:

* Specialized product line sales
* Selling through customer organizations
* Direct-sales organization

To show cost-effective territorial alignments.

To analyze the organization of the local sales office.

INTERVIEW WITH FRANK SMITH

Interviewer: I always got a kick out of the cartoon that depicts two managers with cluttered desks with the caption, "next week we've got to get organized."

Frank Smith: That would be a laugher if it weren't so true. There is some disorganization in all of us.

Interviewer: I've noticed that in most areas, the sales organization simply seems to evolve over a period of years, that as Chandler pointed out, structure must follow strategy.

Frank Smith: Right. It's important that the structure not get in the way of the objectives of the organization, too.

Interviewer: Have you found the structure and organization of most sales organizations you've been associated with to be flexible enough to meet changing needs?

Frank Smith: In the most part I have. A good sales organization always has one ear to the ground and is responsive to changing needs as they occur. For example, if the need arises for more staff people, a good organization provides them. No matter how organized you get, though, you can outsmart yourself if your policies are too rigid.

Interviewer: Good point. One of the things we talk about in this chapter is the typical branch organization. Do you think one model is representative of most firms?

Frank Smith: Yes, more or less. There are more commonalities than differences among most sales branches. Let's take a look at some of the organizational factors in the chapter now.

In most organizations, some overall corporate strategy is developed, and then an organization structure is designed to fit the needs of the firm's strategic approach. It is important that the structure of the organization not lag behind or precede the strategy that it is designed to accommodate. By the same token, certain marketing strategies are developed, and the sales force is organized to aid in the attainment of strategic objectives. This chapter investigates some of the more common approaches to sales-force organization that exist in U.S. business and industry.

CLASSIC SALES ORGANIZATION STRUCTURES

In Chapter 3, we examined the "typical" sales organization, observing at that point that the structure presented was overly simplistic. In sales organizations the product or service sold and the type of customer have a great effect on how the sales force is organized. As a general rule, technical sales organizations are a bit more complex than are the other three, probably because of the relatively large amount of support that is provided by technical specialists, many of whom have no formal authority but do, in fact, have a great deal of informal authority.

In the consultative field, the majority of organizations function on an account basis. The salesperson is assigned certain organizations on a local, regional, or national basis and is expected to become intimately familiar with the workings of those companies. Because it often requires a great deal of time to gain an awareness of the customer and, more importantly, the people in the customer organization, consultative salespeople typically keep their major accounts for a long period of time. Sales managers in the consultative sales field tend to have relatively a broad organization, with several salespeople reporting to one manager.

The sales manager might be in one location and the sales force spread out all over the country, or the majority might work out of the same office. It is sometimes easy to become confused, because consultative salespeople often use the term "manager" in their titles. The term implies that other people report to him or her, but that is not the case. The title is simply used to indicate that the salesperson is the "account" manager or has responsibility for several *accounts*. Actually, he or she is the manager of no one, although the title would imply otherwise. This title is used (or misused) by the majority of consultative-sales firms in describing their sales-force members.

Most of the larger firms in the United States are in an oligopolistic market, the result being that several firms in one industry often have similar sales organization structures. Another characteristic of American industry is that virtually all salespeople who work for large firms are of either the technical or commercial sales type. Although each firm has its own unique sales organization structure, it may be said with confidence that there are a limited number of *types* of sales organization in relatively large firms. A "large" firm is described here rather arbitrarily as falling within the *Fortune* 2000 list of firms ranked by sales volume.

Complete Product or Specialized Product Line Sales

Most organizations sell several different products, and several factors determine which of the firm's products should be sold by its sales force. One important consideration is the amount of capital that a firm has available to support a field sales force. In some cases, one salesperson will sell his or her company's entire product line simply because the firm does not have the resources available to place more than one sales force in the field. Another consideration is whether or not the products being sold require the same or a different selling technique. If a salesperson sells, for example, a complete line of pharmaceuticals, the relative expertise required to sell these products would not be appreciably different if one or more formulas were added to the product line. If, on the other hand, medical electronic equipment were added to the product line, the relative expertise required would probably be appreciably different in both product knowledge and sales technique.

Another factor of great importance in the structuring of a sales organization is the customer who is called upon. Some companies prefer to have their salespeople call at all levels of a customer organization, while other firms prefer to have their salespeople call at only a few different levels. In an interview with the author, a sales manager in the industrial field made the following comments:

> We have a competitor who is about half our size but who competes very effectively with us in several product areas. We sell a pump that is pretty similar to theirs and they sell an extractor that is very close to ours in nearly every respect. The thing that is sometimes difficult to understand is that they use a product specialist to sell the extractor but we use our regular sales force to sell ours. For several years our market shares have been similar and between the two of us, we have a very large market share. We feel as though our people do a good job and I know our competitor is not unhappy with the results they are getting. About six years ago, we tried to use different salespeople who specialized in extractors but it didn't work out at all. Our sales fell, and they didn't get back up until we went back to the old configuration. Their sales manager has told me privately that they were considering doing it our way by using their regular sales force but they decided against it. We're happy with the way we do it, and they're happy with the way they do it. We have two different approaches to the same market opportunity and yet they both work quite well.

It is not unusual to see different organizations use a different sales structure in the same marketplace and both have the same degree of success. As a matter of fact, nearly every major industry is characterized by at least one successful firm that utilizes a different approach to the marketplace. As an example, the publishers of this textbook follow the strategy of using sales specialists who call on professors in specific academic disciplines. The nearest competitor uses essentially the same sales strategy, but the next competitor's salespeople call on professors in every discipline. Yet each of the three firms enjoys a great deal of success in the marketplace. In the consumer products field, one manufacturer of a leading pet food uses salespeople who sell only pet food products to customers. Their two leading competitors, however, use salespeople who sell a complete line of food products, pet food being only one of several. Yet, as in the textbook example, all three firms are successful in selling pet food.

In cases where specialized products require specialized salespeople, it is not unusual for a firm to have several different divisions broken down organizationally with sales offices throughout the country. An example would be PPG Industries. In most cities, there are separate sales offices for the glass division and the chemical division. There are no organizational lines whatsoever, and any contact between the two divisions on the field level is on an informal basis, except with respect to company matters that transcend operational goals, such as a new corporate policy on affirmative action or some other omnibus matter. Du Pont Corporation is broken down in much the same way, with the concession that in many cities more than one division sales office is housed in the same building or in the same suite of offices. In summary, the classic structure of several sales offices in the larger SMSA's is the most widely used structure. On the other hand, corporate considerations may dictate that individual products be sold either by a specialist or a generalist.

Selling through Customer Sales Organizations

Many firms sell products to distributors, who in turn, resell the product to many small customers. Typically, products sold in this manner are consumer products or industrial products that would require an inordinately high number of the manufacturer's salespeople if the product was sold to the end user by the manufacturer.

Clearly, the term "distributor" is somewhat general. If the term is to be interpreted as "someone who distributes something," then a distributor might be very large or very small. As an introductory marketing course points out, there are selective distributors, intensive distributors, and exclusive distributors. The factors determining the type of distributors that the manufacturer will deal with depend a great deal upon the general demand for the product and the distributor's ability to sell it. For the purposes of exposition, we will make the assumption that a company manufacturers and sells pumps, a product used in nearly every industrial application. Most distributors of pumps are firms that also distribute several other industrial products. It should be clear that for the firm to sell the product directly to the end user many salespeople would be required.

In this case, one company salesperson typically has a sales territory that covers several states. His or her title typically includes the term "manager." Even though the salesperson has no subordinates, firms feel that the title implies that the salesperson possesses some additional expertise or corporate authority. The salesperson typically calls on the largest distributors the most frequently and the smallest distributors the least frequently. When a particular account shows signs of developing a larger potential or seems to "push" the product, the salesperson generally spends more time at the account. It is not at all unusual for a pump distributor to handle competing lines; therefore, the salesperson from the manufacturer spends a great deal of time performing an educational function, training the distributor's salespeople and accompanying them on calls. In most cases, the more interest the salesperson shows in the distributor's needs, the more the distributor will "push" the salesperson's product. This formula does not always work, of course, but for the most part the manufacturer's salesperson is in a strong position to influence his or her firm's sales even though the final sale is made by distributor salespeople. In an interview with the author, a sales representative for a midwestern firm selling to distributors made the following observation:

> It's amazing how some distributors are so backward in their sales operations and yet others have a great deal of sophistication. Our field representatives can work with a firm that has little or no sales expertise and put that firm on an equal sales level with a more sales-oriented competitor. That is one of the reasons why our salespeople are so important. They're technical salespeople but they still have to be able to persuade, and for that matter, perform the motivating functions without the authority to back it up. Selling to distributors is a totally different ballgame than a direct company sales force because you don't have the authority to make your customer's sales personnel do anything. They have to be convinced.

Selling a product through other firms is not unusual in selling. Yet there are few industries where every firm in the industry uses the same sales channels.[1] Even the major television set manufacturers employ their own sales force when selling to hospitals and motels.

A second very important customer sales channel is the food broker. Because of the enormous expenditures on food each year, firms in the food brokerage industry are a very significant part of the consumer products industry. Food brokers essentially function as a distributor, except that the broker may or may not carry competing products, depending upon the terms of the agreement between the manufacturer and the broker. The food broker calls on retail and wholesale outlets that sell traditional food and nonfood items. Rather than employ direct salespeople who call on individual chains and stores, some manufacturers prefer to pay a commission to a food broker to sell the manufacturer's products. In some cases, because of the rapport between a food broker and an account, manufacturers find it advantageous to utilize the food broker's services because it is easier (or the only way) to get certain products into stores. Clearly, there are many combinations of possible relationships between manufacturers and food brokers. Although an in-depth analysis of these possibilities will not be made here, we have outlined the essential elements of the manufacturer-broker relationship.

A different type of relationship exists between organizations and manufacturer's representatives. Since "reps" constitute such an important factor in the sales field, an entire chapter will be used to describe the nature of that relationship. Essentially, manufacturers representatives act as agents for firms in place of that firm's own sales personnel, but still remain independent businesspeople, a situation that leads to a relatively complex and sometimes turbulent relationship.

Direct-Sales Organization

The previous section outlined generally the typical sales organization in the consultative, technical, and commercial fields. The typical firm selected was national in scope. In the direct-sales field, a large number of firms are organized on a local level. Because of the high number of firms that enter and leave the marketplace in the direct field, it is difficult to find accurate or timely statistics relating to this field. As indicated previously, life insurance and mutual fund companies make up a substantial proportion of direct-sales firms that are organized on a national level. The automobile industry has more direct salespeople than the insurance industry, but the sales policies of individual dealers vary. The next largest group organized on a national basis is the direct-sales cosmetic field, an industry dominated by three major national companies.

The remainder of the direct-sales field is composed of a few industries in which the major firms are organized on a national basis. These industries are not necessarily ones that have been in existence for a long time. Business opportunities sales, for instance, appear to have supplanted the Florida or Arizona land companies that were as visible a decade ago. Both industries use a sales approach designed to satisfy the consumer's need for financial independence.

The direct-sales field is also composed of a large number of firms that are regional, state-wide or even city-wide in scope. These firms sell a variety of consumer goods and services, ranging from home improvements and basement waterproofing to a variety of services such as airline stewardess training and collections of books on *Great Women in American History*.

The organization of an insurance firm, which sells on a national basis, is more formalized and structured than a locally based direct-sales firm. Most insurance sales organizations consist of hundreds of agencies reporting to regional sales managers for administrative counsel, but the authority relationship between the branch manager or *general agent* and his or her direct supervisor is not the same as it is in most field sales situations. The *general agent* is, in effect, an independent entrepreneur who is supported by the firm to some extent outlined in the contract between the two parties. Contrary to popular opinion, neither the general agent nor the sales-force members are direct employees of the insurance company.

Rather, the salespeople *represent* the insurance company, but they are actually employed by the general agent. Each city has several general agents, but their relationship is not the same as that of, say, two branch managers employed by IBM or Champion Paper. The agents typically have no organizational relationship with each other, unless one of the general agents managers is a satellite unit for the other. On the other hand, all agencies receive extensive support from the home office with respect to training, marketing expertise, and sales communications in general. It can be seen from this description that insurance firms are somewhat specialized in the way they organize their sales forces.

On the other hand, most locally owned direct-sales operations are organized on a very informal basis. There are few lines of authority except between the owner of the firm and everyone else. In many cases, owners communicate directly with salespeople with or without the sales manager's knowledge. Sales managers are, for the most part, supportive of this approach since the absence of a chain of command usually relieves the sales manager from the normal responsibilities that accrue to most sales managers. Indeed, typically the only aspect of the entire sales organization that is truly "organized" is the generation of leads. In many small direct-sales firms, lead generation and administration is often the sales manager's only function. Generally, even though there are probably in excess of 25,000 small direct-sales firms (this figure includes insurance firms), it is very difficult to describe a classic organizational firm.

Cost-Effective Territorial Alignment

In the face of increased gasoline costs, and inflation in general, sales costs have increased greatly over the past few years, resulting in a general reconsideration of the alignment of sales territories. To illustrate the dramatic impact of increasing sales costs, five different cost elements will be examined in historical perspective: the average cost of making a sales call, cost of a hotel room, cost of dinner, cost of renting a car and cost of attending a sales meeting.*

Average Cost of a Sales Call, 1980:

Consultative sales	*$46.00 to $90.00*
Commercial sales	*25.00 to 58.00*
Technical sales	*41.00 to 82.00*

Several organizations provide annual data relating to the average cost of a sales call. Clearly, this cost is higher in some product line areas than others, and it should also be clear that the figures used in determining actual costs might be rough estimates. Nevertheless, the important factor is the *relative* increase in the cost of making a sales call. In the period 1979 to 1980, this figure increased 11

*All figures are from *Sales and Marketing Management,* May 1980.

percent compared to the consumer price index increase of 8 percent over the same period.

Cost of a Hotel or Motel Room, 1980:		
New York City	*$54.72*	*$145.00*
Chicago	*51.00*	*84.00*
Atlanta	*39.50*	*72.00*

The relative increase in lodging cost has increased, on the average, about 9 percent compared to an increase of 8 percent in the consumer price index over the same period.

Median Cost of Dining out for One Person, 1980:	
New York City	*$18.00*
Chicago	*14.65*
Atlanta	*12.60*

The cost of a dinner, usually measured as including the cost of two drinks, has also risen out of proportion to the consumer price index.

Cost of Renting a Car, 1980:	
New York City	*$62.90*
Chicago	*62.10*
Atlanta	*62.70*

Auto rental costs have increased dramatically. Not unexpectedly, these prices have also risen more quickly than the consumer price index.

Median Cost of Attending a Sales Meeting, 1980:	
New York City	*$102.65 per day*
Chicago	*83.90*
Atlanta	*76.95*

One of the major costs of communications in sales organizations is that of providing sales meetings for representatives. This cost has also outstripped inflation.

The purpose in showing the dramatic increases in sales costs over recent years has been to emphasize the need for efficient organization of the sales force. When a sales organization establishes a territory, for example, certain costs will be expended during the year regardless of productivity in that territory. When sales territories have been intelligently aligned so that sales potentials are approximately equal, the greatest cost effectiveness is achieved. At the same time, it is highly important to organize territories in such a way that optimum *profits* rather than optimum sales are derived. The *contribution margin* or difference between sales and variable costs is the cost-related area that has the greatest impact upon determination of profits.[2]

These concepts will be discussed in detail in Chapter 14, but it is important that the reader be aware of the necessity of organizing the sales force on a cost-effective basis.

ORGANIZATION OF THE LOCAL SALES OFFICE

Although every product line requires somewhat different administrative functions to be performed at local or branch sales offices, the basic apparatus for handling administrative requirements is similar. Products or services, whether they are shipped from a nearby or from a distant place, must be delivered to customers in a timely and efficient manner.

Customer inquiries or complaints must be handled courteously and tactfully. Service from both a technical and humanistic standpoint must be provided at the local level. Although billing and collection functions are typically performed at the home office or at the regional level, local administrative management must be sensitive to any and all misunderstandings or communication gaps that could result in loss of revenue and customers alike.

In addition to providing outreach to customers and prospects, a great deal of administrative communications must be passed back and forth to other offices of the organization. Just as an army, if it is to be successful, must have an effective organization supporting its movements, the sales force requires effective administrative support if a wide customer base is to be developed and maintained.

As indicated previously, no two sales offices are alike and no two industries are alike. The sales office depicted in this chapter will be termed "typical," but it should be understood that many differentiating factors render the organization of each local sales office unique. Product line, types of customers, technical expertise of the sales force, and overall mission of the organization all tend to add to that uniqueness. The typical sales office depicted in Figure 9-1 is intended to help describe some of the members of the local sales office team and their duties and responsibilities.

Branch Manager

According to the organization chart in Figure 9-1, the branch manager is the chief executive in the local sales office, with his or her secretary, assistant branch manager, technical or service manager, office manager, and about one half of the sales force having direct reporting relationships. In actual practice, few branch managers feel compelled to use the chain of command in communicating with anyone in the branch. Typically, authority relationships, although very clear, are practiced on an informal basis. It is unusual for any salesperson *not* to have direct access to a branch manager in nearly any sales office.

Figure 9-1

Typical Local or Branch Sales Office

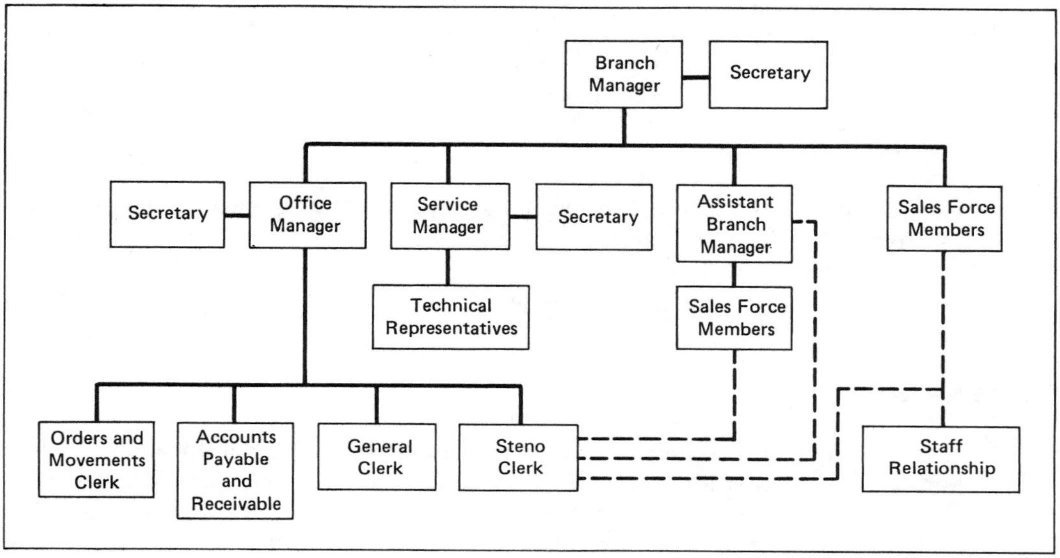

Secretaries

As in most administrative organizations, the secretary to the branch manager typically exercises some authority, either formal or informal, over the other secretaries in the office. This is an important point, because the branch manager's secretary is normally required to use a relatively good deal of judgment and discretion when her supervisor is both in and out of the office. Most salespeople feel that a good relationship with this person is helpful and that a poor relationship is often detrimental to the salesperson's immediate needs.

While the secretary to the service manager is typically responsible solely for service functions, the secretary to the office manager also must exercise a great deal of judgment and discretion from time to time. Often the office manager and the secretary to this individual are privy to information not even known to the branch manager.

Assistant Branch Manager

The position of assistant branch manager is a stepping-stone to the position of branch manager. The assistant manager is normally responsible to the branch manager, and typically about one half the salespeople in the office report to this individual. In some respects this is a unique situation in that the assistant rarely earns much more than an above-average salesperson. The unique nature of the assistant sales manager's position was summed up by an executive in commercial sales.

> Being Assistant Branch Manager in most companies is similar to the kid who graduates from college and goes to work in his father's business. Most people who were there before him have little or no respect for him and the older ones are often openly contemptuous. Even the Office Manager gets called "Mister," "Miss" or "Mrs.," but not the Assistant Manager. Did you ever see a Branch Manager's secretary put the squeeze on the Assistant Manager? It's got to be pretty funny in a sadistic sort of way. I went through it and so did most of the managers in this company. It teaches you a little humility and I never saw anybody who didn't take it with good grace.

Because of the assistant manager's position as a future branch manager, he or she seldom earns more than an above-average salesperson. Despite this person's low status, however, he or she is a very important member of the team, since his or her actions have virtually the same impact on the sales force as those of the sales manager.

Service Manager

This individual reports to the branch manager and is typically accorded very high status in any sales office. The service manager is consistently deluged with requests from salespeople to provide priority treatment, and most service managers usually attempt to accommodate salespeople, even though there is no formal reporting relationship with the salesperson and they are not required to do so. A salesman with a large corporation made the following statement to the author:

> I've been with the company for fifteen years and any office I ever worked in the Service Manager was the one who kept the customers away from our jugular veins. They are all the same—always help you—even when they know you got yourself into the situation. There must be some kind of pill they give Service Managers. They always maintain their cool and get the job done. The salespeople in the competitive firms tell me it's the same way there, too. I'll tell you one thing—I never worked in a sales office where the Service Manager didn't have an enormous amount of respect from everybody in the office.

While there are clearly some incompetent service managers, most sales managers, at least those in firms known for effective marketing policies, would probably corroborate the preceding statement.

Office Manager

The office manager is the ranking administrative executive. In the typical sales office, this person reports directly to the branch manager, but works closely with the service manager, assistant manager, and individual sales-force members. In most sales offices, members of the sales force typically communicate directly with the office manager without going through the branch manager. This type of informal communication often places the office manager in the position of being required to expedite several situations simultaneously, a situation not consistent with sound administrative theory. Salespeople often tend to communicate with the administrative staff directly, bypassing both the branch manager and the office manager. As a rule, certain communications of this type, such as asking a clerk for a delivery date, are encouraged, while other direct communications with the office manager's staff, such as asking for a delivery date *change*, are considered taboo. To maintain the sanity of the office manager, most offices have unwritten agreements between sales and administration as to what can be communicated verbally, what must be communicated in writing, and what communications can be initiated by salespersons to administrative employees.

Administrative Clerks

Although this group occupies the lower level of the branch office pecking order, their influence upon orders and shipments, customer complaints, billings, and other factors that directly influence sales commission payments is great. Salespeople are obviously sensitive to this fact and must therefore treat all the clerical personnel with tact and discretion. In most sales offices a dispute between a salesperson and an administrative clerk normally results in the office manager's taking the clerk's side, with a concurrent lack of sympathy on the part of the branch manager for the salesperson. After one or more confrontations, most salespersons learn to show respect for administrative clerks. Most offices employ a clerk-steno who types salespersons' paper work but does not report directly to sales-force members. Likewise, the other clerks, most of whose work affects the sales force, also have no reporting relationship with salespeople. The net result of this situation is that salespeople can influence, but not change, clerical behavior.

While the preceding description may not simulate precisely every branch sales office, it does provide an idea of the various members of the sales office team and their relative reporting relationships. This type of arrangement is fairly common and has also proved to be effective in most cases.

STAFF SPECIALISTS

Most sales organizations, at either the district or regional level, employ specialists in certain technical areas who visit local offices on a regional basis. These specialists might have a particular product expertise that is used on customer calls with individual salespeople on a first-come, first-served basis. The product specialist is also available to "fight fires" in various accounts, and this function might constitute the specialist's major time priority.

Another specialty area is in sales training. Although this function is the ultimate responsibility of the sales manager, additional help is often provided by a training specialist who either visits periodically or when some additional training is required for the entire sales staff.

Although most managers do not necessarily interpret his or her visits as being overly "helpful," most district and/or regional managers typically have a staff assistant. This individual is typically performing the function of "assistant-to" as a stepping-stone to some line managerial position. Visits by this staff person are often carried out to determine the local manager's effectiveness in both administrative and sales management functions, hence the occasional negative reaction to this individual's visits. Objectively, however, such visits are often necessary and have the effect of tightening up local sales management and company policies as well.

For the most part, staff specialists are considered to be highly beneficial and helpful to sales managers.

SUMMARY

This chapter has examined some of the classic patterns of sales force organization. The structure of the sales organization is greatly determined by the firm's marketing strategies. The classic organizational forms typically include salespeople who sell one product or several products. There are logical reasons why most firms are organized with a particular sales-force configuration.

Organizations sometimes use distributors or other outside organizations to sell their product lines. The factors determining the efficacy of channel relationships of this type are based on specific market, customer, and product characteristics. Some firms also use manufacturers' representatives, and many organizations that sell the traditional grocery store items use food brokers to sell at the store or chain level.

For a firm to effectively organize its sales force, territories must be cost-effectively aligned. Much of the details of cost-effective management will be discussed in Chapter 14.

The organization of a local office is relatively similar in most organizations, with the branch manager acting as the chief operating executive who is responsible for the entire sales and administrative functions. Important nonsales personnel are the service manager and the office manager, each performing critical functions.

Most local offices have available the services of various staff specialists to help solve existing problems or to create an environment where problems are discouraged from arising.

Atlas Power Supply

The newly formed Atlas Power Supply Company sold many hundreds of small semiconductor power supplies of six different types and specifications at prices ranging from as low as $10 to $175 each. They knew they had a state-of-the-art design using new semiconductors and packaging principles and were competing in a vast field with a potential for hundreds of thousands or even millions of units if the price, quality, quantity, and delivery schedules could be properly developed. They had only relatively modest financial backing and would need time to build up credibility in manufacturing and financing generally and costs specifically.

Jay Berkely accepted the challenging post of sales manager with only five year's experience in the component sales field. The new owners asked him to develop a marketing strategy plan that would optimize their short- and long-range growth and profit positions.

He knew this product could be sold directly from the plant through advertising, by direct salespeople in key locations, by manufacturing sales representatives, and through distributors. He also knew if he initially priced his product too low or had too disproportionate a sales program, he might get more orders than they could possibly fulfill at prices that could bankrupt them. On the other hand, if he was not aggressive enough with the proper potential customers, he might irretrievably lose the opportunity to be designed in for the high-volume future.

1. What are the questions Jay should ask the owners to answer regarding their capabilities, plans, and responsiveness and risk taking?
2. What sort of sales organizations should he have initially?
3. Assuming the company proves successful at manufacturing, engineering, and finance, what sort of sales organization should he be planning in five years?

WFMP

WFMP is a small radio station operating out of an old railroad station in Horsheigie, New Jersey. The office staff consists of Sam Nordwick, a combination head disc jockey and station manager and a force of three men and one woman who sell "air time" within a 200-mile broadcasting radius. Each salesperson has the responsibility of making the sale, writing up the copy, sending out invoices, and collecting on overdue accounts.

The station is owned by a president who "always wanted to have a radio station of his own." Since he bought the station, he changed the format from popular punk rock to soft oldies, because in his words, "people with money for advertising don't want to hear that junk." He will often call the station manager if he hears a song with the wrong sort of lyric or beat being played and berate him heartily for trying to put something over on him.

Sam, on the other hand, insists that the president's choice of music is responsible for his dwindling sales volume, which has been decreasing since the stations music format changed. Sam holds weekly sales meetings to try and build up station enthusiasm and boost sales. These meetings consist primarily of Sam ranting and raving at his sales force, threatening to fire them if they don't do better, and in general picking out the low man on the totem pole in terms of selling volume and making him look like a dim-witted fool. This is Sam's idea of sales management.

The sales force, on the other hand, insist their poor performance is not their fault. New customers are just not interested in radio as an effective selling tool or at least not that radio station, and repeat customers insist that they are not getting results from past advertising campaigns. Meanwhile, the president has commented that not only is sales volume decreasing, but the monthly expense accounts turned in have risen alarmingly.

The station as a whole can barely cover the employee's weekly paychecks, and the president has made it clear he has no money for any "fancy" analysis. Weekly meetings are turning into frustrating blind alleys.

1. How could you reorganize the sales force?
2. How can Sam analyze the marketplace?

DISCUSSION QUESTIONS

1. What are the essential elements of a sales force organized by product line?
2. What are some examples of companies that sell by product line?
3. What is meant by the term "distributor"?
4. What are the functions of the food broker?
5. What is meant by the term *contribution margin*? What is its significance in sales?
6. What is a typical branch sales office organization?
7. Where are staff specialists commonly used in sales organizations?
8. What is meant by a classic sales force organized by "account"?

NOTES

[1]E. Jerome McCarthy, *Basic Marketing,* (Homewood, Ill.: Irwin, 1978).

[2]Mack Hanan, Howard Berrian, and James Cribbin, *Take-Charge of Sales Management* (New York: AMACOM, 1976), p. 56.

CHAPTER 10

SALES PLANNING

OBJECTIVES

To discuss various types of sales forecasting techniques:
* Jury of executive opinion
* Use of estimates by salespeople
* Time series analysis
* Econometric techniques

To determine territorial sales potential.

To examine the annual marketing plan.

To investigate the marketing information system.

INTERVIEW WITH FRANK SMITH

Interviewer: Frank, I know that as a branch manager you get involved in planning, but do you think that it's really possible to plan for five or ten years into the future?

Frank Smith: Well, obviously the longer you plan ahead, the less your chances are of being correct. But you don't have to read a textbook to know that.

Interviewer: That's true, but do you have any special formulas at your firm that help you forecast years ahead as to what your sales will be?

Frank Smith: Nobody does. We do, however, try to reduce the parameters. Remember in Economics, you'd hear about conditions of certainty, risk, and uncertainty? What we try to do is reduce our chances from *uncertainty* to *risk*. You never have *certainty*.

Interviewer: What is your opinion of *econometric* techniques?

Frank Smith: Although I'm pretty far removed from home office planning, I find that some mathematical techniques are better than others. For example, we've been fairly successful using one or two fairly sophisticated techniques that most people feel are off the wall. On the other hand, our input at the branch level is very important, too.

Interviewer: Do you think a lot of local sales managers feel that they really don't have any real say in forecasting sales?

Frank Smith: It depends on the firm. I know our forecasts here are considered important at *every* level.

Interviewer: Do you think your ideas are used when your firm develops its annual marketing plan?

Frank Smith: Yes, but I think it would be a little more helpful if we went through the chapter and tried to explain these terms, and then we can see why local managers do or don't get involved to any great extent in the planning function.

The importance of the planning function as one of the key activities of the sales manager was examined briefly in Chapter 3. This chapter will investigate some specific aspects of planning that have an impact upon the sales effectiveness of the local sales organization and, in turn, the effectiveness of the entire organization. The chapter will discuss the sales forecasting function and some relevant techniques, the determination of territorial potential, the marketing plan, and relevant aspects of the marketing information system. All these areas are discussed within the framework of sales management and their impact upon the sales manager and his or her salespeople.

SALES FORECASTING

The longer the term of the sales forecast, the farther removed is the branch-level sales manager from the decision process that determines the type and the sophistication of the firm's forecasting techniques. The sales manager is normally always responsible for providing certain input, however. This section will discuss various specific forecasting techniques and their applications in sales management.

In light of today's instable and inflationary economy, the need for accurate forecasting is critical. There are a fairly wide variety of forecasting methods, and the firm's choice of specific techniques is a function of several factors. Paramount among these factors is the length of time into the future that the forecast attempts to predict. Clearly, the long-term forecast is subject to uncertain conditions. Indeed, the businessperson's inability to cope with unforeseen circumstances prompted Lord Keynes to point out:

> This battle of wits to anticipate the basis of conventional valuation a few months hence, rather than the prospective yield of an investment over a long term of years, does not even require gulls amongst the public to feed the maws of the professional; it can be played by professionals amongst themselves. Nor is it necessary that anyone should keep his simple faith in the conventional basis of valuation having any general long-term validity. For it is, so to speak, a game of Snap, of Old Maid, of Musical Chairs—a pastime in which he is victor who says *Snap* neither too soon nor too late, who passes the Old Maid to his neighbor before the game is over, who secures a chair for himself before the music stops. These games can be played with zest and enjoyment, though all the players know that it is the Old Maid which is circulating, or that when the music stops some of the players will find themselves unseated.[1]

Other factors that determine the kind of forecasting techniques a firm uses are the purpose of the forecast, the risks involved in making an inaccurate forecast, and the cost of using a particular technique. Essentially, three general types of forecasting techniques are used by most business organizations: subjective techniques, time-series analysis, and econometric forecasting.

Subjective Techniques

The least sophisticated techniques have traditionally enjoyed the widest use in forecasting sales.[2] Whether the reason for this has been a general mistrust or a lack of understanding of quantitative techniques, it has only been in recent years that more sophisticated techniques have been growing in use. Nevertheless, the more subjective techniques are still widely used. Among these are three basic approachs that are probably used either exclusively or in conjunction with some other technique in nearly every business organization. These are the *jury of executive opinion* approach, *sales-force estimates,* and the *user or customer expectation* approach.

Jury of Executive Opinion

This is probably the most commonly used subjective forecasting technique. This type of forecast is based upon combining the predictions of many key executives in the firm to obtain a higher-quality decision. Since most executives have a "feel" for their marketplace through experience, this type of forecasting technique leads itself to fairly accurate predictions. The process normally consists of several executives getting together to discuss their individual forecasts and the basis for making the forecast.

Typically, each member of the jury prepares his or her estimate independently, using whatever information is considered to be relevant to the forecast, whether in the form of hard data or of more abstract input, such as a subjective analysis of industry trends or economic indicators.

After each executive taking part in the process has decided upon his or her forecast, the entire group meets to interchange ideas and determine the forecast. Such meetings often require serious research on the part of the members prior to their getting together to arrive at a consensus. The relative weight given to various jury members' input is a factor that must be considered. To take a hypothetical example, suppose an executive vice-president whose forecasts have traditionally been inaccurate is a jury member. How much weight should his judgment receive? The answers to this and other questions that arise are normally determined by the "personality" of the firm and its traditional approach to dealing with such questions.

A method being used more frequently in jury forecasting is the application of probability theory. Use of probability techniques naturally requires some knowledge of the application of theory to practice by the executives involved in the forecast. In actual practice, most members of the jury are not uncomfortable with the use of basic probability theory. The "executive" is usually perceived by students as an impeccably dressed individual with graying temples and a cigar who makes "big" decisions but does not get involved in details. Actually, this perception is inaccurate. The term "executive" normally applies to any line manager past the first supervisory level and any staff member who reports to a manager at or above the previously described level. For this reason, the jury meeting, rather than resembling something out of a movie about the *cosa nostra,* more often consists of an abundance of relatively young, intelligent people who are not bound by tradition to respect every opinion expressed for fear of offending the chief executives.

A widely used group forecasting technique is the *Delphi* method. This approach is used for medium-term forecasting and was developed by Dalkey and Helmar of the RAND Corporation. The essence of this approach is that group opinions that are arrived at on a face-to-face basis are less accurate than those reached by an average of individual opinions without interpersonal contact, because of the possible influence of dominant persons, pressure by the group to force a consensus, and the "noise" or social interchange that detracts from attention to the problem at hand.[3] The Delphi approach attempts to eliminate these factors by keeping anonymous individual input interaction, or feedback to individuals at each stage of the meeting of the other individuals' input, and by taking a statistical average of individual opinions. As long as the individuals taking part are objective and have a feel for the interdisciplinary approach, this technique claims to produce higher-quality forecasts.

IBM Corporation has used this technique with success in forecasting market acceptance of new products. Other firms have used Delphi to forecast the market for toiletries and cosmetics, to determine efficient inventory levels for equipment, and to forecast freight volume by various groups in the railroad industry.

Use of Estimates by Salespeople

Another widely used subjective approach to forecasting is the estimation of future sales by the individual salesperson. This approach is nearly always used for the short term, often as short as three months and seldom any longer than twelve months. The presumption behind this approach to sales forecasting is that sales personnel are in a better position than anyone else in the company to estimate the short-term outlook for sales in their respective territories. Their familiarity with the purchasing policies and plans of customers and prospects should provide high-quality input into the sales forecast.

"I'm not even good in hindsight!"

In cases where companies serve large accounts, information concerning future purchases is relatively easy to determine. Salespeople are normally given a format to follow in discussing buying plans with these customers. In cases where certain accounts purchase from the company on a sporadic basis, salespeople attempt to estimate future sales based upon their subjective judgments.

In situations where a salesperson sells to many customers and nearly every sale is an independent event, as in office equipment and other commercial sales, some probability estimate is used. Salespeople are normally given certain guidelines to use when making sales estimates. Rarely if ever does a firm use these data to determine sales quotas or for any purpose that would be detrimental to the salesperson.

After the sales force has turned in their estimates, sales managers normally review the information and discuss various aspects of the forecast. It is at this stage that sales managers sometimes unwittingly force salespeople into making forecasts that conform to the manager's preconceived notions. This is not a desirable approach, because it tends to force the salesperson to predict what he or she thinks the manager expects, thus taking the grass-roots element out of the forecast. A further refinement of the salesperson's estimate approach develops if the sales manager's supervisor also participates in the process. At this point, the approach becomes even more subjective. In fairness to sales managers, in many firms salesperson's estimates are nearly always less accurate than subjective estimates by the first and/or second levels of sales management. Some firms that experience this situation still request sales-force estimates, but temper them with managerial judgments. The process is often continued to give salespeople forecasting experience. This experience can be valuable in many ways, including giving the salesperson an opportunity to experience some of the sales manager's problems and by forcing individual sales-force members to become intimately familiar with their sales territories.

A great advantage to using sales-force estimates in the forecast is the opportunity to compile many separate estimates into one larger forecast for the entire firm. Naturally, this forecast is only as good as the quality of the input generated by the sales force. If salespeople are overly optimistic or pessimistic, the accuracy of their estimate will clearly be reduced. Unfortunately, overestimates and underestimates seldom cancel each other out with a resultant forecast of relative accuracy. More often than not, salespeople tend to overestimate. Overall, however, this technique is considered to be important, particularly in forecasting industrial products sales, where definite needs are established well in advance. Another positive aspect of this technique is that most salespeople tend to develop reasonably accurate forecasting skills over a two- or three-year period. Generally, firms that find the technique effective tend to continue its use.

OBJECTIVE TECHNIQUES

Time-Series Analysis

The essence of time-series analysis is that elements of the future may be found by looking at the past. This approach is seldom used by firms whose monthly sales are not in the millions of dollars' range.[4] It is also desirable that accurate sales data for one or more years be available. A simplified description of sales forecasting based on time series is that a firm attempts to judge its next period's sales (say a month) by determining a trend. This trend is a function of last years' sales, and then various seasonal, cyclical, and unforeseen events (weather, competition, the economy and other *exogenous* variables) are plugged into the equation. The final result includes four elements; seasonal variations (S), secular trend (T), cyclical variations (C), and irregular variations (I). The basic forecast equation is

$$\text{Sales} = T \times C \times S \times I$$

or for an annual data, where seasonal variations are eliminated,

$$\text{Sales} = T \times C \times I$$

A moving average is then developed, and as the next month's sales are added, the earliest period in the average is dropped.

One of the more popular techniques of time-series analysis is the X-11 method. This is a version of the method used by the Department of the Census and is used by Xerox Corporation to predict copy volume. Another technique is the FORAN system used by PPG Industries. This approach is used to forecast the sales of several different divisions.

More sophisticated time-series techniques such as *exponential smoothing, adaptive filtering* and *Box-Jenkins models* attempt to refine estimation. These techniques are not widely used, but have had some success in certain situations. In general, it may be stated that most time-series approaches depend upon the ability of the forecasters to adequately predict probabilities of unexpected events. This ability is usually reflected in the firm's commitment to time-series techniques.

Econometric Techniques

Econometric techniques are based on the application of regression analysis to business problems. Essentially, a model of relationships between changes in sales volume and changes in other variables is constructed. If the other factors that are presumed to have an influence on sales are known, it is possible to predict the change in sales. An example would be if consumer income had an influence on the sale of a certain product. Then the use of this factor in the equation would tend to give a more realistic answer. Obviously, it is important that the factor(s) used in the regression equation have an influence on the outcome.[5] The basic equation representing the relationships in the regression model is

$$Y^t = a + bX^t$$

where Y^t = dependent variable (sales) at time t
X^t = explanatory variable (income) at time t
a = γ-intercept value (the value of γ when the value of the explanatory variable is 0)

b = the regression coefficient, which measures the change in the dependent variable associated with a unit change in the independent variable

If more than one explanatory variable (e.g, income and monthly freight-car loadings) is used, the model is known as *multiple regression*. Under these conditions, the effectiveness of a forecasting model is clearly a function of the skill of the model builders. If, for example, the forecaster is able to discover several variables that accurately predict the outcome, the model will probably be used as a regular basis. If, on the other hand, it proves inaccurate, either new variables will be sought, or an impatient management might lose confidence in the whole concept of econometric forecasting.

Because of the use of computers and the increasing sophistication of the art of forecasting, the use of econometric techniques is increasing. Many large firms use econometric forecasting to predict long-range sales. The most widely used methods of appraising econometric models are the following:

R^2 or coefficient of determination: *This value attempts to show the variance in the dependent variable that has been explained by the independent variables in the model.*

$$R^2 = \frac{\text{variance in sales explained by the regression}}{\text{total variance in sales}}$$

This value is also called the goodness-of-fit measure.

Reasonableness of the regression coefficient: *This factor relates to the logic or reasonableness of the regression coefficient for each independent variable used in the model. In selling autos, for example, income would be a logical variable because sales would be expected to rise as income rises.*

Comparison of past sales to estimates generated by the model: *Forecasters attempt to find sources of error by analysis of actual versus predicted sales over several periods.*

Significance of regression coefficients: *This is determined by the classic t-test, which usually indicates whether the size of the coefficient is significant or is due to chance.*

Back forecasting: *This technique calls for withholding data for some of the more recent periods in estimating the model. The model is then used to forecast values for the missing periods. Errors revealed in the back forecast are assumed to be attributable to the inability of the model to forecast properly, since actual values are used for the independent variables.*

Generally, econometric forecasts have attempted over the past two decades to associate sales more with the economy than with past sales trends. This technique will continue to grow as new and more sophisticated model-building techniques are developed. It will, however, probably continue to be used more for long- rather than short-range forecasting; thus it will not replace (or even attempt to compete with) the techniques mentioned earlier in this section.

DETERMINING TERRITORIAL SALES POTENTIAL

A sales territory is essentially a group of accounts or a geographical sector assigned to a salesperson. The salesperson is restricted to selling his or her products or services within the territory and receives credit for any sales made within the territory. One exception to the territorial method of assigning salespeople their respective selling areas is in direct sales, where salespeople sell to any and all prospects or customers who can be generated. It would be manifestly impractical, for example, to assign an insurance or automobile salesperson a geographical territory. But most of the other three sales types are assigned a territory based on geography or accounts. Every territory contains a certain number of prospects who are capable of buying the goods and services of the firm. The more qualified prospects there are in a given territory, the greater is that territory's *sales potential*. Territorial sales potential, then, describes the numbers of qualified customers or attainable sales volume within a given sales territory at a given time.

The prevailing theory with regard to assignment of sales territories stresses the importance of assigning territories that are approximately equal in potential. The logic behind this approach is that sales costs will be reduced substantially and that an optimum number of territories can be established. High sales costs occur when salespeople are forced to travel excessive distances and when there are more salespeople assigned to an office than are necessary. Most sales organizations do not carry out this approach very strictly, sometimes for good reason and sometimes because of poor planning. Many companies purposely assign "training" territories to new salespersons—territories that have less sales potential than others in the office but provide a good starting point for new salespeople. As a manager in the office products industry said in an interview,

> Training territories are definitely the best way to break in new salespeople. They can make mistakes and the company doesn't lose any good customers. When I started out, they gave me the Garment District as my territory. Nobody buys new electric typewriters down *there*. The first call I made was in a loft where they were making dresses. I was stupid enough to wait for the owner to come out on the floor. Finally, I saw him and he asked me what I wanted. When I told him what I was selling, he looked at me like I was crazy. "You want me to buy a $600 typewriter when I can't even make a dollar profit on a dress? Get the hell out of here and don't bother me anymore," he said, and walked away. Calling on places like that gave me a chance to sharpen my skills. Even though I didn't sell many typewriters, I got a chance to practice my approach and even learned how to use my hands during a business "conversation."

A second reason why all territories are seldom equal in potential is because many organizations like to reward certain salespeople with better territories because of past performance and because it provides an incentive to other salespeople by giving them something to which they can aspire.

A third and less valid reason for having uneven sales territories is often the organization's failure or unwillingness to treat the equal territory size concept as anything more than an academic or theoretical exercise. The fact is that many firms have not developed accurate methods for measuring sales potential; hence they are unable to equalize territories.

The extent to which a firm decides to equalize territories is, of course, based on corporate objectives and sales policies. There are, however, a few compelling reasons why territory equalization is more than a theoretical exercise.

1. Firms that have wide variations in potential between territories tend to have high sales costs for the reasons stated previously.
2. Firms lose sales because of the tendency of salespeople in high potential sales volume territories to focus their attention on a few high-volume customers, with a concurrent neglect of the remainder of their territories. This procedure is known as "skimming" or "creaming" a territory. As a result, sometimes the poorest performance occurs in the highest sales potential territories and often goes unnoticed because of the large sales volume that *is* produced from the territory.
3. With a configuration of territories that are approximately equal in sales potential, it is easier to compare each salesperson's performance by comparing actual sales to potential sales.

To determine territorial potential, the sales potential for the entire branch or district is determined and then divided by the number of territories assigned. It is sometimes difficult to determine sales potential, but most organizations are able to develop methods that are unique to their product lines. For example, in the construction industry, a measure of potential is square footage of contracts awarded.[6] A good example of this type of determination would be the method used by the Powerlock Floor Corporation of Philadelphia, Pennsylvania. This firm manufactures gymnasium floors. As a result, the marketing department attempts to find out how many gymnasiums are being built and the size of the proposed gym floor. This figure is then divided by the number of salespersons in the firm, and territories with equal potential are assigned.

The figures that are used to estimate potential use, as indicated previously, are unique to each industry. These figures are sometimes referred to as a *market index*. The market index for the floor company is different for a firm that sells wall covering. In this case, square footage of wall space in new buildings would be the most appropriate market index.

To recap, ideally, territorial sales potential is determined by dividing the sales potential for the entire branch or district by the number of sales territories. The sales volume in dollars or other units is determined by the use of the appropriate market index. Although this process might seem elementary, determining accurately the sales volume potential for sales territories is one of the most important elements in marketing planning and, subsequently, in marketing control.

THE ANNUAL MARKETING PLAN

One of the most significant documents for sales and marketing organizations is the annual marketing plan. This plan is the blueprint for the firm's total marketing effort and objectives and also articulates the strategies that will be used to attain those objectives. The usefulness of this document to sales management lies in its spelling out in detail the sales organization's contribution to the achievement of the firm's major objectives.

The development of the marketing plan is typically a top-level responsibility and normally includes the vice-president of marketing, the president, and, depending upon the extent of the firm's commitment to the marketing concept, other functional executives as well. Naturally, sales managers are responsible for a great deal of input to the plan.

The marketing plan typically begins with a statement of objectives in writing. The setting of objective targets allows the firm to ensure that all planning is directed toward common goals. Another advantage of clearly articulated targets is that progress toward the goals may be checked. If current progress has fallen short, corrective action may be taken. This process will be discussed in the following chapter. At any rate, setting objectives provides a guide at the beginning of the planning process and provides a yardstick for measuring results at the end of the planning process.

To be effective, a marketing plan must be converted into *action programs*, which are specific strategies that will be implemented to reach the stated objectives. It should also include a timetable that indicates when each function should be completed. The plan should also indicate which individuals are responsible for each function.

Included in the marketing plan are several important financial considerations: budgets, resource allocation, and projections of profits. These figures must be determined well in advance of the final drafting of the document. To develop such a document, then, it is critical that all deadlines be met and that all participants in the plan prepare their contributions accurately. This condition requires not only the strong support of top management, but a recognition by the firm that the marketing plan carries top priority for its development and implementation.

THE MARKETING INFORMATION SYSTEM AND SALES PLANNING

In its simplest form, the marketing information system is a means of getting the right marketing data to the right people at the right time and in the right form. The kind of data provided can be as simple or as sophisticated as the marketing executives of the organization prefer. As a generalization, it can be safely said that larger firms tend to oversupply data, while smaller firms as a rule tend to supply too little input to their respective marketing information systems.

The concept of the marketing information system is interesting. The system reaches into every functional area of the marketing organization and, in its advanced form, requires input from virtually every department in the firm. Detailed analysis of the system, however, is beyond the parameters of this textbook. Our discussion will be limited to the system and its impact upon the local sales manager and his or her organization.

A simple example of the practical use of the marketing information system to the sales manager is the *monthly sales summary*. While each firm has its own nomenclature for this report, its purpose is to provide the sales manager with a useful and meaningful documentation of the relative performance of his or her salespeople. In many cases, it also provides information related to the performance of other branches as well, thus allowing the manager to compare the results of his or her efforts to those of other managers during a given month. The monthly sales summary is typically in the form of a computer printout, and individual salespeople are also provided with a printout of their own performance, typically a tally of sales with debits and credits to particular accounts, which eventually total up to that month's first commission payment. (About the only thing common to all salespeople with respect to this printout is that the final commission figure determined by the firm is always less than the figure determined by the salesperson.)

Source data for the sales analysis is based on information taken from call reports and sales results tabulated at the branch level and forwarded to the home office. This report is typical of the kind Frank Smith referred to in the interview. The need for prompt attention to deadlines should be apparent to the reader. As a sales manager remarked during an interview with the author,

> There's an old saying about garbage-in and garbage-out. I'll tell you though, that little system is set up so that you can't beat it. If you feed it a lot of phoney calls, it will feed you back a higher number of calls per sale. Then your boss says to you, "what's the matter boy, your salespeople dumb? don't you know how to train them, or am I getting phoney sales calls, which?" Ain't no difference what you tell him, you're wrong. That is, unless you are doing a pretty good job. Before we had this little old computerized summary, we were in a hell of a shape. Couldn't really make an honest objective analysis at all. Now we have several areas where I can just look at this printout and say "uh-oh, this old boy needs some training." Another thing it helps me do is spot consistency. I'd rather spend my time with those who need it. You can tell from that monthly report who the strong ones really are. It might be a pain in the neck getting together our reports, but it sure pays off when we get back this little old monthly sales summary.

Most sales and marketing managers would agree that, as long as unnecessary data are kept to a minimum, companies with a strong marketing information system have a clear competitive advantage.

SUMMARY

The planning function is a key activity of sales managers. Without planning and setting of objectives, no effective sales strategies can be developed or maintained.

There are several different methods for forecasting sales. Subjective methods include *jury of executive opinion, sales-force estimates,* and the customer *expectation* approach. All these approaches utilize a great deal of judgment, but they also require experts to use available quantitative data, so they are fairly reliable techniques.

Objective techniques are *time-series analysis,* including *exponential smoothing, adaptive filtering,* and *Box-Jenkins models*. Another type of objective forecasting is through the use of econometrics, but there is no guarantee that any of the "objective" techniques will be accurate in forecasting long-range sales.

Analysis of territorial sales potential allows sales management to determine intelligent and legitimate quotas. An objective approach to sales territory determination requires the adoption of appropriate measures, and it is not a simple process.

Marketing information systems provide a highly objective and reliable document to be used in sales planning and control programs. Often the major problem faced by management is the dissemination of too much data, but when effectively handled, a marketing information system provides the firm with a strong competitive weapon.

Planning Ahead

Three brothers, Ebeneezer, Bjorn, and Shaun are in charge of several small factories scattered throughout the southern states that sell plant products and accessories. Started by the older brother ten years before the plant business boomed, Ebeneezer considers himself the "brains" of the business.

Bjorn, however, feels that it's time for a change. He wants to branch out into having their own showrooms, rather than dealing through small, local stores, and he wants to expand their line of products to include wicker furniture, lawn equipment, small tractor trailers, and roto-tillers.

Shaun has ideas of his own also. He wants to start a mail-order business associated with the original plant product line.

Ebeneezer wants nothing to do with either of these and emphatically considers it best to keep the status quo and take no chance of diluting a going operation.

Bjorn and Shaun want to use forecasting techniques to get a realistic estimation of future sales to help them with the decision of how best to proceed. They are aware that a jury of executive opinion will keep them at a standstill, considering Ebeneezer's controlling interests as senior partner.

1. What forecasting technique would you recommend?
2. How would you implement the forecast?

Moving Pipe

An asbestos cement (A/C) pipe manufacturer in Detroit has, over the past 18 months, witnessed a sharp decline in sales. Management believes that the decline in sales volume has been due to (1) the recent surfacing of an asbestos cement health issue, (2) the general decline in the construction market, and (3) a new pipe product (PVC pipe) entering the market for first time. The new product consisting of PVC resin carries no health hazard.

price per foot of A/C pipe = $0.90
price per foot of PVC pipe = $1.00
installation cost of A/C pipe = $0.10 per foot
installation cost of PVC pipe = $0.20 per foot

When the construction market is at its peak, there is not sufficient combined A/C and PVC capacity to handle all sales requirements.

1. What do you believe will be the best forecasting technique to project (a) A/C sales for the next 12 months, and (b) A/C sales for the next 5 years?
2. What are the advantages and disadvantages in parts (a) and (b) of question 1 for (a) subjective techniques (which subjective technique is best), (b) time-series analysis, and (c) econometric forecasting?

DISCUSSION QUESTIONS

1. What is the value of accurate sales forecasting?
2. What are the two major groups of sales forecasting techniques?
3. What are the most commonly used subjective techniques?
4. What are the advantages and disadvantages of the jury of executive opinion technique?
5. What are the advantages and disadvantages of the salesperson's estimates approach to sales forecasting?
6. What are some of the more sophisticated of the time-series techniques?
7. Why is a knowledge of territorial sales potential critical to sales organizations?
8. What is the annual marketing plan and why is it critical?

NOTES

[1]J. M. Keynes, *General Theory of Employment, Interest, and Money* (New York: Harcourt Brace Jovanovich, 1935), pp. 155–156.

[2]Stanley J. PoKempner and Earl L. Bailey, *Sales Forecasting Practices; an Appraisal,* (New York: Conference Board, 1970).

[3]David L. Hurwood, Elliott S. Grossman, and Earl L. Bailey, *Sales Forecasting* (New York: Conference Board, 1978), p. 12.

[4]Ibid., p. 47.

[5]Frank M. Bass, "A Simultaneous Regression Study of Advertising and Sales of Cigarettes," *Journal of Marketing Research,* August 1969.

[6]Richard D. Crisp, *Eight Keys to Sales and Profit Expansion* (New York: McGraw-Hill, 1967).

CHAPTER 11

SALES CONTROL

OBJECTIVES

To enumerate some well-known sales control techniques.

To analyze the impact of sales control on profits.

To discuss the concepts of the marketing information system.

To discuss the concept of penetration analysis.

INTERVIEW WITH FRANK SMITH

Interviewer: Frank, I suppose sales control is another one of the important functions of the sales manager. The only problem is that the word "control" is so pervasive.

Frank Smith: You are quite right. Not unlike Kipling's story about the elephant, it means many things to many people.

Interviewer: What does the term "control" mean to you, Frank?

Frank Smith: A lot of people associate the word "control" with some kind of manipulation. As a matter of fact, in business, control is, or should be, associated with making sure that you are on target. Or keeping a tight ship. It should be viewed as being a *positive* thing.

Interviewer: Do you use a lot of formal control devices in a positive way at your firm?

Frank Smith: Very decidedly so. We have a sensible, built-in control system so that we can follow up on meeting our objectives, and we even have certain controls that are pretty flexible.

Interviewer: What are some of the control devices you use, Frank?

Frank Smith: Well, to put it in a simple framework, we have control devices such as paper-work requirements that help the salesperson keep up with his or her stated goals. We also have a very sophisticated management information system, which helps us sales managers meet our targets.

Interviewer: In your experience as a sales manager, have you developed control systems for your firm's salespeople?

Frank Smith: Yes, I certainly have. In fact most of them are similar to the ones we will be looking at in this chapter. Let's see what they have in store for us today.

One of the basic functions of the manager is controlling. Plans are made and certain procedures are instituted to provide the manager with the greatest possible assurance that these plans will be realized. From time to time, certain action must be taken to correct deviations from planned progress toward specific goals. *Control* is usually described to include any activity taken by the manager to ensure that plans are realized and goals or targets are met. Specifically, this function might range from instituting a follow-up on sales call reports to terminating poor performers. This chapter will investigate some of the basic control activities that are performed by most sales managers.

SALES-CONTROL TECHNIQUES

The term "sales control" has a somewhat ominous sound for the individual becoming acquainted with the sales management profession. Many students have indicated that this term implies an enigmatic and sophisticated approach to problem solving, nearly always employing some mathematical or heuristic set of tools. It is certainly true that more sophisticated control techniques are used in the home office, particularly in larger firms, but control techniques at the local level are typically based on a series of policies that are promulgated verbally, as well as through written reports.

In most firms, control measures begin when actual performance is compared to planned performance during a given period. If the "actual" meets or exceeds the "planned," typically no action is taken. If the "planned" exceeds the "actual," however, attention is directed toward this fact and corrective measures are taken. This section will investigate some of the more widely used control techniques and explain their usefulness to sales managers.

Measuring Territorial Sales Performance

A key sales-control activity is measurement of territorial sales performance. This measure provides management with an indication of the relative effectiveness of each sales territory. To have an understanding of performance effectiveness, it is first necessary to know territorial potential or opportunity. Several techniques are available to sales management to measure potential; they are peculiar to specific product areas or industries. There is a strong relationship between planning and control that is based upon an accurate estimate of territorial potential. Without an accurate measure of sales opportunity, any planning or control technique employed is more often guesswork than fact. *It cannot be emphasized strongly enough that adequate estimation of the real potential of each territory is essential to any sales management control technique.* The essence of all control systems is bringing to the attention of management any variations between expected results and actual results. These results might be measured in terms of sales, profits, new accounts, expenses, or a variety of related areas.

An objective evaluation of the sales potential of individual territories is often likely to disclose enormous variations among territories. It is not at all unusual to find a territory that has five or ten times the potential of a different territory. By the same token, it is not unusual to find a similar range in *performance effectiveness* among different territories. *Performance effectiveness* refers to the sales results in a given territory *in terms of the territorial potential available.* Suppose for example, territory A has the potential for sales of 1000 units and territory B has the potential for sales of 2000 units. Let us further assume that territory A has sales of 500 units and territory B has sales of 600 units:

Territory	Potential	Sales	Sales/Potential
A	1000	500	0.50 (500/1000)
B	2000	600	0.30 (600/2000)

In our example, territory A has more effective performance, even though the sales of territory B were greater. This is because A sold 500 of its possible limit of 1000, or 50 percent of its potential, while B sold 600 of its possible limit of 2000, or 30 percent of its potential. Clearly, the performance in territory A was greater than in territory B. If the sales manager was not aware of their respective potentials, territory B would appear to be more effective because its sales were greater than those of territory A. An example of what happens in such a case is illustrated by a sales manager in the sporting goods industry:

> We had two salespeople selling the same item in two different territories. One territory was the state of Texas, the other was a territory consisting of Arizona, Nevada, Utah, Montana and New Mexico. Year after year, the Texas salesman sold about three times as much as the other one, and always collected a big bonus for it. When I came here, I made an update of the potential in the two territories. The Texas salesman, who was selling three times as much as the other one, should have been selling about ten times as much. Evidently a lot of business had moved to Texas over the past ten years but nobody bothered to take it into account. A year later I fired the Texas salesman and put the other one in his place. Sales increased by about seventy percent.

The preceding example indicates the value of a sales control system. By knowing the performance effectiveness of each salesperson, the manager was able to initiate a favorable change. It should be noted that the relative potential of each territory had not been measured for quite some time. For many reasons, it is not unusual for managers to receive a shock the first time territories are measured for sales potential. The classic reason for the shock is that salespeople with "juicier" territories tend to expend less effort in chasing marginal sales than do salespeople with "leaner" territories. Salespeople with the better territories normally have higher sales, which tend to look good on paper until a realistic tabulation of potential is made by management.

A control of territorial sales potential has enormous value, since problems like the preceding are usually solvable. The result of remedial action in such situations is nearly always increased sales and profits. Sales managers who are able to recognize differences in territorial sales effectiveness have several options available to them to narrow those differences. The causes of poor performance can be analyzed and corrective measures taken. In some instances, if not most, the firm or the sales manager has unwittingly exacerbated the problem by allowing it to continue. In a sense, it is difficult to pass judgment upon ineffective salespeople when management ineffectiveness caused the problem initially. In most cases, a more equitable arrangement results when management acts upon such situations, negating the need for extreme measures such as terminating salespeople. Further training or an exhortation to work harder often results in increased sales effectiveness. Both the salesperson and management benefit from increased earnings, higher profits, and a new emphasis on the salesperson's *management* of his or her territory, rather than simply selling in it.

Index of Competitive Performance

The previous control technique is used by many sales managers to improve territorial effectiveness in relationship to the other salespeople in the office. It is also desirable to develop some control techniques to recognize and improve effectiveness with respect to competition. Developing such a technique is relatively difficult for an office or for an individual territory. For a company or for one of a company's product lines, it is less difficult. To determine this measure of effectiveness, it is necessary to know what competitors' sales were over a given period, typically on a monthly basis. These data are usually available through industry trade associations.[1] In some industries the data are more reliable and accurate than in others. Unfortunately, it is usually difficult to determine what sales were in smaller subunits as sales office or territory. When such information is available, a valuable control tool can be developed that will indicate the firms sales versus those of the market in general. This information is most helpful when sales have increased or decreased significantly. A monthly index can be computed by taking the firm's sales growth (or decline) and comparing it to the industry as a whole. As an example, suppose firm A increased its sales by 9.6 percent for a particular month compared to the previous year. This would indicate an increase in sales effectiveness. Assume, however, that the industry increased sales by 6.8 percent over a similar period. On this basis, actual increase was 109.6/106.8 or 103. The firm actually performed at a higher rate than the industry as a whole. If the competition has performed at a greater rate than the firm, then certain measures must be taken to determine where and why the changes took place.

Concentration Patterns

In Chapter 14 it will be shown that in many sales offices about 20 percent of the customers account for 80 percent of the sales volume. Such a large amount of volume concentrated in relatively few accounts requires certain control tools to show the degree of such concentration. These control tools are known as *concentration patterns*. Another important fact about concentration is that two thirds or more of all business is conducted in the top 250 or so metropolitan areas.[2] In fact, about one third of the U.S. population, retail sales volume, and effective buying income is concentrated in the top twenty marketing areas (see Table 11-1). Sales managers attempt to identify the concentration patterns that have the most relevance for their specific sales area and customer configuration. Through the development of concentration patterns, sales managers are able to control the most important elements in their respective sales structures.

An excellent example of the practical use of the concentration pattern as a control device is in the building materials industry. As in most product areas, there

TABLE 11-1

Concentration of Standard Metropolitan Statistical Areas (SMSAs)

New York–Northern New Jersey
Los Angeles–Long Beach, California
Chicago, Illinois
Philadelphia–Southern New Jersey
Detroit, Michigan
Boston–Lowell-Lawrence–Brochton, Haverhill, Massachusetts–New Hampshire
San Francisco–Oakland, California
Washington, D.C.–Maryland–Virginia
Nassau–Suffolk, New York
Dallas–Fort Worth, Texas
St. Louis, Missouri–Illinois
Pittsburgh, Pennsylvania
Houston, Texas
Baltimore, Maryland
Newark, New Jersey

is a major metropolitan market concentration pattern in this industry. As of 1979, both residential and nonresidential construction had about the same percentage of concentration as retail sales, buying power, and population in the top twenty metropolitan areas. In measuring *individual* marketing area concentration, however, there is a wide range of difference in the relationship between the aforementioned demographic factors and construction. Use of population or any of these factors as an index of nonresidential construction concentration could involve an error range of about 100 percent in *individual* marketing areas. In residential construction, the relationship is even more meaningless.

As a result, many sales managers break down concentration of construction by analyzing specific porjects. For example, on a project-sized basis, the top 25 percent of projects underway included about 80 percent of all construction of schools and colleges during the late 1960s, a peak period for institutional construction of this type. Similar concentration patterns exist in *every* industry. The construction industry is used in this example because data are readily available from the F. W. Dodge Corporation.[3] With these data in hand, a sales manager for a blackboard manufacturer is in a position to assign specific projects to specific salespersons and to compare sales results to potential on a project basis. Much of the data available in other industries are readily available if the sales manager is willing to look for it. Nearly every sales manager uses some type of concentration pattern as a control tool in selling his or her products.

Sales Control and Its Impact on Profit

Most marketing textbooks describe the process of marketing as evolving through a series of time periods or "eras," such as the progression from the *pro-*

duction era to the *sales era* to the *marketing department era* to the ultimate—the *marketing company era.* One of these time periods, the *sales era,* is characterized by an emphasis on *sales volume* rather than on *profits.* Unfortunately, many business organizations still operate under the premises of the sales era, where profits are conceived as a residual from all sales. This is not to say that firms do not want to make profits; however, they simply assume that higher sales mean higher profits. When profits recede, firms typically embark on drastic cost-cutting programs. People and budgets are slashed to reduce "organization slack," but often at the expense of long-run objectives. For example, one of the first cost reductions during a slack period is in the advertising budget. Indeed, it is not at all unusual for companies to reduce their advertising effort to a minimum. An advertising manager for a large entertainment firm recalled in an interview,

> I used to work with _____ Corporation during the '50s. Things were great during the Korean War for the company, but when we hit the recession in '55, they cut the ad budget in half. The Director of Advertising and Sales Promo was unceremoniously let go—he found out when he came to work and his drawers were emptied and the contents laid on his desk—and about two-thirds of his staff were let go right along with him. It's funny on Madison Avenue, you can be fired or lose an account at 10 a.m. and by noon everybody in the advertising world knows it. That's when you go to any bar for lunch on Madison Avenue and everybody you see excuses themself and gets the hell away from you. It's as though you had leprosy or something. Believe me, in Advertising, you carry your resume in your hip pocket at all times.

Although some people doubt the value of advertising or, more often, certain advertisements, the long-run value of advertising is beneficial to most firms. Cutting the ad budget and engaging in other short-sighted, even punitive, cost-reduction programs is often counterproductive, as it can lead to even lower profits.

A positive approach to increasing profits is to operate within a fair but tight budget to begin with, and then increase sales while keeping sales costs constant. This approach is, of course, easier said than done. Most high-level sales executives, however, achieved their status because they were able to accomplish this objective.

One of the oldest maxims of business is that "you have to spend money to make money." This old saw certainly holds true in most sales situations. Investment in an ample-sized and highly skilled sales force is usually considered good strategy by most sales managers. Even when effective salespeople have been hired, it is necessary for the sales manager to maintain certain controls to ensure that maximum effectiveness is gained by most or all salespeople. Obviously, this situation hardly ever exists. The extent to which it does usually determines how profitable a sales effort will be.

The sales manager is ultimately responsible for the results attained by all salespeople; therefore, the control procedures set up should apply to the entire sales force. It is necessary that all salespeople have a specific understanding of what they are expected to do and how to go about it. To provide that understanding, the manager must convey the information and develop a set of controls to ensure that the results desired are actually being attained. Control of the relationship between the sales manager and salesperson can be covered in a checklist specifically designed to identify sales-control factors. The following management functions are indicative of these factors:[4]

1. Development of specific objectives, in writing, to be accomplished by salespeople.
2. Division of salesperson's job into major categories, with a description of approximately how much time should be spent in each category.
3. Review of territorial sales coverage and allocation of geography and/or accounts.
4. Placing salespeople geographically near a large customer concentration in his or her sales territory.
5. Programming with individual salespersons a sales coverage plan that allocates his or her time to various portions of the sales territory in proportion to potential in each portion.
6. Development of sales call frequency standards for salespeople.
7. Ensuring management follow-up on sales leads and requiring feedback on disposition of lead.
8. Developing objective performance standards for all salespeople.
9. Providing for full and clear communication from manager to salesperson and from salesperson to manager.
10. Development of an information system whereby nonroutine performance is called to the attention of management.

Through the establishment of program policies and procedures that result in these above control devices, profitability may be improved greatly. A good deal of the material in this textbook is directed toward these specific factors.

The Marketing Information System

One of the basic principles of management is *management by exception*. This fundamental is based upon the fact that the modern manager has such an enormous "inside" and "outside" work load that it is impossible for him or her to analyze every report from his or her subordinates in great detail. For this reason, certain standards are established so that exceptions to the norm literally standout to be called to the manager's attention. Some of the reports that come across the desk of most sales managers include information on call frequency, sales volume, territorial performance, personnel data, and any number of *performance versus standard* types of information.

Since most sales organizations utilize a large number of salespersons, it would be manifestly impractical to tabulate and aggregate all the information required for a sales manager's needs (or perceived needs) manually. Hence, data-processing systems are used in the preparation of the necessary management reports. Every firm has its own marketing information system (MIS) but a few examples of data common to most will be mentioned. Sales call frequency, a report of calls made by individual salespersons based on a daily or weekly average, and usually compared to some standard, is used in virtually all MIS documentation. Likewise, sales volume in terms of actual versus quota and sales by product line are popular favorites among sales managers. Chapter 10 will discuss the marketing information system in greater detail. It is important, however, that the student be aware of its critical nature as a control device.

Penetration Analysis

Sophisticated marketing executives and analysts are acutely aware of the need to know the relationship between the firm's product sales and the sales of the total product market. If known, these sales figures will reveal the extent of *penetration* into the market by the particular product. Like many other numerical relationships, these figures are best used to define relative changes over certain time periods. Mere knowledge of a firm's market share, for example, is not helpful. But if the previous two or three years' data regarding product market share are available, the manager is able to evaluate relative performance and take appropriate measures. If market data are available, penetration analysis can be a powerful control tool. Although most industry data are available on a national basis, it is often difficult to determine total sales of a product by all manufacturers in a relatively small sales territory.

Let us say that in a certain marketing area (A) the annual sales of a firm's product are $4 million. The total sales potential in that area is estimated to be $50 million. Dividing actual volume by sales of $50 million results in a penetration of 0.80 or, expressed another way, $8 of sales was attained for every $100 of sales potential. In area B, the sales potential was $25 million and annual sales of the product were $2.75 million. Using the same formula, area B attained 0.11 or $11 of sales per $100 of potential. During the period then, area B sales had more effectively penetrated the market than sales in A. As indicated previously, a single time period of a quarter or even four quarters may not be conclusive evidence that territory B is more effectively managed than A. These data do call to the attention of the regional sales manager the fact that one area is outperforming the other. At this point, the manager would seek to discover *why* there is a difference in penetration between the two areas. Table 11-2 depicts a similar analysis in a branch sales office.

According to Table 11-2, salesperson Briggs has the lowest penetration and salesperson Kean has the next lowest, with the "average" penetration for the office being $7.20. Since all the figures are based upon objective evaluation (sales versus sales potential), size of territory or potential is not a factor in determining degree of penetration. In this example, salespersons Kean, Aron, Briggs, and Decker are below the office average, and salespersons Kean and Decker are well below the average. It is very possible that there is some reason beyond the salespersons' control that is responsible for their low penetration. The sales manager must now investigate the situation and discover the reason. The existence of this type of control report makes such analysis possible.

TABLE 11-2

Sales Penetration by Individual Salespeople in a Branch Office

Salesperson's Name	Territory Potential	Actual Sales	Penetration
Alberg, S.	$300,000	$25,000	$ 8.30
Stecklow, S.	200,000	18,000	9.00
Parry, J.	250,000	25,000	10.00
Kean, R.	400,000	20,000	5.00
Aron, C.	350,000	21,000	6.00
Sultan, A.	450,000	36,000	8.00
Briggs, J.	550,000	25,000	4.50
Decker, B.	250,000	17,000	6.80
			$ 7.20 average

Final Comments on Control

There are hundreds of phrases that are variations on the theme that it is easy to lie with statistics. Nowhere is this more true than in control reports. For one thing, the composition of a territory is such that large customers' buying habits can change at any given time, competitors might suddenly become very aggressive, or a host of other factors might manifest themselves. A salesperson might not be made aware of these conditions until it is too late. In short, there are many plausible, realistic reasons why a salesperson's penetration could be low when compared to the group. The purpose of control reports is not to punish salespersons, but to bring to the attention of management problem areas through the management by exception technique. Each sales organization has its own set of control reports. What works for one firm may not necessarily work for another. This chapter showed only a few of the underlying principles connected with control reports. It is fair to say, however, that nearly all control reports and procedures are instituted for essentially the reasons outlined here.

SUMMARY

A basic function of the manager is controlling. As planned activities deviate, measures must be taken to achieve the intended targets. Most control techniques are in the form of written statements designed to help isolate problem areas through the management by exception principle. A basic foundation for all control activity is that sales territories be divided and allocated based on a knowledge of realistic sales potential. Without this information, any subsequent reports are meaningless and, in fact, tend to compound errors in estimating sales effectiveness.

One control device is an index of *competitive performance.* This measures relative movements in actual sales effectiveness. *Concentration patterns* show the degree to which larger customers pervade a sales territory. This control information allows sales managers to place an emphasis on the more important geographical or account customer bases.

As important as making a sale is making a *profit*. Over the past several decades, managers have become increasingly aware of developing *profit-oriented* rather than *sales-oriented* control strategies. Most successful firms are highly involved in this philosophy. As a result of the need for a profitable sales configuration, *marketing information systems* have been developed which pinpoint sales elements that need to be improved upon. These elements might be individual sales territories, branches, or even sales districts.

One of the more sophisticated tools used by sales managers is the concept of *penetration index*. Based upon recent historical data, a manager can determine which sales territories are making the highest degree of market penetration.

Control tools are numerous, and each firm has developed its own methods. As in any other statistical comparison, mere numbers do not tell the whole story. By the use of control reports, however, the management by exception principle is used to great advantage provided that reports are analyzed in a positive and meaningful way.

Reliable Products

Reliable Products has been in the building industry for fifty years. The company has always done well in the past; it has been continually able to show its stockholders a profit and to pay upper management a nice yearly bonus. Recently, the company's name has been linked with controversial disposal of dangerous substances and with the use of below-grade materials, but none of these accusations have been proved.

Owing to a decline in the building industry as a whole, soaring inflation rates, and an uncertain economy, Reliable Products has, for the first time, shown a decline in profits. The president of the company, however, is unwilling to use these factors as justification for poor performance and has made a strong push to institute stringent control measures. He has asked the heads of each department to review their performance and to indicate what steps they feel should be taken.

In response to this, the advertising department manager has suggested initiating a program to push the solar-energy related line of their products in an effort to take advantage of a new market that can offer long-term financial benefit to its customers. The advertising manager would also like to start a "people-oriented" outlook for the company's advertising campaign in an effort to clear its image, but the president is seriously considering cutting back drastically on the entire advertising budget.

1. What concrete suggestions from sales managers could help turn the company's financial situation around?

2. What facts could the market information system provide that would be useful in this connection?

The Advanced Electronic Control Co.

The Advanced Electronic Control Company makes sophisticated microprocessor controls and sells them to electronic manufacturers all over the world for inclusion in all types of finished equipment. The United States is divided into five regional areas with a sales manager and three to six direct salespeople, depending upon the territory. Each salesperson submitts detailed forecasts by customers, which are supposed to be very specific in the current months and year, becoming more abstract for later years. These are updated monthly, and pressure to meet or beat quarterly forecasts is quite severe.

The older units, which were being phased out, used hundreds of discrete components and were comparatively limited in their flexibility and performance. However, these were designed in equipment that was presently in mass production, and it would be costly and time consuming to redesign these established units electrically and mechanically.

The new units have much superior performance with a far lower cost per function because of the new large-scale-integrated circuits and sophisticated microprocessors being used. They require knowledgeable hardware engineers and software programmers to be used effectively, and this takes more time as well as greater support and skills than many of their customers appreciated.

The sales manager and salespeople are faced with the problem of keeping the old product orders as high as possible to meet short-term revenue, while introducing the limited quantities of new product to obtain sufficient orders, thereby verifying its credibility and preparing for future revenue growth as the older products decline.

How should the sales manager train and guide the salespeople under this common situation? What questions and support should the salespeople face the salesmanager and the plant with? What factors will favorably and unfavorably influence the salespeople's performance against quota? What sympathy will management give a salesperson who tries to justify poor performance at the end of the year in either or both categories? How can the salesperson anticipate and avoid this?

1. What factors will influence the salespeople's performance against quota?
2. What kind of a control system would you suggest?

DISCUSSION QUESTIONS

1. Why is a knowledge of territorial sales performance necessary for adequate sales control?

2. Describe the index of competitive performance.

3. Describe concentration patterns.
4. What were the four eras that characterized the evolution of marketing?
5. What are the functions of a marketing information system?
6. What is the purpose of penetration analysis?
7. What are some major sales control report documents?
8. What are two approaches to the advertising budget as a sales expense?

NOTES

[1]Individual firms' sales figures by product line are seldom disclosed in these figures.

[2]David S. Schwartz, *Marketing Today*, (New York: Harcourt Brace Jovanovich) 1981 p. 122

[3]*Dodge Reports*, McGraw-Hill Corporation.

[4]Richard Crisp, Marketing Research, (New York: McGraw-Hill) 1959, pp. 272–8.

CHAPTER 12

EVALUATING SALES PERFORMANCE

OBJECTIVES

To examine the major types of performance appraisal techniques for salespeople:

* Subjective methods
* Objective methods
* Performance-based methods

To analyze some of the problems associated with sales performance appraisal programs:

* The program itself
* The manager
* Exogenous factors

To discuss the components of a practical sales performance evaluation program.

INTERVIEW WITH FRANK SMITH

Interviewer: It seems as though every time we come to a new function of sales management, it's "one of the most critical functions." Is this true of performance evaluation?

Frank Smith: There is no doubt about it. Measuring a person's performance is an awesome responsibility. *How* you do it is as important as *what* you are doing.

Interviewer: I don't envy you. Nobody likes to give criticism.

Frank Smith: It's got its good side too, don't forget. Most of the time my salespeople perform well, and I enjoy discussing their evaluations with them.

Interviewer: What part do you find the most difficult?

Frank Smith: Well, if you give someone criticism and then you can't back up what you say to his or her satisfaction, then you've got a disgruntled employee on your hands and it can certainly affect his or her performance.

Interviewer: Does this happen often?

Frank Smith: Not with me it doesn't. We use a very objective system, and most of the time our salespeople are shown *exactly* why they are being criticized. Some other firms I know of have pretty loose performance appraisal systems, and they aren't always able to communicate with the salesperson being evaluated as much as they would like to.

Interviewer: What are some of the methods you use?

Frank Smith: Why don't we get into the chapter, and we can take a look at the philosophy of performance appraisal, some of the general techniques and then we can look at some specific programs. I think that would be better than having me explain it now.

Interviewer: Fine, but one last question. Do you think most sales managers are objective when they evaluate their salespeople?

Frank Smith: I think they *want* to be. Unfortunately, if a lot of subjective judgments are required, even if the sales manager is right, he or she still has to convince the salesperson. Let's get into the chapter. I'll show you what I mean.

To promote, train, and even fire salespeople, the sales manager must have knowledge of that person's performance. The methods used by sales organizations to measure their salespeople's performance are often diverse, complex, confusing, and controversial. Some companies measure performance by sales relationships exclusively, others use a combination of subjective and objective criteria, while still others depend upon the manager's subjective judgment to evaluate their salespeople.

Most large organizations and many medium-sized firms use some type of formal appraisal tool. Smaller firms, for the most part, do not. There are essentially three methods of formal performance appraisal. Many sales managers use a combination of the three. The first method, the *subjective method,* is based on the evaluation of the salesperson on the basis of certain qualities, traits, or behavior deemed necessary for effective performance. The second method, the *objective method,* is based upon mutual planning in which the manager and salesperson participate in the setting of specific targets to be attained during a specific time period. The third type, the *performance-based* technique, is related to a salesperson's performance in several different areas already predetermined by the organization, such as meeting a sales quota.

Since the *subjective* or *rating method* does not always focus adequately on results, while the *objective method* tends to lack analysis of a salesperson's personal characteristics, a combination of both methods is often used in formal sales performance programs, usually in conjunction with some performance-based criteria.[1]

In addition to formal performance programs, sales performance is often evaluated on the basis of certain objective and subjective factors. The objective factors are related to data used in the firm's marketing information system, and the subjective factors are related to personal observation by the sales manager. Although the use of objective data based on sales results would appear to provide a rational basis for evaluation, there are certain conditions that must be, but not always are, present in order for the evaluation to be fair. Territorial potential, for example, must be known. Likewise, competitive and external conditions should be programmed into the model if sales-related data are to be used solely as the basis of the evaluation. In many cases, the results of subjective evaluation comprise a valid basis for evaluation. Unfortunately, if the salesperson does not agree with the sales manager's observations, the performance evaluation will not only be rendered useless, but probably will have negative results.

The process of performance evaluation is indeed complex, yet it remains a vital function of sales management. Evaluation of a performance program itself is extremely difficult and time consuming. Because of the complexity of the process, no panacea has yet been discovered. Probably the nearest that researchers and practitioners have come to an "answer" to the problem of the development of effective performance evaluation are the following generalizations.[2]

1. Criticism appears to have a negative effect upon goal achievement, but praise seems to have little if any positive effect.
2. Performance appears to improve when specific goals are established.
3. Defensiveness caused by criticism nearly always has a negative effect upon a salesperson's performance.
4. Coaching should be performed daily, not once or twice a year at formal performance evaluation interviews.
5. Mutual goal setting, not criticism, tends to improve performance.
6. Interviews held to evaluate performance should not include discussions about compensation.
7. Participation in goal setting by the employer is critical in the process.
8. Appraisals should be based on job responsibilities, not personal characteristics.
9. Managers should be thoroughly trained in the administration of performance evaluation.

This chapter will investigate some of the different techniques used by the sales manager to evaluate performance and will also discuss some of the reasoning behind the preceding generalization.

FORMAL PERFORMANCE EVALUATION PROGRAMS

In most organizations, salespersons are subject to a periodic formal evaluation of their performance. This appraisal is conducted by the sales manager and should answer the following questions for the salesperson:

How am I doing?
How can I improve?
Where do I go from here?

An effective performance appraisal program should provide the sales manager with a rational basis on which to make judgments with respect to promotions, identification of training needs, and the personal growth and development of individual salespeople. Formal performance appraisal programs should *not* be used as a basis for dispensing rewards and punishments. Like most other management techniques, performance appraisal is not a simple process, and what might appear on the surface to be a well thought out system could very well end in disaster.

Formal performance evaluation programs essentially consist of an evaluation interview between the manager and the salesperson and should provide answers for questions raised earlier. The interview is supposed to improve communications and provide *positive* feedback to both parties. It is *not* supposed to lead to hostility, resentment, and/or misunderstanding. There is ample evidence that many formal performance evaluation programs tend to enhance the relationship between manager and salesperson. Programs of this type are well thought out and carefully administered.

Because of the typical human being's reaction to criticism, however, even some well thought out performance appraisal programs fail to achieve positive results. One can well imagine the harm that can be caused by a poorly conceived program.

Unlike most occupations, sales is numbers oriented. No matter how well or how poorly a sales manager feels a salesperson is performing, the monthly sales figures inexorably determine that person's worth over the past thirty days. Whether or not the salesperson's performance *should* be judged by sheer numbers is another matter. There exist many compelling reasons why absolute sales might *not* be an equitable criterion of sales performance. Most of these reasons will be discussed in this chapter. Other things being equal, however, many fair and objective measures of sales performance are tied in with sales figures.

As a result of this numbers orientation, the sales manager should find it easier to justify his or her evaluation of a subordinate's performance than should an accountant or a research administrator. Unfortunately, the sales manager must not only *justify* his or her analysis of the salesperson's performance, but must also gain agreement from the salesperson if the evaluation is to have positive results. To gain this agreement, the program must be easily understood, eminently fair, and should utilize objective criteria whenever possible.

"Hi! I think it's time we had a little talk."

Reprinted with permission. © by *Sales and Marketing Management*.

It should not be inferred from the preceding paragraph that a performance evaluation consists simply of an annual or semiannual interview. A manager is constantly evaluating his or her salespeople. The formal performance review interview is intended to document the manager's appraisal and to provide a forum for the salesperson's analysis of his or her performance.

MECHANICS OF FORMAL PERFORMANCE EVALUATION PROGRAMS

Formal programs normally require five elements: the salesperson, the sales manager, the evaluation technique or instrument, the evaluation interviewer, and the place where the appraisal form is sent at the conclusion of the interview.

In most instances, the sales manager is required to hold the formal evaluation by a certain date. Because of other commitments and because of the disinclination of most sales managers to "play God," evaluations are often held later than they should be.[3] For this reason, the evaluation interviews are typically required to be held and a copy of the form sent to the sales manager's boss by a certain date.

Since both parties are aware of the time and the purpose of the interview, each normally comes prepared to support his or her contentions. Some firms require the salesperson to fill out a self-appraisal form in terms of the same criteria used by the sales manager in the evaluation. The organizational environment fostered by management normally determines the objectivity of the salesperson in self-appraisal. If, for example, he or she thinks the information will be used against him or her at a later date, the salesperson will normally omit any weaknesses or data that could be interpreted in a derogatory way.

Depending upon the objectives of the performance appraisal program, the appraisal form (see Figure 12-1) may or may not be sent up to the next level of sales management. If, for example, recommendations for promotion, dismissal, or salary increase are involved, the appraisal form might go through several levels of management. If, on the other hand, appraisals are held strictly for personal development or improvement purposes, the form may not even be entered in the salesperson's personnel file. For the most part, however, appraisals are normally sent to the next level above the sales manager.

Most appraisals are made on an annual or semiannual basis. As indicated earlier, the manager constantly appraises his or her salespeople, but normally does not discuss these daily appraisals with them. As a general rule, the more frequently formal appraisals are held, the more smoothly the development of the salesperson will run. The primary reasons for this are that the lines of communication between the manager and the salesperson are assured of staying open, and a clear understanding of the salesperson's needs and the sales manager's requirements usually results.

The justification of salary raises is *not* an objective of the performance appraisal. A sales manager in the chemical industry explained why:

> As far as I know, there has never been an evaluation form designed that's perfect. Let's say they *did* put salary increases as an objective of the appraisal—imagine if you have a lot of good reasons why you want to give one of your salesmen a raise, but you know that the form has to read "outstanding." What happens is that you give him a higher rating than he really deserves just so you can get him a raise. You are not only doing a disservice to your firm by painting a false picture, you're doing a disservice to the salesman too. At this point he's going to actually believe that he's great. What do you do—tell the guy you're rating him *excellent* but he's really only *good*? That kind of stuff is precisely what subverts a lot of performance evaluation programs.

Salary increases for salespersons are normally based on sales performance results. Criteria of this type will be discussed later in this chapter.

The type of form used to evaluate the salesperson is, of course, related to the type of evaluation scheme used. If, for instance, the sales manager "rates" salespeople on the basis of certain characteristics, a rating type form is used.[4] This type of form (see Figure 12-2) typically lists various traits or qualities that management associates with sales success. The sales manager then rates the intensity of each trait. In an essay-type appraisal, certain questions are asked and space is left blank for the manager to fill in according to his or her perception of how the employee

Figure 12-1

Typical Rating Form

PERSONNEL

PERFORMANCE FEEDBACK PROGRAM

Exempt Performance Review

NAME	EMPLOYMENT DATE
TITLE	MOST RECENT PROMOTION
Due ______ PAST PERF. REVIEW	LAST SALARY REVIEW

> Let your employee know several days in advance that you will be discussing past performance and goal setting. Have your employee study his/her job description and current plans for the unit and come up with suggestions on improving performance. See your PFP-Guide for ideas on making this review a success.

CODE EACH BOX BELOW TO INDICATE YOUR APPRAISAL OF PERFORMANCE IN THESE AREAS DURING APPRAISAL PERIOD.

- [5] Exceptional Performance – Constant top quality, with little room for improvement.
- [4] Outstanding Performance – Usually above standard, very few errors.
- [3] Satisfactory Performance – Usually meets requirements and standards.
- [2] Uneven Performance – Less than satisfactory, not consistently up to standard, but improving.
- [1] Poor Performance – Improvement required within time limit set.

CONTROLLING – The ability to make planning work. Regulating and scheduling activity to attain desired results. Adhering to budgets. Handling emergencies and preventing problems.	
LEADERSHIP – The ability to motivate and organize subordinates or peers to obtain desired results, Properly delegating authority and responsibility. Developing subordinates to increase their competence and achievement.	
PLANNING – The ability to determine how objectives (Div., Dept., Unit or personal) will be achieved. Deciding how to organize activity of self and others to obtain desired results.	
COOPERATION – Assisting other company groups or individual employees to achieve results. Willingness to give special effort in critical situations.	
COMMUNICATION – The ability to report upward and keep subordinates well informed. Keeping up-to-date in area of job skills and knowledge and sharing useful information.	
ADDITIONAL COMMENTS (use separate sheet if necessary):	

P–12 E (REV.) 1/75

Figure 12-1 (Cont.)

Analyze the results of planning and goal setting from last appraisal.	A
List specific, agreed-upon actions to be taken or objectives to be met by (1) next performance appraisal or (2) next salary review. Note interim timetables where appropriate. (Describe plans to remedy problems cited on reverse side.).	B
Suggestions for self-development of this employee (further education, training, etc.). Has employee set any personal goal (s)?	C
In opinion of reviewer, the following position (s) would be next logical promotional step for this employee. Position Title ______ Paygrade ______ Position Title ______ Paygrade ______ Reviewer Signature ______ Manager/Divisions Officer ______ Personnel ______	D
EMPLOYEE COMMENTS (any areas of specific disagreement with ratings on reverse side or items A B C or D above should be noted here in employee's handwriting.) (Do you understand clearly 1. Your job duties; 2. The objectives you must meet in the following months; 3. How your performance will be measured by your supervisor? What you must do to prepare yourself for promotion?) Employee Signature ______ Date ______	

Figure 12-2

Free-written statement

PERFORMANCE ANALYSIS

What are, in your opinion, the salesperson's strengths?

Mr. Jones is an excellent closer. His presentation is strong on the molychrome assembly unit.

What are the salesperson's weaknesses?

Mr. Jones does not follow up on the R-2 Adapter presentation. His product knowledge in this area is weak.

How would you evaluate the salesperson's paperwork?

Mr. Jones turns in all reports on time and is generally very capable in this area.

What can the salesperson do to improve his or her performance?

Stronger product knowledge in the R-2 product line should help to improve Mr. Jones performance.

When, in your opinion, will the salesperson be ready for increased responsibility?

Mr. Jones is about two years away from serious consideration for management.

Signed Frank Smith
Sales Manager

has performed. In an objective type of appraisal, the salesperson selects certain objectives that are entered into the evaluation form, and so on. While the mechanics of performance appraisal are important and must be well planned and implemented to ensure a smooth interview, simply providing well-thought-out "mechanics" in no way assures that the evaluation will be effective. Probably the most important element of the process is a mutual agreement of (1) ***what is being evaluated*** and (2) the evaluation criteria.

Subjective Evaluation Techniques

Before a sales manager can rate a salesperson's performance, there must be an articulated policy of what is being measured. Since effective performance is presumed to be associated with various degrees of certain qualities exhibited by the salesperson, these qualities must be identified.

In a recent study, sales executives chose ten characteristics of salespeople in the following order of priority:

Enthusiasm
Self-organization
Obvious ambition
High persuasiveness
General sales experience
High verbal skill
Specific sales experience
Highly recommended
Follows instructions
Apparant sociability

Not surprisingly, most sales performance formats attempt to measure the extent of some or all of these characteristics. The effectiveness and validity of the particular evaluation format used depends upon the precision of that instrument. Whether or not the *rating* technique is the best method to use is open to some question.

In most rating systems, the most commonly used format is probably the *graphic scale*. This technique records on a continuum the sales manager's opinion of the intensity of a particular quality or trait.

The advantage of the graphic scale technique is that the adjectives or short statements describing the factor tend to pinpoint the sales manager's evaluation. As long as there is a common understanding of these descriptions, the evaluation is understandable. Unfortunately, it is difficult to attain a universal understanding of how good "good" is. Similarly, descriptions such as "needs improvement" fall short of describing accurately precisely how much improvement the manager feels the salesperson needs.

The *check-mark* technique is used in some rating scales where only two ratings, such as "acceptable" or "not-acceptable," "satisfactory" or "unsatisfactory," or "good" or "bad" are used to describe some attribute of the saleperson's performance. Examples of these attributes might be, for example, "makes enough cold calls," or "turns in reports on time." Because of the specific nature of the attributes in question, the check mark is probably the most accurate of any rating criteria. Unfortunately, it, too, is and can be subject to different opinions by the manager and by the salesperson.

Another popular method of rating is the *critical-incident report*.[6] This technique requires the sales manager to record any specific example of good or poor performance observed. At the end of the period, the manager produces from a "little black book" a written summary of observed incidents. The problems with the *critical-incident* technique are (1) incidents observed by the sales manager amount to only a small fraction of the salesperson's time, and (2) only extreme performance is documented, eliminating most of the salesperson's normal performance.

A third commonly used subjective technique is the *free-written statement*.[7] This method requires the sales manager to write a narrative report on an employee's performance. The literary ability of the sales manager is, unfortunately, a major element of this technique and is often subject to misinterpretation or open to dispute by the salesperson. A further problem with the free-written statement is that all sales managers may not discuss the same factors when evaluating salespeople. This becomes an especially difficult problem when a third party, such as the sales manager's boss, tries to compare evaluations of different salespeople made by different managers.

Objective Appraisal Systems

Subjective evaluation techniques are used by many firms, the "rating" method being the most popular. Much time and effort has gone into the preparation and analysis of the aforementioned techniques, yet there is a great deal of controversy about their validity because of the subjective judgment of the sales manager which is an intrinsic part of these systems. Opponents of subjective types of systems are quick to point out that there are too many factors like reliability and halo effect that can influence a sales manager's judgment.[8] The alternative most commonly offered by advocates of objective performance appraisal systems is the management by objectives (MBO) technique.[9] Although used in various formats, the essential focus of this method is that the salesperson and the sales manager agree on certain performance targets. At the end of the period when the salesperson has either attained or not attained those targets, there can be no confusion as to the fairness of the standards, because theoretically both parties agreed at the outset that the targets were mutually agreed upon.

The MBO approach is basically a process of "contract" negotiation between the sales manager and the salesperson with respect to the latter's specific duties and responsibilities during the upcoming six- or twelve-month period. There are basically five steps in the process:[10]

1. The salesperson drafts a written statement of specific sales, administrative, and personal objectives to be performed during the period, based on quantitative measures, such as "$250,000 in net sales," "45 new accounts opened," and so forth.
2. The salesperson presents the proposal to the sales manager. They meet, negotiate, and agree in writing on the salesperson's final goals and objectives. The final outcome constitutes a "contract" between the two parties.
3. They meet periodically to discuss and review progress, referring to specific items.
4. At the end of the period, the salesperson is evaluated vis-a-vis the goals and objectives that were previously agreed upon.
5. New goals and objectives are set for the following year, which should upgrade the previous year's targets.

According to proponents of the MBO approach, there are several advantages:[11]

1. Salespeople know in advance the precise basis upon which they will be evaluated.
2. The sales manager and the salesperson agree *in writing* on what the latter's job entails.
3. The program takes place within the confines of the supervisor-subordinate relationship, a condition that should strengthen the relationship.
4. Challenging, yet reachable, targets may be set.
5. Training needs, if any, are isolated during as well as after the evaluation period.
6. Performance is judged without regard to personality or other nonoperational characteristics.

An example of an MBO format is shown in Figure 12-3.

To date, the MBO approach is most often used by very large firms.[12] As its supporters point out, there is a great deal of merit in its philosophy. The following statement made by one of its staunchest advocates presents a strong case for its merits:

> The conventional approach [rating scales], unless handled with consummate skill and delicacy, constitutes something dangerously close to violation of the integrity of the personality. Managers are uncomfortable when they are placed in the position of "playing God." The respect we hold for the inherent value of the individual leaves us distressed when we must take responsibility for judging the personal worth of a fellow man. Yet the conventional approach to appraisal forces us not only to make such judgments and to see them acted upon but also to communicate them to those we have judged. No wonder we resist.[13]

Although the MBO approach eliminates to a great extent manager subjectivity and halo effect, this method is not without its shortcomings. In the first place, the MBO approach requires a very strong commitment on the part of management. The enormous amount of paper work generated by this program alone results in a great deal of administrative time and cost. Because of the nature of the commitments made by both parties, such as deadlines, targets, and benefits expected, salespeople have a tendency to become very skeptical of the program if the sales manager does not appear to follow it with great vigor. A third problem generally true of MBO, but necessary in sales, is that it is often difficult to set quantitative targets for many jobs. Because of these problems and others, MBO has proved to be less than a panacea in many firms where it was introduced with great promise. In spite of these shortcomings, however, the MBO approach to performance appraisal has many advantages. A sales manager for a leading data-processing company made these interesting remarks in recalling an incident for the author:

> I got promoted to my first Sales Management position about fifteen years ago. At that time we were using, and still use, a variation of the MBO performance evaluation.
>
> I had led the office in a lot of sales categories and had generally done an outstanding job. In all modesty, I must say that management used excellent judgment in appointing me as the first black sales manager.
>
> I come from the city here, and I met my wife when we were going to Columbia, but she comes from a little town in South Carolina. Right after I got promoted, we went on vacation to visit her family. While we were there I met her grandfather, a man who had been used to some pretty hard times, if you know what I mean. Anyway, somebody told him that I had just gotten promoted and he said to me, "you mean *you* gonna be boss over a bunch of white fellows?" Obviously, he assumed that a lot of racial tension existed up North and my being a black supervisor would exacerbate the problem. I tried to explain to him that my job wasn't "boss," but "Sales Manager" and that not all, but most people in the office were pretty open-minded. He looked very suspicious and finally said "well, I don't know nothin' about them machines you sells or them fancy words you uses, but I do know one thing—*you* tell some of them white boys they ain't doin' a good job, and there gonna be a lynching right in New York!" We all laughed at the time and I remember thinking, "uh-oh, where are they going to lynch me—in front of Friday's?" Afterwards, though, I started to reflect on what the old fellow had said. You know, if we didn't have a very objective method of performance appraisal, I could have had a tough time convincing certain people that they needed improvement in certain areas. The problem would have been that maybe I wouldn't have had the credibility that was needed to get close to them so I could really *help* them. I've moved ahead here and done very well since I first got promoted. I'm not saying I didn't have some luck, but for the most part I got where I am now because my salespeople produced. Again, in all modesty, I feel I've helped develop a lot of people around here, and I've been told more than once, that I never tried to B.S. my people. In my opinion, the most difficult thing a sales manager has to do is sit down and tell a salesperson that he or she needs improvement. I don't care if you're black or white or yellow or orange or chartreuse, if you are critical that person on the other side of the table is going to resent what you say, and if you don't have ammunition to back up your statements, they'll never believe that you're trying to help them and that you're not out to get them. And once they think *that,* you might as well fold up the file on them, because they'll never trust or believe you again.

Figure 12–3

MBO Type statement

WHAT ARE YOUR OBJECTIVES FOR THE NEXT TWELVE MONTHS IN EACH AREA?

Sales Volume:

I expect to sell 185 units from January 1, 1982 through December 31, 1982.

New Accounts:

I will open thirty-two new accounts during this period.

Sales Calls:

I expect to increase my average number of sales calls to fifteen per week during this period.

Sales Expense:

My average weekly expenses will be approximately $85.00 during this period.

ADMINISTRATIVE GOALS

Sales Activity Summary Reports:

These reports will be turned in no later than Monday afternoons.

Quarterly Competitive Reports:

These reports will be turned in no later than the fifth day of the appropriate month. Sales forecasts will also be turned in no later than the fifth of the month.

Figure 12-3 (Cont.)

SELF-DEVELOPMENT GOALS

During this period I will attend all branch seminars and will take an evening college course in Sales Management.

I will also make at least two presentations in sales techniques at sales meetings.

MISCELLANEOUS

During this period I will help to train at least two new salespeople in sales techniques and product knowledge.

Signed ______________________________
Territory Representative

Approved ____________________________
Branch Sales Manager

Most sales managers would agree with the preceding sentiments. Indeed, because of the nature of the job, salespeople are generally quite sensitive and perceptive. Unfortunately, salespeople's egos are also probably a little stronger than those of people in most occupations, and it is often quite difficult for them to accept someone else's opinion that their performance might need improvement. Unless objective performance figures *that the salesperson knows are credible* are forthcoming, his or her willingness to accept the sales manager's conclusions is limited severely. In the final analysis, the primary *purposes* of the performance appraisal are related to not only *measurement*, but *improvement* and *personal development*. If these purposes are not achieved, there is, simply stated, no reason to waste the time and money on a performance appraisal program. It is therefore, of critical importance that the credibility of the method used be instilled and maintained in the minds of the sales force.

All objective measures of evaluation use *performance-based* criteria. The most commonly used are the following:[14]

Percentage of sales quota attained
Sales volume attained
New accounts opened
Profitability
Selling expense versus sales
Territorial efficiency
Number of calls per week
Number of cold calls per week
Number of customer calls per week
Time analysis
Dollar size of average order
Balance of product line sold

The order of priority of these criteria should reflect the needs and objectives of the firm at a given time. Suppose, for example, a firm is attempting to enlarge the market share of a product. Then "sales volume attained" would be a more significant measure of good performance than would profitability. Accordingly, an emphasis on "new accounts opened" would have increased importance since the company is trying to build up its sales base. Because so many different performance criteria can be used to evaluate salespeople, the sales manager must be very careful and discriminating as to the priority of these measures.

Most firms use some form of a *marketing information system* (MIS). The MIS is essentially a periodic document that reflects sales activities and relationships in some or all of the sales performance categories just listed. An MIS for a firm could range from a monthly computer printout documenting results in all areas for each salesperson to a quarterly report on only a few categories, such as total dollar sales. Most firms use some form of MIS for documentation of sales information. In most cases, the specific type of reports used are based on the peculiar needs of the firm and were, in most cases, arrived at through a trial-and-error process. The typical basis for MIS information is source data received from salespeople and sales managers with respect to number of orders received, dollar sales volume, types of calls made, and other input data. This information is then compiled, printed out, and distributed in the form of relationships, such as number of calls per week, number of calls per sales, average order size, or any others required by management. When setting up the MIS, most sales managers tend to require too much data or information that has no real value. In some cases, these reports continue in existence even after the sales manager has moved on. Most experienced salespeople can wryly relate incidents of unnecessary reports being perpetuated; for the most part, however, most MIS systems are sooner or later cut down to the useful essentials.

The information used in making up the MIS reports is critical to the validity and usefulness of the system. The term "garbage in, garbage out" is used by computer specialists to describe the value of reports based on erroneous or inaccurate data. If, for example, a salesperson enters on his or her call report more calls than were actually made, the monthly ratio of calls made in relationship to sales will appear to be higher than it actually is. This, in turn, has the result of making the salesperson appear to be less effective than he or she actually is. Another problem of this type could occur if a salesperson enters fictitious calls for certain product lines; for example, if product A is easier to sell than product B, but management requires a certain percentage of calls to be made selling product B, many salespeople will simply mark on the call report that some calls that were actually made selling A were made selling product B. This type of "doctoring" of call reports has the result of making the B product line look more difficult to sell then it really is.

Although most sales managers expect a certain amount of "judging" on call reports, a significant deviation between reported calls and calls actually made can render the MIS less than an effective tool based on the "garbage in, garbage out" principle. In an interview with the author, a sales manager in the building supplies industry sums up the problem this way:

> I've found over the years that management pretty much gets the kind of sales force it deserves. If you put a lot of pressure on them to make extra calls they're going to be making "ghost calls." Most of the time this happens, it's because somebody on top pushes a panic button and wants the sales force to make some enormous sales increase *now* because somebody upstairs screwed up. What it amounts to is that the sales manager has got to make sure of not putting them into a position where they're forced to cheat on call reports. Usually if a salesmen's call frequency is down, there's a *reason*. I used to have a sales manager who'd tell us "I want to see *eight calls a day* on those call reports." What he was saying was that even if you didn't make them, to make sure they're on the report to take the heat off him. This is bound to happen occasionally and if they fired every sales manager who ever did it, there probably wouldn't be many left. To do this kind of thing though is ridiculous because it just undermines the whole reason for any kind of reporting system. If it can't be constructive, then why the hell even use it?

To avoid the final point made by the foregoing manager, many firms train their sales manager to emphasize the positive aspects of honest, open communications. In the final analysis, any information system is only as good as its input, and the MIS is no exception.

Sales Quotas

For many firms, small and large, the salesperson's value depends upon attainment of sales quota. Firms like IBM and Xerox, for example, have annual recognition meetings for salespeople who have attained 100 percent of quota. In many firms, the salesperson's compensation, recognition, and whole future with the company are based on attainment of quota, although most large firms do use some other evaluation method as a supplement. The concept of *quota performance* is based upon the salesperson's achieving a certain sales target, normally described in dollar volume or in units of sale, for a given period. Quotas are almost always set up on a monthly basis *and* on an annual basis. There is seldom any subtlety about the salesperson's performance in relation to quota in sales organizations. If he or she attained 100 percent or more, it was a good year. The only ingredient about quota that varies among firms is the emphasis placed on its attainment. Firm A, for example, might tolerate less than 100 percent quota performance for several years if the salesperson appears to possess other valuable assets; firm B might have a policy to automatically dismiss any sales representative who misses 100 percent quota attainment for two consecutive years.

Implicit in assigning the salesperson a quota to be attained is the assumption that the sales manager has assigned a quota that is fair and equitable. Firms like IBM and Xerox use many sophisticated techniques in customer analysis and forecasting to determine actual territorial potential. An extremely careful and painstaking process is required to be used by sales managers before assigning quotas. Many firms, however, have neither the instruments nor the expertise to make accurate estimates of territorial potential. In Chapter 10, the importance of accurately estimating sales potential was pointed out, and unless a firm is able to make accurate estimates, the chances of assigning fair quotas are diminished greatly.

Assuming that the sales manager *has* (and in many cases, even if he or she *has not*) assigned fair quotas, the technique as an important criterion of sales performance has long been popular with most firms. One reason for this is that there appears to be an inescapable logic attached to the use of this standard. The salesperson either came through or did not. And if the salesperson did "come through," how much better did he or she perform than the rest of the sales force? Another advantage to the *quota* technique of evaluation is that, once it is set, it is rarely adjusted. This usually gives the salesperson an entire year to make up for lean months. As indicated previously, if quotas are not set fairly, the chances of losing good salespeople and rewarding marginal performances are greatly increased. There are also many situations in which sales quotas are used unjustifiably, for example, with new products where management does not yet comprehend sales

"Yes, J.B., everyone here was absolutely stunned, too, by the news of another price increase!"

potential. Most organizations, however, have always used and will continue to use sales quotas as a criterion of performance.

PROBLEMS OF SALES PERFORMANCE APPRAISAL

Most, if not all, sales managers realize that no performance appraisal program is or will be perfect. At best, an appraisal program performs the functions for which it was intended (assessment of job performance, improvement of personal growth and development, isolation of training needs, improvement of communications). If most or all of these functions are enhanced by the program, it should be considered a success. Unfortunately, some programs actually have a negative effect and produce results counterproductive to their stated objectives. These problems are typically associated with the program itself, the manager, or, to a lesser extent, with exogenous or outside factors.

The Program

A traditional problem of performance evaluation is the program itself. If, for example, a program is used to simultaneously provide a written justification for a salary increase and to motivate a salesperson to improve performance, these conflicting purposes will tend to render the program valueless. The discussion will tend to focus around the justification for a monetary reward, while the appraisal discussion will have little or no influence on future performance.

A second problem inherent in many programs is the existence of built-in subjective features. In *rating* methods particularly, a pseudoscientific approach is too often taken. The format of a program, for example, might list several traits of a salesperson to be objectively evaluated by the manager. "Enthusiasm" and "verbal skill," for example (two attributes mentioned by executives as being important in the evaluation of salespeople), are not subject to the same interpretation by any two sales managers; no matter how thoroughly trained they may be in the administration of the program, lack of precision in defining the extent of the salesperson's competence in *any* attribute will in fact tend to diminish the precision and therefore the value of evaluation. If, two managers cannot agree, how will the salesperson agree, particularly if the evaluation is in any way critical.

A further problem of performance evaluation programs is the controversy generated by them. Even if a program is well thought out and implemented properly, general skepticism of its value will normally diminish its utility. Skepticism of formal programs occurs when the sales force perceives that the firm's management (not necessarily their own sales manager) is using the program in some manipulative way, such as an excuse to "clean house" or to reduce territory size. In cases of this type, the firm must improve communications with the sales force and regain their confidence before any positive results from the program can be expected.

The Manager

Although many programs are well thought out and well designed, they fail because of shortcomings of the manager administering them. Most of the problems associated with the manager are caused by a lack of expertise in the administration of the evaluation. Probably the most common problem in this area is the sales manager's subjectivity in evaluating the salesperson. Since many firms use rate-form techniques, it is very easy for the manager to form his or her own judgment as far as standards of performance are concerned. Since it is difficult, if not impossible, for a firm to adequately describe what "good" or "excellent" means, most managers develop their own interpretations. This problem is difficult to overcome, even when the firm makes a strong commitment to manager training.

A second problem with performance appraisal programs caused by sales managers is the setting of unfair sales quotas. Many sales managers are unwilling or unable to do the research necessary to determine accurately the sales potential of each territory. Yet quotas are expected to be met, and the salesperson's performance is judged in relation to the established quota. In many cases, sales managers simply add a figure like 10 percent to the previous year's quota and proceed to evaluate salespeople accordingly. This problem can only be overcome if a sales manager is willing and able to develop and use techniques like the ones discussed in Chapter 10.

A further problem is the manager's unwillingness to "play God." In many cases, particularly where rating scales are used, sales managers tend to rate certain employees higher than they deserve. The manager does this for several reasons. Probably the most common reason is that the manager wants to give the salesperson the "benefit of the doubt." Lacking concrete indisputable facts to back up critical comment, a lot of managers tend to allow a "halo effect" to enter into the evaluation, favoring high sales producers and often disfavoring low producers. A second reason is that many managers who know better are afraid that, since negative criticism will probably adversely affect the salesperson's performance, a positive evaluation might stimulate sales performance. These problems and other manager-associated problems can often be reduced by extensive training in the administration of the evaluation program.

Exogenous Factors

Even the most well conceived performance appraisal programs can go haywire when unforeseen incidents occur. The bulk of these uncontrollable factors are associated with undetected changes that take place during the evaluation period. Examples are as follows:

1. *Competitive conditions:* an increase in competitive activity can result in lost sales.
2. *Windfall sales:* A large unexpected order can result in making the salesperson's performance look more effective than it really is.
3. *Physical changes in territory:* The movement of a large customer or a number of smaller customers in or out of a territory can have either a favorable or unfavorable impact upon the salesperson's quota achievement.
4. *Outside support:* A large expenditure on advertising or sales promotion in a territory may greatly affect the salesperson's statistics.

Exogenous or outside factors similar to the preceding have the effect of making the salesperson's performance look better or worse than it really is. To reduce the effect of these factors, sales managers require their salespeople to report on changes as they occur. A problem exists when such factors go undetected. Unfortunately, a certain amount of outside influence occurs in every territory that is never known by either the manager or the salesperson. Most managers hope that a combination of positive and negative factors will tend to offset each other over a given period of time. Obviously, this fatalism may or may not be well founded. There is, however, a limit to the resources that can be expended to uncover sales territory changes.

The Practical Sales Performance Evaluation Program

This chapter has set forth most if not all of the various types of sales performance appraisal programs, both form and informal. An accompanying anaysis of the advantages and problems of these programs has indicated that there does not appear to be any one foolproof program that has been developed to date. The past two decades of research, however, have uncovered certain relationships between evaluation and sales performance that suggest some workable evaluation programs. There is little doubt that further refinements can probably be expected in the future, but the state of the art favors flexible evaluation programs that incorporate the strongest aspects of the various types of format.

Objectively based programs provide a qualified basis on which to measure or compare sales performance with expected sales, but behavioral criteria, many of which are of critical importance, may not be evaluated easily. On the other hand, subjective appraisal techniques such as rating scales provide an indication, albeit subjective, of the salesperson's behavioral and personality "performance." Because of the need for performance data in *all* areas, the most practical evaluation programs tend to incorporate aspects of both objective and subjective techniques. Many companies, in fact, tend to use an MBO approach supplemented by the sales manager's filling out graphic rating scales to supplement the objective data. In addition to these two evalution tools, sales quotas are also assigned. Determinants of weights attached to each technique depend primarily upon the goals and strategies of the sales organization. If, for example, a salesperson is being considered for promotion or dismissal, the manager's rating of his or her personal traits would provide an important supplement to the objective instrument that would be used. If, on the other hand, the employee is being considered for a salary increase, sales performance statistics would be emphasized.

The most important aspect of performance appraisal is its credibility. If the salespeople being evaluated are cynical, skeptical, or diffident about the program itself, the reasons for its use, or its fairness, the program will probably hinder rather than help the effectiveness of the sales organization. If, on the other hand, the program does what it is supposed to do and measures performance fairly, facilitates personal growth and development, lets the salespeople know where they stand, and improves communications, its value to the sales effort will be outstanding.

SUMMARY

There are several ways in which organizations measure sales performance. Subjective methods reflect the manager's perceived judgment based upon his or her observation of the salesperson. Objective methods are based upon impartial setting and consequent attainment of certain targets, and performance-based techniques are based upon certain bench-mark goals already installed by the organization.

Formal programs should answer the questions related to the salesperson's progress and should not be used as reward or sanction criteria. Some of the more commonly used evaluation techniques are the rating system, graphic scales, check-mark scales, critical-incident reports, and free-written statements. The former techniques are subjective-type evaluations. Some of the more commonly used objective techniques are management by objectives types of programs or other variations of participative techniques in which the salesperson has some influence over how he or she will be judged.

Most performance-based criteria lend themselves to a marketing information system in which data in the form of a report are fed back to sales management on a regular basis. These criteria are related to sales volume, calls made, expense control, and other regularly measurable data.

Although it is difficult to make general statements because organizations have different approaches to the selling function, the most practical method of performance evaluation should be objectively based. The advantage of a program of this type is that the salesperson has helped to set his or her targets and must accept the responsibility for their attainment. The technique then becomes a control technique, as well a performance evaluation tool. No matter how comprehensive the performance appraisal technique is, however, some performance-based criteria are *always* used in conjunction with other evaluation criteria.

Performance appraisal programs are sometimes limited by the structure of the program itself, by the manager who administers the program, and by various outside factors such as competition, changes in the nature of the territory, windfall sales, and the extent of outside support.

Marketing Systems Corporation

Marketing Systems Corporation (MSC) is in the time-sharing business. The company owns a large computer and sells space in the computer and also performs accounting, payroll, and other functions for clients. Because of heavy competition, the firm trains its salespeople to be highly aggressive in the selling of their services. Jon Anderson was hired by the company about 18 months ago. He graduated from college and went into pharmaceutical sales. After about a year, Jon wanted something with a little more action, so he went to work with an office products firm and was very successful selling to commercial accounts. Since the selling of MSC services is roughly similar to selling the office equipment, the branch manager of MSC, Steve Howe, was delighted to hire Jon and indicated that it would be possible for Jon to become a manager within 6 months if he came with MSC.

From the start, Jon was an excellent performer. He was 30 percent over the sales quota, worked long hours, and was helpful in many ways around the office. His paperwork was always on time, and several of the older salespeople often asked his advice. After he had been with MSC for 6 months, Jon approached Steve and reminded him of his "promise" to promote him if he performed well. At that time, Steve told Jon that the 6-month time span was an estimate, not a certainty. He told Jon to sit tight and that his chance would come.

When Jon had been with the firm for about a year, his performance was still outstanding, but one of the older salespeople, Sheila Young, was promoted to branch manager at another location. Sheila was obviously a good choice, but her sales performance was nowhere near as effective as Jon's. Jon went in to see Steve and complained about his not getting the promotion. Steve told Jon that Sheila got her promotion because there was pressure to appoint female managers. "Besides," said Steve, "you're making as much money as you would if you were manager, and there's a lot less aggravation." Steve further advised Jon that, although he was an excellent salesperson, there was little indication that we would perform well as a manager.

When Steve came in to the office one morning about two weeks later, there was a letter of resignation from Jon on his desk.

1. If you were Steve, how would you have handled the situation?
2. If you were Jon, what would have been your approach when you were hired?

The Scottie Optical Company

Douglas MacPherson is sales manager for Scottie Optical Company, a manufacturer and distributor of eyeglass frames. The firm imports some frames in addition to its own line so that it carries a full range of frames at all prices.

Connie Kruse is the leading salesperson for the organization. During 1980 her sales volume was roughly $200,000 against a quota for $100,000. This volume accounted for about $120,000 in gross profit from the firm. Additionally, Connie's call frequency was about 20 percent higher than the average. She worked from 8 A.M. to 9 P.M. on most days, since most of her customers and prospects were open at night. She also led the sales force in new accounts and in lowest number of returns. Since Mr. MacPherson insisted that salespeople pay their own expenses, there were no records kept of expense control.

Salespeople at Scottie are paid on straight salary plus a bonus to be paid upon "overall performance." The decision for bonuses is made by Mr. MacPherson at an annual performance review. The firm uses a rating form, which the sales manager fills out. The salesperson is allowed to see the rating form and discuss it with the manager. Connie's performance evaluation came up in February, and she was presented with the following form:

Characteristics	*Rating* 5	4	3	2	1
Adaptability			x		
Cooperation		x			
Appearance	x				
Handling objections		x			
Closing		x			
Prospecting			x		
Interest in job			x		
Creativity				x	
Judgment				x	
Reporting and paperwork		x			

Comments:
Should improve on creative selling and prospecting. Somewhat stubborn in approach to certain accounts. Could use better judgment in voicing opinion at sales meetings.

Recommendation:
Bonus of $250. Raise salary from $200 per week to $220.

Key: 5 = excellent; 4 = good; 3 = average; 2 = poor; 1 = unacceptable.

When Connie read the form, she and Mr. MacPherson had the following conversation:

Connie: I'm really surprised that you gave me such a low rating, Mr. MacPherson; after all, I *was* your top salesperson in 1980.

Mr. MacPherson: Oh, I gave you a very good rating, Connie. It's just that I don't give out 5's willy-nilly like some of our younger managers.

Connie: Well, the only thing is, even so, don't you think I deserve more than a $250 bonus? Jimmy got $1000 and he didn't sell half of what I sold.

Mr. MacPherson: Jimmie's been with us for ten years, Connie. When you show that you're a real Scotties man, I mean, heh-heh, Scottie's *person,* you'll be ready for a big bonus too.

Connie: But Mr. MacPherson, I have two little children to support and a housekeeper to pay to watch them and other expenses. At $220 a week, I can barely make it. I don't want to bring this up again, but Jimmy makes $350, and there's just him and his wife.

Mr. MacPherson: Well Connie, we at Scottie feel that people should be paid on performance, not need. This is a free-enterprise system, not socialism.

Connie: Oh, Mr. MacPherson, I'm not asking for anything I don't deserve. I just think that maybe my evaluation should have been a little better.

Mr. MacPherson: Well Connie, at least that shows that you have some ambition. Keep selling and maybe next year after you're here a little longer, we'll see what we can do.

1. How would you evaluate the Scottie performance appraisal system?
2. If you were Connie, what would be some specific questions you would ask Mr. McPherson?

DISCUSSION QUESTIONS

1. What is the purpose of a formal performance evaluation program? What questions should it address?
2. Describe the mechanics of a formal performance review.

3. What are the advantages and disadvantages of the following appraisal methods: (a) subjective method; (b) objective method; (c) performance-based method?
4. Why should a performance review be separate from a salary review?
5. What is management by objectives (MBO)? What are the advantages of this approach as the basis for appraisal?
6. In a performance-based review, list objective measures of evaluation in order of priority for a specified case history.
7. What are the external factors generally outside of a salesperson's control that can influence major factors of favorable or unfavorable performance? How are these to be handled in reviews?
8. You have a severe personality and communications problem with your boss. What can you do about it? Describe the alternatives in some detail.

NOTES

[1]See, for example, the sample evaluation forms used in this chapter.

[2]These "principles" have evolved over the past two decades.

[3]Alva Kindall and James Gatza, "Positive Program for Performance Appraisal," *Harvard Business Review*, July–August 1962, pp. 125–34.

[4]Paul Pigors and Charles Meyers, *Management of Human Resources* (New York: McGraw-Hill), 1973.

[5]Bob Arnold, "People and Management," *Marketing Times*, November/December 1979, p. 3.

[6]See "How to Select a Sales Force that Sells," H. R. Chally Group, Inc., 2600 Far Hill, Dayton, Ohio, p. 12.

[7]See A. M. Speers and D. G. Spencer, "Achievement Needs and MBO Goal Setting," *Personnel Journal*, vol. 57, no. 1 (January 1978), pp. 26–28.

[8]A convincing argument for objectivity in performance evaluation is made by Douglas McGregor in "An Uneasy Look at Performance Appraisal," *Harvard Business Review*, May-June 1957, p. 89.

[9]See George Odiorne, *Management by Objectives* (New York: Pitman, 1965).

[10]Gordon Storholm, "An MBO Approach to Placement Office Effectiveness," *Journal of College Placement*, Summer 1978, p. 53.

[11]Ibid.

[12]See David Hopkins, Marketing Performance Evaluation Information Bulletin 53 (New York: Conference Board February 1979).

[13]Douglas McGregor, *The Human Side of Enterprise* (New York: McGraw-Hill), 1960.

[14]Frank Eby, *How to Increase Sales and Profits through Salesman Performance Evaluation* (New York: Dartnell Corp.), 1974.

CHAPTER 13

SALES PERFORMANCE PROBLEMS AND SOLUTIONS

OBJECTIVES

To analyze causes of poor sales performance:

* Poor self-organization
* Limited selling ability
* Inadequate self-motivation
* Personal problems
* Organization and supervision
* Poor attitude
* Organizational change

To identify solutions to sales performance problems:

* The administrative apparatus
* Sales training
* The sales management

To provide the reader with a basic understanding of the most common sales performance problems:

* Poor self-organization
* Limited selling ability
* Inadequate self-motivation
* The organization
* Poor attidude
* Organizational change

To analyze some widely used solutions to sales performance problems:

* The administrative apparatus
* Sales training
* The sales manager

INTERVIEW WITH FRANK SMITH

Interviewer: Frank, let's talk about improving sales performance. Can a sales manager develop specific programs in this regard?

Frank Smith: Yes, you certainly can. The thing that has to be understood is that every case is different because every personality is different. There are, however, many instances of implementation of programs that improved the performance of many salespeople in an organization. All sales managers have seen this happen.

Interviewer: That would imply, then, that there was something wrong with the sales policies of the organization to begin with, and that after certain changes were made salespeople were able to perform more effectively.

Frank Smith: That's probably true in most cases. You have to remember, though, no sales organization is perfect. The worst approach to improving sales performance is to be judgmental. Find the problem, then try to correct it. What happened in the past is over and done with. I think it is to an organization's credit that it can find out where it went wrong and then correct the problem.

Interviewer: Right. You said that every case is different. Are you saying that sales managers need to understand the problems that each salesperson faces?

Frank Smith: Unfortunately, yes. It's true that a few people are hired poorly and shouldn't even be in sales. Also, a small percentage of salespeople develop such a negative attitude that they should get out of the business; but for the most part, salespeople have specific problems that stand in the way of their performance, and it's the job of the sales manager to discover what the problems are and try to correct them.

Interviewer: Do you find that there are patterns; for example, experienced people have one set of problems and new people have different types of problems?

Frank Smith: Generally, I would say yes. First of all, and make no mistake about it, experienced salespeople definitely consider themselves professionals. I know a few professional athletes and musicians, and they have a lot in common with top salespeople as far as their egos and insecurities are concerned. On the other hand, new people can develop problems that are more job-centered initially, like handling objections or prospecting, but because these skill problems retard their performance, the salesperson becomes very discouraged. Then you have an attitude problem.

Interviewer: Then what's the difference between motivating salespeople and improving their performance?

Frank Smith: They are mutually exclusive. Motivation is positive; it's a process that the sales manager attempts to provide *everyone* with. People also motivate themselves. Improving performance is tied in with something more negative, I'm afraid. We're not talking about making a .325 hitter into a .350 hitter. You have to have a performance letdown or problem before you *improve* it. Therefore, you can't talk about improving performance unless you analyze the causes or contributing factors.

Interviewer: Do you think that all salespeople have problems from time to time?

Frank Smith: Oh yes, definitely. The really top performers normally get themselves out of slumps. Can I make an analogy between a par golfer and a good salesperson? Sometimes one or two lessons point out a few simple changes that have to be made, and the golfer is shooting par again. With a really good experienced salesperson, there's a close correlation to the good golfer. On the other hand, with a less effective salesperson, it's not so simple.

Interviewer: Then you feel that this chapter will give us some insight into the various reasons why you have subpar performance, right?

Frank Smith: Exactly. And through an understanding of these causes and conditions, we can look at some different ways in which performance can be improved.

Two of the most time consuming but important functions of sales management are the identification and elimination of the causes of poor sales performance. Sales as an occupation has a very high rate of personnel turnover when compared with most other white-collar occupations. The primary reason for this high turnover is poor sales performance. Part of the reason lies in the unique nature of the selling job. The rate of rejection, for example, is very high. Another unique aspect of selling is its lack of closure. Salespeople are very frequently independent of any supervision and are not required to be at a desk all day as in many occupations. The need to be a "self-starter" is yet another characteristic of sales that is unique. These and other factors, all of which are considered highly desirable by most salespeople, can be sources of problems as well. It can often take several weeks, or even months, for example, before poor selling skills or work habits are discovered by the sales manager. Often, by the time these problems have manifested themselves, extensive application is required to overcome them. Specific performance problems are not the only impediments to effective selling; personal and organizational causes also contribute. Fortunately, many problems of poor sales performance are solvable. This chapter will investigate some of the causes, effects, and contributing factors to ineffective selling and possible remedial action.

CAUSES OF POOR SALES PERFORMANCE

It is somewhat presumptuous to cite a specific set of causes of poor sales performance in the same way that a General Motors manual cites a finite set of causes of poor engine performance. Clearly, when dealing with human factors, the process of identifying causes of any type of behavior is much more complex. Indeed, a *combination* of causes and contributing factors normally exists, a factor that can complicate the process of finding the root of the problem. A starting point or frame of reference is needed, however, and there appear to be about seven general sources from which the majority of sales performance problems emanate. The order of importance of each causal factor is clearly impossible to determine. In specific organizations, however, certain causes tend to arise more often than others.

Poor self-organization
Limited selling ability
Inadequate self-motivation
Personal problems
Organization and supervision
Poor attitude
Organizational change

This section will discuss the nature of these problems (see Table 13-1) and how they affect sales performance. Some steps toward a solution or toward temporary remedial action will be discussed later in the chapter.

Poor Self-organization

The selling profession requires that the successful practitioner be extremely well organized. Most studies indicate that the typical salesperson spends only about 15 to 25 percent of his or her time in front of a qualified prospect, depending upon the industry and type of products or services being sold.[1] In most cases, a deviation from this norm of 25 percent one way or the other can make the difference between being a mediocre, or even poor, salesperson and an effective one. For example, if an industry and company average of time spent in front of qualified prospects is 2 hours per day, then a 25 percent differential would extend this range from 1½ hours to 2½ hours. This differential of 1 hour would make the difference between unacceptable sales performance and outstanding sales performance.

Specific data on productive time spent by salespeople will be examined more closely in Chapter 14, and it is not our intention, at this point in the text, to get involved in an in-depth analysis of how salespeople spend their time. Suffice it to say that very few salespeople spend more than 2½ hours per day actually *selling*. To achieve this standard, it is necessary for the salesperson to be highly organized and to possess an uncommon amount of self-discipline in his or her daily work habits. This self-organization extends to highly detailed aspects of the selling job, such as performing paper-work functions, returning telephone calls promptly, planning out calls for the coming week, and a multitude of other seemingly mundane tasks. Yet, unless the salesperson has a planning system to accomplish these requirements, he or she cannot maintain the effectiveness required to be a top producer. Many salespeople do not have such a system. The personality characteristics of the "typical" salesperson do not lend themselves to strong attention to detail.[2] Many salespeople find that a commitment to a meticulous and well-planned schedule is an unnatural act.

TABLE 13-1

Causes of Poor Sales Performance

Poor Self-organization: Lack of discipline, lack of application, poor planning.
Limited Selling Ability: Lack of confidence, easily intimidated, poor application.
Inadequate Self-motivation: Failure to set targets, lose interest, not "hungry."
Personal Problems: Professional, family, health, tension.
The Organization: Inadequate training, lack of marketing orientation, paper work.
Poor Attitude: Rejection, peers, negativist.
Organizational Change: New manager, new territory, new products.

Sales managers find that in many cases some of their most talented salespeople are poorly organized, a factor that inhibits effective sales performance. No matter how much training these people are given, they seem to become well organized only for a short period of time and then fall back into their old disorganized ways. Unfortunately, it is nearly impossible for the salesperson to lack effective self-organization skills and still be able to spend the required time in front of qualified prospects on a consistent basis.

Limited Selling Ability

Many salespeople simply lack the requisite skills to become anything more than marginal producers. The phrase often used by salespeople to describe the lack of selling expertise of a peer is that "he or she couldn't close a door!" This is, unfortunately, an unkind but essentially accurate statement. Without the recognized selling skills, it is difficult for any salesperson to become a compelling factor in the sales manager's achievement of his or her objectives. There are several reasons why many salespeople are unable to utilize effective selling methods.

Lack of sales skill is normally more prevalent in newer salespeople. The primary reason is lack of confidence. This is a common problem in many cases where a salesperson has not been successful. A vicious cycle manifests itself; lack of success leads to one's lack of confidence in his or her ability to sell. This lack of confidence is reflected in the sales presentation and has the effect of detracting from the salesperson's credibility or in some other way "turning off" the customer. The salesperson might also lack confidence because of inadequate knowledge of the product or its applications. In either case, the salesperson's lack of confidence has a negative effect, usually resulting in lost sales.

Some salespeople are easily intimidated by certain customers. While most effective salespeople thrive on meeting top executives, others are intimidated by their status and usually "blow" the sales presentation through nervousness or through temporary loss of verbal and persuasive skill.

In some cases, salespeople have a basic lack of confidence in their product or possibly even in selling as a profession. It is not surprising that such convictions tend to impede the aura of sincerity and conviction that is necessary to obtain credibility with prospects.

Whatever the specific reason for it, sales managers agree that lack of expertise in selling ability accounts for a great deal of lost sales.

Inadequate Self-motivation

In Chapter 6 the subject of individual motivation was discussed. Certain people have a strongly felt need to achieve, which drives them toward accomplishment of predetermined goals, and the sales profession seems to provide a logical occupational base for these persons.[3] While this personality characteristic certainly appears to be present to some degree in a large proportion of salespeople, it by no means applies to everyone in the field. A large number of salespeople who have the ability to perform well simply do not possess the internal drive that is necessary for effective sales performance on a consistent basis.

A primary reason for this lack of internal drive is the failure of the salesperson to set clear, attainable, and realistic goals. Without applying a candid assessment of one's abilities and resources to a commitment in terms of tangible expected results, it is quite easy for salespeople to slip behind in sales performance. This problem often arises when the salesperson becomes so enmeshed in customer service, paper work, and other nonselling activities that he or she tends to forget, at least temporarily, about the critical nature of setting targets and concentrating on sales as his or her priority. This tendency exists with experienced salespeople, as well as new ones, and is an easy trap to fall into, but not an easy one from which to extricate oneself.

Another problem associated with target setting exists when salespeople have little or no influence upon the goals they must reach. In many sales organizations, management sets the quotas to be reached by sales-force members. These quotas are usually assigned from the national to the regional level until the sales force, as the last remaining group, are assigned the branch quota, broken down on an individual basis. The logic of assigning quotas in this fashion may be impeccable from a mathematical point of view, but it fails to take into account the somewhat illogical mentality of the individual salesperson. It is a well-documented fact that most salespeople usually perform more effectively when they have some say in setting their own sales targets.[4] Unfortunately, many sales organizations take the viewpoint that sales quota assignments are the result of some arcane knowledge of the top executives and must be inflexible. This kind of attitude often impedes rather than encourages sales performance.

A further problem associated with poor self-motivation is lack of interest by the salesperson in his or her job, product, or customer base. In certain selling situations, particularly in technical or commercial sales, where salespeople call on the same customers and prospects year after year, salespeople tend to develop an insensitivity to sales opportunities. This may come from the salesperson's conviction that he or she is so familiar with the territory that there is little more that can be done to influence sales. Salespeople often become complacent in this type of situation, and their approach to the territory is one of boredom rather than interest.

A widely accepted reason for lack of self-motivation is the salesperson's apparent loss of the "killer instinct." When a sales manager complains that a salesperson is not "hungry," he or she is referring to the same general condition. This condition is associated with the presumption by many sales executives that salespeople tend to become lazy when they do not have an immediate need for cash. This theory is, in many cases, an oversimplification, because it overstresses the importance of money as a motivating factor. There are, however, many cases where the theory seems to be totally justified, particularly in direct-sales situations.[5] It is not an unreasonable assumption that many salespeople tend to ease their efforts when they no longer have a great need for money, and nearly any sales manager can relate one or more classic examples of this phenomenon that he or she has observed.

Personal Problems

In sales, as in any other occupation, individuals have personal problems to cope with that tend to affect their work performance. At one time or another, every person goes through some emotional crisis, and it is unrealistic for managers to discount their occurrence. Women go through menopause, men experience some sort of "mid-life crisis," and younger people experience specific emotional trauma at various times. Individual personal problems have, for some reason, always been pushed into the background by sales managers. There has been a presumption that mention of personal problems as a debilitating factor might be contagious to the rest of the sales force. There are also implications of shame and embarrassment, which cause people to hide personal problems. Instead of facing them squarely and dealing with problems as they arise, American business and industry have had an implicit policy of pushing problems to the background. This policy simply builds up tension and typically has the effect of exacerbating the problem rather than reducing it.

Family problems are a rather common occurrence in sales. One familiar with sales could suggest that at least some of the characters on the contemporary soap operas be salespeople instead of medical people. As with most professionals, changing attitudes, inflation, and the pressures to maintain a contemporary life-style have resulted in various family problems for salespeople. The incidence of teenage alcohol and drug use and the relatively high rate of marriage breakup are contributors to less than optimal sales performance.

Physical health problems likewise tend to reduce many salespeople's production. To begin with, sales requires more physical stamina than most occupations. Most salespeople either drive or walk considerable distances as part of their job. Others log an inordinate amount of time on the road, not always obtaining proper diet or rest. Smoking also seems to be highly prevalent in certain sales occupations, particularly in direct sales. In many selling jobs, it is customary for salespeople to have one or more drinks at lunchtime on a regular basis. Given the normal curve of physical tolerance (or intolerance) to poor diet, lack of rest, smoking, alcohol, and tension, it is not surprising that a certain percentage of nearly any sales force is apt to be operating at less than peak efficiency at least part of the time.

The Organization

In many cases, an organization's own policies tend to be counterproductive to its sales efforts. The most shortsighted policy in this area is, of course, the failure of companies to commit adequate funds to sales training. In most cases of this type, sales managers are well aware of the problem and its consequences, but are unable to convince the company hierarchy to spend the necessary dollars. Many executives feel that a large portion of training expenditures are unnecessary frills and that good salespeople possess the necessary skills without additional training.

A second company-induced performance problem arises in firms that do not have a marketing orientation. Many administrative people view the sales force as a necessary evil and are quite insensitive to customer needs that are brought to their attention through salespeople. Problems such as delivery, pricing, billing, and delay in quotation are avoidable and militate against the salesperson's and the firm's credibility. Eventually, the customer goes elsewhere for a supplier.

Many extraneous paper-work and other nonselling activities are forced upon salespeople, nearly always at the wrong time. Without a rational administrative apparatus, a sales force will cease to function efficiently, but many organizations allow executives to require reports, information, and other nonselling work that is either unnecessary or poorly thought out. In either case, the information is normally gained or the project carried out at the expense of sales volume.

The practice of paying salespeople late has a demoralizing effect and in most cases causes diminished sales activity. This practice is widespread in direct sales, but is by no means limited to this sector. Most often, sloppy clerical administrative reporting is responsible for delays. Lack of a clear marketing orientation of clerical personnel normally causes this problem. There is a great deal of evidence to support the contention that salespeople tend to perform less effectively when they are not paid on time.[6] Yet many firms persist, either accidently or by design, to pay commissions long after salespeople have earned it and their "momentum" has waned.

Poor Attitude

Unlike most occupations, selling requires an almost unrealistic or naive belief that most prospects can be sold. In an environment where rejection is the rule rather than the exception, it is very easy to become discouraged and develop a negative attitude toward one's job. In many occupations, a positive mental attitude is not necessary. In noncompetitive positions like accounting, personnel, and finance, for example, a negative attitude will not necessarily stand in the way of effective performance. In sales, however, a negative attitude not only inhibits the salesperson from performing enthusiastically, but also rubs off on the prospect or customer. The high incidence of rejection in selling causes many salespeople to develop a negative or defeatist attitude. This attitude in turn keeps the salesperson from performing well, which in turn leads to greater discouragement and further attitudinal problems.

In some cases, particularly with a newer, more impressionable salesperson, peer group attitude has a strong impact on his or her outlook. In group discussions among peers, many salespeople make cynical comments about the organization and the sales manager or voice their complaints about company products. Whether the complaints are valid or not, they often create doubts in the mind of the new salesperson and lead that person to develop a negative attitude.

In other cases, salespeople have a negative attitude because they have been thinking in negative terms most of their lives. This attitude should become apparent to the sales manager prior to hiring the negative individual. Unfortunately, for various reasons, some negativists are hired anyway. There is ample evidence that such salespeople are usually a liability to the sales force, yet nearly every sales force has its share of negative thinkers.

Organizational Change

The contemporary literature in the fields of administrative management and organization behavior virtually abounds with the effects of organization change upon the individual. Salespeople likewise find that through the initial shock waves of change their productivity often suffers. Most sales managers should expect this condition and be prepared for it.

The most common type of organization change that affects salespeople is the appointment of a new manager. As in other change situations, fear of the unknown tends to permeate the environment in most sales offices. Until some rapport is developed with new managers, salespeople often tend to take a very tentative approach to performing their duties. Eventually, the sales force adapts to the new manager and the environment is one of "business as usual," but it is not uncommon to see the performance of some salespeople decline somewhat in the interim.

The assignment of new sales territories is another example of organization change that often has an impact upon sales performance. Until the salesperson has had an opportunity to become familiar with his or her new accounts and even the new logistical arrangements, sales may be expected to decline.

Introduction of new products may also contribute to a decline in production. Salespeople, in attempting to develop markets for new products, sometimes do so at the expense of existing product sales. It is not unusual for firms to devote more of their resources to the introduction of new products, leaving less time available for the pursuit of solid business in existing areas.

In addition to changes in management, territory, and products, there are many other types of organizational change that result in either long- or short-run sales performance decline.

According to an interview with Jack R. Dauner and Eugene Johnson, their survey shows that the problems that plagued sales managers over 20 years ago are similar to contemporary problems (see Table 13-2). In an extensive survey sponsored by Sales and Marketing Executives International, sales managers were asked to list in order of priority *problems with salespeople that trouble sales executives most* and *reasons for firing salespeople* (see Table 13-3). The results of the studies in 1979 and 1959 were startling similar. Except for a perceived drop in the quality of sales training, the major problems that existed in 1959 seem to exist today.

The study outlined in Table 13-2 would seem to indicate quite clearly that selling is a profession requiring a great deal of self-discipline. It is interesting to note that the same problems exist while training capability or expertise has declined. Whether or not a cause-and-effect relationship exists cannot be determined from the available data. It is certain, however, that a great deal of attention must be given to individual salespeople and their shortcomings.

SOLUTIONS TO POOR SALES PERFORMANCE

The first part of this chapter discussed various causes of poor sales performance. This section will deal with approaches to solutions to both general and specific types of problems, to the extent that solutions do, of course, exist. It must be recognized that certain problem areas have *no* solution. An attempt to solve a problem must be weighed from the standpoint of costs and benefits. It may appear callous to suggest, for example, that the cost of reshaping a salesperson's negative

TABLE 13-2

Major Problems with Salespeople

Problem Area	Rank 1979	Rank 1959
Poor utilization of time and planned sales effort	1	1
Inadequacy in sales training	2	21
Wasted time in office by salespeople	3	6
Too few calls in work hours	4	3
Inability of salespeople to overcome objections	5	5
Indifferent follow-up of prospects by salespeople	6	7
Lack of creative, resourceful salesmanship	7	2
Meeting competitive pricing	8	15
Lack of sales drive and motivation	9	8
Recruitment and selection of sales personnel	10	11

TABLE 13-3

Major Reasons for Firing Salespeople

Problem Area	Rank 1979	Rank 1959
Poor work habits	1	1
Lack of resourcefulness, initiative, fact finding	2	2
Inability to sell from beginning to end (closing)	3	8
Unwillingness to canvass and establish new contacts	4	3
Inability to meet objections; slow, unresponsive	5	10
Lack of self-evaluation and self-betterment	6	6
Refusal to prepare and use required reports	7	14
Lack of vision and creative thinking	8	4
Lack of self-confidence and sustained enthusiasm	9	7
Negative attitude, lack of sales interest	10	13

attitude is too high to justify continuance of that person's employment. Nevertheless, many business decisions must be made with a view toward what will be best for the firm's overall effectiveness, rather than in terms of humanistic considerations.

In sales as in other fields where there exists a great dependence on human factors, a problem in one area often has a way of causing problems in other areas. For example, an inadequate and inflexible compensation plan can cause salespeople to become discouraged enough to slow down their sales efforts and to develop a poor attitude with respect to prospecting efforts or customer follow-up. This attitude can in turn have an effect upon how the salesperson performs *all* of his or her functions.[7]

In seeking solutions to sales problems it is necessary to recognize that there might be more than one causal factor involved, and that sometimes the solution of one specific problem will also solve other problems as well. We will analyze performance problem solutions by looking at three possible remedial sources: the administrative apparatus, training, and the sales manager (see Table 13-4).

TABLE 13-4

Factors in Sales Performance Improvement

Administrative apparatus:	A rational system of policies and procedures.
Sales training:	An ongoing committment to providing training at periodic intervals.
Sales manager:	Providing this person with the tools to become part of the solution rather than part of the problem.

The Administrative Apparatus

A rational approach to administration presents one of the most effective ways of preventing sales problems from occurring and presenting a solution to existing problems. An administrative system that requires only necessary descriptive, reporting, and control paper work tends to discourage many problems caused by too much paper work. Part of the rational administrative process is a marketing orientation on the part of all service, administrative, and sales-support personnel; often a predilection for conforming to rules and bureaucratic guidelines on the part of nonsales personnel tends to work against the customer and the salesperson, as well as the organization. Providing these employees with an understanding of the need for a marketing-oriented approach is a vital step in the establishment of a rational administrative apparatus. A rational administrative system also prevents a great deal of needless time spent in the office by salespeople.

An understandable compensation plan that pays commissions soon after sales will also tend to prevent many sales problems. The surest way to induce negative attitudes toward a firm is for the firm to take its time in making commission payments to its sales representatives.

For the most part, an analysis of the administrative system as a potential problem or solution to sales-force performance should be taken on a periodic basis by all sales organizations, particularly in periods of anticipated organization change.

Training as a Solution

There is an old maxim in the Navy that says "if it's standing still, paint it; if it moves, train it." To some extent, this old saw holds true in sales. Many experienced salespeople feel that there is no such thing as too much training. The specific types of problems that can be solved or partially solved by training are those that are related to lack of self-confidence and to "mechanical" types of problems, such as shortcomings in product knowledge, sales techniques, and in self-organization. In many cases, salespeople lack expertise in performing their functions because they lack the confidence that they are taking the right approach. In most cases, this lack of confidence emanates from a weakness in one or more of the preceding areas, hence, the concentration by many firms on additional training in specific problem areas. The following examples are typical of some sales-force problems and their consequent solution through training methods:

A branch manager with Pitney-Bowes Corporation, a firm which manufactures and markets office equipment, found that Jim, a salesman he had hired about six months ago, was experiencing poor results in selling office copiers. Jim appeared to have all the characteristics required of a good commercial salesperson and gave excellent demonstrations of the product both in the office and when they made joint sales calls. One of the leading salespeople in the office developed a test of competitive products in certain areas to be given at a sales meeting. It developed that, although Jim had a good superficial knowledge of competitive copiers, he lacked the in-depth knowledge that is often required to close sales. The unfortunate part of the situation was that Jim did not realize that the information he lacked was readily available. After studying certain material and several role-playing sessions, Jim's knowledge of the competition was quite extensive. He began mentioning copiers on every sales call, and within three months his new-found copier sales expertise moved him from fifteenth to third in total copier sales. Evidently, he had been suffering from a lack of confidence in his ability to sell the product because of his superficial knowledge of the competition.

The branch manager of the Chemical Division of PPG Industries in a major city found that Andy, a veteran technical salesman, was experiencing difficulty in maintaining a high sales volume and also servicing present customers. Andy had recently taken over a large geographical territory. His previous territory consisted of a few customers in a concentrated geographical area. Because of his strong sales ability and his technical expertise, Andy was given the new territory, one that presented a real challenge. The territory contained several potentially good accounts that were currently buying from competitors. No one else had "cracked" the territory, and it was felt that Andy could. True to form, in his first month in the territory, he "stole" two medium-sized accounts away from the competition. He generally made things happen throughout the territory by giving quotes, presentations, and following up service requests. After about three months in the territory, Andy told the manager that perhaps part of the territory should be given to someone else because there were too many complaints of late follow-up. The branch manager instead instituted an intense logistical program on management of time. The program not only solved Andy's problem but problems of many other salespeople. Apparently, the firm had not spent much time training its salespeople in the efficient use of time. It had stressed the importance of setting priorities but had never provided training in the specific area of how to set up one's day so that the maximum number of customers and prospects are called upon.

One sales manager for Deltona Corporation, a firm that sells and develops homesite property in Florida, was experiencing difficulty with Jane, one of his top salespeople. Jane was an excellent direct salesperson. She possessed all the right sales tools and was very strong in the most important area of all—closing the sale. Over the past several months, Jane closed more sales than anyone else in the office, but also received more cancellations than anyone else. The manager was convinced that, even though Jane was a real professional and had the best command of sales technique in the office, somewhere there was a flaw in her presentation. Feeling that his presence might impede Jane's presentation, his reluctance to accompany her on sales calls was understandable. Finally, he felt there was no other way to approach the problem, so he scheduled himself to accompany her on several sales calls. On the first call, she made a sale that made her about $400 commission. The next two calls were on people who could not afford the product and the next call was on a couple who were interested in going to New Mexico to retire, but Jane sold them on Florida. The manager was certain that Jane had overcome whatever problems she had, but, to his dismay, both orders were cancelled by the end of the week. In frustration, he began to read a book on basic selling and the problem became apparent. Jane was neglecting the *follow-up* function. After the sale was made, she left the house and never contacted the customer again except to ask for referrals to other customers. The manager gave training to the entire branch on various follow-up techniques, and within two months Jane's cancellation rate dropped 80 percent and the overall office rate of cancellations was reduced by 50 percent. The main problem was that even a professional group of salespeople was neglecting, to a person, one of the most important aspects of the selling process. Upon reflection, the manager realized that he had hardly ever stressed the importance of this function, assuming that all the salespeople were well versed in the follow-up process.

These instances are fairly typical of how training can provide a solution to many sales problems. The cases depicted here may not seem very dramatic, but neither are most business success stories. Most effective sales organizations got that way because several individual salespeople were taught how to overcome certain shortcomings.

Role of the Sales Manager

A company's administrative philosophy and the use of the necessary training techniques both have a strong impact upon the solution of certain selling problems. Undoubtedly, the key factor in this process, however, is the involvement of the sales manager. He or she can be part of the problem or part of the solution.

It would be a wonderful thing if all sales managers were endowed with an abundance of the skills necessary to perform each of their many functions. Unfortunately, such is not the case. It is not unreasonable to expect that some small but significant proportion of the sales management community lacks one or more of the skills required for effective performance. To the extent that a sales manager lacks abilities in the important areas of training and motivation, the situation is one of the blind leading the blind. As a highly respected consultant in the field of marketing put it in an interview with the author,

> Just as you have incompetence in government, business and any other human contact situation, you have to expect a certain amount of incompetence in sales management. How did these people get the job? In some cases, they were the bosses' favorite; in many cases, the promotion was simply given to the best salesperson, often a classic enunciation of the Peter Principle if I ever saw it. In other cases, the company didn't use objective methods to determine who should be manager—they left it to the subjective judgment of a regional manager. In some other cases, the job is only perceived as one of paper shuffling by the sales force and nobody wants the job—in these cases it often goes to the least qualified individual. Oh, I can give you plenty of horror stories about situations where the firm promoted or hired incapable sales managers. After all, about half of my business is helping companies straighten up the mess left by one of its mistakes.

These remarks were made by a free-lance individual whose background includes teaching sales management at a university, as well as having been a very successful regional manager for a well known corporation. It is his contention, as well as that of many other sales professionals, that many organizations are strongly in need of comprehensive training programs that teach sales managers how to perform effectively. This book will not dwell on the shortcomings of sales managers. There are, however, a few classic managerial areas of weakness that often cause or exacerbate problems in sales performance (see Table 13-5).

Lack of Experience A true understanding of sales problems and their solution can often be grasped only after the manager has spent a certain amount of time performing sales management functions. Many companies promote a salesperson directly to the manager's position and allow him or her to sink or swim in the job with no prior experience or training. It is not surprising that under these conditions many people fail to perform up to expectations.

Misperception Perception is a highly subjective characteristic and can often be misleading. First impressions, for example, tend to be lasting and often misleading. Yet many sales managers seek to validate initial judgments by perceiving only actions and qualities that confirm their first impression of a salesperson. Other sales managers have a tendency to ignore cues that could be critical in understanding certain salespeople. In any event, lack of perception is usually a very important shortcoming in sales management.

Lack of Respect by Salespeople Without the respect of the sales force, the manager cannot function as a leader. We have already discussed leadership traits, situational leadership, and various motivating characteristics in Chapter 6. Unless a manager can function as a leader, this lack of respect unfortunately results in a general lack of confidence in the manager's ability and judgment. This lack of confidence becomes an informal norm for the sales force and, even though the man-

TABLE 13-5

Common Sales Management Problems

Lack of experience:	Firms move persons into management positions too quickly with inadequate training.
Misperception:	Inability or lack of awareness to visualize situations as others do. "Shooting from the hip."
Lack of respect by salespeople:	Inability to establish oneself as a source of support, expertise, and leadership.
Lack of scope:	Failure to pay attention to all aspects of sales management.
Uncompromising disciplinary approach:	Overemphasis on power and authority characteristics of management position.

ager may not deserve it, his or her credibility will be low. The inexorable result of such a condition is less effective performance by most sales-force members.[8]

Lack of Scope This characteristic applies to sales managers who are unable to visualize the entire scope of their job. Invariably, the manager who lacks scope is preoccupied with two or three functions, paying little or no attention to others. A classic example of this condition is the manager who is preoccupied with (1) his or her own advancement, (2) sales output, and (3) avoidance of looking bad in the eyes of his or her boss. Most of the time effective sales managers are able to blend these three important requirements into the needs of the sales force so that the proper balance between the salespeople's and the manager's needs is fulfilled. Without the proper scope, sales managers tend to place the needs of the sales force in a subordinate position. This is immediately perceived by the sales force, and the result is invariably lower sales effectiveness.

Uncompromising Disciplinary Tactics This condition exists primarily as a result of certain personal needs. The uncompromising disciplinarian is normally preoccupied with standards and controls, often showing little understanding or interest in the personal needs of salespeople. Unfortunately, many regional or national managers often mistakenly attribute effective sales-force performance under martinet types to the harsh tactics of these managers. Sometimes harsh methods will "wake up" a sales force, but their effect is temporary. Continuance of harsh methods invariably results in hostility, defiance, defensiveness, and lower sales volume.

During a career in sales, every salesperson will observe managers with at least one of the preceding characteristics. Additionally, few managers perform every function perfectly. In many cases, shortcomings can be rectified if they are recognized and accepted by the manager. Unfortunately, unless some member of the management hierarchy with more authority is also aware of a need for change in managerial style, it is probably unrealistic to expect the manager's problems to be met head-on with objective understanding and subsequent remedial action.

The preceding section has dealt with the role of the sales manager as part of the problem. Fortunately, the sales manager also presents the best solution to ineffective sales performance. Very few problems are identical, and there are no troubleshooting manuals with simple solutions to sales performance problems. There are however, many symptoms and problems that can be recognized and treated through the following classic and time-proven means:

Clear and objective standards.
Personal interest in salespeople.
Improvement of perception.
Effective communication.
Spending adequate time with sales-force members.

Making Standards Clear and Objective Performance standards should be made clear at all times. In addition to formal standards to be used in performance evaluation, other requirements such as paper work and administrative responsibilities should be made equally clear. It is important for managers to extend standards to all sales-force members. Many of the problems that emanate from unclear objectives from inconsistent administration or from favoritism to sales-force members can thus be eliminated.

Personal Interest in Salespeople Many earlier principles-of-management textbooks stressed the importance of the manager's maintaining an arm's-length relationship with subordinates. In sales, quite the reverse is true. It is of great importance that sales managers know and understand their salespeople. It is equally important that the manager take a sincere personal interest in that person's career objectives. Salespeople are generally quite perceptive and are normally able to sense whether a manager has a sincere interest or is simply attempting to manipulate sales-force members. A personal knowledge of the salesperson's makeup enables a manager to provide the kind of support that is needed. Perhaps most important, salespeople normally recognize and appreciate the manager's awareness of, and attention to, the salesperson's particular problems and opportunities.

Improvement of Perception A sales manager's ability to see other people objectively is an important quality in improving sales performance. The concepts of stereotyping, forming a "halo effect," and depending upon first impressions in personal relationships are well known to most students. The recognition of the need to avoid such tendencies provides a strong basis for improvement of perception. Sales managers who can evaluate people logically are better able to understand a salesperson's true deficiencies and can usually improve performance significantly.

Effective Communications The term "communications" has been widely used and misused over the past two decades. Essentially, the basis of effective communication is two way rather than one way. Effective communications programs always allow for feedback from the sales force to the manager. Without this two-way communication, it is difficult if not impossible for a manager to know what sales-force members want or need. And the manager must know what these wants and needs are if he or she is to implement effective sales programs that will receive sales-force support.

A few of the specific aspects of developing communications include a consistent interpretation of rules and regulations, norms, and standards.[9] Inconsistent interpretation of policy and procedure tends to reduce a manager's credibility, and in turn, his or her effectiveness. It is equally important, particularly in the more egalitarian 1980s, for the managers to conduct interpersonal relationships with the sales force as colleagues rather than in the traditional superior-subordinate fashion. This posture does not represent a contemporary fad; it has been the rule rather than the exception for effective sales managers to manage through logic rather than through the use of power. Sales-force members still respect the manager's authority but are generally more responsible when their individual dignity and human worth are recognized. There was a time when "talking down" to employees was the accepted mode of communication in business. These days, however, are over.

It is equally important to effective sales management that the sales force be kept informed at all times. An information gap with respect to anticipated changes, new products, new procedures, or *any* aspect of their jobs nearly always results in not only a great deal of rumor, but in the strengthening of the informal grapevine that carries them. It is actually desirable for a group of salespeople to meet informally to "blow off steam." This condition exists in every sales force and will continue to exist. When salespeople are not kept informed, however, these informal meetings often take the form of a "gripe-session," and rumors circulated tend to draw the salesperson's concentration away from the job and toward conjecture of impending change. An honest and open approach to the dissemination of information not only allows salespeople to know where they stand, but also lessens the undesirable effects of the informal grapevine.

Spending Adequate Time with the Sales Force In a very credible recent study, it was shown that sales managers spend more time responding than in directing.[10] Unfortunately, a great deal of this time is spent responding to the sales manager's boss than to the sales force. It is axiomatic that if the major aspects of a sales manager's job are interpersonal the majority of his or her time should be spent with the sales force. Yet nearly any sales manager at the field level will readily admit that his or her paper work or other information requirements from above are so great that they result in an infringement upon time that must be spent with the sales force. Unfortunately, this is one of the reasons why effective sales managers find 50- to 60-hour weeks not uncommon. In an analysis of most problems or impediments to effective sales performance, the intervention of the sales manager at the beginning solves a great deal of them. Unfortunately, the sales manager is not ubiquitous, and it is impossible for him or her to detect all danger signals. But with a manageable sales-force size and a willingness to spend most available time in the field, the task of spending a good deal of time with all sales-force members is an attainable goal.

SUMMARY

This chapter has dealt with an analysis of some of the major sales-force problems and an approach to their solution. The major problems occur in the areas of *self-organization, selling ability, motivation, personal problems, organization and supervision, attitude,* and *organizational change*.

The solutions to these problems lie in the administrative apparatus, sales training, and most importantly, the approach taken to problems before and after they occur by the sales manager. Many sales managers are hindered by lack of experience, misperception, lack of the sales-force's respect, lack of scope, and taking too narrow an approach to discipline. The primary approaches to improving sales-force effectiveness lie in setting clear and objective standards, taking a personal interest in sales-force members, improving one's perception, communicating effectively and spending adequate time with sales-force members.

There does not appear to be any easy panacea to the improvement of sales performance, and a good deal of hard work is required. Attention to the preceding factors has proved to be an effective approach.

Floyd Pinkerton Janitorial Products

David Gilmour was recently appointed as branch sales manager for the Floyd Pinkerton Janitorial Products Corporation. Salespeople with the organization call on industrial and institutional accounts, selling a variety of compounds for use in cleaning. Dave noticed that Roger Waters, one of his sales representatives, was experiencing a severe sales slump. Roger's sales volume began to fall in December, and failed to pick up during January and February. March, normally a good month for sales, was even worse than January and February. In a conversation with his regional manager, Richard Wright, Dave indicated that Roger's performance had been poor. Mr. Wright asked Dave to elaborate, and the following conversation took place:

Gilmour: I don't know what's the matter with Roger lately, he just doesn't seem to take the interest he had or to show his old enthusiasm.

Wright: That's hard to understand, Dave. Roger's been with us for what, at least seven or eight years, hasn't he?

Gilmour: More like ten years, Dick. I've never seen him behave this way before. I don't think he has any personal problems but you never know with a lot of these people.

Wright: Let's start from the beginning—did anything happen in November or December that you know of?

Gilmour: Not really. I changed the territories around in November. Roger was complaining that it hurt his chances to make 100 percent of quota for the year, but I actually gave him a *better* territory than the one he had.

Wright: How did Roger end up the year?

Gilmour: Well he *almost* made it—he wound up at 98 percent.

Wright: I see. What was your reaction?

Gilmour: I told him if he had tried a little harder he could have gone to Acapulco with the rest of us, that a little extra effort would have made the difference. Not that I want to sound callous, but maybe if he had made one more call on a Friday afternoon instead of bugging out early to see that kid of his in the hospital, he'd have had that 100 percent.

Wright: What does he act like on sales calls in his new territory?

Gilmour: I haven't had any feedback on Roger from customers, so I guess he's doing all right.

Wright: How often do you go out on calls with him?

Gilmour: We went out together in December right after he got his new territory. I wanted to introduce him to some of his new customers. I've had so much paper work that I haven't been able to go out with him since.

Wright: Do you notice anything else about Roger?

Gilmour: Yeah Dick, I notice that his paper work is late, too. I've been meaning to have a talk with him. I'm going to raise his quota to get him moving and if he doesn't start to sell more, we'll have to let him go.

1. If you were Mr. Wright, what would be your analysis of the situation?
2. What could Dave Gilmour have done to possibly improve Roger's performance?

Aerospace Dynamics Ltd.

Aerospace Dynamics Ltd. markets a line of parts to customers in the aerospace industry. The company had seen its position in the industry drop from the leader to the number 3 position and its market share reduced from 20 to 15 percent. The directors of the organization attributed their problems to sales performance and, as a result, George Marino and Barry Rogers were hired as marketing manager and national sales manager, respectively. Both George and Barry had been with competitors and were intimately aware of the industry and the type of selling involved.

Their first step was to analyze the sales operations of the firm. With the help of an outside consulting firm, George and Barry administered several questionnaires to the sales force. The relationships disclosed by the questionnaires were the following:

1. The turnover rate of salespeople was double that of three years ago.
2. Average compensation was 5 percent lower than last year.
3. Average number of calls made per salesperson was 17 percent lower than last year.
4. Most salespeople had changed territories on the average of three times over the past two years.
5. An attitude survey showed that most salespeople considered their sales manager's credibility to be low.
6. Most salespeople doubted that the firm was interested in their welfare.
7. Older salespeople were particularly cynical of sales management's motives.
8. Over 30 percent of the sales force planned to leave the company in the near future.

Faced with these disquieting results, George and Barry have called you in to help them with their difficulties.

1. What could be some of the causes of the eight problem areas?
2. How would you advise George and Barry to approach an improvement program?

DISCUSSION QUESTIONS

1. What are the causes of poor sales manager performance?
2. How does each causes in question 1 affect salespeople with regard to their performance and motivation?
3. How can a sales manager help others with problems? What are some of the limitations here?
4. You have been given an impossible or highly unfair quota and/or territory. What can you do about it?
5. What aspects of training will help a relatively inexperienced salesperson? experienced salesperson?
6. What are the positive and negative factors of a strong disciplinary approach?
7. Discuss effective communications from a sales manager's approach with his superiors; with his peers; with his salespeople.
8. What are the major reasons for firing salespeople?

NOTES

[1]Gordon Storholm, "Trait Theory and the Salesman' unpublished working paper, Department of Economics, Rutgers College, New Brunswick, N.J.

[2]Ibid.

[3]Steven X. Doyle and Benson P. Shapiro, "What Counts Most in Motivating Your Sales Force?" *Harvard Business Review*, May–June 1980, p. 136.

[4]David Hopkins, *Marketing Performance Evaluation*, Information Bulletin No. 53 (New York: Conference Board, 1979).

[5]Ross Webber Management: *Basic Elements of Managing Organizations* (Homewood, Ill.: Irwin, 1979), p. 78.

[6]Bob Arnold, "People and Management," *Marketing Times*, November/December 1979, p. 3.

[7]Mack Hanan and others, *Take-Charge Sales Management* (New York: American Management Association, 1976) p. 23.

[8]Ed Roseman, "How to Manage Problem Salesmen and How to Manage Problem Sales Managers: A Casework for Sales Managers" (New York: Sales Builders Division, a division of *Sales Management Magazine*, Communications, Inc. 1975), p. 21.

[9]See Herbert R. Northrup and Gordon R. Storholm, *Restrictive Labor Practices in the Supermarket Industry*, Chapter 10 (Philadelphia: University of Pennsylvania Press, 1967).

[10]See Ross A. Webber, *Time Is Money* (New York: Free Press, 1980).

CHAPTER 14

TIME AND TERRITORY MANAGEMENT

OBJECTIVES

To investigate the major concepts of time management.

To analyze the cost of sales time.

To develop the fundamentals of territory management.

To enumerate the important factors involved in key account selling.

INTERVIEW WITH FRANK SMITH

Interviewer: Frank, it has been said that the most valuable asset a salesperson has is his or her time. Would you agree?

Frank Smith: Yes, I certainly would. Since sales performance is often measured in term's of revenue, it's not an exaggeration to say that *time is money*.

Interviewer: Funny you mention that. A good friend of mine who is highly respected in business and academic circles, Ross Webber, just published a book with that exact title.

Frank Smith: I know. I read the book. I ordered a copy for all my salespeople. The concept that a salesperson's time utilization is directly proportional to his or her effectiveness has been taught to salespeople for a long time. You would think that it would be a number one priority, a way of life, with salespeople. But it isn't. We all have our bad habits when it comes to time management.

Interviewer: To what extent do training programs help?

Frank Smith: Well, there's no doubt about their being a considerable help. The salesperson has to consistently be aware of the need to seek out new ways of using time to the best advantage.

Interviewer: Will this chapter deal with some of the specific ways that salespeople save time?

Frank Smith: Yes. This is not a text in "how to do it," but this chapter does point out some specific solutions. Let's take a look and see what it has to say.

One of the greatest problems and opportunities facing the sales manager is the development of programs for the effective utilization of time. There is no question that the salesperson's most valuable asset is his or her time, yet many experienced professionals continue to waste many hours each week. To develop programs or work habits that will result in more efficient use of this precious commodity, some modus operandi must be developed that can be followed easily and naturally. Most sales organizations spend a good deal of time and money on seminars, meetings, and other formal gatherings drawn together for this purpose.

To render time-saving ideas operational and workable, the manager must also design sales territories with the need for time conservation a paramount criterion. Unless the daily work pattern design is conceived to maintain a closer geographical proximity between accounts, too much time is wasted in travel time. In some cases, where a salesperson's territory is necessarily spread out geographically, greater creativity must be used to conserve time. This chapter will study the areas of time management and territory management as possible joint solutions to the problem of effective sales territorial coverage.

TIME MANAGEMENT

The manager is responsible for developing effective time management methods for himself or herself, as well as for individual sales-force members. One of the greatest concerns common to all sales managers is that only a small portion of the salesperson's time is spent in front of prospects and/or customers. How to increase this selling time has been and will continue to be one of the sales manager's greatest challenges. In the face of increasing costs of transportation, communication, and other costs associated with selling, this challenge continues to be a growing one and is not likely to diminish in importance in the near future. This section will investigate in depth some of the specific problems and opportunities in the field of time and sales territory management that are faced by contemporary sales managers.

Cost of Sales Time

There are many ways in which the cost of a salesperson's time may be calculated. The method of calculation used will obviously determine the relative size of the cost of time. The most popular method used is to determine the cost of the "average" sales call. Depending upon who is to be impressed with this information, the base data for determining this figure will include more or fewer items. If the firm wants to show a large figure, then the salesperson's salary, fringes, all sales costs, and even overhead will probably be used in arriving at a final figure. Overhead can include rent, sales manager's salary, service salaries, and any or all branch cost figures. A typical cost of a sales call could be arrived at by the two following examples utilizing a salesperson who earns $500 a week.

$$\text{Cost of sales call} = \frac{\text{salesperson's salary} + \text{overhead}}{\text{number of sales calls per week}}$$

$$\text{Overhead} = \frac{\text{all branch costs}}{\text{number of salespersons in branch}}$$

Assume that all branch costs are $80,000 per month and there are 20 salespeople in the branch. Assume further that fringe costs for the salesperson equal $100 per week. If a salesperson makes 10 calls per week during an average week, then

$$\text{Cost of sales call} = \frac{\$500 + \$100 + \dfrac{80{,}000}{20}}{10}$$

$$= \frac{4600}{10} = \$460 \text{ per call}$$

If overhead is not counted, then

$$\text{Cost of sales call} = \frac{\$500 + \$100}{10}$$

$$= \frac{600}{10} = \$60 \text{ per call}$$

These two examples are extreme, but the computations show that the cost of an "average" call depends upon the criteria used to determine what "cost" means. A few well-known organizations compute average sales call costs on an annual basis and distribute the findings throughout the sales community. Since one of these organizations is a publishing firm, it would seem that a high cost would be depicted, showing implicitly the logic for higher advertising expenditures.

A firm or branch trying to impress some public constituency or board of directors of the effectiveness of its sales force would be able to contrive a lower figure. Essentially, a firm can compute a "cost of a sales call" figure using any criteria it wishes. Ironically, it makes little difference which criteria are used as long as they are meaningful and are used over a long period of time, since this kind of data has most value when used as a *relative* measure.

Some of the applications of these data are for comparison of time effectiveness among salespeople or groups of salespeople. The use of "cost of an average sales call" is a good measure of, for example, trends in sales branch office policies, procedures, and training programs. If, other things being equal, there appears to be a significant decrease in the cost of sales calls after changes in the nominal routine, it can generally be concluded that the new techniques are working. On the other hand, this figure cannot be relied upon accurately for comparison among branches or salespeople because of different environmental conditions in territories, as well as in branches. For example, it is cheaper for a salesperson to travel 2 miles in Pocatello, Idaho, than in New York City.

Of the sources that provide cost of sales call data, the one used here is from *Sales and Marketing Management* magazine.[1] These figures are broken down by different sales type and are based on extensive field research. Based on the findings of this organization, sales call costs have risen at a higher annual rate than inflation over the past several years. According to this source, 1980 average sales call costs ranged between $46 and $82 (see Table 14-1).

TABLE 14-1

Average Cost of a Sales Call

Consultative sales	$46–90
Technical sales	$41–82
Commercial sales	$25–58
Direct sales	Not available

Source: *Sales and Marketing Management*, May, 1980.

As can be seen in Table 14-1, it is relatively expensive to "field" a sales force. The least expensive of the three categories is, as would be expected, commercial sales, and the highest is in consultative sales. These figures are based on direct costs, which include sales compensation, fringes, and other expenses, including automobile. In view of these figures, it is clear that an increase in sales-force effectiveness in terms of getting salespeople in front of prospects and customers can lead to dramatically reduced costs and, therefore, to increased profits.

Opportunity Cost of Time

On the basis of the foregoing data, keeping unproductive salespeople in the field would seem to be not only expensive, but, at today's costs, virtually suicidal. On the other hand, the leverage involved in more efficient utilization of time is substantial. For example, if a salesperson increases his or her time per day spent in front of customers and prospects from three hours to three and three quarter hours, the increase in his or her productive time is increased by 25 percent.

For this reason, sales organizations spend a great deal of time and money trying to improve the effectiveness of salespeople in time management, as well as in sales technique.

As in the estimation of the cost of a sales call, different organizations have from time to time attempted to document how salespeople spend their day. The breakdowns in Tables 14-2 and 14-3 depict two different analyses:

TABLE 14-2

How a Salesperson Spends His or Her Day

Activity	Hours	Minutes	%
Traveling and waiting	2	45	32
Nonselling activities	1	40	19
Service calls		35	7
Selling	3	40	42
	8	40	100

Source: McGraw-Hill Publishing Company.

TABLE 14-3

How a Salesperson Spends His or Her Day

Activity	Hours	Minutes	%
Traveling and waiting	2	30	30
Nonselling activities	2	00	25
Service calls	1	30	15
Selling	2	30	30
	8	30	100

Source: Sales and Marketing Executives Club, Philadelphia, Pa.

The amounut of time a salesperson spends in nonselling activities clearly depends upon the type of sales he or she performs. Consultative salespeople, for example, are often required to spend hours and even days of backup time just to spend one hour with a prospect. Commercial salespeople, on the other hand, can canvass from one office to the next. If he or she cannot see a decision maker, however, the canvassing time spent is normally not too productive. Unless some other person provided useful information that will be useful on subsequent calls, this time is similar to traveling time.

As transportation costs have increased dramatically over the past few years, there has been an increased emphasis on the use of the telephone, not only for the purpose of making appointments, but for selling products, as well. Maintenance chemicals, light bulbs, auto transmission parts, and other industrial products are presently being sold successfully by phone. In Europe, some insurance firms are successfully selling life insurance through a three-step process of newspaper advertising, direct mail, and telephone selling. It is expected that the cost of video phone communication will soon be low enough to be used on a regular basis.[2] A buyer will be able to plug into a standard television console and have visual access to the salesperson and his or her products. This process is expected to be operational within the next two to three years. These and other techniques are being utilized not only to save fuel but to save time as well.

Because of the nature of selling, the only one who knows exactly how many sales calls are being made, the amount of time taken for lunch, and the amount of time worked is the salesperson. It has been estimated that about 30 to 35 percent of the day is spent actually selling[3] (see Tables 14-2 and 14-3). Anything that can be done to increase time spent in actual face-to-face selling is literally money in the pocket of the salesperson. By the same token, any nonproductive time that can be put to better use can also be translated into dollars and cents. An example of turning nonproductive time into productive time would be spending waiting time preparing for a sales interview. Time spent on an airplane, as a further example, could be spent the same way, instead of watching a movie or conversing with a fellow passenger.

As can be seen from Tables 14-2 and 14-3, the importance of a salesperson's time can hardly be overestimated. The only truly productive time is spent in front of a customer/prospect, yet the greatest part of the salesperson's day is spent in support activity, traveling, or in dubious activities. There is an old maxim in sales that top producers do not work *harder*, they work *smarter*. Since self-organization and time management is the key to working "smarter," managers and sales-force members alike find it necessary to set time priorities into a daily plan and then follow through with the plan. Although the value of a salesperson's time is sometimes overstated, in most cases the opportunity cost of pursuing any support activity is highly expensive if not prohibitive.

Field sales-force members are not the only people who have problems with time management. Sales executives also face the frustration of the inability to come to grips with this pressing problem. In many cases, lack of time to perform necessary functions is the most immediate problem of sales executives. It is not uncommon for a manager to work 60 hours or more a week, yet even then relatively little might be accomplished.[4] It would appear that the sales manager who would help others become organized must become organized first.

In a recent study, a national sales manager, who was considered to be typical, made a log on how his time would be spent during the coming year. He accounted for 390 days, a clear indication that there was not enough time for him to perform the functions he considered necessary.[5] After an analysis of his functions, a group of other sales executives concluded that the executive could have solved his problem through the following:

1. Delegating more work to field managers to cut down time spent in field.
2. Restrict field visits to the regional level.
3. Practice management by exception, a technique whereby all routine work is handled according to a certain procedure, and only unusual variations from the norm are brought to the executive's attention (see Chapter 3).
4. Hire an effective administrative assistant.
5. Clarify lines of responsibility and authority so that each person performs his or her job and not someone else's.

As a result of the group's recommendations, the busy sales executive was able to cope with his responsibilities more effectively. This example shows how certain changes can result in time savings. Essentially, the executive restructured his interface with other people, as well as his time priority schedule.

In most cases, the demands upon executives are so heavy that an individual could work an 80-hour week and still not be finished with his or her responsibilities. The problem is not so much a lack of capability, but a lack of self-organization. Many executives fail to recognize that they are not well organized. In most cases, recognition of this problem is an excellent first step toward solution. The best approach to a solution to the time management problem is normally associated with a detailed analysis of his or her job, both in content and in the ways in which duties and responsibilities are carried out. In either case, there are positive steps that can be taken to rearrange the time-consuming aspects of the job.

In effect, time is a constraint on the executive's job.[6] Because of lack of self-organization or being uncomfortable in delegating authority, many sales managers spread themselves too thinly. Because of the increasing cost of executive time, however, a great deal of attention has been focused upon techniques for preserving this scarce resource. Formal seminars, printed material, and training programs regarding this subject have increased substantially over the past decade. As a result, many or most sales organizations seem to be concerned with the problem of time management for sales managers as well as for field sales personnel.

TERRITORY MANAGEMENT

As was indicated previously, management of the salesperson's time is not sufficient. Without a concurrent effort to manage the sales territory, the problem of time conservation is not being addressed completely. Recognizing that the goal of time and territorial management programs is to provide the salesperson with more face-to-face selling time, it is incumbent upon sales managers to help salespeople develop and implement a well thought out approach to optimal utilization of resources. This section will describe some of the basic strategies used by sales managers to better manage sales territories.

Sales Territory Alignment

It was indicated in Chapter 8 that territories should, in most cases, be equal in sales potential. Such a configuration allows objective comparison and evaluation of sales-force members and provides them with similar income opportunities. A second factor of importance in territorial alignment is sales expense, not only in terms of money, but also in terms of time. As one sales manager stated in an interview:

> The most valuable thing a salesperson has is his or her time. We have estimated that based *only on salary and commission* the time spent in front of a customer is worth about $75 an hour. It's easy to work up all kinds of figures, but this one is legitimate. As a result, we are very careful about the logistics of our sales territories. We even have time and management games with prizes at our sales meetings. These efforts are all aimed at reducing time spent between sales calls. We have hired consultants in this field to work with our managers and the money was well spent, believe me.

Most sales managers would agree that time is of inestimable value to a salesperson. Given that productivity is, in the aggregate, directly related to number of effective sales calls made, selective time management would appear to be a determining variable to success in the sales field. At a recent seminar, which included sales managers from several types of industries, a questionnaire was distributed asking the managers as to what they considered to be the most important characteristic related to sales success. The number 1 factor, almost unanimously selected, was "effective utilization of time." The sales managers felt that this trait or talent was not only helpful to success, but that its absence almost certainly guaranteed failure.

For these reasons, most sales managers organize territories in such a way that maximum exposure to customers is accomplished.[7] In a metropolitan area, it is clearly quite easy for a salesperson to see many people in a short period of time. In suburban and rural areas, however, the task is not so easy, particularly if the salesperson has an "account" territory rather than a geographical one. Priorities must be set and a specific call pattern must be established in accordance with the salesperson's priorities. The more active the territory, the better organized the salesperson must be. It is certainly no coincidence that more effective salespeople tend to create more activity and hence have more practice at self-organization than ineffective salespeople.

Many firms have an unusually wide variation in sales potential among their sales territories. This condition results in a situation where no matter how active some good salespeople are they cannot adequately cover their territories because there are simply not enough hours in the day to do so. Eventually, a salesperson in this situation no longer tries to cover the territory completely. Instead, he or she "skims" by focusing on accounts that appear to have the greatest sales potential. Because the sales-cost ratio is low in such territories, sales managers often overlook the fact that a good part of the territory has been overlooked and potential sales have been lost. Essentially, the firm typically does not achieve a high market share in such territories; indeed some of the poorest performance can occur unnoticed if territories are not monitored. Other territories often tend to have relatively low potential, a situation resulting in high sales costs. Salespeople tend to call on the same customers with excessive frequency or, as one sales manager pointed out, might develop into low-handicap golfers.

It was mentioned earlier that, theoretically, at least, territories should be equal in sales potential. It is interesting to note that, in situations where wide variations in sales territory potential exist, it is likely that the sales manager is running a loosely controlled operation. In view of the situations described previously, wide variations in potential lead inexorably to high sales costs. To organize sales territories that are equal in potential, the manager must know the current sales potential in each territory. Chapter 10 discussed some techniques for accurate determination of specific potentials. When the manager is aware of true sales potential, he or she can decide exactly how many salespeople to employ. Without accurate knowledge of potential, it is impossible to *know* the optimum number of salespeople to employ. *These strategic moves can make or break a sales manager.* Once territories are assigned, some managers encourage salespeople to break down their territories into smaller "control groups." Each group represents a segment of the territory that is (1) either relatively homogeneous, such as several accounts in similar industries, or (2) a geographic subdivision, such as a country or a town. When this breakdown is made, salespeople find it easier to focus attention upon "problem centers."

Along with the preceding considerations, sales management must decide which type of territory provides the optimum in time and expense utilization. In addition to the traditional geographic and account territories, management should consider the implications of market-specialized territories, including many firms in the same business with similar problems, which translate into sales opportunities. Because of the function of the salesperson as a marketing-oriented problem solver, this type of territory breakdown might be desirable. IBM, for example, has used this approach successfully for several decades. Another possibility is the sale of a single product by each salesperson. The merits of this approach were discussed in Chapter 9.

In dividing territories, sales managers must also take into consideration the needs of the salesperson in the territory. In larger geographical areas, for example, there is often a tendency for many salespeople to concentrate sales calls in an area near where he or she lives. There is also a tendency to cover the outer limits, since it is a foregone conclusion that the salesperson must stay overnight in the territory in order to adequately cover his or her prospects and customers. There is, however, an area in between where salespeople find it difficult to spend the day without returning late or rising early. The distance, however, is not far enough away from the salesperson's home to justify the expense of an overnight stay. This part of the territory is often responsible for less sales volume because it is seldom "worked" nearly as hard as the two parts. Figure 14-1 illustrates these points.

With a growing emphasis on "quality of life" and other humanistic considerations, sales managers are becoming more cognizant of the personal requirements of salespeople. Yet the caliber of the sales organization and optimal development of resources must be maintained. A sales manager for a division of a publishing firm recently lamented to the author:

> As you know, we have hired a lot of sales*women* over the past few years. What do you do about overnight travel? I'm supposed to go with them sometimes. A lot of the time—I should say most of the time—their husbands or boyfriends are not especially thrilled about our staying in the same motel. Not to mention my wife. Yet, I can't just give the females territories close to their home and put all the guys on the road. I suppose they could have one male and one female manager, but that defeats the purpose of setting up optimal sales cost controls. I'll tell you, the job keeps getting harder and harder.

While most sales organizations eventually find some balance between personal considerations and efficient deployment of salespeople, growing attention is being given to this situation by most, if not all, sales organizations.

Figure 14-1

Traditional Coverage in a Geographic Territory

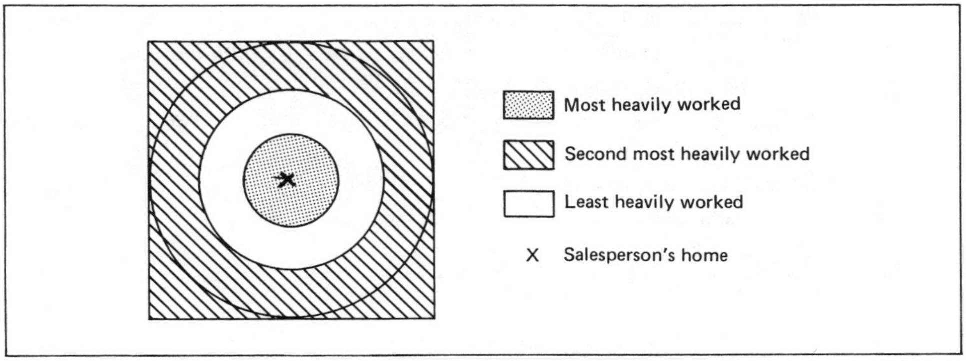

The Importance of Key Accounts

There is an axiom in sales management called the "80-20 rule."[8] This principle states that up to 80 percent of sales come from approximately 20 percent of the customers. Clearly, the 80-20 rule does not apply to every sales territory. Nor does it apply to every product line or to every company. By and large, however, most sales managers attach a great deal of credibility to this principle, and a good case for its application in many sales situations could probably be advanced if hard evidence were required to prove that it works.

If the 80-20 or some similar approach to sales territorial alignment is taken, it is important for sales managers to encourage their salespeople to make maximum penetration into the heavy user accounts, as well as to develop those accounts that show strong potential for becoming key accounts. A well-organized, consistent approach should be taken in calling upon these accounts; otherwise, an enormous amount of time may be wasted.

Sales managers are well aware of these accounts in all sales territories and normally have some organized strategy for their exploitation. Buying in key accounts is influenced by many executives in various departments, and the salesperson must have a good understanding of the customer's organization, the functions of its various departments, and who are the major and minor buying influences within those departments. It is also critical that complete records concerning the development of sales within key accounts be kept so that any salesperson turnover will not result in the necessity to "start over" again. (In some smaller accounts, it is often desirable to do so, but not, as a general rule, in large key accounts). Records kept on key accounts should provide the following information:

- *Heavy use departments*
- *Departmental executives*
  - *Name*
  - *Title*
  - *Attitude toward firm*
  - *Actual buying influence or authority*
- *Analysis of growth opportunity by department (or lack thereof)*
- *Problems that have arisen and their solution*
- *Justification for use of our products and what is needed to expand or keep account*
- *Competitors*
  - *Weaknesses*
  - *Strengths*
- *Products sold*
  - *Monthly*
  - *Quarterly*
  - *Annually*

Benefits to customers
Major opportunities for expansion of sales to the account

Most salespeople attempt to develop a few "information centers" in their key accounts. These people are not necessarily in high places of authority, but are in a position to know the inner workings of the department or the company. It is a known fact that many salespeople do not like to disclose these sources as they consider them something akin to their private property. A sales manager whose territories included several major firms made the following observation during an interview with the author:

> All of my good salespeople, without exception, have developed very good sources of information in their accounts. Most of them consider these people to be "insurance policies" and they don't like to bring me around to meet them. I don't encourage it, either. Obviously, I know who the sources are, because their names come up on expense accounts pretty often. Most salespeople have a relationship with their sources of information that is a true personal friendship. The salesperson is scared to death of doing anything to make that individual feel that he or she is being exploited, so they very seldom introduce me. It's funny, too, most of the time, these people with all the information are not very high in the corporate pecking order, but they provide an enormous amount of help to the salesperson. And they feel important because the salesperson is always attentive and ready to provide any kind of moral support required.

By the same token, most salespeople who have been calling on key accounts have a highly placed executive who from time to time helps the salesperson sell his or her products. In selling to key accounts, it is therefore necessary for most salespeople to be fairly sophisticated with respect to initiating and developing helpful contacts within customer organizations. It is interesting to note that a salesperson can "oversaturate" a customer with sales calls, as well as not make enough calls.

Most sales managers insist that call records be maintained indicating frequency and quality of sales calls on a cumulative basis. Because of the large sales and profits generated from key accounts, it is not surprising that sales managers tend to look upon these calls as being slightly more important than sales calls on some smaller unprofitable accounts. Because of the size of the orders generated in key accounts, a high degree of leverage is attained from a profit standpoint, not only because large quantities of high-unit-profit items are sold, but also because sales costs are normally lower.

First, most products have some life cycle of profitability to the firm that sells them. A new product that is highly desirable to users attains "brand" status, and the firm is then able to set prices that result in high profits because of the product's exclusivity. After time, however, competitors enter the marketplace, often with lower prices, and the profits generated by the formerly unique product will begin to fall if inroads are made by competition.

As an example, IBM and Xerox continued to maintain profits in certain product lines even though competitive products in the marketplace were similar. The ability of these two firms continually to sell high profit lines to the larger accounts has been one of the major marketing accomplishments of the past two decades. They were able to do so because of an extreme emphasis upon the needs of the customer. A sales manager for an office products firm in competition with IBM and Xerox made the following comments in an interview:

> As long as I can remember, and I've been in this business since 1956, IBM has always been the class of the field. Even though they go to such great lengths to advertise the superiority of their products, most of them [IBM products] are no better than anyone else's. Their salespeople are all college graduates, but that doesn't necessarily make them any smarter. The thing that they were always able to pull off in spite of their higher prices was to convince the customer that he got (1) his money's worth and (2) that IBM would never leave a customer unsatisfied. When Xerox started with the 914 in the early sixties, their philosophy was identical to IBM's. Hell, half of the sales managers they brought in during the early sixties had been with IBM. Both firms did get good people, though. Despite the fact that we kid a lot about required conformity in those two firms, they both encourage creativity. It is impossible to argue with the success of either firm and when you look at their organizations, they are capable, competent, people from the top to the bottom. Some competitors get a smug feeling of satisfaction to see them fighting it out in copiers, automatic typewriters, and other product areas, but to me it's like being in a golf tournament with two Jack Nicklauses instead of only one.

Over the years, IBM and Xerox were able to keep their customers convinced of the exclusivity of their products to the extent that those products were perceived by the customers as "brands" rather than "commodities." The greatest benefit that accompanied the product was probably the IBM or Xerox name, and there was an implicit assumption that either firm would go to any length to keep customers satisfied. Clearly, their customer cadre, which included the majority of the Fortune 500, understood enough of the technical aspects of office equipment to recognize that competitive products were about equal in quality or result (with the exception of Xerox, who maintained a virtual monopoly on the bond paper copy until the early 1970s). They also recognized the enormous contribution they made to IBM's and Xerox's profit structure. Yet they continued to give large orders to those firms, primarily because the IBM and Xerox images perpetuated a certain mystique and their products were perceived as "exclusive." It has often been suggested that successful firms prefer to do business with other successful firms. If this maxim is true, it would seem to account for at least part of the reason for the nearly legendary success of IBM and Xerox over the past few decades. In any event, key account selling has proved to be the major factor in the success of these two highly profitable firms. Although every sales manager does not work for an IBM or a Xerox, there is a strong body of evidence that effective management of key accounts can make or break his or her career.

SUMMARY

One of the greatest problems and opportunities that faces the sales person is time management. The cost of a sales call is high in some jobs and prohibitive in others. The opportunity cost of time is, therefore, enormous.

Finding adequate time for seeing customers is the major objective of effective territory management. Positive approaches taken include effective assignment of territories and key account selling. One reason why IBM and Xerox have been so successful is because of their efficient approach toward selling key accounts.

Edgemont Industries

Edgemont Industries is the exclusive manufacturer of the Kom-pakt-Jim, a combination exercise machine and multistation weight-lifting apparatus. Russ La Rosa, the general manager of Edgemont, has been dissatisfied with the past few months' sales results. After a long discussion with Jack Hartzell and Paul Austin, his two top sales executives, Russ decided that he would take a trip to all eight sales offices and gain a firsthand view of what the sales force was doing right and wrong.

Russ found that three types of prospects composed about 85 percent of all sales potential:

1. *Institutional accounts:* This group consists of schools, colleges, military bases, and prisons. In nearly every case, an order for equipment could be submitted only once each year by the unit desiring the equipment.
2. *Sporting goods distributors:* This group consists of approximately 80 firms nationally who buy products like the Kom-pakt-Jim and sell the product under their own brand name. These organizations can place an order at any time. It is important that salespeople calling on these firms reach a decision maker.
3. *Sporting goods retailers:* These organizations are local in nature. They buy products like the Kom-pakt-Jim to sell to schools or even to consumers who have a gym in their garage or basement. Many of these retail firms are in poor financial condition and would not be approved for credit even if the salesperson were able to make a sale. There are about 25,000 sporting goods retailers in the United States if the sporting goods departments of large department stores are counted.

After making sales calls with approximately 30 different salespeople around the country, Russ decided that better organization of selling time is needed.

1. What would be some specific areas where it would be possible to waste a substantial amount of selling time?
2. What in your opinion would be some general rules to be followed by salespeople to maximize selling time?

Kwipp Systems Ltd.

Robin Mallory is the River City branch sales manager for Kwipp Systems Ltd., a firm that markets computer terminals used in the transportation and freight industry. Any firm that has loading facilities for trucks is a good prospect for Kwipp's products. Each unit of sale is about $2000 and does not require a high-level purchase decision. Typically, the Kwipp salesperson explains the economic advantages to the executive in charge of distribution, and then puts a unit in on trial. The equipment is used by one or more dispatchers during the trial period (typically one week). At the end of the trial period, the salesperson should see the distribution executive again and get a "yes" or "no" as to whether or not the prospect wants to order the unit. On the same call, the salesperson is to pick up the unit if the prospect does not wish to place an order and install it in another trial location. If the prospect does place an order, the unit is left on the customer's premises, and a new unit is requisitioned from the branch inventory. The new unit is then brought to the new customer, and the trial unit is taken and placed in the new prospect's location. Each salesperson is responsible for three units. Sales in River City have been dropping off slightly lately, and Robin recently had the following conversation with Bob Brooking, the assistant branch manager:

Robin: You know, I can't understand it. We've got trouble right here in River City, Bob. I went to the Chamber of Commerce meeting today and everyone at the luncheon said that their sales have been going up lately.

Bob: Well, that's true. On the other hand, ours have only been dropping by about 2 percent over the past two months.

Robin: That's all well and good, Bob, but I just know we should be selling more. There is a lot of potential out there, so we need to make a few more sales. What do you think is the trouble?

Bob: I know what the trouble is, Robin. Our people aren't making good enough use of our time.

Robin: You're right, by gosh! You know, I never thought of that possibility, I'm glad you said that.

Bob: Come on, Robin. You knew that was the reason for the problem before you called me in. What do you want me to do?

Robin: You're right. I was only teasing. But at least we both agree. I know for a fact that some units are staying in too long and others are sitting in trunks of cars when they should be in prospects' buildings. I want you to put together a list of trouble spots that our people can run into with the present systems, and then I want you to find a solution for each problem. Have it ready for the meeting Wednesday, okay?

1. If you were Bob, what would you list as some of the major potential problem areas?
2. How could each area be improved to effectuate better time utilization?

DISCUSSION QUESTIONS

1. Why do most sales managers consider time to be the salesperson's most valuable asset?
2. What is a method of determining the cost of a sales call?
3. What are the major time-consuming activities of salespeople that are considered to be nonselling in nature?
4. What are some ways in which sales managers can help their salespeople make better use of their time?
5. What are the major problem areas associated with poor time management?
6. What are some positive steps that can be taken by sales managers to increase territory management effectiveness?
7. What is the 80-20 rule?
8. What are some reports that can help increase territory effectiveness?

NOTES

[1]See "Significant Trends," *Sales and Marketing Management*, September 15, 1980, p. 140.

[2]M. Rodgers, "Ford Aerospace Makes Connection with Picturephone," *Telephony*, vol. 198, no. 11, February 11, 1980.

[3]Results of survey of Philadelphia Chapter Sales and Marketing Executives International, June 1980.

[4]N. Howard and S. Antilla, "Thank God It's Monday," *Dun's Review*, vol. 115, pp. 46–50, June 1980.

[5]See R. Alec Mackenzie, *The Time Trap* (New York: American Management Association, 1972).

[6]See R. A. Webber, *Time is Money* (New York: Free Press, 1980).

[7]See Mack Hanan, Howard Berrian, and Jack Donis, *Take-Charge Sales Management* (New York: American Management Association, 1978).

[8]Hanan, *Take-Charge*.

CHAPTER 15

MANAGEMENT OF INDEPENDENT REPRESENTATIVES

OBJECTIVES

To describe the nature and structure of the manufacturer's representative organization.

To describe the relationship between manufacturer's representatives and principals.

To analyze some of the traditional problems faced by principals.

To analyze some of the traditional problems faced by representatives.

To investigate positive approaches to the principal-representative relationship.

To outline the typical representative association.

INTERVIEW WITH FRANK SMITH

Interviewer: Frank, you don't deal with independent representatives, do you?

Frank Smith: Well, I don't right now, but I used to. Even though our firm uses its own salespeople exclusively, however, we still use, as you say, *independent representatives* in a few places. Personally, I use the term "rep" to describe the group we're going to discuss. So do most other sales managers.

Interviewer: I guess the key term is "independent."

Frank Smith: That's for sure. They are about the most independent bunch I ever met. I say that in an admiring way. Most of these people ground it out to get where they are and I don't begrudge them their rewards one bit.

Interviewer: That's true, Frank. Most "reps" are entrepreneurally inclined and are fiercely independent.

Frank Smith: Right. That's why you have some conflict once in a while. The firms they represent are usually small, and the people who run those firms are usually just as independent as the reps. Here you have a situation where there's bound to be a little friction.

Interviewer: Would you describe the relationship generally as one of mutual dependence?

Frank Smith: Yes, I think that's a good way of putting it. They are most definitely dependent upon one another. Most of them recognize it, too. The result is that you have a professional approach by both parties, even though every now and then you might hear some rep or some principal squealing like a stuck pig.

Interviewer: You used to be a rep yourself, didn't you?

Frank Smith: I certainly did. I've been on both sides of the table, and it has never been dull from either standpoint.

Interviewer: Is there anyway in which you feel that reps are different from the typical salesperson?

Frank Smith: Well, I've heard it said that as a group they tend to have a higher need for achievement and that they might be a little more intelligent than the typical salesperson, but I don't know that there is any evidence to back those statements up. One thing I would say based on my own experience is that they seem to make a little better use of their time than the typical salesperson. If this is true, it's probably because they run their own business.

Interviewer: What is the best reason for using reps?

Frank Smith: There are several. First of all, you only have to pay a rep commission on what he or she sells. Another advantage is that they have a built-in initiative. In a sense this is a talent they need in order to survive. I think we're getting ahead of ourselves, though. Let's take a look at the chapter, and we'll hit all these questions point by point.

Thus far we have described the salesperson as an individual who works as a full-time employee for the same firm as the sales manager and reports directly to him or her. There are, however, large numbers of salespeople who are self-employed but who represent various firms by selling their products and services. This kind of relationship between independent representatives and business organizations has existed for so long that it is considered to be a marketing institution.

This institution in the marketing process is known as the *manufacturer's representative*. Today there are about 50,000 manufacturer's representatives in the United States. About 60 percent of all sales managers will deal with manufacturer's representatives sometime during their careers. Yet very little has been written about this important element in the marketing channel network. This chapter will investigate in depth its functions and significance.

The term "manufacturer's representative" refers to salespeople who are self-employed and represent, on an independent basis, various firms, known in the jargon of the relationship as *principals*. The principal is typically a manufacturer, hence the term "manufacturer's representative." There is a traditional contractual agreement between the principal and the manufacturer's representative, which defines the specific nature of the relationship. This contract will be examined in depth later in the chapter, but the essential elements of the agreement are associated with commission structure, territory and customers terms of delivery, length of contract, and other terms that prudent parties would want to put in writing. This contract spells out the exact terms and conditions between the principal and the manufacturer's representative.

A term that is also used to describe the manufacturer's representative is *manufacturer's agent* or, simply, agent. This term is most often used in contracts and formal documents. In everyday parlance, however, the most widely used term to denote a manufacturer's representative or agent is the term *rep*. This term is probably used verbally about one hundred times for each time either of the other two terms is used. As a matter of fact, rep is so widely used that some sales managers might have to think twice when the term "agent" is used. A few typical statements to denote the context of usage of the term "rep" are as follows:

Our company sells through (or goes through) reps instead of using our own sales force.

Do you go through your own people or do you use reps?

We've been doing better (worse) since we started using reps.

Although the term "rep" might sound ambiguous since most companies refer to their full-time company-employed salespeople as "sales representatives," sales managers seldom if ever confuse the two categories of salespeople by the use of the term "rep." Because of the widespread use of the term, we will use it hereafter in this text to denote the manufacturer's representative or agent.

It has been estimated that reps are responsible for as much as 70 percent of sales to small- and medium-sized manufacturers in the country.[1] Selling to manufacturers often requires a technical sales background, and many reps are former technical salespeople who wanted to get into their own business. On the technical side, the number of male reps overwhelmingly outnumbers females. There are a variety of reasons for this phenomenon; first, several years' experience in technical sales is nearly always necessary before one is able to start up one's own business. The need to "pay dues" as a technical salesperson is required because contacts must be developed, a knowledge of the product and competition must be assimilated, and a substantial amount of capital must be saved before entering business. This amount can vary anywhere between $10,000 and $50,000. From a realistic standpoint, one would not expect to see many female reps in the manufacturing fields, mainly because there are simply not that many female technical salespeople who have enough experience to meet these criteria. As females are assimilated into technical sales jobs, there will undoubtedly be an increase in the number of female reps, with a lag period of five to ten years from entry into technical sales to becoming a rep. There is little reason to believe that there would then be a significant difference between males and females with respect to the ratio of technical salespeople versus percentages of this occupation who become reps.

Besides selling to industrial firms, reps also sell a large share of the consumer goods market. Examples of different industries that are characterized by large numbers of reps are men's and women's clothing, sporting goods, hardware, jewelry, china, and a multitude of other products classified as *merchandise*. In the merchandise sector, a much larger proportion of female reps is in evidence. In the merchandising product line areas, a large number of rep organizations consist of a husband and wife team. Husbands typically perform the more difficult and complex functions such as wining and dining customers, writing orders, and playing golf with prospects, while the wives perform the simpler and more mundane tasks of paying the bills, making collections from late-paying customers, handling complaints, and straightening out accounts with the principal's home office personnel.

The concept of the independent manufacturer's representative began on a large scale in this country during the period when the railroads began to expand. At one point during the nineteenth century, the railroads purchased an enormous amount of goods and services and were in fact the largest industrial consumers of many products. Predictably, there was an even larger amount of graft, corruption, and favoritism in the purchasing behavior of most railroads. It was not uncommon for a relative or friend of the railroad purchasing agent to represent one or more firms doing business with the railroads and, more specifically, with the purchasing agent in question. At the same time, there were many entrepreneurially oriented salespersons who legitimately sold through their own efforts, although bribery and coercion were not strangers to any of them.[2]

Such a person was James Buchanan (Diamond Jim) Brady. Better known for his propensity to shower lady friends with gifts and for his voracious appetite than for his sales effectiveness, Brady was one of the first reps who truly made it big. In the 1880s Brady was able to negotiate an exclusive contract with the Leeds Forge Company of Great Britain to sell their trucks for use under railroad cars. The product turned out to be a breakthrough in the railroad industry and Brady's exclusive contract, which gaven him sales rights for the entire United States and Canada, made him an instant millionaire. It is unfortunate that history records Brady more as a parvenue than as a businessman. While it would appear that "Diamond Jim" enjoyed life to the fullest in moments of relaxation, he was apparently a highly intelligent person with a reputation for integrity in his business dealings during a period when one's word was not always to be relied upon.

Brady and others like him were probably the earliest examples of the manufacturer's rep as we know the term today, although the function of the independent sales representative has undoubtedly existed for at least 2000 years.

NATURE AND STRUCTURE OF THE REPRESENTATIVES ORGANIZATION

According to the most recent survey, a breakdown of product fields represented are as follows:[3]

Original Equipment	29%
Technical goods	18%
Capital products	15%
Mill supplies	9%
Consumer products	8%
Other	20%

Although consumer products amounted to 8 percent of the products represented, dollar value of these products amounted to approximately 30 percent of all sales volume of products sold by reps. What should be apparent to the reader from these data is that it is highly possible for a sales manager to be associated with reps in any given industry.

The typical manufacturer's representative organization consists of an agency of 4.5 people. Many rep organizations consist of one person and some of the larger ones might employ as many as 25 or 30 salespeople. A rep organization typically begins when a salesperson decides to leave his or her company to go into private business. From the demand standpoint, the rep has one or two contacts with buyers so that he or she is assured of a certain amount of business. On the supply side, it is equally necessary to negotiate a contract with the principal for an exclusive rep territory. From the start, the rep attempts to add additional related, noncompeting lines so that he or she will have more than one product to sell when making sales calls. At this time, the rep can seldom afford to hire administrative help, and since most of his or her time must necessarily be spent in the field, a spouse who can type and perform the required administrative duties is a valuable asset.

Normally in two to five years the rep has either built up the business substantially or has become discouraged and dissolved the business. If he or she has been successful enough and fortunate enough to build up the business, it is literally impossible to spend enough time in the field calling upon customers. By this time, his or her spouse has probably become tired of performing the administrative functions, so the next stage of development, the initial expansion stage, normally requires a relatively large investment of capital. The additional expenses might be to hire a full-time secretary and to move the offices from the rep's home into rented or purchased space. The most critical decision to be made at this point is how to go about hiring a salesperson. If the rep has been in business without a partner, forming a partnership with another rep presents a good possibility. The advantages of such a move are related primarily to an increased customer base, depending upon the lines the other rep carries, and lower costs based on larger sales vis-a-vis fixed costs such as office, secretary, and other such basic items.

Aside from the legal aspects, there are, however, certain disadvantages of entering into a partnership for most reps. Decisions, for example, must be made jointly, and acquiescence may be a difficult pill for many reps to swallow. This loss of flexibility in decision making applies to everything from financial matters to the kind of desks in the office. Given the independent nature of most small business owners, it is not surprising that many reps consider it disadvantageous to enter into a partnership. A second alternative is to hire one or more salespersons. If this is done, the relationship between the rep and the new salesperson is as employer and employee. The new salesperson is *not* considered to be a rep. It is difficult to find good salespeople, and, to complicate matters, new salespeople are generally paid on the basis of straight commission. If the rep continues to be successful, more salespeople will be added to the staff until a fairly large organization has been built up. Although the average rep agency consists of about four salespeople, some organizations have forty or even more salespeople. An example is the Ralph Libonati Agency in New Jersey, which sells sporting goods. Libonati employs about forty full-time salespeople representing lines such as Adidas, Puma, Spalding, and others.

Once the rep organization has become established, there is normally a continual active or inactive search for new lines. Some manufacturers, as they expand, replace reps with their own salespeople. Other lines are seasonal and yield little or no revenue to the rep organization except at certain times of the year. For these and various other reasons, it is considered prudent for the rep to be constantly evaluating the prospects for adding new lines. Most rep organizations feel that it is better to represent several lines, even if it is necessary to add more salespeople, than it is to depend upon a few perennial products from which all income must be derived.

PRINCIPALS AND REPRESENTATIVES

Many sales managers treat the principal-rep relationship as an unholy alliance. To indicate here that all or even most arrangements between these two parties are always amicable would be sheer nonsense. As one can imagine, when there are geographical differences, communication gaps, and a general dependence of one party on another for financial information, it is not unreasonable to expect some amount of friction to result. Certain common problems tend to cause resentment by both parties to the relationship.

Consider the two following quotes, each from the national sales managers of firms who sell their products primarily through reps:

> Doing business with reps is not the same as having your own sales force. They are concerned with one thing—maximizing their own sales—and they could care less about representing *you*. They might try to sell your line and they might not. It all depends on what *you* can do for *them*, never the other way around. Most of those guys would shoot their parents to go to the orphan's picnic. I trust a rep about as far as I could throw an elephant. Naturally, I'm sociable with them and most of them are good guys personally, but if we were in a position to have our own sales force instead of reps, there's no doubt which way we'd go.
>
> We have been dealing through reps for about thirty years. In the ten years I've been here, we've made plenty of adjustments, but overall, we're very satisfied with the type of rep we have. Most of them are fair with you if you're fair with them. Reps aren't "good" and "bad" necessarily—a lot of it has to do with how comfortably your product line fits into his business. The match has to be right. Actually, if you can find a good rep, you're probably better off than having your own direct sales force.

These two statements are fairly typical of the ambivalent posture of sales managers toward reps. The first sales manager had clearly been "burned" in his relationship with reps, hence his antipathy toward the entire group. The second sales manager, on the other hand, had obviously enjoyed a profitable relationship with reps. If there were such a thing as an "average" attitude of sales managers toward reps, it would probably range somewhere between the two expressed here. Not unlike a marriage, it would be unrealistic to expect the relationship between manufacturer and rep to be without its ups and downs, and since certain problems are manifest in all such relationships, we will examine the more prevelant ones from the point of view of the principal and then from the point of view of the rep.[4]

TRADITIONAL PROBLEMS FACED BY PRINCIPALS

There appear to be three major areas of complaint expressed by company sales managers about reps. It should be understood that these complaints are by no means expressed by all sales managers, nor do they apply to the majority of reps. They are, however, a real part of many manufacturer-rep relationship, and a realistic examination of the relationship must include them. The three major areas of complaint are the following:

1. Divided loyalties.
2. Lack of effort in representing manufacturer's products.
3. Inadequate feedback from rep to principal.

Divided Loyalties

Most reps carry as many product lines as they are physically able to handle. The typical product configuration consists of several noncompeting but allied lines. An example would be a rep who sells truck mufflers to truck distributors. An allied product would be a truck tire jack or a portable truck loading platform. The purpose of carrying allied lines is to enable the rep to present more than one product on each sales call. This arrangement is mutually beneficial to both parties in that it provides the rep with a chance to sell *something*, and the manufacturer has his product shown. An illogical product line configuration would exist, for example, if the same rep also carried a line of kitchen appliances. It would be necessary for the rep to call on different types of industries, and the advantage of selling two or more products on one sales call would be lost.

Most manufacturers resent their reps acquiring unrelated lines because they feel that the attention given to the new product will greatly exceed the attention given by the rep to the manufacturer's existing product. As we will see later in the chapter, most reps are somewhat secretive about their activity, a condition that makes manufacturers even more dubious about the amount of attention being given their product. In many cases, a rep will spend the bulk of his time selling the most profitable products to the exclusion of others. Manufacturers are therefore keenly aware of the rep's opportunity to divide his or her loyalties depending upon which product sells the quickest. In some cases this fear by the manufacturer is justified, and in many cases the problem is an imagined one rather than a real one.

A further problem associated with loyalty is that the rep must necessarily owe his primary loyalty to the customer rather than to the principal. This is understandable since the customer is the lifeblood of the rep's business. Principals, however, often feel that they should have top priority in the rep's relationships with is or her various constituencies.

Lack of Effort in Representing Manufacturer's Products

One of the continuing functions of the rep is to be on the lookout for new products to represent. Since his or her livelihood depends upon the amount of goods or services sold, dependence upon one or two products can easily lead to disaster in the event the product becomes obsolete, a recession causes a slowdown in purchasing, or if any one of a multitude of other factors intervenes. For this reason, most reps are anxious to add new lines. In some cases, however, reps tend to keep a line "in reserve" rather than give up the line, even though they may spend very little time attempting to sell the manufacturer's product. As can be expected, manufacturers are highly concerned about the existence of such a possibility. Because of the reluctance of many reps to divulge more than a minimum of information regarding their selling activities, manufacturers tend to develop anxiety when sales of the product are lower than should realistically be expected. One of the conclusions invariably arrived at, whether justified or not, is that the rep is "sandbagging," or exerting less than a fair effort to sell the product.

Actually, it is very difficult for a rep to obtain a well-known or a fast-selling product. When such lines are obtained, the contract typically sets standards of minimum performance that must be maintained as a condition of the rep's continuing to represent the firm. "Sandbagging," when it does occur, is nearly always done with products that are not particularly sought after by customers.

Inadequate Feedback from Rep to Principal

The most valuable asset that every rep has is his or her time. Any time not spent in front of a customer is considered to be nonproductive, even though the alternative use of time might be spent performing some very important function, such as consulting with a customer's personnel to prepare a proposal or develop a price quotation. Because of the exceptionally high value of his or her time, reps normally do not report to their principals unless the communication is associated with a sale. Call reports or other such communications from the field to the principals are considered by most reps to require too much time to bother with. Principals on the other hand, develop anxiety over the rep's activity (or lack of it) concerning their products. Realizaing that reps carry several product lines, a natural reaction of the principal is to feel that the rep is spending the bulk of his or her time promoting some other product, and lack of communication from the rep often only reinforces this assumption. The only obvious solutions for this problem are for reps to communicate in a timely and systematic manner or for principals to maintain full confidence in the rep's willingness to promote the principal's product line. Both of these solutions are somewhat simplistic. Many principals and their reps have reached an understanding on the meaning of adequate communication from the field, but in many principal-rep relationships the problem still persists.

TRADITIONAL PROBLEMS FACED BY REPRESENTATIVES

If principals have been slow to adopt a close-knit relationship, reps have been equally diffident about their association with manufacturers. Consider the following quotes from two experienced reps:

> I've been handling various lines for about twenty-one years and have represented about twenty different firms over that period. Most of the time things worked out very well. I've had a few complaints now and then, but I think most firms will treat you well if the parties can fill each other's needs. I am very careful before I take on an additional line. Just as the principal wants to be sure of me, I want to be sure of him. If there is any doubt about our ability to work together and to communicate, then I investigate further. Once I take on a line, I commit myself and the three salespeople I have to making that product successful. This isn't always a bed of roses between our principals and ourselves, but overall I'm satisfied and I think most of our principals are too.
>
> There's an old joke about a husband and wife being related only by marriage.

To an extent, this describes the "marriage" between a rep and a principal. In my opinion, their objectives are bound to conflict. I'm not saying that every principal is out to screw every rep, either. For the most part, the sales managers I deal with are honest and decent people. Business is business, though, and a firm's objectives are realistically opposed to those of the rep. For example, from an economic standpoint, a firm figures it can let a rep build up a territory and then take it away from him and put in its own salesperson. I don't mean to sound paranoid, but a lot of executives in small- and medium-sized firms really resent reps. They feel that the rep is overpaid, too independent, and strictly self-centered. Notice I didn't say that was the attitude of most sales managers, but they have to do what they're told to.

The rep has to look out for himself because he has only what he sells. It's also difficult for a rep to make out call reports. Yet, the firm practically *requires* unselfish reps who communicate daily in order to have a successful marketing effort. Somewhere there must be an accommodation made, and it is seldom pleasant for either party.

Both of the reps who made these statements have been successfully representing various principals for approximately twenty years, and both are considered to be well thought of in their profession. The questions that are raised by the second rep are related to certain drawbacks of the principal-rep relationship. These drawbacks, which are perceived by many reps to constitute the major problem areas in dealing with principals, are the following:

1. Reduction or removal of sales territory.
2. Incomplete or late communication of information to the field.
3. Failure to provide adequate sales and/or product training.

Reduction or Removal of Sales Territory

One of the rep's worst nightmares is that he or she will build up a sales territory from nothing into one that produces a large sales volume, only to have the principal terminate the contract and substitute the rep with a company salesperson. Unfortunately for reps, this situation is not an uncommon one. From the rep's standpoint, the principal's actions are typically considered disloyal, ruthless, unethical, and shortsighted. Having build up the sales territory, the rep feels, and in most cases justifiably so, that he or she should be permitted to reap well-deserved rewards.

From an economic point of view, however, it is not difficult to understand or even accept the principal's actions. Assume, for example, that at some time territorial sales increase from 0 to $200,000. If the rep's commission is 10 percent, it would cost the company a total of $20,000 in sales commissions to keep the rep in the territory. Since it would undoubtedly cost the firm more to hire, train, and manage a full-time employee in the territory, the firm could probably still justify keeping the rep in the territory, assuming that the company salesperson's ability to devote full time to selling company products would be offset by the rep's personal contacts. As the volume increases, however, the prospect of replacing the rep with a full-time company salesperson becomes increasingly more attractive to the company. At a sales level of $400,000, the firm is required to pay the rep $40,000. But the cost of maintaining its own salesperson in the territory would probably amount to only $25,000 or $30,000. Taking into account the fact that a firm may have as many as twenty or thirty sales territories, the policy of replacing reps with company salespeople can have a substantial impact on company profits.

As a result of this situation, there is a temptation for reps to "sandbag" or to refrain from writing the maximum amount of business possible in order to keep the principal from replacing the rep with company salespeople. This dilemma can only be overcome by a sincere commitment by both parties to maintain the working relationship in such a way that guarantees are made by both parties. These guarantees normally require the firm to keep the rep in the territory as long as certain sales objectives are achieved.

Incomplete or Late Communication to the Field

These problems occur more often in the technical fields, where custom-made equipment requires a request for a price quotation (RPQ) from the field to the plant. As indicated previously, large numbers of home office technical personnel are not as marketing oriented as they might be; hence they tend to disregard or procrastinate on requests from reps in the field. While urgent production needs at the plant might weigh heavily in the priority order, customers are seldom interested in knowing reasons why a rep is unable to address their needs in short order. Indeed, a customer who provides a large share of the rep's business often feels justifiably or not, that such requests should receive top priority.

Most company sales managers understand fully the gravity of such situations and are usually sensitive to the rep's needs. Unfortunately, most company sales managers are often traveling and are not present when requests from the field are received. As a result, personnel who are not as sympathetic often tend to delay in providing the necessary information.

From the rep's standpoint, failure of the principal to get the information out quickly can be disastrous since the rep's own credibility is often at stake. A customer often buys several products from a single rep, and failure to deliver from one firm is often interpreted by the customer as a weakness on the part of the rep and can result in a general undermining of confidence. Since conditions of this type are repugnant to reps, they are generally very hesitant to provide RPQ's to anyone in the principal's organization other than the sales manager. The following quotation from a midwestern rep fairly well summarizes the posture of most reps in this unenviable situation:

> I have this customer in Dearborn who has depended on me for certain auto assembly parts for the last fifteen years. It seems to me that every buyer they put in for my particular product line gets more and more skeptical about my ability to de-

liver. Last week I go into this place and the regular buyer is on vacation and they get this new guy they're training to move in as a buyer. Most of the time they are pretty reasonable and realistic about meeting RPQ dates. Well, this guy breaks my chops like there's no tomorrow. When you gonna deliver? Why can't you get an RPQ for me by Monday? What kind of company you work for, man? Well, I'll tell you, if the regular buyer doesn't come back from vacation, I lose the account. I told him very frankly, I value your business more than you'll ever know, but if I have to put up with this kind of stuff much longer, I'll be a basket case pretty soon. He reassures me and makes me feel pretty good when he says "Look Milt, don't worry about it, we know you do your best all the time," but I have to feel that if that girl in RPQ at the home office does that to me one more time, I can kiss this account good-bye.

A rep from Texas with a similar complaint indicated that the problem might be a pervasive one with the following insights.

I've been calling on this firm ever since 1958. My buyer is a good old boy. I guess we hit it off initially because we were both in the 82nd Airborne. He respects me and I respect him. He introduced me to the president of the organization and it was even more solid because his wife and mine were both involved in the Baptist Scholarship Fund. Everything was fine until one time they needed an RPQ for a particular part for a Jupiter milling assembly. Well, I'm here to tell you, the last time old Jupiter made a milling assembly, Harry Truman was still running a men's clothing store in Missouri. I told the buyer "Hey Gideon, you want me to get you all something easy like an autographed picture of Robert E. Lee or maybe Joe Namath's jersey when he played for Alabama or something simple like that, you got it—but a *Jupiter milling assembly*—they haven't made them for fifty years. He looks at me and says "Bobby Joe, the man says that's what he wants and he also told me to tell you that if you ain't man enough to deliver, he reckons he might be able to find some old boy who will." I said, "there ain't no way that old B.J. can't give a good customer anything he asks for" (after I gulped a few times). The buyer said, "Well that's good, Bobby Joe, because we really have taken a liking to you and so when the Man said to me the other day 'I don't know about that old Bobby Joe, he looks like he been gettin' fat on this account' I said to him, swear to the Lord, Bobby Joe, I told that old boy, I said 'Sir, there ain't no way old B.J. won't deliver anything you specify.' So he says to me, "Boy, if he don't you both gonna be in deep trouble." "So you see, B.J., we're both in trouble if you don't deliver." So I called up the sales manager, and he wasn't there, naturally, he was out in Provo, Utah, checking out some other poor rep. I got this guy on the phone who tells me the only way I'm gonna get a Jupiter is if I make one myself. About this time I felt pretty low. But I say, "no sir, old B.J. ain't gonna give up this easy. I tell my wife to track that sales manager down wherever he is. That old girl could find a penny in a cow pasture, so finally she finds the sales manager in a motel in Shreveport. I told him, 'Look Jimmy Ray, I got this problem,' and I proceed to tell him the whole story. He says, "Bobby Joe, I got the exact part you want back in the parts room. I'm gonna call home office right now and tell them where to find it and ship it air express. Anything else I can do for my best rep while you got me on the phone?" Well sir, he gets the part for that old Jupiter machine to the account in about 48

> hours. I'll tell you something else, too. Anybody else comes around trying to squeeze me out of that account, I feel sorry for him. The buyer said when he told the man he had the part *on the unloading dock* that old boy liked to drop over with relief. He took me fishing about a month later and told me, "Bobby Joe, y'all the best rep we ever had. Ain't but one thing you can't do and that's to walk on water." And I thought, "uh-oh, I wonder what he's gonna ask for now."

These situations are not at all atypical and serve to point out the importance of the principal's sales manager to its reps. The importance of a commitment to the marketing concept is paramount. Most sales managers recognize this fact; nevertheless, reps have been known to lose accounts because of a principal's personnel's lack of sensitivity to the need for expeditious attention to field requests.

Failure to Provide Adequate Field Sales and Product Training

This problem normally manifests itself in rep organizations where the rep employs his or her own salespeople. Most rep organizations simply do not have the resources that large- or medium-sized firms have at their disposal. As a result, much of their time is spent "fighting fires" rather than developing long-run programs, and there has been a traditional dependence upon principals to provide sales and product training for salespeople. Although most principals recognize the importance of this function, other priorities often pre-empt this critical responsibility. As indicated in Chapter 7, inadequate sales training can have devastating consequences. In rep organizations, these consequences are even more devastating, since there is seldom anyone available to provide adequate backup when a rep's salesperson is unable to provide a customer with adequate information. A discussion with a rep from southern California elicited the following anecdote:

> As you know, we sell to the sporting goods trade, and we've been pretty successful because we fill our customer's needs and we never overload anybody. We have everything from tennis rackets to jogging equipment, and the market is quite fragmented for this type of merchandise. We were looking for something to sell to the college and school market for quite a while because most of our lines are too upscale and we could never crack that market because of bidding procedures where price was always the dominant factor. Then, finally, these two guys from Pittsburgh developed this ten-station exercise machine that was *fantastic*. As you probably noticed, every other building out here is either a body building gym or some kind of exercise salon. There are three things that we institutionalized in Southern California—divorce, the Beach Boys, and physical fitness. We figured we could get this thing into every school in the state because it was unique and nobody could bid against it. I went to Pittsburgh for an interview and met the principals, these two brothers named Stanley and Walter something too long to pronounce. I used to play football in high school and college and consider myself to be in fairly good shape, but these two guys looked like they were both probably too big and too tough to even play for the Steelers. Aside from an annoying trait that they both had where they called you "stud" instead of using your name and

> kept punching you on the arm or shoulder in a friendly way, they seemed to be pretty knowledgeable about the market. They kept telling me about this sales manager they were bringing in who had all the answers. We signed the rep agreement and they shipped me literature and a sample right away. After that everything went downhill. Evidently, the sales manager hit the road and worked his way West through all the other forty-nine states before he got to California. Naturally, my sales force just *had* to try to sell the unit before they really understood what they were selling. We got plenty of orders and miraculously they were able to ship everyone of them within thirty days. The problem was, nobody could figure out how to *use* the bloody thing. Every time I called Stanley and Walter up, they were running around in circles. Nobody in our organization knows about "kinesthetics" or "forced tension" or any of that crap. To make a long story short, after we burned them with that damned machine, we couldn't get into another college or school if we were *giving* them our products. This was about ten years ago. We still haven't seen the sales manager and the last I heard Stanley and Walter went bankrupt and were back working in a steel mill. I just hope they don't get mad at the foreman and decide to tear the place apart.

Although most field sales and product training problems are normally of a more subtle nature than the preceding situation, many reps have high anxiety about the possibility of similar situations arising.

POSITIVE APPROACHES TO THE PRINCIPAL-REPRESENTATIVE RELATIONSHIP

The preceding sections have documented the role of the rep, the structure of the agency, and some problems that arise from the principal-rep relationship. The problems described previously do not apply in all or probably even in most cases, but are the most common ones that do occur. This section will investigate the more positive aspects of the relationship between reps and principals and the tools that are used to develop and maintain a viable working arrangement between the parties.

Manufacturer's Representative Associations

William Gomberg, the well-known labor relations philosopher and consultant, once described a profession as "an organized conspiracy against the public." The accuracy of Gomberg's tongue-in-cheek assessment of doctors, lawyers, and the clergy is clearly open to subjective interpretation, but the relevant term would seem to be *organized*. Not unlike any other professional group, manufacturer's reps have banded together for mutual protection and for the maintenance of certain economic standards unique to the profession. As in most cases of mutual survival pacts among competitors, a certain code of behavior has evolved, often referred to as a statement of professional ethics. Without lengthy analysis, there appear to be a few iron-clad rules that are observed by most if not all reps.[5]

1. Mutual exchange of information among reps concerning principles or any other trade information of mutual interest.
2. Nonuse of questionable tactics to take a line away from another rep.
3. Agreement not to accept less than the going rate of commission for any product line.
4. Not to split commissions with a principal's representative.
5. Not to take on any lines that will not be aggressively sold.

As in any other professional ethical code, these standards of conduct are designed to protect other reps, not principals. Clearly, there is another set of ethics that reps and principals are expected to observe in their business dealings with each other.

Conduct of Rep toward Principal

1. To comply with the policies, procedures, and standards set down by the principal.
2. To aggressively pursue the sale of the principal's line.
3. To avoid misrepresentation.
4. To give the same loyalty to the principal that is expected from the rep's own employees.

Conduct of Principal toward Rep

1. Agree to pay going rate of commission.
2. Not to modify the terms of a rep agreement except by mutual consent.
3. Not to withhold rep's commissions.
4. Agree to arbitration of disagreements between rep and principal.

The preceding codes of standards are, in the main, observed by most principals and most reps. Without such standards of conduct, an orderly marketplace could not exist. The maintenance of such standards is virtually assured because reps are in close communication with each other and because principals are in equally close contact. The vehicles by which close communications are maintained are the formal organizations in which either reps or, in some cases, both reps and principals hold membership. There are formal rep organizations for practically every product line grouping. Sporting goods reps, for example, belong to the Association of Sporting Goods Manufacturers Representatives, with offices in Chicago, Illinois. Principals in the sporting goods industry belong to an organization known as the Sporting Goods Manufacturers Association of Miami, Florida. As indicated, nearly every product line group has formal associations, and an enumeration of the various organizations would be unnecessary, since most of them are designed to serve the aforementioned purpose.

A very important function of the principal-rep organization is the use of an *information exchange*. Essentially, this data bank documents information received from the field regarding both parties. If, for example, a principal feels that a rep has not lived up to the terms of their agreement, he might want to report this fact to the association. The same procedure would hold true if, for example, a rep had not received commission checks on a timely basis. The association's information exchange documents these kinds of occurrences and in this respect performs an important function.

A rep from Montana made the following comments about the concept of an information exchange:

> A lot of times you hear a rep crying about the screwing he got from some manufacturer, but most of the time if he spent the time investigating the principal's past relationships with other reps, he probably wouldn't have entered into the deal to begin with. That's one good thing about the information exchange we have. Suppose a principal has a history of not paying his reps on time. You don't have to call every rep in the country to find out about him. By the same token there are a lot of honorable principals who have been burned, too. I know that service has helped a lot of people on both sides avoid a lot of disappointment.

Another service of such organizations is legal assistance in providing both reps and principals with standard contract guidelines that are beneficial to both parties. Most rep agreements are composed of the following essential elements:[6]

1. Exclusive sales representation
2. Territory and customers
3. Commissions payable
4. Handling and acceptance of orders
5. Selling aids, promotion, sales training
6. Handling of inquiries
7. Selling effort required
8. Termination
9. Handling of disputes between principal and rep

The somewhat lengthy but comprehensive sample standard form of agreement shown in Figure 15-1 details these contractual elements. Agreements of this type are typical of most principal-rep relationships.

In addition to the foregoing services, most associations also provide an apparatus for collection of overdue commissions and information concerning events of interest in federal and legal legislative arenas. Larger organizations even provide group medical plans, discounts in advertising, various statistical surveys, a nationwide list of attorneys and accountants who specialize in problems affecting reps and principals, and periodic workshop seminars.

Manufacturer's Representative Councils

In recent years, the rep-principal relationship has become more sophisticated. In most cases, both parties recognize the need for each other and attempt to adopt measures that will ensure a continuing viable and profitable partnership. One of the more interesting and more effective steps being taken by many enlight-

Figure 15-1

Agreement for Exclusive Sales Representation

(Standard Agreement Form Officially Approved by the Sporting Goods Agents Association)

This AGREEMENT dated the _______day of______________________,

19____, by and between _______________________________________

______________________, a ______________________________
corp., partnership, or individual proprietorship
___________________________, having its principal place of business located at ____

______________________, in the State of ____________________,

hereinafter called the COMPANY and/or their assigns, _________

____, a __________ corp., partnership, or individual proprietorship
____, having its principal place of business located at______________________

___________________________, in the State of______________,

hereinafter called the AGENT.

WITNESSETH:

That the COMPANY does hereby appoint the AGENT as a Sales Agent, and the AGENT does hereby accept the appointment subject to the following terms and conditions:

FIRST: The AGENT shall faithfully, diligently and to the best of his ability, endeavor to promote and extend the sales of the COMPANY and its products to the customers both existing and prospective in the territory hereafter described.

SECOND: The territory of the AGENT shall be as follows:
____
____
____

THIRD: The AGENT shall be the sole and exclusive agent of the COMPANY within said territory for the sale of its products, both wholesale and retail, without exclusion unless specifically negotiated with and agreed upon by the AGENT in advance of any offer to the market or any actual transaction.

FOURTH: The AGENT shall be entitled to receive a commission upon all shipments in his territory whether by the AGENT or by direct orders of the customers to the COMPANY or otherwise.

Figure 15-1 (Cont.)

FIFTH: It shall be the responsibility of the AGENT to provide the COMPANY with active and continuous sales representation in his territory by actual salesman contact with the customers both existing and prospective. The AGENT further agrees to maintain procedures and records to assure systematic, repeated and complete coverage of his territory.

SIXTH: It shall be the responsibility of the COMPANY to provide products and customer services which are reasonably competitive with those offered by other sources with respect to quality, price and design concept. Further, it shall be the responsibility of the COMPANY to adequately support the sale of its products with such trade and consumer advertising, and such other promotional assistance as may be required by the prevailing standards of the competition.

SEVENTH: The AGENT shall keep the COMPANY properly advised and informed as to the general conditions which pertain to or affect the sale of its line. The AGENT agrees to comply with such directives as may be issued by the officers of the COMPANY to carry out its policies in dealing with the customer trade, provided and insofar as such directives are not inconsistent with the terms, conditions and understanding of this Agreement. The AGENT shall cooperate with the COMPANY to the best of his ability in obtaining credit and financial information regarding the customers, and in reporting this and other pertinent information to the COMPANY and otherwise assisting in the orderly processing of orders.

EIGHTH: The COMPANY will keep the AGENT informed of all communications between it and the customers; will furnish the AGENT with copies of all customer correspondence; and will promptly furnish the AGENT with copies of order acknowledgements and customer invoices. The COMPANY, at its own expense and including delivery charges, shall furnish the AGENT with all necessary sales supplies such as catalogs, price lists, display material and all other sales aids in sufficient quantity to fulfill the requirements of his territory.

NINTH: The COMPANY shall pay to the AGENT a commission of ______________________ percent upon all shipments as indicated in paragraph FOURTH above. The term "Shipments" shall mean orders for merchandise accepted by the COMPANY but not including transportation costs. Commissions shall be paid to the AGENT regardless of the customer's payment for "Shipments" to the COMPANY.

TENTH: The COMPANY shall furnish the AGENT with a detailed commission statement once each month. The commission on shipments shall become due and payable on or before the 15th day of the month following the month of shipment.

2

Figure 15-1 (Cont.)

ELEVENTH: The COMPANY shall furnish adequate samples to the AGENT on memorandum invoice. The title and ownership of such samples shall remain with the COMPANY. The AGENT shall exercise reasonable care to account for all samples in his possession, for all samples periodically returned to the COMPANY, and for all samples disposed of in any other manner. In those cases where samples are expendable or not of significant value the requirement of accountability on the part of the AGENT is hereby waived. Samples, which in the sole judgment of the COMPANY, have significant value must be returned by the AGENT or disposed of at a price set by the COMPANY and the proceeds promptly remitted to the COMPANY.

TWELFTH: The term of this Agreement shall be for a period of________________________ from ________________________ to________________________. Such Agreement shall be automatically renewed for a similar period or periods, unless a notice of cancellation in writing is sent to either party by the other via certified mail return receipt requested at least ninety (90) days prior to the end of the period of this Agreement. The COMPANY shall not without good cause take any of the following actions:

(1) terminate or fail to renew a contract or other binding agreement with AGENT who is soliciting business on behalf of such principal from an account;

(2) reduce the size of the geographical territory assigned to AGENT; or

(3) reduce the rate of commission paid to AGENT.

"Good cause", when used with respect to the termination of, or failure to renew, a contract or other binding agreement between COMPANY and AGENT, means a termination or failiure to renew by COMPANY which is based upon the following:

(1) an act of God, an act of war or insurrection, a strike, or any action by an agency of Government;

(2) a continuing decline in the volume of sales of merchandise with respect to which AGENT solicits business on behalf of COMPANY, if such decline is more than temporary in nature; or

(3) conduct on the part of AGENT with respect to the COMPANY which constitutes--

(a) fraud, dishonesty, or criminal activity;

(b) a material breach of the contract or other binding agreement between AGENT and COMPANY;

3

Figure 15-1 (Cont.)

THIRTEENTH: Any COMPANY who violates any of the above provisions of Section 12 shall be liable to AGENT assigned to the account involved for the payment of compensation in an amount equal to the amount of any commissions which such AGENT would have received from COMPANY if the violation had not occurred. The period for such compensation shall be:

(1) The period during which AGENT solicited business from such account before such violation occurred; or

(2) Two (2) years; whichever is longer.

FOURTEENTH: After this Agreement has been terminated in accordance with the provisions hereof (except in cases of termination by the agent or for good cause) the COMPANY shall pay to the AGENT an amount equal to ____________________percent of all sales upon which the AGENT would have earned a commission in accordance with paragraphs 4 and 9 herein for a period equal to the period the AGENT and COMPANY have been bound by this Agreement.

FIFTEENTH: It is further understood and agreed that the AGENT is an independent contractor and that neither COMPANY nor AGENT shall assume any liability whatsoever, each for the other, directly or indirectly. It is also agreed that this Agreement shall not under any circumstances create the relationship of joint venture between the parties hereto. Notwithstanding the above, COMPANY agrees to name AGENT as an additional insured on its liability insurance policies under broad form vendor's endorsement and agrees to hold AGENT harmless and defend AGENT from any and all claims for personal injury and property damage made in connection with its products.

SIXTEENTH: Any controversy or claim arising out of or relating to this contract, or the breach thereof, shall be settled by arbitration in accordance with the Rules of the American Arbitration Association, and judgment upon the award rendered by the Arbitrator(s) may be entered in any Court having jurisdiction thereof.

SEVENTEENTH: Any COMPANY who enters into this contract or other agreement with the AGENT under which the AGENT solicits orders for the merchandise of the COMPANY shall give the AGENT access to the records of the COMPANY for the purpose of verifying any information supplied to the AGENT by the COMPANY in accordance with this agreement.

EIGHTEENTH: This Agreement is made and executed in the State of ______________________ and shall be construed under the laws thereof.

IN WITNESS WHEREOF, the parties hereto have set their hands and seals the day and year above first written.

______________________________ ______________________________

______________________________ ______________________________

______________________________ ______________________________

______________________________ ______________________________

4

ened firms and their reps is the institution of the *manufacturer's representative council*. This term is used to refer to a committee formed to communicate the needs of both parties to the other. A typical council is composed of several executives of the firm and several reps who sell for the organization. Inputs are received from all members of the group, and a stronger understanding usually evolves from such councils. Just as in any other relationship of this type, the positive results that come from open communication depend upon the sincerity of the parties involved and their commitment toward the achievement of a synergistic outcome. With a strong commitment, the results are typically beneficial to both parties. Lack of strong commitment typically reduces the functions of such committees to a meaningless sham, and often tends to weaken the relationship rather than to strengthen it.

The most important commitment must, of course, come from top management. Other things being equal, the company should be represented by at least the president, all the major marketing executives, and preferably also by the appropriate production and distribution executives. It is also necessary that these parties take an active part in the proceedings rather than be there for "window-dressing" purposes.

One example of a very successful council is the one instituted at the Hoffman Air Filter Corporation.[7] The council at this organization consists of a board composed of the president, the marketing manager, the production superintendent, the national sales manager, and several technical executives of the Hoffman Corporation. Representing the agents are seven reps from various geographical regions who are intimately familiar with the organization, its products, and its sales philosophy. These reps are also in regular communication with the remainder of Hoffman's rep force and are aware of problems that are common to individual representatives.

The rep council has been responsible for instituting several new departures, such as developing a product film for customers, making the service level more responsive, a new sales training program, and several other positive changes and additions. The Hoffman Council has developed a very comprehensive and specific charter of its functions and objectives, which is shown in Figure 15-2.

Advances in the profession, such as rep-principals associations and the manufacturer's representative councils, have contributed greatly to the effectiveness of firms and reps alike.

SUMMARY

This chapter has provided a realistic appraisal of the importance of the manufacturer's representative as an institution and of the nature and structure of the relationship between the firm and the manufacturer's representative. From the standpoint of terminology, the manufacturer's rep is typically referred to as a *manufacturer's agent* in writing and simply as a rep in verbal usage.

Figure 15-2

HOFFMAN'S ADVISORY BOARD CHARTER

Purpose of the Board

The purpose of the Hoffman Air & Filtration Systems Representatives Board is to provide advice and make recommendations to Hoffman management on marketing policies and programs. The primary objective of the Board is to assure maximum customer orientation of these marketing programs to the mutual best interests of the Hoffman Air & Filtration Systems Division and its representatives. To accomplish this purpose, the Board is to provide uninhibited individual commentary on proposed policy and programs.

Composition of the Board

I. The Board will consist of six (6) members, each of whom will serve for a period of three (3) years. Membership will be rotated so that one-third of the membership will be succeeded by new members each year. The term of each Board will be one (1) year, beginning on January 1 and ending December 31. Each member will serve three (3) terms, except the first Board which will have two (2) members with one (1) term, two (2) members with two (2) terms and two (2) members with three (3) terms. No member will serve more than three (3) consecutive terms.

II. Selections for Board membership will be made by Hoffman management within the framework of the criteria noted below. Selections arre based on these criteria in order to provide a Board membership with broad experience and an understanding of the problems involved in the highly diversified marketing areas served by the Hoffman Air & Filtration Systems Representative organization.

III. Invitation to membership will be extended to the individuals who have exhibited an active participation and interest in the marketing of the Hoffman Air & Filtration products, the exercise of good business judgment and practices in their respective businesses, and individuals whom we feel will make a contribution to the mutual growth and profits of the Hoffman Air & Filtration Systems Division and our representatives.

IV. For purposes of geographical selections, the United States has been broken down into four (4) geographical areas as follows: South, East, West, and Central as supervised by each Regional Manager. The Board will generally consist of one (1) member from each area plus two (2) other at large members.

V. Hoffman membership on the Board will consist of the following Divisional Personnel:
   - Division President
   - Division Vice President
   - Marketing Manager
   - Executive Engineer
   - Technical Managers (3)

VI. Invitations will be extended from time to time to other representatives and members of Hoffman Air & Filtration Systems who can make significant contributions to the Board.

Procedures

I. The Board will meet at least once a year, generally in Syracuse. Board members will be advised of the meeting at least two (2) months prior to the date of meeting. Meetings may occasionally be held at other locations.

II. The formal meeting will be of two (2) days' duration. Members will have an

Figure 15-2 (Cont.)

Hoffman's Advisory Board Charter

opportunity to get together informally at activities arranged for the afternoon and evening preceding the meeting in order that new members of the Board may become better acquainted with other members of the Board prior to the meeting.

III. The Board members may act as spokesmen of other representatives in their area. However, suggestions and recommendations made by the Board will be considered as individual opinions of the members, acting as a group.

IV. A preliminary agenda will be prepared in advance of the meeting and mailed to members for their suggestions as to agenda changes or additions. Copies of the final agenda will be mailed to each member at least two (2) weeks prior to the meeting.

V. A copy of the Minutes will be sent to each member. At the beginning of each meeting, the Minutes of the previous meeting will be read. As the Board is advisory in nature, the preparation of the Minutes is not intended as a commitment that all of the suggestions and recommendations can, or will be adopted into Hoffman's marketing programs or policies.

VI. In the preparation of the agenda, particular emphasis will be placed on basic policy matters and marketing programs and not on detailed practices. The Board should not be hampered in discussing the details of day to day business practice, but must necessarily be concerned with broader areas of mutual interest.

VII. From time to time, throughout the year, problems or situations may develop which require immediate advice and suggestions from Board members. In such cases, the Board's services will be utilized and advice and suggestions solicited through correspondence. By this means, the services of the Board will be available on a continuing basis.

VIII. Travel expenses of members to and from the annual meeting will be absorbed by Hoffman Air & Filtration Systems, and members will be the guests of the Company while in Syracuse, or in any other meeting location.

IX. Election of a Chairman for a one year term takes place by secret ballot before the Annual Fall Meeting. All members with one year's service on the Board are eligible for the office of Chairman. Six to eight weeks prior to the annual meeting, the Board selects one of these members to represent them as Chairman for the coming year.

The rep as a viable marketing institution in the United States probably began during the nineteenth-century era of industrialization. Today the size of the typical rep agency consists of about four persons.

Possibly because of the independent nature of both reps and the owners of the small- and medium-sized firms they represent, certain problems have traditionally characterized the relationship. Many owners of business, or *principals,* have traditionally complained that reps have divided loyalties, sometimes expend little effort to sell products when it is not their advantage to do so, and provide as little feedback from the field as possible.

On the other hand, many reps feel that principals will reduce or take away rep territories without regard to the effort invested by the rep in building them up, that certain firms provide inadequate field assistance, and that incomplete or late communication of information to the field, often in the form of price quotations, has caused problems with important accounts.

There is no doubt that many of these problems exist and will continue to exist. There is, however, ample evidence that the manufacturer's rep has achieved professional stature. Formal, well-organized associations for the mutual advancement of the needs of both parties exist for nearly every product group. Associations such as MANA (Manufacturers and Agents National Association) have helped to define codes of ethics in business transactions, to establish standard territories, and to develop standard contractual forms, as well as providing other important services to both parties. A further innovation has been the manufacturer's representative council, a committee approach to common problems. Essentially, the advances mentioned here, along with the integrity of both parties, have solidified the relationship between principals and reps. That the manufacturer's representative approach has become a viable and important marketing institution has been established, and consistent efforts are being made by both parties to further strengthen the relationship.

U-GARD-IT Systems

Ed Murphy is president of U-GARD-IT Systems, a firm that manufactures and markets safety devices for armored trucks and cash storage centers. His products are used by many of the major security firms, and with the exception of an incident in Boston in 1951, where one of his devices failed and a gang of thieves stole some money from one of his customers, Ed's products have enjoyed a good reputation.

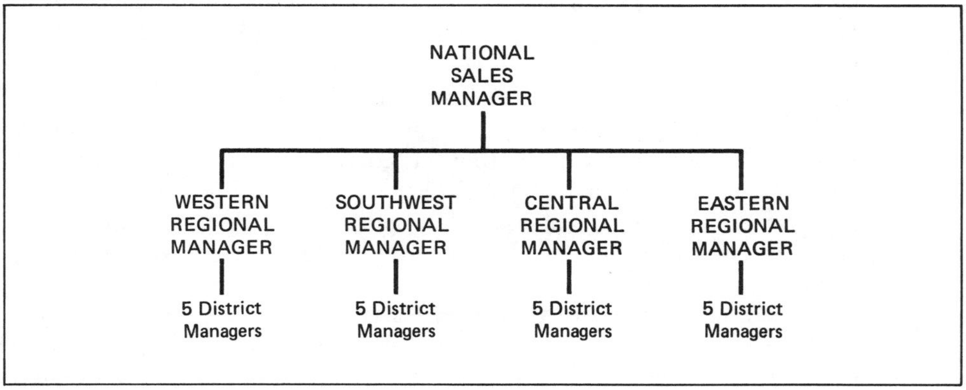

The sales organization consists of a national sales manager, four regional managers, and twenty district managers.

Although the district managers are called managers, they actually perform the selling. Most DSMs make about five or six sales per year. DSMs receive a base salary of $25,000 plus expenses, plus a commission of roughly 5 percent of gross sales.

In recent years, the median income of the twenty DSMs has fallen from about $45,000 to $35,000. Aggressive inroads by competition have been the primary reason for the sales and income decline. Ed feels that U-GARD-IT is getting a large enough share of the market, but that sales costs have been too high. He has called you in to help him develop a solution to his problem.

1. What possible changes would you suggest to Ed Murphy?
2. What would be the specific benefits of these changes?

Jesse's Dilemma

Jesse Morris has been selling tractor trucks and semitrailers for the past seventeen years. Although he has been fairly successful and is considered a solid performer by his manager and the owners of the firm, Jesse has been finding his job less challenging in recent years. When the recent recession caused a dip in sales, Jesse felt that the time had come for him to consider moving on into a situation where he could achieve greater personal growth and a more interesting career path. Although he complained about reduced income potential, he had been through difficult times before, and he knew that money was an excuse, not a reason, to seek a new opportunity.

After considerable investigation, Jesse decided that the manufacturer's representative profession appealed to him. He had always been a loner, was well organized, and had the financial resources to weather the uncertain start-up situation he anticipated. In deciding what kind of lines to carry, he discussed the situation with Dick Simon, a manufacturer's representative in medical instruments, and Marty Golden, president of a well-known and highly profitable fabric firm.

Dick advised Jesse to carry as many lines as he could. He also pointed out that they should be noncompeting but compatible. He explained that many principals resent their reps and that he needed several lines to protect himself from arbitrary action by the principal. He also advised Jesse to be careful not to sell too much of any one product; otherwise, the principal would take the line away and put his own salesperson in the territory.

In discussing the situation with Marty, Jesse was advised to set up a reporting relationship with all principals to keep them informed of all sales calls. Marty also told Jesse that he should keep the number of lines he carries to a minimum, since "most principals want loyalty from their reps." Jesse has come to you to help him decide what advice to take.

1. What are the pros and cons of Dick's and Marty's advice?
2. What advice would you give Jesse?

DISCUSSION QUESTIONS

1. What are the major functions of the manufacturer's representative?
2. Why do firms use manufacturer's representatives?
3. In which product areas are females most prevalent as manufacturer's representatives?
4. What are the major problems faced by companies using manufacturer's representatives?
5. What are the major problems faced by the manufacturer's representatives in their relationships with principals?
6. What are some positive approaches to the principal-rep relationship?
7. What is the purpose of the manufacturer's representative council?
8. What types of companies typically use manufacturer's representatives?

CHAPTER 16

ETHICAL IMPLICATIONS OF SALES MANAGEMENT

OBJECTIVES

To examine some of the established ethical principles in business.

To identify some of the ethical dilemmas faced by sales managers:

* In selling
* In hiring
* In training
* In service
* In motivation

INTERVIEW WITH FRANK SMITH

Interviewer: As the chapter starts out, Frank, "For centuries scholars have been wrestling with the concept of ethics in business." Do you have a specific set of standards that you subscribe to in transacting business?

Frank Smith: I don't like to sound sanctimonious, but, yes, I do. I don't lie to customers, I don't do anything that I personally consider dishonest or shady. Fortunately, I work for a firm whose ethical approach is pretty similar to my own.

Interviewer: Do you agree with the statement that it's good business to be honest and ethical?

Frank Smith: I certainly do. I can't emphasize strongly enough how important one's reputation is in business. The kids in college see all this ABSCAM and similar stuff going on and conclude that most people are dishonest. The funny part is that it's just the opposite—most people in business are honest.

Interviewer: Do you have an established policy with respect to, say, disparaging competitors?

Frank Smith: We have very strict policies regarding all areas of ethical conduct. We are careful that we don't leave gray areas for the salesperson to wink at the policy and then go ahead to do something he or she shouldn't.

Interviewer: What areas do you think are reasonable to associate with ethical implications?

Frank Smith: That's really hard to answer. There is no pat answer. Let's look at the chapter. I think we do a good job of getting our point across even though we are discussing a very nebulous area.

For centuries scholars have been wrestling with the concept of ethics in business. Probably the most enduring statement of ethical conduct in the Western World has been the injunction to "do unto others as you would have them do unto you." Despite the simplicity of the Golden Rule, business organizations have found it necessary from time to time to document acceptable codes of behavior. Various opponents of the capitalist system, for example, have declared that there exists a direct contradiction between business and ethical conduct. Even certain groups within the structure of the American government spend a good deal of their time seeking ways to expose the businessperson's failings to their constituencies. That there is often good reason for protestations from various groups is an established fact. But is business bad per se? In her monumental work *A History of Business*, Miriam Beard wrote:

> Few really horrid crimes, without rational motive, may be imputed to businessmen Seldom have they put out the eyes of competitors with hot irons or burned rival salesmen at the stake. Even early Italian financiers, though they resorted to the stiletto at times when certain industries appeared overcrowded, were cautious

> and methodical despite their Latin temperament, and did not murder other bankers just for fun, or throw away monopolies for love. To be sure, businessmen were often drawn into violence as fighters, slavers or pirates, and they did evil in their own way: they robbed widows and orphans and the Indians; the oppressed whole populations with monopolies and usurious practices and cheated the State, by selling it rotten ships, as the Romans did in the Punic Wars or Vanderbilt in the American Civil War, or by outfitting its enemies with arrows or airplanes. But as a class, they were not wanton in barbarity; they have not engaged in the fantastic cruelties, the *crimes passionnels* and massacres for pleasure which endeared other kinds of men to the general public.[1]

The impact of a business decision on other groups depends to a great extent upon subjective interpretation. Clearly, the businessman who sets fire to his own store to collect the insurance is guilty of wrongdoing in virtually everyone's eyes. On the other hand, who is to determine the distinction between legal and ethical business strategy? A case in point is typified in the following incident. During the late 1960s, a disturbance was created in a New Jersey discount store on a busy Friday evening when the protagonist, a professor at a well-known Eastern University, had driven his eight-year-old son some distance to buy a high-quality fishing reel at a very low advertised price. When told rather abruptly by a somewhat pompous assistant manager that there were no reels available, even though the ad appeared for the first time that day, the professor sarcastically inquired how many were originally for sale. When the assistant manager replied, with a superior look and an evil grin, "three," the normally quiet and reserved professor expressed his indignation by leaping over the counter and chasing the surprised, but agile clerk through the store, shouting obscenities and threatening bodily harm. When finally subdued by security guards, the assailant was heard to mutter something related to false advertising.

This incident points out how a business firm can set out to deceive while still operating within the limits of the law. The consumer in the incident, who clearly should have known better, chose to vent his frustration in a most basic way. Less irascible types, however, have attempted to come to grips with the problem of ethical business conduct by more thoughtful and constructive processes. Yet it is doubtful that anyone will ever articulate a description of what is ethically acceptable business behavior that is satisfactory to all or even most parties involved. This chapter will investigate some of the reasons why ethics in business and, specifically, in sales management are so difficult to objectively determine. It will also examine some of the ethical dilemmas that are faced by most sales managers on a regular basis.

CORPORATION VERSUS CONSCIENCE

According ot Clarence B. Randall, a well-known former chief executive officer of a major corporation, the business executive should quit his job rather than take an action that is repugnant to his or her own conscience, whatever the personal consequences might be.[2] This course of action is probably the most practical "solution," since a person with a strong conscience must live with the distasteful reality that he or she has "sold out." There are, however, ways in which actions that are contradictory to one's normal sense of integrity may be rationalized, and it is within the framework of relative values that one's own action is typically judged.[3] Probably the greatest dilemma of all is that most ethical questions in business fall within some gray area that can be interpreted as being either "right" or "wrong" according to one's subjective interpretation. Indeed, it is difficult enough to set standards for oneself; yet some individuals feel compelled to set standards for others as well.[4]

Setting aside individual judgments of people who set standards for others, standards for human conduct within the corporation, rightly or wrongly, are usually set at the highest levels of the organization. If a commitment to high standards of ethical conduct in both letter and spirit is made at the top, these standards normally become a mandate for other members of the corporation. There is no guarantee that if the executive cadre practices what it preaches that all employees will do likewise, but their conduct has a great influence on others. It scarcely need be mentioned that if the top executives do not observe their own rules, very few employees will, either. Within any kind of pluralistic society, however, *somebody* must set standards and codes of behavior, and in the corporation, this task falls upon its leaders.

In light of the many public scandals of the past decade, public confidence in politicians, doctors, lawyers, and businesspeople has eroded (one observer of the scene commented sarcastically that college professors would probably have been included in the list, except they lacked the imagination to do anything to cause a scandal). It is not at all surprising, therefore, that the public at large is hesitant to accept professional codes of ethics as serving anyone except the professionals who devised the codes, and in no one does the public have less confidence, as a general rule, than in businesspeople.

Most corporations, at least the larger ones, have documented some general sets of standards that are to be followed in the transaction of business. In some cases, these guidelines are quite pretentious; in other cases, some very sensible general rules are laid down.

The larger question of the impact of the individual's conscience on decision making must be examined from a more specific viewpoint. Novels and plays ranging from Herman Hesse to Jean-Paul Sartre have been written on the subject of the individual's integrity versus the organizational imperative, typically culminating in hero's trading of pleasure for pain in a final gesture of maintaining individuality. Situations in the corporate milieu are seldom as dramatic or as black-and-white as represented by T. S. Eliot and Kierkegaard. The sales manager, in fact, is seldom "ordered" by his or her supervisor to engage in some activity that is blatantly antisocial, illegal, or immoral.

More often than not, situations requiring ethical decisions seldom arise by

"Where do I draw the line between good and evil?"

design. While ethical dilemmas are present in all areas of business, this section will examine specifically the ones that are associated with selling, hiring, training, service, and motivation. Some of the more frequent situations that arise will be examined, along with examples of how managers traditionally deal with these issues.

ETHICAL PROBLEMS IN SELLING: MAKING UNTRUE STATEMENTS TO CUSTOMERS AND PROSPECTS

Selling is described in this text as a one-to-one relationship between the customer and the salesperson. Our textbook approach has been that salesperson and customer alike are honest and above board in their dealings. Yet it was recently reported in the prestigious and widely circulated weekly, *The National Enquirer*, that most salespeople tell "at least five white lies" to their customers every day.[5] The value difference between a white lie and an outright untruth will not be weighed here, but some of the more common ones will be described. Whether or not an untruth is told with the tacit or expressed approval of a sales manager, or even without his or her knowledge at all, the sales manager is nevertheless responsible for all statements made by salespeople, and it is the manager who must rectify any situations caused by reliance on such statements.

Probably the most common "white lie" salespeople are guilty of is quotation of delivery dates. Because a long delivery date might be used as a wedge against closing a sale, quoting the customers too-early delivery dates seems to be a common problem among salespeople. The primary reasons for this appear to be associated with keeping the customer "on the books" or discouraging him or her from canceling an order. This practice is normally engaged in by newer salespeople or by salespeople who lack confidence in themselves or their products. Like most other untruthful statements, misquoting delivery typically results in a lessening of credibility.

Another practice of making untruthful statements is detracting from a competitor's product with incomplete knowledge of the facts. "Knocking" the competition is generally frowned upon by most sales managers. In some cases, the product sold by a competitor is superior, and there is a temptation for the manager as well as the salesperson to overstress some flaw or to imply that some detriment will accrue to the user. This practice in some ways is analogous to "pirating" a competitor's employees. Most managers recognize its damaging effects and are also aware that competitors have the opportunity to retaliate. As one sales manager said to the author,

> Lying about a competitor's product is a very bad practice to indulge in. I tell my people that if it comes to my attention that a salesperson has lied about a competitive product by an outright statement or by inneuendo, that this will have a detrimental effect upon his or her career. The results can be very bad. It's almost like a "war" in the Mafia, where they never bother each other's wife or kids, not for humanitarian reasons, but because the retaliatory possibilities are so repugnant.

It is also a fact that in most informal sales status systems unfair disparagement of the competition denotes a definite lack of sales expertise.

The opposite approach, one that is taken by some salespeople, is overstressing the performance capabilities of products or services. This practice is often engaged in with the approval of sales managers and is known as "puffing." Clearly, this practice results in returns and customer ill will. Many products sold to consumers are "puffed up" by salespeople because of the one-shot nature of the sale and the unlikelihood of ever seeing the customer again. In consultative, technical, and industrial sales, this practice is, among other things, eminently impractical, since most sales organizations in these fields tend to take a marketing-oriented approach rather than a production-oriented approach.

One of the more blatant areas of lying to customers is in the quotation of prices. In many firms a certain price is set at the home office and the price is rigidly adhered to by all sales units. Most national concerns operate in this fashion, and quantity or trade discounts are part of an orderly price structure. Other organizations, however, charge whatever the market will bear. Once again, this practice is most prevalent in industries that sell to the ultimate consumer.

One of the more widely practiced pricing techniques is the "par" approach. This method is most often used in service industries such as home improvements. The salesperson is provided by the company with a cost or "par" figure for a given measure of a service to be performed. Using aluminum siding as an example, a "square," or 100 square feet of siding, might be "costed out" by the company at $175. This means that at this figure the salesperson earns no commission whatsoever. If the customer pays $225 per square, the salesperson receives $25 and the company receives $25 per square. Assuming that a particular house requires 2000 square feet of siding, or 20 squares, the salesperson is free to quote whatever price he or she feels that the customer will pay. The commission structure is then based on the arrangement shown in Table 16-1.

TABLE 16-1

House Requires 20 Squares

Price per Square	Sales Commission	Company Profit
Less than $175	Company will probably renege on the contract or attempt to receive more money for job. Salesperson would most likely be fired.	
$175.00	$ 0	$ 0
200.00	250.00	250.00
225.00	500.00	500.00
250.00	750.00	750.00
275.00	1,000.00	1,000.00
300.00	1,250.00	1,250.00
325.00	1,500.00	1,500.00
35.00	1,750.00	1,750.00
375.00	2,000.00	2,000.00

The insidious and cynical nature of such a pricing scheme scarcely needs mentioning. Yet a large proportion of contractors providing various home improvement services have relied traditionally upon some variant of this approach. The practice is particularly reprehensible in that those who can least afford it, particularly senior citizens and members of certain minority groups, are the ones who are typically victimized. It would be a mistake, however, to assume that most middle-class white Americans are too sophisticated to fall into the par-based pricing trap. As a direct sales manager indicated to the author,

> A mooch is a mooch. Whether they're white, black, hispanic, young, old—it doesn't make any difference. They all want to get rid of their money. I never moralize about it. After all, don't some of our most cherished establishments continually rip off their constituencies? Doctors, lawyers, our duly elected representatives in government—give any of them a chance, and they'll walk away with the gold in

your teeth. At least I render a service and do a good job. So they pay a little more than the going rate? Big deal. If I didn't get their money, they'd just spend it on the horses, the lottery, drugs, booze, or something else. As I said, when I get it, at least they have something tangible to show for it.

A final area where a good deal of lying takes place in some industries is in prospecting. Most people reading this textbook have probably been taken in by some subterfuge utilized to get a salesperson into the home. Telephone soliticitation by some firm "conducting a survey" has become institutionalized as part of our society's noise pollution. Prospecting gimmicks are also used in advertising and in direct mail, promoting a free gift or some other ploy intended to place a salesperson in front of some unwitting prospect. Although many of these subterfuges are formalized and are used by "reputable" firms, the untruthfulness factor continues to exist.

There are, of course, other areas than those mentioned here where salespeople have been known to tell less than the truth.

ETHICAL PROBLEMS IN RECRUITING AND HIRING

One of the sales manager's greatest assets in his or her sales force. As a result, the ability to recruit and hire successful salespeople is one of the most critical performance factors.

While recognizing a salesperson's potential is an important aspect of successful hiring, the manager must also be able to persuade the salesperson to join the organization. It is in this area that ethical questions can arise. The primary focus of ethics in sales recruiting and hiring is how the manager portrays or "sells" a position to a potential salesperson.[6]

Just as salespeople can "puff" the attributes of a particular product or service, a sales manager can likewise oversell the attributes of a particular sales job. This situation creates an environment highly charged with ethical overtones, since the salesperson's career can be greatly affected by the outcome of the interview. Questions regarding the salesperson's career objectives versus the manager's short-run need for increased sales can often be solved by expressed or implied promises by a sales manager. Unfortunately, sales managers often make these promises without being able to deliver on them at a later date.

The most common promise of this type is in projecting future earnings. Even in the most reputable blue-chip firms, some sales managers have a tendency to overstate the amount of money a salesperson can realistically be expected to earn. Many times a manager will stress to a candidate the earnings of the top salespeople, neglecting to point out that most members of the sales force earn considerably less. In other cases, managers quote the average salary but tell the candidate that he or she is "obviously" capable of earning considerably more than the average salesperson. In other cases, the realistic barriers to sales, such as lack of territorial potential, are omitted from the interview, leading the salesperson to believe that earnings opportunities are greater than they really are.

An even more serious ethical problem in the hiring process arises in discussions of a salesperson's future progression within an organization. As should be expected, a great number of salespeople have high need for achievement or power and, as such, can reasonably be expected to become dissatisfied with a career in territory sales. The possibility or even actuality of high earnings is normally not a stimulating factor in this type of salesperson's decision to make a long-term commitment to an organization. Promotion to a position of greater responsibility, however, will often motivate him or her to put in inordinate amounts of time on the job. In sales, the extra effort expended, particularly in a systematized and organized fashion, invariably leads to greater sales. If the increased sales help the sales manager but do not result in fulfilling the salesperson's needs, there is no question about the relationship's benefiting only one party.

Another ethical problem in hiring is the proselyting or "pirating" of a competitor's salespeople. Although the recognized ethics of this practice vary somewhat among the many divergent industries, there are a few practices that are considered to be unethical in virtually all industries. The most blatant of these practices is approaching a competitor's salesperson with a job offer. This breach of ethics is widely practiced, and there are many rather transparent techniques used to theoretically avoid the letter, if not the spirit, of this unwritten law. One such method is to have a member of the sales force "accidently" meet the unwitting candidate and point out the benefits of working for his or her firm. Another technique sometimes used is to retain an executive search agency to contact the individual. In almost every case, the overture made to the individual consists of describing the job and then asking the individual if he or she "knows of anyone" who might be interested in interviewing for the position. The phrasing is relatively innocuous, but its meaning is unmistakable to even the most naive.

ETHICAL PROBLEMS IN TRAINING

When a new salesperson begins his or her career with most organizations, a great deal of time, money, and effort are expended in training the new employee. And companies are understandably anxious to have their new sales personnel go into their new jobs exuding enthusiasm and confidence New sales employees are trained in the sales process, features, benefits, and mechanics of their products or services, and in those of their competitors as well. Unfortunately, a few firms encourage sales trainers to overemphasize the appeal of products and services to the trainees, often resulting in discouragement and disillusion. One of the most common areas of this type of intentional "overselling" is characterized by depicting unrealistically favorable customer reactions that the trainee can expect when he or she goes into the field to sell.

Sales trainers have also been known to overemphasize flaws in competitor's products, creating an unrealistic image of the product in the mind of the trainee. This often results in the trainers' unfair but unwitting disparagement of competitive products. A further problem is that trainees are often taught how to disparage a competitor's product by innuendo, a highly unethical practice that can and does result in the development of a devious approach to selling.

Certain ethical considerations also arise in field sales training situations. When sales managers delegate the sales training function, they still maintain responsibility for the conduct of the trainer, as well as for the trainee. It is impossible to delegate this responsibility, although some sales managers attempt to wash their hands of any unethical sales training tactics employed by the person performing this critical function. Some of the unethical tactics performed in this area range from teaching the trainee questionable sales tactics to instilling in him or her negative or cynical attitudes.

While the majority of sales organizations probably conduct ethical and above-board training programs as a matter of policy, it is not difficult for breakdowns in this system to occur when individuals take it upon themselves to engage in the practice of misinforming trainees. Unfortunately, in some cases these practices are well known to sales management.

ETHICAL PROBLEMS IN SERVICE

"We service what we sell" is the well-known motto of a very well known national organization, highly regarded for its high-quality products and service. In an age of technological innovation and planned obsolescence, malfunctions or breakdowns of products are to be reasonably expected. The possibility of purchasing or leasing a "lemon" is an ever-present possibility for both the consumer and the industrial firm, and virtually no organization can boast of flawless products. As a result, the service aim of the company often conveys the image and credibility of that organization to an equal or greater extent than the sales department. Problems often occur, however, in organizations where the service manager reports to the sales manager rather than maintaining, at least theoretically, equal organizational status. Some typical sales service structures are depicted by Figure 16-1.

It is not unusual for a service manager to report to a branch sales manager; in fact, any other relationship in a field sales situation would probably be unwieldy and unrealistic. Nevertheless, when service departments do not maintain an independent posture, it is possible that they might be unduly influenced by the sales department, sometimes to the detriment of the customer. One of the more common examples of this is when a sales manager unduly influences a service manager to recommend to service personnel that products be replaced rather than repaired. A service manager in the office equipment industry reported in an interview that

> Since I started working for this firm, I've been a lot happier. At the last place I worked, the sales department put a lot of pressure on me and on my tech reps to

Figure 16-1

Two Traditional Reporting Relationships of Service Managers in Marketing Organizations

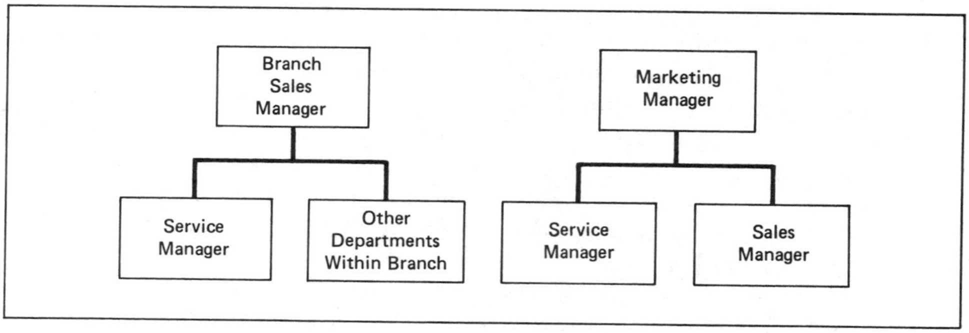

recommend that broken equipment be "surveyed" [replaced]. There were a lot of cases where the items were fixable and I just wouldn't let my people tell the customer that they couldn't be repaired. Now most sales managers at this company would accept my judgment, but over there [the former company], they really gave me a hard time about it. When there was a sales contest on, they wanted *everything* replaced. I might not be a college graduate like a lot of sales managers, but I know the difference between right and wrong, and I just wouldn't do it. Finally, I quit and came here. I report to the branch manager and he tells me, "Bob, what you say, goes." The two sales managers in our office know it and we get along fine and have the utmost respect for each other.

A second problem associated with the ethics of service is the follow-up (or lack of it) that a firm provides once the product is sold. Certain firms, for example, are notorious for poor service. Many people have expressed extreme dissatisfaction with the service provided by particular automobile dealers. Because salespeople are compensated only for sales, they often tend to rationalize or even ignore customer complaints. As a matter of fact, many if not most direct-sales organizations tend to downgrade the importance of the service function. This lack of attention to customer service needs, which was responsible for part of the stimulus for the consumer movement that began in the 1960s, is extremely short sighted and in the long run typically results in lower sales. If consumers express reluctance to buy a particular firm's products, it is not inconceivable that the firm may find it necessary to close its doors.

ETHICAL PROBLEMS IN MOTIVATION

A leader is envisioned by most people to possess certain positive qualities that instill in subordinates a desire to follow. Unfortunately, some managers push and shove instead of lead. Others manipulate instead of motivate. The ethical dilemmas inherent in the motivation process are a significant factor to be considered by the sales manager.

One specific problem arises in the use of the reward-punishment approach. Practical aspects notwithstanding, certain moral questions arise from the use of fear as a motivator. The primary question is a philosophical one. Is the manager endowed with the right to frighten the people he or she is responsible for? If so, by whom? While it is true that some sales managers appear to consider themselves "anointed" to use any kind of motivational tactics they desire, the overwhelming majority of sales managers find the use of fear tactics repugnant. As a sales manager in the sweater industry stated to the author,

> The day when the sales manager scared the hell out of his charges is over. To begin with, the people today don't scare that easily. This isn't the 1930s where there's no place else to go. People get pushed around too much, they leave. Hell, everybody leaves. The guy who was here before me tried to use scare tactics. The president of our company, who came over from the other side, hated to see that stuff. One day he said to him, "So one Hitler wasn't enough?" Not only is scaring people right out of the Dark Ages, but it's bad business. People get too scared, they ram the products down the customer's throat and everybody loses. Me, I couldn't scare anybody if I wanted to. Most people in the business are human beings despite what you read in the novels.

These comments notwithstanding, intimidation is still used by some sales managers to "motivate" their salespeople.

Manipulation is a way of getting people to do things through the use of devious or questionable means. Making or implying promises that cannot be met is a common manipulative device. In essence, "using" people to achieve one's own needs is considered to be manipulation and is a highly unethical practice, even though it is used extensively in business. A major practical problem of manipulation is that people are able to quickly analyze the motives and from then on are highly mistrustful of these managers.

As a general rule, more insecure managers tend to utilize manipulative techniques. Effective sales management requires that salespeople be treated as human beings who need to grow, rather than as tools to be used to help further a manager's own ends. The same can be said for ethical and above-board behavior. Invariably, the sales manager who finds it necessary to violate company, industry, and business codes that have been purely and objectively laid down has a great deal of difficulty in coming to grips with the reality of effective management.

SUMMARY

This chapter has discussed some of the ethical implications of business in general and sales management in particular. Unfortunately, ethical conduct is not black or white, and subjective interpretation is more the rule than the exception.

The modern corporation, in its pursuit of profit maximization, often tends to create ethical dilemmas for its managers, as well as for its salespeople. And the conscience of the individual to a great extent determines that individual's interpretation of right or wrong "business" behavior.

Some specific areas where ethical dilemmas are apt to arise are in selling, hiring, training, service, and motivation. It would be impossible to enumerate all the possible situations that could arise to cause conflict in the individual. Some of the more common situations, however, were depicted.

Fleetwood Products

Christine McVie is the sales manager for Fleetwood Products, a manufacturer and marketer with advertising specialties. Part of her responsibilities include the recruiting and hiring of salespeople.

An opening for a territory salesperson was advertised and several applications were received. Among the applicants were several people with experience in the advertising field and a few applicants with no experience.

Christine narrowed the field down to two applicants who had worked in the industry, had good sales records, and also had apparently justifiable reasons for wanting to leave their present employers. The day before Christine was going to invite the applicants in for further interviews her manager called her and inquired about the status of one of the applicants that Christine had previously rejected.

After going through the applicant's paper work, Christine pointed out that he was considerably less qualified than either of the two people she had settled on. Her manager then told her that the firm had recently been concerned about the relatively small number of black salespeople on its staff. The manager suggested that Christine reconsider the previously rejected applicant, who was a black person.

Christine said she would call her manager back later that day to tell him what she planned to do.

1. If you were Christine, what would you do?
2. What are some of the ethical problems Christine faces in this situation?

E-Z- Duz-It

Paul Dobleman is the branch manager for E-Z-Duz-It (EZDI), a computer service organization that specializes in setting up payroll and accounts-receivable systems for various manufacturers. Paul came from a strict family background and attended New York University on a basketball scholarship. All his life, Paul observed certain standards that he set for himself regarding honesty and moral conduct. Even though he had strict standards for himself, he recognized that most people have different philosophies, and he was very careful not to be judgmental about people. His sales meetings and directions to salespeople were that all business must be conducted in an upfront manner. No half-truths or any kind of questionable behavior were to be tolerated.

During March, Paul's office was just below quota and an additional $20,000 of business would put the office at 100 percent of quota and would also qualify Paul for a $2000 quarterly bonus. Paul's wife, Stella, had been very sick recently and had to quit her job. Paul wanted very badly to send her to Florida for a couple of weeks to speed up the recuperation process.

On March 29, Fred Ferkokta, the leading salesperson in the branch, brought in an order for $28,000 from a local manufacturer. Paul was jubilant until he noticed that he date on the order blank was April 15. "Fred, this order isn't good until the middle of next month" said Paul; "we can't count this deal in this month's business." Fred said, "Paul, listen. The buyer told me that they will definitely issue a purchase order in April and backdate it to March 29. All we have to do is put in the order now in the month's business, Paul replied, "Yeah, that's all well and good, Freddy, but what if it backfires and they change their mind?" "Paul, you don't understand," Fred said, "It's not gonna bounce, and even if it did, we have nothing to lose. All the other managers do it. Besides, with this order I make quarterly bonus. You're always talking about how important it is to make quarterly quotas. Well, here it is—what are you going to do?"

1. If you were Paul, what would you do?
2. What would be some of the consequences if Paul decided to include the order in March business?

DISCUSSION QUESTIONS

1. What are the difficulties involved in describing a universally accepted code of business ethics?
2. What are some of the pressures put on the sales manager by his or her organization that can cause ethical dilemmas?
3. What are some specific ethical problems involved in selling?
4. What are some specific ethical problems involving in hiring salespeople?
5. What are some specific problems involved in training salespeople?
6. What are some specific problems encountered in the area of customer service?
7. What are some of the ethical implications involved in motivating salespeople?
8. What is meant by manipulating people?

NOTES

[1]Miriam Beard, *A History of Business*, Vol. 1 (Ann Arbor: University of Michigan Press, 1938).
[2]Clarence Randall, *The Executive in Transition* (New York: McGraw-Hill, 1967), pp. 137-138.

[3]See Leon Festinger, *A Theory of Cognitive Dissonance* (New York: Harper & Row, 1957).

[4]See Harold W. Beckman, "Corporate Ethics: Who Cares?" *Journal of the Academy of Marketing Science* (Summery 1977), pp. 154-167.

[5]*National Enquirer,* May 1978.

[6]See Albert Z. Carr, "Is Business Bluffing Ethical?" *Harvard Business Review,* January-February 1968. This was one of the most controversial articles ever written regarding business ethics. Carr drew an analogy between telling less than the truth in business and bluffing in a poker game. Because of the environment, he felt each was expected behavior and therefore permissible. In one of the many letters to the editor in the May-June 1968 issue, Leon P. Chemlen of Stonehorn, Massachusetts, remarked "Fortunately, Mr. Carr's view does not appear to be the prevailing view, except, perhaps, along the few remaining frontiers of civilization, such as the upper Amazon."

CHAPTER 17

CAREERS IN SALES MANAGEMENT

OBJECTIVES

To provide an understanding of the important aspects of a sales career:

* Starting salary
* Student organizations
* Contact with sales managers

To enumerate the basic steps necessary to a sales management career:

* Trainee stage
* Territory salesperson stage
* Experienced salesperson stage
* Dependable experienced salesperson stage
* Sales manager trainee stage

To investigate careers in the four sales sectors:

* Consultative sales careers
* Technical sales careers
* Commercial sales careers
* Direct sales careers

To discuss the opportunity for women and minority group members in sales.

To make a concluding statement on a career in sales management.

INTERVIEW WITH FRANK SMITH

Interviewer: Well Frank, we're getting to the home stretch.

Frank Smith: Don't think it hasn't been fun. The only problem is that by this time the semester is nearly over, and the people reading this have one thing on their mind—*when is the semester going to be over*?

Interviewer: Then why don't we make it short, interesting chapter and leave them with something to think about.

Frank Smith: That makes sense. I hope everybody who reads this book wants to get into sales. Obviously, not everyone will, but we hope this chapter gives you some feel for the possibility of a career in the field.

Interviewer: Thanks for coming through the book with us, Frank. It was a pleasure having your comments and the benefits of your experience.

Frank Smith: We could never cover *everything* we'd like to; the book would be too long. I think we covered the major points, though. Remember, certain things change from year to year, like the job market. This chapter should give you a handle on the present. Good luck to all of you. I sincerely hope that you find some work that makes you happy, productive, and well rewarded, whatever it is.

Most students in business administration, like those in engineering, computer science, and other technically oriented major fields, view a college or university education as a springboard to obtaining employment with some business organization. Basic courses in economics, accounting, finance, and quantitative methods are typically followed by specific major courses, such as sales management. It should be pointed out here that, although such specific major courses are valuable, the "core" courses such as English, public speaking, and similar ones are at least as important. By the same token, there is no reason why colleges should not perform the function of providing "vocational" courses like sales management. This chapter discusses the realities of a career in sales management, making the assumption that the reader is a college student.

THE STUDENT AND SALES CAREERS

For several years there existed a stigma on many college campuses regarding a sales career. Particularly during the 1960s and early 1970s, selling was looked upon as a rather mundane job objective. Many students wrongly perceived the high-pressure tactics found in certain direct-sales situations as being characteristic of the entire profession. At the same time, neither teachers nor college professors tried particularly hard to change this mistaken impression. The very people who exhorted students not to judge entire groups based upon the actions of a few exercised the kind of bias they found distasteful and unacceptable in others. As a result, sales became "tainted" on most campuses, and it was often fashionable for students to disparage the profession, in many cases, the same profession that paid for their educations.

The pullout in Vietnam, the recession of 1972, the oil embargo of 1973, and the subsequent tightening up of corporate personnel requirements all had an impact upon recruiting at college campuses. At the same time, a resurgence in enrollments in engineering and business administration brought about a new attitude toward sales as a viable option. By the late 1970s, ample evidence existed that college students had indeed shifted their perceptions regarding a profession in this field. It would appear that there will be strong competition among college students for sales jobs in the 1980s.

The Illusion of Starting Salary

There is an old adage that if an individual had his head in a refrigerator and his feet in an oven his average body temperature would be very comfortable. In a sense, a survey of "average" salaries produces a similar result. Chapter 8 showed average salaries for all types of sales jobs. Unfortunately, it is impossible to determine in advance whether one will receive an "average" salary. It is an incontrovertible fact that success and, therefore, income in sales is a function of the individual's attitude. There are very few occupational choices for the college graduate that allow him or her to receive significant income increases after only one or two years of school as does sales. By the same token, lack of success in some selling jobs can lead to the same or an even lower income over a similar time period.

There is a strong relationship between degree and risk and income in sales. In the technical sales field, for example, many new salespeople find that it may take four or five years before they begin to receive significant income increases. Yet in the office equipment industry it is not unusual for a salesperson to increase his or her starting salary by 50 percent or more at the end of the first year. Very few college graudates enter the direct-sales field, with the exception of insurance sales. Starting salaries in this field have been only slightly lower than those in technical or commercial jobs. Yet some new salespeople are able to double or even triple this figure during their second and third years out of college. An unusually high proportion of people in this field, however, fail to *make it* to their second or third year in the profession. According to reliable sources, the college graduate entering commercial sales can expect to be offered a starting salary of about $13,000 to $15,000 per year. When compared to other starting salaries, for example, for computer science graduates, engineering graduates, and some critical areas for MBA's such as finance, this figure would seem to be quite low. When put into perspective, however, starting salary disparities are often less than one would imagine.

Income taxes, for example, are quite high. After "Uncle Sam" takes his share of gross earnings, the gap in real income is narrowed. State income taxes, social security, and other taxes also have a tendency to reduce take-home income. In many cases, the salesperson receives a company car or remuneration for expenses, both of which are tax free and are very important budget items. Last, the salesperson's starting salary can usually be supplemented by bonuses or commission. As one manager in the technical sales field told the author,

> For years I've been trying to explain to new college graduates that it's the *take-home,* not the gross, that counts. With the kind of wild government spending programs we've been experiencing over the past few decades, we'll be lucky if any of us have anything left. Seriously, though, by the time you deduct taxes, fringes, pensions and social security, a single college graduate actually gets about 60 percent of his or her gross as take-home pay. If they're married without kids and don't own a home, it's probably even higher. We give them a company car, which saves them about three thousand a year. That's only part of it though—they would have to earn about *six* thousand to make it up. Then they don't have carfare, their lunches are usually on the house, and most of them get a bonus of about two thousand at the end of the year. This may sound illogical, but today *two* thousand in one sum is better than *three* thousand spread out over twelve months because they'll just spend it unless they have a very disciplined spending program. Also, we have a national sales meeting in Florida once a year, all expenses paid. Most of them take their vacation then too. When you compare it to a regular job that pays five grand more, there is actually very little difference, when the smoke clears. In my opinion, they're probably better off with us.

Many sales managers in the commercial and technical fields would agree with the preceding observation. On the other hand, a company car, expense account, and bonus are relatively "sure things." Sales jobs that base their income or a good deal of it on commission are not as secure, and bear close scrutiny. One student who had graduated and taken a sales job reported the following experience to the author:

> The sales manager was really great to me. Most of those people have very nice personalities and are very persuasive. The statement he used, was, "our average salesperson earned $22,000 last year. Now, do you consider yourself to be average?" I answered that I considered myself to be above average, and he replied in a conspirational way "You know, Lester, I agree with you. Frankly, we have some people here who really could do a lot better, if they worked harder. I can tell that you're the kind of person who will give one hundred percent. Those are the kind of people who make a lot of money and usually wind up as managers." Naturally, I was flattered and took the job. They told me it was commission, but don't worry—I'd be making more than anybody I graduated with before long. Without going into details, I didn't make much money, and it was a very discouraging thing. I can conclude one thing; if a company won't pay you a starting salary, then that's about what they think you're worth.

Fortunately, Lester found another sales job and was successful. This experience, however, in effect represents the exact reason why many students have some trepidation about the sales field; they are afraid that they will experience a similar situation.

There would appear to be some reason to question an organization's motives if the student is offered a straight-commission sales job. Indeed, many firms in industries where straight commission is the only feasible method of payment (e.g., life insurance sales) provide their new employees with some kind of income guarantee, such as a salary or drawing account for the first year or until they have established themselves financially.

Lester's experience notwithstanding, the student should make a very careful examination of the starting salary when he or she is considering a career. In many cases, it is a good idea to discuss this situation with an objective, impartial third party. Clearly, if the individual does not have two or more offers from which to make a choice, this starting salary dilemma does not exist. If the graduating student does have a choice, these are some of the questions that should be answered before making a decision.

What are the long-run prospects of the job? Is the starting salary high because it is a dead-end job? Is the job with the lower starting salary likely to yield higher second-year earnings?

Will I be required to move geographically or can I continue to live at home and sponge off my parents?

Are there additional commission or bonus possibilities in addition to starting salary?

Are there other benefits involved? If there are, how much are they worth?

What are the income-tax implications of the relative positions?

What are the fringe benefits offered by each firm? How much are they worth? Are they important to me? For example, tuition remission might add up to several thousand dollars, particularly when the tax implications are considered. A profit-sharing plan, for instance, might even be of greater value than current income.

Am I sacrificing the prospect of an interesting, fulfilling job for the sale of a few thousand dollars, which add up to very little on a take-home weekly basis?

Am I allowing my peers to exert undue influence over my decisions or am I deciding what to do in light of my own best interests? (Most graduates will never see their classmates again, and when they do, it will usually be when the former classmate wants something from them).

Am I considering my own qualifications and other factors (e.g., a recession economy, tight job market) realistically? Do I have an honest evaluation of my own usefulness to an organization? Am I underestimating or overestimating this usefulness?

There are clearly a multitude of questions that one can ask regarding starting salary and job opportunity. Like a multiple-choice examination, the correct answer may or may not be the first choice. A certain amount of rigor should be used in making a choice. But many people have found by experience that the position offering the highest starting salary may not be the best choice.

Student Organizations

Some students join organizations because they have the desire to be leaders or may even be strongly in need for power. Others join student organizations because they desire to work off a high level of energy, and others join simply to put the application on their resume. Whatever the reason, recruiters for sales positions are favorably impressed, and this reason alone, ignoble, but realistic, should be enough for any serious job candidate to strongly consider membership in some organization related to sales. Very few organizations exclusively for future salespeople exist on college campuses. Since many or most students interested in sales major in marketing, organizations are typically formed for the benefit of all marketing students and are given the name of the Marketing Club, the Marketing Society, or some such appellation. These organizations are typically funded by nominal membership dues and by various fund-raising activities such as car washes, Las Vegas nights, suitcase parties, and a host of other schemes. Organizations of this type are generally highly beneficial, and most students become actively involved whatever their original motivations for joining.

There also exist a few regional and national organizations that were formed for the benefit of future salespeople. One of the most prominent college and university organizations of this type is Pi Sigma Kappa, the national sales and marketing service fraternity (although it is co-ed organization). This organization is headquartered in New York City and receives administrative and financial support from the Sales and Marketing Executives International. Pi Sigma Kappa has over 100 chapters on various college campuses and was formed to provide all kinds of assistance to students interested in a sales and, to a lesser extent, marketing career. Because of the influence of SMEI, members of this group have experienced an unusually high rate of job offers during the period of the late 1970s, when there was a definite job shortage. Annual awards are presented to certain chapters based upon their meeting various performance criteria.

On the whole, most students who belong to *active* campus marketing and sales organizations tend to receive a strong extracurricular exposure to the sales field. Probably because of the relatively high achievement motivation innate in sales managers, student organizations of this type tend to receive a great deal of support from most sales managers if they are made aware of the organization and its purpose. Typically, there is a strong relationship between the effort expended by the student and the benefits gained from membership in these organizations.

Contact with Sales Managers

As in any other profession, contact with effective practitioners would seem to provide a solid foundation for making a career choice. Medical and premedical students work with doctors and law and prelaw students attempt to work during the summers with law firms. By the same token, it would seem to make more sense for a future salesperson to seek out part-time and summer jobs in sales than in nonselling occupations. As in medicine or law, it is probably necessary for the student to come in contact with sales managers before he or she can expect to work in the profession. There are a variety of ways in which sales managers may be met by students. Student organizations normally invite several speakers to participate in meetings. Student projects and term papers often provide students with the opportunity to come into contact with sales managers. However the contacts are made, face-to-face discussions with sales managers are vital to learning about sales as a profession. During the 1980s there are expected to be many opportunities in sales management, and there is every reason to believe that the best-prepared students will be best able to cope with the demands required to be a successful sales manager.

STEPS TO SALES MANAGEMENT

Very few jobs in sales management exist for college graduates without selling experience. As a matter of fact, there are even very few formal training programs that are designed to transform college graduates into sales managers. Most organizations hire graduates as salespeople on a "no promises" basis with respect to advancing to sales manager. The reasoning behind this practice should be fairly obvious after reading the previous chapters of this text; it is expected that would-be managers must themselves be capable of being considered for promotion. The whole process from being hired to becoming a sales manager consists essentially of six steps. For various reasons, one of the steps might be omitted, but for the most part, this process consists of the following:

1. Sales trainee stage
2. Territory salesperson stage
3. Experienced salesperson stage
4. Dependable experienced salesperson stage
5. Sales manager trainee stage
6. Sales manager

Most large firms tend to hire salespeople out of the ranks of college graduates, while smaller firms tend to place less importance on a college degree as a hiring criterion. Consequently, more sales managers in larger firms are college graduates, and the majority of sales managers who are *not* college graduates work for smaller firms. On the whole, larger firms tend to have more formalized training programs than do smaller firms. It is therefore conceivable that the six-step process from hiring to sales management might vary somewhat from company to company.

Sales Trainee Stage

This stage of the process is the most concrete, formal, and clearly defined. Sales-force members must undergo a period in their career when their primary responsibility is in assimilating knowledge. Chapter 7 investigated various aspects of the sales training process and pointed out specific techniques and procedures to be followed. When the new salesperson is in the *trainee* stage of his or her career, no performance expectations exist. In some firms, the trainee stage is relatively short, lasting only one or two weeks; in other firms it may be of several months' duration.

Territory Salesperson Stage

At this stage of his or her sales career, the salesperson attempts to put into practice the theory learned in sales training. The salesperson is assigned a quota and is expected to produce results, but performance expectations are not high. Although the salesperson must depend to a great extent upon others, this stage is characterized by a growing competence on the part of the salesperson. A subtle change in techniques, attitude, and sales results marks the conclusion of this stage and the movement to "experienced salesperson." The territory salesperson stage might last from six to eighteen months in most sales situations.

Experienced Salesperson Stage

At some point, the salesperson is recognized by the manager and by the rest of the sales force as being an important resource. He or she is expected to meet sales quotas and provide advice to new salespeople. At sales meetings he or she is expected to participate and even to provide presentations upon occasion. This stage might last for the remainder of the salesperson's entire career if he or she is unable to grow into the next stage. Depending upon the firm and the particular branch, a salesperson might find that this stage lasts only a few months. It should be stressed that the transformation from this stage to the next is informal.

Dependable Experienced Salesperson Stage

This stage of the salesperson's career is probably, in most cases, the most professionally rewarding. It is also the stage where the salesperson enjoys the highest degree of status among colleagues and managers alike. Salespeople in this phase of their career are expected to exceed quotas and to provide informal leadership to the sales force. On the positive side, salespersons at this stage of their career can provide a great deal of support to managers by their actions and their opinions, which are usually respected by most other salespeople. On the negative side, these salespeople might disagree with the sales manager's methods or tactics, in which case they can influence other salespeople in a manner detrimental to the manager. From a practical standpoint, salespeople at this stage are normally highly supportive of most managers and provide a great deal of help in "straightening out" the manager when his or her techniques are counterproductive or ineffective. This stage of the salesperson's career either continues indefinitely or subtly changes if he or she is interested in a managerial job.

Sales Manager Trainee Stage

This stage is perhaps the most interesting for the salesperson. There are essentially two ways in which the salesperson moves to this stage. Either it is earned, or the salesperson is "pushed" or "helped." In certain organizations, many management jobs are available because of expansion or promotion. In situations of this type, salespeople are usually designated as managerial material from the "experienced salesperson" stage. In firms that have a formal training program for managers, the transition from salesperson to manager is formalized. In firms that do not have formal management training programs, most salespeople at this stage are recognized by the majority of sales-force members as future managers. Realistically, there are some cases where a favored salesperson is appointed to the managerial risks. Most of the time, the future manager has distinguished himself or herself through superior performance in certain areas.

Sales Manager

This position is the culmination of the various career stages previously described. Although most new salespeople at the trainee stage aspire to be managers, it would probably be surprising to the student if he or she were told that most salespeople tend to change the focus of their career as they move from one stage to the next. There are many reasons why the majority of sales-force members decide not to pursue a career in management. In some cases, the financial opportunities are greater in sales and in other cases salespeople do not want the responsibilities, pressure, or time constraints involvement in management. For those who do want to be managers, this step is the beginning of an interesting and rewarding career.

OPPORTUNITIES FOR POTENTIAL SALES MANAGERS

Virtually no jobs are available in sales management for new graduates. There are, however, many opportunities for entering the six-stage "obstacle course." This section will investigate careers in the various sectors of sales, as well as careers for specific groups.

Careers in Consultative Sales

Because of the nature of consultative sales, a great deal of experience in dealing at the top levels of organizations is normally required. There is also a certain amount of expertise and sophistication required, which is usually acquired from several years of dealing with higher-level executives. In spite of these requirements, a knowledge of various types of consultative sales jobs is helpful to the graduating student. Discussions with salespeople in the consultative field will often reveal certain factors of interest that will help the student prepare for a job in consultative sales in the future. Unfortunately, the outlook for sales managers in the consultative field is rather bleak. Since most firms in this field are small and very specialized, there are few managerial jobs available, and those that do exist are often held by principals of the firm. On the other hand, sales management jobs in this field often provide less opportunity to utilize managerial skills than the other three sales fields.

Careers in Technical Sales

In periods of relative prosperity, the technical products field virtually abounds with sales opportunities for college graduates. In periods of economic recession, the majority of these opportunities are offered to engineering and technical graduates. There are, however, many jobs available for nontechnical graduates as well. Most entry-level sales opportunities in the technical sector exist with fairly large organizations. These positions, in the classic tradition, offer a good starting salary, excellent benefits, and a company car. The scope of the technical sales job includes about six to nine weeks of formal training, with the assignment of a sales territory at the end of the initial training period. The next year is typically characterized by frequent visits to customers with the sales manager, other salespeople, and product specialists. The first year is also marked by frequent training sessions with various company personnel. Because of the specialized nature of most technical firms' product lines, the sales territory usually consists of a finite number of accounts. The salesperson is expected to develop sales within those accounts. For the individual who is interested in a career in technical sales, discussions with salespeople would probably be the most effective way to investigate the pros and cons of this professional career path.

Careers in Commercial Sales

The largest number of salespeople work in commercial sales. Predictably, the majority of employers visiting college campuses are also in the commercial sales sector. Most firms in this sector seek experienced salespeople, but there are still many hundreds of firms that recruit at campuses at the national, regional, and local levels.

Because of the nature of commercial sales, colleges and universities provide a very good source of talent. Very few commercial sales jobs require any particular skill that cannot be learned after being hired. For the most part, commercial sales firms recruit at the sales trainee level. This allows the firms to break in their salespeople according to their own philosophy. There is a great deal of speculation in this field that new college graduates have open minds and can be taught good work habits. Many sales managers believe that it is easier to teach the "company way" to inexperienced trainees than to experienced salespeople who have already developed their own set of work habits.

Most commercial sales positions pay the going rate as a base compensation, with supplements such as commissions and bonuses that can be earned but do not have to be depended upon. Some firms also provide company cars, while most provide extensive fringe benefits. While the recent demand for commercial sales trainees has been low in recent years, it is expected that there will be significantly more openings at the trainee level during the next few years.

Careers in Direct Sales

Since most direct-sales firms compensate their personnel on a straight commission basis, there are few firms in this field that recruit on college campuses. Most successful direct salespeople are experienced and have acquired persuasive skills, a talent that must be developed over time. Most students stay away from direct-sales positions upon graduation, and very few direct firms make an effort to recruit new college graduates.

One exception to this general condition is the life insurance industry. Many if not most firms recruit on campus for sales trainees. A state license is required to sell life insurance, and a great deal of preparation is required to not only learn but to stay current with its legislative, actuarial, and technical aspects. The turnover rate of life insurance sales is quite high, but it is difficult for the graduate to determine whether or not he or she would succeed in this industry without making an attempt at it. Like most direct-sales jobs, a great deal of selling must be done at night, because both husbands and wives must be "pitched" in order to make a sale. Consequently, the hours spent in this type of selling are long. If successful, the financial rewards are very high, but there is a certain amount of satisfaction that must be gained by the salesperson from this type of selling; otherwise, he or she would not be able to sustain the high level of activity required. Although some insurance sales managers attempt to hire graduates in order to get them to sell their friends and relatives, most sales managers in the insurance field are quite professional and do a good job of providing an environment to help trainees succeed.

It should not be concluded that other kinds of direct selling are bad per se. The main problem in direct sales for new college graduates is that the amount of time required to become an accomplished professional is very long and can be a demoralizing experienced for the individual not sophisticated in the ways of direct selling.

Women in Sales

Over the past decade, there has been a great increase in the number of women in the sales field. In some industries, such as industrial products, the concentration of women is about 5 percent, while in college textbook sales, this figure is about 50 percent. Most male sales managers find that there is very little difference in the general performance level of males versus females in sales. Opportunities for women, however, do seem to vary among industries.

The cosmetic industries and sales of "party plan" items employ women practically on an exclusive basis, but it would be unfair to use these industries as indicators of equal employment opportunity, since women have traditionally comprised the sales forces. By the same token, there are some industries, for example, many services, where women have only recently been given an opportunity and have proved to the satisfaction of most males that they are as qualified, effective, and competent as males. In most industrial sales jobs, there are still a considerable number of firms that prefer to hire males, and there are few females who are really interested. On the other hand, female technical graduates have found that firms are very interested in hiring them.

Most college placement officers appear to recognize the need of female graduates to prepare themselves to show employers that they are capable of performing as well as male graduates. By the same token, there is considerably less emphasis upon hiring either one sex or the other; sales managers are interested in hiring salespeople who will meet their objectives and make the manager look good. It is almost inconceivable that very many sales managers in 1981 would turn down a good candidate because of their sex.

On the other hand, the same condition does not appear to exist for minority group members in general. Sales managers have tended more often to hire minorities *because* they were members of a particular group over the past several years. It can only be concluded that the decision *not* to hire certain minority group individuals has also been motivated by racial or national characteristics. Some sales managers still tend to impute lack of intelligence or perception to certain minority groups in general, primarily because of traditional lack of educational opportunity for the groups in question. By the same token, minority group members are, in general, considerably less agressive in seeking sales employment than women. Most sales managers who care about this situation feel that a positive approach providing information to individuals about the benefits of a sales career is necessary as a starting point. Further career counseling and guidance as the student passes through high school and into college would provide a greater degree of interest in sales as a profession to all groups, regardless of sex or race. To indicate here that employers in this country observe the spirit and the letter of equal opportunity would be hypocritical and misleading. On the positive side, however, the sales field is certainly one of the most egalitarian of the business professions, and there is reason to believe that future trends will continue in this direction.

CONCLUSION

The student who has some interest in the possibility of a sales manager career should investigate all the available sources to ascertain whether or not this profession might be a viable alternative. He or she should be careful not to let the financial opportunities in sales cause a myopic view toward a career. Discussions with professionals, interviews, tests, and even spending time on the job with sales-force members and managers should be undertaken. Membership in student sales and marketing organizations should likewise be of interest to the potential sales manager. All the disadvantages as well as the rewards of a career in this field should be examined. If the individual then decides to pursue sales as a choice, every effort should be made to find a job that will be emotionally satisfying. The other rewards will follow.

Ron Jackson

Ron Jackson is a senior at Egon College and is majoring in marketing. Most people who know him would attest to his intelligence and his up-front approach in dealing with other people. During the first semester of his senior year, Ron spent very little time looking for employment or even developing a workable plan for entering the job market. The placement office provided seminars for seniors designed to help them in career development, but Ron had heard from some of his friends that the seminars weren't too stimulating, so he chose not to participate in them. During the semester break he went to Florida with a few friends to, as he put it, "catch a few rays."

On March 1, Ron was talking to a few of his friends and one of them remarked that very few students on campus had been able to receive any assurance that there would be a job for them when they finished school. When he went back to the dorm that night, Ron asked Marty Laughlin, the resident advisor and a graduate student also in marketing, how to best go about searching for a job. The following conversation between them took place:

Ron: Where do you think I should go first, Marty?
Marty: Well, what kind of work do you want to do, Ron?
Ron: I don't know, something in management, I guess.
Marty: Like what, Ron? Maybe president of IBM or something like that? How about board chairman of AT&T?
Ron: Come on, Marty, be serious. My parents are getting kind of uptight about the whole thing. As a matter of fact, I'm kind of concerned myself.
Marty: The first thing you have to do is decide what field you want to get into. What did they tell you at the career development office?
Ron: I didn't go to the seminars.
Marty: Probably somebody else told you they were no good, right?
Ron: Yeah, how did you know?
Marty: Never mind. What courses did you like, if any?
Ron: I kind of liked some of the phys ed courses, and a couple of the marketing courses weren't bad.
Marty: Out of the marketing courses, which ones did you like the most?
Ron: I liked sales management, advertising, and personal selling as much as anything else.

Marty: Do you think you'd like selling?
Ron: I don't know. I never tried it.
Marty: Ron, if I were you, I would go and talk to somebody who can tell you about selling. First, you'd better learn to sell yourself.

1. If Ron came to you looking for advice and asked you to be candid, what advice would you give him?
2. Does Ron sound like anyone you know?

Macro-Copy

Bill Hartman is the branch sales manager for Macro-Copy, a well-known brand of office copy machines. The firm has traditionally hired recent college graduates to enter its sales training program. The program consists of extensive field and classroom training, followed by assignment of a sales territory and, ultimately, sales quota responsibility. Macro has estimated that it costs about $15,000 to train a new salesperson during the first year. If the salesperson leaves the firm during the first eighteen months, however, the cost to Macro is closer to $35,000.

On this basis, branch managers are encouraged to be highly selective in new trainees into the firm. Bill has been evaluating college seniors for a trainee position. He has narrowed the field down to three candidates and is ready to make a selection. He has compiled a list of attributes and impressions he received during interviews. The list reads as follows:

Mike Hayes: Mike makes a good appearance, appears to be well groomed and is reasonably articulate. During the interview he indicated that his goal is to be president of the company. Since he has never had a job in business, he doesn't exactly know how he would achieve this goal. Some of his past accomplishments were membership in the Marketing Society, and he played on the basketball team. When asked how he thought he would like selling, Mike candidly answered that he wasn't sure.

Cynthia Warren: Cindy was very businesslike and her appearance was excellent. She had made contact with the company on her own, having too low a number in the lottery to get an interview. Cindy had interviewed with several other firms as the result of a media-blitz type approach she took to a job search. She felt that she could do well in sales because she was well organized, had a good sense of responsibility, had worked long hours in the past, and was therefore able to understand what was required. Her goal was to do a good job as a sales representative and perhaps move into a supervisory position sometime in the future.

Warren O'Brien: Warren was a very gregarious and outgoing person. He told

Bill that he had "at least 200 friends" and would do well in sales because he liked people. Although he was well-dressed, his smoking cigarettes during the interview was somewhat distracting. His goal was to be in management, although he hadn't considered where in management he might want to work. His attitude was positive and he seemed to be a sincere person.

1. If you were Bill Hartman, who would you pick and why?
2. If you were interviewing college seniors for a position in sales, what criteria would you use in your evaluation of candidates?

DISCUSSION QUESTIONS

1. What is meant by "the illusion of starting salary"?
2. What has been the attitude of students toward careers in sales from the 1960s to the present?
3. What is the relationship between risk and income in sales?
4. What are the major questions that should be asked before making a decision as to which position to accept?
5. What is the value of belonging to student organizations with regard to a career in the sales field?
6. What is the value, if any, of having contact with sales managers before graduation from college?
7. What are the basic steps involved in a sales management career?
8. Will there be more or fewer women in sales in the future? Whyor why not?

INDEX